Techno-Orientalism

Asian American Studies Today

Series Editor: Huping Ling, Truman State University, Series Editor

This series publishes scholarship on cutting-edge themes and issues, including broadly based histories of both long-standing and more recent immigrant populations; focused investigations of ethnic enclaves and understudied subgroups; and examinations of relationships among various cultural, regional, and socioeconomic communities. Of particular interest are subject areas in need of further critical inquiry, including transnationalism, globalization, homeland polity, and other pertinent topics.

Jennifer Ann Ho, *Racial Ambiguity in Asian American Culture*

Jun Okada, *Making Asian American Film and Video: History, Institutions, Movements*

David S. Roh, Betsy Huang, and Greta A. Niu, *Techno-Orientalism: Imagining Asia in Speculative Fiction, History, and Media*

Techno-Orientalism

Imagining Asia in Speculative Fiction, History, and Media

EDITED BY DAVID S. ROH, BETSY HUANG, AND GRETA A. NIU

Rutgers University Press
New Brunswick, New Jersey, and London

Library of Congress Cataloging-in-Publication Data

    Techno-Orientalism : imagining Asia in speculative fiction, history, and media / edited by David S. Roh, Betsy Huang, and Greta A. Niu.
        pages   cm.—(Asian American studies today)
    Includes bibliographical references and index.
    ISBN 978–0-8135–7064–8 (hardcover : alk. paper)—ISBN 978–0-8135–7063–1 (pbk. : alk. paper)—ISBN 978–0-8135–7065–5 (e-book)
    1. Science fiction—History and criticism. 2. Asians in literature. 3. Asians in motion pictures. 4. Asians in mass media. 5. Technology in literature. 6. Asia—In literature. I. Roh, David S., 1978– editor. II. Huang, Betsy, 1966– editor. III. Niu, Greta A., 1969– editor.

PN3433.6.T43 2015
809.3'8762—dc23

2014027494

A British Cataloging-in-Publication record for this book is available from the British Library.

This collection copyright © 2015 by Rutgers, The State University
Individual chapters copyright ©2015 in the names of their authors
All rights reserved

No part of this book may be reproduced or utilized in any form or by any means, electronic or mechanical, or by any information storage and retrieval system, without written permission from the publisher. Please contact Rutgers University Press, 106 Somerset Street, New Brunswick, NJ 08901. The only exception to this prohibition is "fair use" as defined by U.S. copyright law.

Visit our website: http://rutgerspress.rutgers.edu

Manufactured in the United States of America

For my mother and father. —DSR

For David Logan: The real relation, the underlying theme. —BH

For Kathleen, Gregory, and Kenneth Niu, Evan Lowenstein, and Lyndon Lowenstein-Niu. —GAN

Contents

Acknowledgments — ix

Technologizing Orientalism: An Introduction — 1
DAVID S. ROH, BETSY HUANG, AND GRETA A. NIU

Part I Iterations and Instantiations

1. Demon Courage and Dread Engines: America's Reaction to the Russo-Japanese War and the Genesis of the Japanese Invasion Sublime — 23
KENNETH HOUGH

2. "Out of the Glamorous, Mystic East": Techno-Orientalism in Early Twentieth-Century U.S. Radio Broadcasting — 40
JASON CRUM

3. *Looking Backward*, from 2019 to 1882: Reading the Dystopias of Future Multiculturalism in the Utopias of Asian Exclusion — 52
VICTOR BASCARA

4. Queer Excavations: Technology, Temporality, Race — 64
WARREN LIU

5. I, Stereotype: Detained in the Uncanny Valley — 76
SEO-YOUNG CHU

6. *The Mask of Fu Manchu*, *Son of Sinbad*, and *Star Wars IV: A New Hope*: Techno-Orientalist Cinema as a Mnemotechnics of Twentieth-Century U.S.-Asian Conflicts — 89
ABIGAIL DE KOSNIK

7	Racial Speculations: (Bio)technology, *Battlestar Galactica*, and a Mixed-Race Imagining JINNY HUH	101
8	Never Stop Playing: *StarCraft* and Asian Gamer Death STEVE CHOE AND SE YOUNG KIM	113
9	"Home Is Where the War Is": Remaking Techno-Orientalist Militarism on the Homefront DYLAN YEATS	125

Part II Reappropriations and Recuperations

10	Thinking about Bodies, Souls, and Race in Gibson's Bridge Trilogy JULIE HA TRAN	139
11	Reimagining Asian Women in Feminist Post-Cyberpunk Science Fiction KATHRYN ALLAN	151
12	The Cruel Optimism of Asian Futurity and the Reparative Practices of Sonny Liew's *Malinky Robot* AIMEE BAHNG	163
13	Palimpsestic Orientalisms and Antiblackness; or, Joss Whedon's *Grand Vision of an Asian/American Tomorrow* DOUGLAS ISHII	180
14	"How Does It Not Know What It Is?": The Techno-Orientalized Body in Ridley Scott's *Blade Runner* and Larissa Lai's *Automaton Biographies* TZARINA T. PRATER AND CATHERINE FUNG	193
15	A Poor Man from a Poor Country: Nam June Paik, *TV-Buddha*, and the Techno-Orientalist Lens CHARLES PARK	209
	Desiring Machines, Repellant Subjects: A Conclusion DAVID S. ROH, BETSY HUANG, AND GRETA A. NIU	221
	Bibliography	227
	Notes on Contributors	245
	Index	251

Acknowledgments

As is often the case, the genesis of this volume is rooted in a conference (the 2011 Association for Asian American Studies Conference in New Orleans), for which we organized a panel called "Techno-Orientalism: Speculative Media and Asian American Corporeality." During the rich discussions that ensued, it dawned on us that there was a strong interest in a subfield that was frustratingly nebulous and that there was more work to be done. And so, building on the work of the field's trailblazers mentioned in our introductory chapter, we sought to define and deepen our understanding of "techno-Orientalism" with the book that you now hold in your hands.

Of course, we couldn't have undertaken such a task without a strong support network. In addition to the contributors who answered our call, we would like to thank the following people whose aid, fellowship, and encouragement have made the experience of editing this book not only possible, but pleasurable: King-Kok Cheung, Clare Counihan, Jennifer Ho, Yunte Huang, Sue Kim, Paul Lai, Jim Lee, Julia Sun-Joo Lee, Stephanie Li, Evan M. Lowenstein, Jane Park, Jennifer C. Rossi, and Stephen Hong Sohn.

We are grateful to the people at Rutgers University Press for their interest and investment in this project—particularly Katie Keeran, editor par excellence, and series editor Huping Ling, for granting us the vanguard position in the Asian American Studies Today series. Carrie Hudak has been instrumental in our stumbling journey from manuscript to book. Many thanks go to the anonymous readers, who read our manuscript with care and keen insight—we are in their debt.

We would like to thank our contributors for entrusting their work to us, for their energetic writing, and for their thoughtful participation in this field. It has truly been a pleasure to work with each and every one.

This collaboration has cheered Greta to no end—she has been particularly thrilled to meet various family members (including pets) through the medium of numerous video meetings—and she would like to thank Dave and Betsy for their intense intelligence, calm patience, and fantastic humor.

David would like to thank Betsy and Greta for relenting to his pestering, humoring his harebrained schemes, and indulging his OCD tendencies.

And Betsy remains in awe of Dave's otherworldly unflappability, smarts, and file organization chops; of Greta's stunning eloquence and endless equanimity; and, if she may, of the collective accomplishments of Team Davie, Besty, and Great.

Technologizing Orientalism

An Introduction

DAVID S. ROH, BETSY HUANG,
AND GRETA A. NIU

A century has passed since British author Sax Rohmer introduced the character Dr. Fu Manchu, whose particular brand of Eastern mysticism wedded with Western science both terrorized and titillated readers and audiences alike. Appearing in 1912, the character is perhaps one of the earliest and most potent instances of techno-Orientalist expression. A figure of unnatural, unknowable peril who must be kept from acquiring knowledge lest it be used against the Western subject, Dr. Fu Manchu is at once brilliant and technologically challenged. In one part of the serial, Dr. Fu Manchu plots to strengthen China by kidnapping European engineers, suggesting the Orient's lack of technological prowess and desire for Western technology. Yet, in another, he is described as possessing "all the cruel cunning of the entire Eastern race, accumulated in one giant intellect, with all the resources of science, past and present."[1] Both of the past and the future, his monstrous form captured Western ambivalences toward what it regarded as the mysterious power of the East, manifesting in strange contradictions.

Throughout the twentieth century, variations of that premodern-hypermodern dynamic in speculative visions of Asia and Asians have been recycled numerous times.[2] Exemplars include the villainous Khan Noonien Singh in Gene Roddenberry's *Star Trek* universe, the leader of a group of superhumans who attempt to take control of the *Starship Enterprise*; the Chinese scientist Dr. X in Neal Stephenson's novel, *The Diamond Age* (1995), a counterfeiter using "a gallimaufry of contraband technology" (73) to steal Western innovations; and most recently The Mandarin in *Iron Man 3* (2013), a clear revival of Dr. Fu Manchu played cleverly by Ben Kingsley in a tongue-in-cheek fashion.[3] But Western speculations of an Asianized future are not always consolidated in a singular fictional figure as in Fu Manchu, Dr. X, or The Mandarin. The yellow peril anxiety of an earlier, industrial-age era embodied by Fu Manchu found new forms across cultures and hemispheres as Asian economies become more visible competitors in the age of globalization and rapid technological innovations. One needs to witness only the speculative fictional worlds of Maureen McHugh's novel *China Mountain Zhang* (1992), Joss Whedon's television series *Firefly* (2002), and Gary Shteyngart's novel *Super Sad True Love Story* (2010) to trace persisting anxieties over the past three decades of a China-dominated future. All of these worlds feature Western protagonists struggling to navigate a sociopolitical landscape in which China is the dominant global empire with a superior technological edge. Beyond the focus on China, paradigmatic works such as William Gibson's Japan-based oeuvre (including *Neuromancer*), Ridley Scott's *Blade Runner*, and the Wachowskis' *The Matrix* films have also burnished in the Western consciousness Asian-influenced visions of the future underpinned by a familiar yet estranged mixture of Orientalist sensibilities.

These examples perfectly illustrate our definition of techno-Orientalism: the phenomenon of imagining Asia and Asians in hypo- or hypertechnological terms in cultural productions and political discourse.[4] Techno-Orientalist imaginations are infused with the languages and codes of the technological and the futuristic. These developed alongside industrial advances in the West and have become part of the West's project of securing dominance as architects of the future, a project that requires configurations of the East as the very technology with which to shape it. Techno-Orientalist speculations of an Asianized future have become ever more prevalent in the wake of neoliberal trade policies that enabled greater flow of information and capital between the East and the West. Substantial criticism of techno-Orientalism emerged in the mid-1990s when cultural theorists began to trace its manifestations and theorize its causes and implications. Kevin Morley and David Robins, Toshiya Ueno, and Kumiko Sato, principal trailblazers of the field, laid much of the valuable groundwork. Morley and Robins's *Spaces of Identity: Global Media, Electronic Landscapes, and Cultural Boundaries* (Routledge, 1995), in which a definition of "techno-Orientalism" first saw print, remains the most cited in critical assessments of technological and Orientalist discourses; however, Ueno has probably written most extensively about techno-Orientalism as a discursive cultural phenomenon in the era of what he identifies as the "post-Fordist social environment of globalization" (223). "The basis of Orientalism and xenophobia is the subordination of Others through a sort of 'mirror of cultural conceit,'" Ueno explains. "The Orient exists in so far as the West needs it, because it brings the project of the West into focus" (223).

Whereas Orientalism, as a strategy of representational containment, arrests Asia in traditional, and often premodern imagery, techno-Orientalism presents a broader, dynamic, and often contradictory spectrum of images, constructed by the East and West alike, of an "Orient" undergoing rapid economic and cultural transformations. Techno-Orientalism, like Orientalism, places great emphasis on the project of modernity—cultures privilege modernity and fear losing their perceived "edge" over others. Stretching beyond Orientalism's premise of a hegemonic West's representational authority over the East, techno-Orientalism's scope is much more expansive and bidirectional, its discourses mutually constituted by the flow of trade and capital across the hemispheres. As Ueno observes, techno-Orientalism is first and foremost an effect of globalism. "If the Orient was invented by the West," he writes, "then the Techno-Orient was also invented by the world of information capitalism" (228). Technological developments, driven by the imperial aspirations and the appetites of consumerist societies on both sides of the Pacific, propel the engines of invention and production. In its wake, Western nations vying for cultural and economic dominance with Asian nations find in techno-Orientalism an expressive vehicle for their aspirations and fears. Our volume, *Techno-Orientalism: Imagining Asia in Speculative Fiction, History, and Media*, documents past and current constructions of the role of Asia in a technologized future and critically examines this proliferating phenomenon.

Dr. Fu Manchu illustrates just one way in which techno-Orientalist imagery pervades Western cultural productions in the early twentieth century. The principal locales of techno-Orientalist projects as they developed in the late twentieth century have primarily been Japan and China. Ueno, whose influential analyses of "Japanimation" in the mid-1990s seeded the field of techno-Orientalist studies, observes, "In Techno-Orientalism, Japan is not only located geographically, but is also projected chronologically. Jean Baudrillard once called Japan a satellite in orbit. Now Japan has been located in the future of technology" (228). Morley and Robins put a finer point on the temporal dimension of the spatial construction: "If the future is technological, and if technology has become 'Japanised,' then the syllogism would suggest that the future is now Japanese, too. The postmodern era will be the Pacific era. Japan is the future, and it is a future that seems to be transcending and displacing Western modernity" (168).

Whereas Japan's dubious honor as the original techno-Orient was bestowed in the eighties with the help of the cyberpunk movement, the techno-Orientalizing of China occurred roughly a decade later.⁵ China was not yet a competitor in the global economy in the 1980s, when the West focused its wary gaze on what it saw as an invasion of Japanese capital investments and imports into Western economies. When China was recognized as a newly industrialized country (NIC) in the 1990s and its influence in the global economy increased, it, too, became once again a target of techno-Orientalist fashioning. The discourse on China's "rise" in the U.S. context, consistent with techno-Orientalist contradictions, has focused on constructing its people as a vast, subaltern-like labor force *and* as a giant consumer market whose appetite for Western cultural products, if nurtured, could secure U.S. global cultural and economic dominance. This dual image of China as both developing-world producers and first-world consumers presents a representational challenge for the West: Is China a human factory? Or is it a consumerist society, like the United States, whose enormous purchasing power dictates the future of technological innovations and economies?

Japan and China are thus signified differently in the techno-Orientalist vocabulary. Both are constructed as competitors and therefore threats to the U.S. economy; but while Japan competes with the United States for dominance in technological innovation, China competes with the United States in labor and production. To put it in starker terms, Japan creates technology, but China *is* the technology. In the eyes of the West, both are crucial engines of the future: Japan innovates and China manufactures. And as Asia, writ large, becomes a greater consumerist force than the West,⁶ its threat/value dualism commensurately increases. These differences in the technological signification of Japan and China manifest themselves in the fictive forecasts of the Asian-tinged future. If Japan is a screen on which the West has projected its technological fantasies, then China is a screen on which the West projects its fears of being colonized, mechanized, and instrumentalized in its own pursuit of technological dominance.

India, another NIC, has also found itself under the techno-Orientalist gaze as a consequence of U.S. outsourcing practices. As a much maligned business strategy, outsourcing has provoked extremely negative public sentiments in the United States. These opinions find expression in a particular strand of techno-Orientalist discourse that consolidates China and India as the chief threats to the U.S. service and labor sectors. These Asian nations serve as the scapegoats for corporate decisions to move service and manufacturing jobs abroad and bear the brunt of the resulting xenophobic antipathies. Chinese and Indian workers, for instance, are routinely portrayed in techno-Orientalist and technophobic vocabularies; call center employees in India adopt Western Christian names and mimic the linguistic and idiomatic style of Americans, a practice so ubiquitous as to be parodied cinematically in romantic comedies such as *Outsourced* (2006), conjuring images of Dickian androids (or *Blade*

Runner's "replicants") who simulate human behavior and threaten the distinction between "real" and "fake" Americans. Glossy spreads of endless rows of Chinese workers in corporate factories and towns in mainstream magazines such as *Time* and *Wired* seal the visual vocabulary of Asians as the cogs of hyperproduction. In the NIC contexts, techno-Orientalist discourse constructs Asians as mere simulacra and maintains a prevailing sense of the inhumanity of Asian labor—the very antithesis of Western liberal humanism.

Discursive Conspicuity, Critical Invisibility

As this collection demonstrates, techno-Orientalism occurs across genres and disciplines—history, art, literature, film, television, video games—but the majority of the *criticism* coalesces around literature and film, particularly in the genre of speculative fiction (SF). This is unsurprising; techno-Orientalism finds some of its most pervasive expressions in SF because of the genre's futurist *esprit* of contemporary existential, racial, and technological anxieties. Nevertheless, we identify a disciplinary narrowness to SF in the extant scholarship that our project attempts to broaden.

Even as techno-Orientalism in SF has been documented by several incisive studies in recent decades, critical studies of Orientalism in the long history of

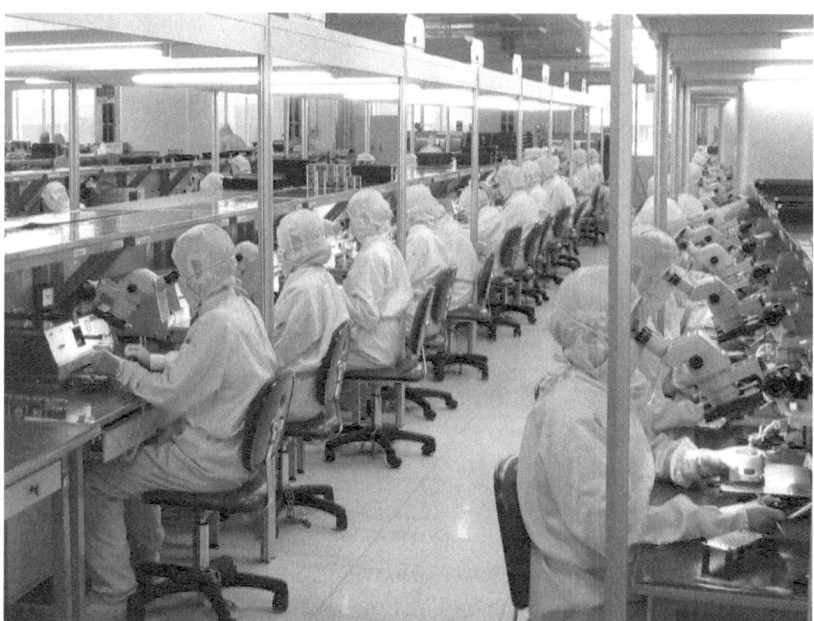

FIG. 0.1. Factory workers in China. *Source:* Photo by Steve Jurvetson. Licensed under Creative Commons 2.0.

SF are scarce. A survey of the essays published in the genre's flagship journal, *Science Fiction Studies*, founded in 1973, confirms the critical neglect. A search with the term "Orientalism" in the journal's archives yielded only nine substantive essays that address Orientalism, four of which are book reviews. A search with the term "techno-Orientalism" yielded, even more negligibly, two review essays. Similar searches in *Extrapolations*, another major academic venue for SF criticism, yielded equally scant results. And when *PMLA*, the lingua franca of academic scholarship in literature and languages, published a special issue on science fiction in May 2004, no mention of Orientalism could be found—this despite the fact that SF's propensity for projecting and amplifying contemporary racial and imperialist attitudes is well documented.[7] Indeed, the conceptualization of techno-Orientalism as a recognizable discursive effect of the postindustrial age may have been the clarion call for addressing this gap in the genre. Orientalism in SF during the pre-cyberpunk era may have suffered critical neglect because of the perception that the "yellow peril" has been kept in check by the mechanisms of immigration and exclusion acts that were in place for much of the midcentury. It took the repeal of the immigration acts in 1965, coupled with the entrance of Japanese capital and imports into the U.S. economy in the late seventies, to precipitate a renewed wariness toward all things Asian, onto which the West once again projected agendas of cultural hegemony and technological dominance. Cyberpunk, with its fetishizing gaze upon Japan as a seductive and contradictory space of futuristic innovation and ancient mystique, sharply focused the SF critical and creative lenses upon Asia.

Substantial criticism of techno-Orientalism thus emerged in the mid-1990s with the contributions of Morley and Robins, Ueno, and Sato. Critical momentum continued with Takayuki Tatsumi's 2000 historiography of Japanese SF in *Science Fiction Studies* (*SFS*), and a 2002 special issue of *SFS* on Japanese speculative fiction, guest edited by Takayuki Tatsumi, Christopher Bolton, and Istvan Csicsery-Ronay, Jr., introduced Japanese SF and cyberpunk visions to the Western audience. Sato's important and incisive 2004 intersectional analysis of what she describes as "the four different categorical spheres, namely, Western cyborg philosophy, American cyberpunk, Japanese cyberpunk, and Japanese theory of uniqueness known as *nihonjinron*" (335–336) and Christine Cornea's chapter "Techno-Orientalism and the Postmodern Subject" in Jacqueline Furby and Karen Randell's *Screen Methods: Comparative Readings in Film Studies* (Wallflower Press, 2006) sustained the necessary critical interest in the field.

These studies, however, constitute the bulk of the critical history of techno-Orientalism. Other studies in recent years, such as Mimi Thi Nguyen and Thuy Linh Nguyen Tu's *Alien Encounters: Popular Culture in Asian America* (Duke, 2007), Wendy Hui Kyong Chun and Lynn Joyrich's 2009 special issue of *Camera Obscura*, "Race and/as Technology," Chun's *New Media, Old*

Media: A History and Theory Reader (Routledge, 2005), and Lisa Nakamura's *Cybertypes* (Routledge, 2002), made significant contributions to critiques of Orientalism in popular culture and mainstream media. Yet, despite techno-Orientalism's growing prevalence in the Western cultural consciousness, and in SF more specifically, it has been generally ignored in academic and popular cultural spheres.

A special issue of the literary journal *MELUS*, titled "Alien/Asians" (2008) and edited by Stephen Hong Sohn, expanded the critical scope of the phenomenon and drew it closer for theoretical scrutiny. Sohn's introduction persuasively conveys the urgent need for vigilant documentation and analysis of the ever-growing techno-Orientalist vocabulary. The eight essays in the issue examine a range of techno-Orientalist instantiations in SF within U.S., Japanese, Chinese, and Indian contexts, from "a cyberpunk-inflected Asian future" to "the cyborg technologies intertwined with Asian American bodies" (Sohn 15). The essays, Sohn writes, "investigate how alternative imaginaries provide fertile terrains to consider the prospects of racial subjectivity and identity" (15). The essayists take a hard look at the work of SF luminaries such as Philip K. Dick, Ursula K. Le Guin, William Gibson, Neal Stephenson, and William S. Burroughs, whose work consciously or unconsciously traded in techno-Orientalist tropes, as well as the work of Asian American and Asian Canadian writers such as Karen Tei Yamashita, Amitav Ghosh, and Larissa Lai, who mount metafictional critiques of techno-Orientalist tropes in SF.

Techno-Orientalism: Imagining Asia in Speculative Fiction, History, and Media, therefore, has two objectives. The first is to continue the work begun by the aforementioned predecessors, to "consider the prospective thesis that cultural production is still invested in parsing out how the yellow peril continues to be a mode to draw from, write against, challenge, negotiate, and problematize" (Sohn 6–7). The volume argues that while Orientalism defines a modern West by producing an oppositional and premodern East, techno-Orientalism symmetrically and yet contradictorily completes this project by creating a collusive, futurized Asia to further affirm the West's centrality. The second objective is constructive. While we critique the dehumanizing effects of the techno-Orientalist gaze, we also see an opportunity for critical reappropriations in texts that self-referentially engage with Asian images; indeed, as an example, Asian SF writers have already taken to the trope to create the SF cottage industry in which the subject and setting are Eastern. There is of course the danger that Asian and Asian American creators might internalize techno-Orientalist patterns and uncritically replicate the same dehumanizing model. However, thanks to its global and mass appeal, the speculative imagination in television, graphic novels, or science fiction is by no means the purview of single national traditions. Even as techno-Orientalism has become more pervasive, it has also engendered counterdialogue in those same cultural and political spaces.

Global Consumption

While Orientalism as a critical lens describes how Western discourse discursively catalogues or frames the East, it has always been trained on domestic—that is, Western or U.S.—configurations against the Orientalized Other. Edward Said notes his "real argument is that Orientalism is—and does not simply represent—a considerable dimension of modern political-intellectual culture, and as such has less to do with the Orient than it does with 'our' world" (12). *Techno*-Orientalism, with a vision of the future that is global in scope and reach, adds a wrinkle to the critical commonplace that Orientalism actively produces and reproduces an oppositional East to cement Western hegemony. Particularly within the realm of SF, techno-Orientalist tropes have been absorbed, reenvisioned, and replicated by other sites of cultural production, with interesting geopolitical implications.[8] For example, Sato writes that Japan's entry into cyberpunk SF reinvigorates *nihonjinron*, the idea of an essentialist Japanese superiority that was integral to its imperialist project. With Japan's surrender in 1945, however, the idea of *nihonjinron* lost currency—that is, until it was reenabled by cyberpunk fiction in the 1980s. Sato observes that it was cyberpunk that resurrected the idea of Japanese essentialism: "This proud announcement of revived Japaneseness requited through the cutting edge of American culture means that the two separate histories of the West and Japan—the former modernizing, the latter behind—coincide in the discovery of Japan in American cyberpunk" (346). That proves troublesome, she argues, because it assumes Japanese essentialism as the primary reason for Japan's economic and technological achievements. For example, two paradigmatic cyberpunk works, *Ghost in the Shell* (1995) and Chōhei Kambayashi's novel *Yukikaze* (1985), have strong female cyborg leads paired with weaker, male companions. While Western cyberpunk seeks to claim liberal humanist subjectivity and modernity, having a female cyborg subject allows Japan to circumvent the question of subjectivity and modernity altogether. In both works, the male (Western) subject is deflated and removed from the center, while the cybernetic female embraces technology over humanity, allowing the insertion of Japan-as-signifier of futurity based on the constructed image of the West's Othering of technology and Asia. In other words, a Japan manufactured by the West can further ethnocentric or nationalist projects on both fronts. Techno-Orientalist discourse, in this case, has been reified in another nationalist context, further demonstrating its discursive hegemony as it serves a site other than its point of origin.

The Western fixation on Asian futurism indicates just how important it is to approach techno-Orientalism from several vantages. William Gibson is perhaps the most renowned exemplar of the West's fascination with the technologized Asian subject, evident in his unapologetic rhapsodizing in a 2001 issue of *Wired*, but even he merits a second look: "Dining late, in a plastic-draped gypsy noodle stall in Shinjuku, the classic cliché better-than-*Blade Runner* Tokyo street set, I scope my neighbor's phone as he checks his text messages. Wafer-thin, Kandy Kolor pearlescent white, complexly curvilinear, totally ephemeral looking, its screen seethes with a miniature version of Shinjuku's neon light show.... Tokyo has been my handiest prop shop for as long as I've been writing: sheer eye candy" (Gibson, "My Own Private Tokyo"). Gibson's meditation touches upon the multipronged reach of techno-Orientalist discourse—he references the dystopic, Asianized cinematic vision of Los Angeles; he admits drawing upon Tokyo's luminescence for his literary well; and it is the "ephemeral looking" mobile phone that inspires him to imagine new media, as he did with cyberspace in *Neuromancer*. Essentially, Gibson admits that the futurism he reads in Tokyo is largely superficial ("sheer eye candy"); the phone appears to be futuristic simply because of its alien surroundings, and his own somewhat tautological belief in Tokyo as his futuristic "prop shop."

But more interestingly, Gibson credits Japan's encounters with the West as the central reason for its present status as a site of the future. He explains, "[T]he nation of Japan [swallowed] whole the entirety of the Industrial Revolution. The resulting spasms were violent, painful, and probably inconceivably disorienting. The Japanese bought the entire train-set: clock-time, steam railroads, electric telegraphy, Western medical advances.... The result of this stupendous triple-whammy (catastrophic industrialisation, the war, the American occupation) is the Japan that delights, disturbs and fascinates us today" (Gibson, "Modern Boys and Mobile Girls"). That is, to understand Japan as the site of the future, one must first read its historical introduction to technology by (and, to the Western eye, its embrace of) the West. In a wonderfully circular way, Gibson touches upon the tautological aspect of techno-Orientalism: the Japanese are technologically advanced and therefore culturally fascinating now because of past Western modernizing interventions in the Eastern sphere. In Gibson's history, the West has created a hyperfuturistic Japan; and in this vision, Japan is now, in a sense, more West than the West, a simulacrum that threatens the foundational fiction of the West as Future.

It would be easy to dismiss Gibson's liberties with Japanese culture as a symptom of his misreading of his muse, but our instinct tells us that would be too simple. Instead, we are interested in the potentials for contrapuntal dialogism in such engagements. Parodic and reciprocal appropriations of techno-Orientalism in Asian cultural productions, for example, have opened up spaces for artistic and intellectual critique. Yet some remain skeptical of the effects of such appropriations. Ueno regards techno-Orientalism as a metanarrative that has become "an epistemological apparatus for Japanese to misunderstand themselves, and for Westerners to misunderstand others" (qtd. in Oda 250).

Elaborating on Ueno's skepticism, artist and cultural anthropologist Masanori Oda observes in an essay on what he calls "the present Post-Orientalist moment," "Japanese *anime, manga,* and *games* are becoming a kind of 'contact zone' for the West to meet the latest Japan/ese. What is different from the old Orientalism is that both parties (Japanese and Occidental) hold a kind of reciprocity. This means that the Japan/ese often appear as 'as you like,' self-fashioned figures to the West, not only to satisfy their own gaze, but to disguise the real portrayal of their own nature or desires, as if to say, 'This figure is not so bad for me'" (250). Oda's skepticism rests chiefly with the mediatory capacity of techno-Orientalist discourses. "There may be a contact between both parties," he cautions, "but there is never an encounter, much less an uncanny experience. Thus, mutual misconceptions accumulate" (251). Indeed, numerous examples of Oda's notion of "contact without encounter" are identified and critiqued in the essays collected in this volume. It is this effect of "contact without encounter" produced by techno-Orientalist discourses that our volume seeks to call out and counteract. If technology has come to mediate "contact" between East and West through techno-Orientalist discourses, how, then, might we fashion representational technologies that engender "encounter" rather than empty contact?

Expanding the Fields: Techno-Orientalism and Asian American Studies

If SF and its variants in historiography, cinema, and new media provide the content of techno-Orientalist expressions, we believe that Asian American studies equips us with the best critical and theoretical toolboxes for documentation and interrogation. Asian American studies has always attended to constructions of culture, race, and the body partly because U.S. techno-Orientalist imagination has its roots in the view of the Asian body—the Chinese body, most specifically—as a form of expendable technology, a view that emerged in the discourse of early U.S. industrialization.

From the earliest era of Asian peoples in the United States, their technical abilities were both lauded and erased. An exemplar is the Chinese men who composed more than half of the labor force that completed the transcontinental railroad's western portion over the high Sierra Nevada mountains to Promontory, Utah, in 1869. In the campaign to extend the Chinese Exclusion Act of 1882, the American Federation of Labor argued in their publication, *Some Reasons for Chinese Exclusion, Meat vs. Rice, American Manhood against Asiatic Coolieism: Which Shall Survive?* (1902), that the Chinese male body differed radically from the American male body. The publication argued that the Chinese laborer could withstand physical deprivations that American and

European laborers could not (American Federation of Labor et al. 5, 14, 16, 18). This constructed difference rationalized discriminatory policies against Chinese railroad workers. *Meat vs. Rice* did not argue the Chinese had particular technical skills that were *valuable* for constructing the transcontinental railroad. On the contrary, the publication claimed the Chinese body simply did not require the conditions of safety, sustenance, and shelter that bodies of European descendents required. Implicit in their argument is a threat to the superior European laborer's way of life or culture by a kind of unfeeling superhuman antithetical to the West's liberal humanist credo.

The U.S. techno-Orientalist imagination is thus rooted in this view of the Asian body as a form of expendable technology—a view that emerged in the discourse of early U.S. industrialization and continued to evolve in the twentieth century. In 1982, a twenty-seven-year-old Chinese American named Vincent Chin was beaten to death by two white men in Detroit. The attackers, Ronald Ebens and Michael Nitz, were autoworkers in a U.S. auto industry that was losing market share to Japanese cars. Though Chin, a drafter, did not work in automobiles, Ebens and Nitz viewed him as representative—indeed, an embodiment—of Japanese auto manufacturing as they beat him with a baseball bat, reminiscent of Americans smashing Japanese-made cars in reaction to increasing auto imports in the early 1980s.[9] The callous brutality of Chin's death evinces something more than racial hatred; Chin not only was perceived as a convenient stand-in for the Japanese automotive industry, but embodied its traits—unfeeling, efficient, and inhuman. In Ebens and Nitz's eyes, they were Luddites striking down the automatons that had been sent in to replace them. Techno-Orientalist discourse completed the project of dehumanizing Vincent Chin by rendering him as not only a racialized Other, but a factory machine that had to be dismantled by Ebens and Nitz to reclaim their personhood, subjectivity, and masculinity.[10] The shock and outrage over Chin's murder served as a critical rallying cry under which a coalition of ethnic-specific groups joined as *Asian Americans*.

In the twenty-first century, the perceived economic threat of Japan and its automobiles has given way to China. Despite the fact that China does not have a particularly strong reputation as a high-tech nation, techno-Orientalism's robust flexibility allows for seamless transplantation to another national site. China's rapid economic rise is largely credited to its vast manufacturing base, which, coupled with cheap labor and less regulation, has made it an attractive production location for many tech companies, including Apple and Dell. And although the vast majority of Chinese cannot afford the iPads and iPhones they produce, we see in U.S. media a representational shift, using techno-Orientalist conventions, transforming Chinese from mindless workers to sinister agents. For example, in October 2010, a U.S. PAC called Citizens Against Government Waste uploaded a commercial titled "Chinese Professor" on YouTube.

FIG. 0.2 *Chinese Professor*. Citizens Against Government Waste. *Source:* YouTube.

Set in Beijing, China A.D. 2030, the commercial depicts a male professor lecturing in a large hall accompanied by high-tech gadgets. The lecture consists of conservative talking points regarding the decline of the United States. As colorful images of fallen nations scroll behind him, the professor explains, "America tried to spend and tax itself out of a great recession. Enormous so-called 'stimulus spending,' massive changes to health care, government takeovers of private industries, and crushing debt." He concludes, "Of course, we owned most of their debt, so now they work for us." With echoes of Fu Manchu, the professor smiles directly into the camera, eliciting his students' mirth. By presenting the Chinese professor, the students, and the lecture as moving seamlessly between the lecture hall technology and the tablet screens that students hold in their laps, this video implies that China now leads the world in technological production *and* consumption. The encoded secondary message of the commercial sidesteps the reality of China's still developing technological penetration by projecting a present-day existential fear into a vision of the future, with technology supposedly rooted in U.S.-based innovation. It is an elegant solution that effectively alarms the uninformed viewer by using a pan-Asian technological conflation to elide reality and implicitly accuse China of stealing U.S. intellectual property. Thus, although the national actors and the details are quite different from the automobile industry of the 1980s, we have a similar techno-Orientalist narrative: U.S. jobs and manufacturing are being stolen by inorganic, technologically infused persons who threaten not only our economic but humanistic integrity.

SF's techno-Orientalist tendencies have become so common as to merit incisive parody. The animated series *Futurama* takes place a thousand years in

FIG. 0.3 *Futurama*. "Attack of the Killer App." *Source:* Comedy Central.

the future, and both skewers and pays homage to SF conventions. In an episode from the sixth season, *Futurama* depicts the launch of the new "EyePhone," a jab at Apple's handset, as a pillory of modern consumerism. The series' white protagonist, Fry, asks a retail clerk of South Asian descent, "you're from one of those ethnicities that knows about technology; why is it called an EyePhone?" (Sandoval). Depicted in the show as having an intelligence level on par with Homer Simpson, Fry is not meant to be taken seriously, and often acts as a vessel for twentieth-century ignorance in a progressive future. What is notable in this exchange is how the producers of *Futurama* have Fry explicitly verbalize a familiar techno-Orientalist trope—Asiatic bodies functioning as gatekeepers, facilitators, and purveyors of technology. In this episode, the South Asian clerk literally acts as the final node on the assembly line that has been largely produced by robotic arms—the clerk reaches through the drapes to pull an EyePhone from a pile and we see mechanical limbs swinging about the factory. He is an assembly line automaton with a human skin, and his affectless, bored intonation belies his true nature as a machine. A less self-aware show might leave it at that, but Fry's graceless pronouncement underscores the techno-Orientalist trope, taking SF to task while simultaneously paying ironic homage to the genre.

This same technologizing convention that *Futurama* so sharply satirizes is found in numerous literary works, including David Mitchell's *Cloud Atlas* (2004). Mitchell's six stories link together characters and narratives spanning past, present, and distant future. Consequently, Mitchell's novel has the unenviable task of repeatedly establishing the framing for each separate story line. An economical method for quickly thrusting the reader into the speculative future is to use a technologized East Asia, as he does in the story "An Orison of

Sonmi-451." The setting of Nea So Copros, the "corpocracy" of what appears to be a unified Korea sometime after the twenty-second century, is where we are introduced to our enslaved narrator, Sonmi-451, a cloned "fabricant" designed to serve in a fast-food restaurant. Mitchell paints Korea as the setting for high technology, enforced consumption, and excessive advertising; and his larger social critique lies in the mirroring of the fabricants who must serve and the "purebloods" who must constantly consume, a master-slave dialectic that relies on cannibalism, erased from view, and technology, projected into high visibility. Sonmi-451 eventually gains self-awareness, knowledge, and power to create a declaration of rights for enslaved fabricants and oppressed classes, but only after she reads the classics of Western civilization (187, 193). Thus, Mitchell's novel reinforces both the perception of Asia as the definitive site for technophilic and technophobic speculations of an oppressive future and the view that only a Western-coded subject can truly realize liberal humanism in such an environment.

Digital spaces abound with reinscribed racial tropes and stereotypes; these are sites in which racialization is more likely to be reinforced than challenged (Nakamura, *Cybertypes* 227). However, we argue that techno-Orientalist conventions in new media are complicated by the fact that the medium is closely associated with Asia on several levels—as a manufacturing base, as a source of technological innovation, and as a conduit for cultural exports. In new media, the Asian subject is perceived to be, simultaneously, producer (as cheapened labor), designer (as innovators), and fluent consumer (as subjects that are "one" with the apparatus). This has the effect of schizophrenic significations of the techno-Orientalized subject in the realm of new media—games in particular. In 2011, for instance, Blizzard Entertainment announced an expansion

FIG. 0.4 Screenshot from "Mists of Pandaria" expansion pack. *Source:* Blizzard Entertainment.

pack, called "The Mists of Pandaria," for their immensely popular MMORPG (massively multiplayer online role playing game) *World of Warcraft*. MMORPGs generally have strong roots in the fantasy and SF genres, which grant room for characters and creatures with attributes that often reflect racial stereotypes.[11] The Asian-themed world of Pandaria—described as "mysterious" and "ancient"—and its high-flying, kung-fu-fighting Pandaren—warriors in a nonthreatening form—continue in the tradition of portraying Asian culture and subjects as exotic realms to be explored and manipulated. Within the same game is a curious mirroring of globalization, in which first-world gamers looking to accrue in-game capital (gold) more quickly hire gamers—many of whom are young Chinese men—to "farm" gold, thereby miming offline conditions in which first-world consumers gain economically by cheapened high-tech labor. At the same time, an acceptance of the Asian subject's reputed digital literacy brings about a sense of wonder and even admiration of their gaming skills—the global rankings of gamers are often dominated by Korean players, for instance. We question, however, whether that is not another symptom of the stereotyping of Orientalized cyborg bodies predicated on a presumed seamlessness with technology.

But not all accounts of Asia's development of machine, computer, and robot technologies can be said to bear the stamp of techno-Orientalism, of having been authored or mediated by the Western techno-Orientalist lens. Japan's own narrative accounts of its postwar national renaissance, for instance, have always emphasized its status as a premier robotics innovator in the global context; such accounts cannot always be read as appropriations (self-conscious or not) of Western techno-Orientalism. The International Robot Exhibition (IREX), the largest robot trade fair in the world, has taken place biennially in Tokyo since 1973. The 2013 Expo slogan, "Making a Future with Robot," expresses Japan's construction of itself as the author of the future, to be written with the technology with which it has almost become synonymous. The slogan not only resonates with Nam June Paik's famous declaration "the future is now," but also reverberates throughout East Asia as China and South Korea vie for leadership in high-tech innovation and consumerism.[12] Is techno-Orientalism still Orientalist if contemporary techno-discourse is being authored principally by Asians, seemingly without regard for the Westerners who look on with a mixture of anxiety and envy? Can its patterns be adapted to preserve and facilitate an ethnocentric discourse with its own set of problematic racial politics?

Instantiations and Reappropriations

Our volume provides an array of cultural and media reference points from which to interrogate and negotiate representations of "Asia" in our projections of the technologized future. The essays in Part I document and analyze instantiations of techno-Orientalism over time and across genres, while those in Part II examine ironic and self-referential texts that seek to recuperate anti-imperial, anti-Orientalist critical and representational stances via techno-Orientalist reappropriations.

Part I begins with Kenneth Hough's "Demon Courage and Dread Engines," an examination of how early techno-Orientalist discourse during World War II exaggerated the military technology and prowess of Imperial Japan—some of which was completely fabricated—and promoted wartime hysteria with techno-Orientalist tropes, including automaton-like Japanese soldiers forming human pyramids to scale walls. Jason Crum follows with "'Out of the Glamorous, Mystic East,'" in which he traces a different strain of wartime Orientalism in a discussion of U.S. radio serials from the 1920s to 1940s. Unlike the exaggerated rhetoric that Hough documents, Crum argues that these programs deny rather than exaggerate the technological prowess of Asian Others and depict Asian subjects as culturally fixed in the past.

Whether Asians figure into U.S. speculations of a future utopia at the onset of the Industrial Revolution is the subject of Victor Bascara's "*Looking Backward*, from 2019 to 1882." Bascara juxtaposes the complete absence of Asians in the late twentieth-century future envisioned in Edward Bellamy's 1887 speculative novel *Looking Backward 2000–1887* with their pervasive presence in that of *Blade Runner* (1982), directed by Ridley Scott, to make the point that for both Bellamy and the film, Western utopian futurity is contingent on "the obviation of racialized and/or immigrant labor." Warren Liu picks up a similar gesture of erasure in his examination of William Gibson and Bruce Sterling's *The Difference Engine*. In "Queer Excavations," Liu insists that techno-Orientalism's presence need not be signified by Hong Kong's neon skyline or Shibuya's noodle bars; instead, he reveals that the very absence of Orientalist images underscores an obsessive conflation of race and technology that has been sublimated into the key technological plot device—time travel—and the very structure of the novel.

In "I, Stereotype," Seo-Young Chu bridges Masahiro Mori's theory of the "uncanny valley," used to describe the unease of viewing human-like figures bordering on verisimilitude, with the stereotyping of Asian bodies. Chu contends that while technology may be used to create humanoid robots that fall short, stereotypes as *techne* have the opposite effect—rendering entire peoples less than human. In each case, the viewer's humanity is reassured, due to the existential anxiety produced by the very presence of an uncanny Other. Like Chu, Abigail De Kosnik traces the ways in which American popular cinema functions as what she calls "mnemotechnics," or "memory technology," by registering the evolving stages of anti-Asian sentiment over the course of the twentieth century. De Kosnik constructs a persuasive historiography of the ways in which *The Mask of Fu Manchu*, *Son of Sinbad*, and *Star Wars* capitalized on the antagonisms of the decades in which the United States was at war with an Asian nation by deploying techno-Orientalist tropes.

Jinny Huh's "Racial Speculations" provides an illuminating reading of the cult television series *Battlestar Galactica* (2003–2009) within the rhetoric and practices of contemporary assisted reproductive technologies. Huh argues that the series engages in a speculative exercise in determining the look of a future master race by resolving anxieties about racial mixing via a future populated by the offspring of acceptable gendered racial pairings (i.e., Asian female-white male) and by expunging blackness, both male and female, from the process.

Steve Choe and Se Young Kim's "'Never Stop Playing'" offers a chilling look at the discursive powers of techno-Orientalism in rendering Asian video gamers as objects of knowledge for Western subjects. In their examination of *StarCraft* and professional South Korean players, Choe and Kim note the ways Western journalists and gamers seek to comprehend, while belittling, the popularity of video gaming as a national pastime. And finally, Dylan Yeats's "'Home Is Where the War Is'" reminds us that in the U.S. entertainment industry, techno-Orientalism remains a unidirectional exercise. Drawing on Said's view of the Orient as a Western fantasy, Yeats explains that the smooth switch from "space wars" to "cyber wars" indicates the primacy of U.S. policy in creating an enemy Orient.

If the essays in Part I reaffirm Orientalism's stranglehold on representations of Asia in the technological age, the essays in Part II provide vital, sharp counterdiscourses via ironic, self-referential, and recuperative narrative strategies. Julie Ha Tran, in "Thinking about Bodies, Souls, and Race in Gibson's Bridge Trilogy," contests prevailing techno-Orientalist criticism by arguing that William Gibson creates a self-aware dialectic between Eastern and Western conceptions of posthumanist subjectivity. Tran reworks techno-Orientalism by arguing that Gibson self-consciously reflects techno-Orientalist discourse back onto itself as a bidirectional force.

Kathryn Allan's "Reimagining Asian Women in Feminist Post-Cyberpunk Science Fiction" contrasts cyberpunk fiction, which objectifies and Orientalizes female cyborgs, with works that attempt to reposition them as the subject. In a reading of Tricia Sullivan's *Maul* and Larissa Lai's *Salt Fish Girl*, Allan articulates a "feminist post-cyberpunk" subgenre that creates a space for non-white characters due to globalization and reorients the subject matter around issues of gender and race, moving such characters from the periphery to the center. In "The Cruel Optimism of Asian Futurity and the Reparative Practices of Sonny Liew's *Malinky Robot*," Aimee Bahng also moves the periphery to the center by examining forms of survival, if not reappropriations, necessitated by the human cost of the spread of neoliberalism in Asian economies in recent decades. Drawing on Lauren Berlant's elucidation of the fallacies of "aspirational normativity" in *Cruel Optimism*, Bahng's reading of Sonny Liew's graphic anthology *Malinky Robot* (2011) teases out the ways in which techno-Orientalism and neoliberal policies have colluded to produce an Asian future in which dispossession and displacement of a permanent underclass are rationalized.

Douglas Ishii's "Palimpsestic Orientalisms and Antiblackness" takes Joss Whedon to task for rendering settings infused with techno-Orientalist artifacts but troublingly depopulated of Asian people in the cult television series *Firefly* and *Dollhouse*. In these Orientalist palimpsests of future Whedon-verses, Ishii argues, Asians and blacks remain illegible, subjugated, instrumentalized, or objects of emancipatory efforts in order to evoke and rationalize white-defined human rights discourses and liberationist fantasies—or, as Ishii puts it, "to keep freedom white." Like Ishii, Tzarina Prater and Catherine Fung target techno-Orientalist influences in cult films by reading Larissa Lai's short story "Rachel" (2004) and her poem "rachel" (2009) as critical reappropriations of the Orientalized android in *Blade Runner* and in Philip K. Dick's novel *Do Androids Dream of Electric Sheep?* (1968). Prater and Fung challenge what they call the "tyranny of the lens" by asking, "How does one contend with the history of image making in which one is the abject object?" They situate *Blade Runner*'s and Dick's female replicants and male characters of color within transnational racial contexts, with an illuminating connection to British "blackness," as signifiers of all who are not labeled "white" and therefore not human.

Perhaps the most self-referential and potently parodic gestures toward techno-Orientalist imaginaries can be found in the work of media artist Nam June Paik. Charles Park examines how Paik's work illustrates the creation of hybridity and "the fluidity with which cultural and technological exchanges occur" across transnational sites. Park argues that Paik, as an artist who practiced uncanny "self-Orientalizations," is not simplistically trying to bridge East and West, especially as the distinction itself fixes the two in time and place, but instead illustrates what Park calls "multiple cultural modalities" that encompass a variety of cultural exchanges.

Such modalities, we believe, constitute the current state of the techno-Orientalist discourse as it circulates and evolves with the flow of cultural and informational capital across the hemispheres. And precisely because it continually evolves with the vicissitudes of globalization and technological advancements, techno-Orientalism must undergo continual assessment and critique.

Notes

1. Sax Rohmer, *The Mystery of Dr. Fu-Manchu* serial (1912–1913).
2. For a discussion and more examples of premodern Orientalist tropes in postwar

and contemporary U.S. science fiction, see Betsy Huang's "Premodern Orientalist Science Fictions."
3. The original comic book version of The Mandarin is bereft of satire—he is portrayed in earnest as a maniacal villain from China.
4. See Niu's "Techno-Orientalism, Nanotechnology, Posthumans, and Post-Posthumans in Neal Stephenson's and Linda Nagata's Science Fiction" (74).
5. We could argue that the fear of Chinese command over science and technology began in the nineteenth century concerning the Chinese men who built the transcontinental railroads in the United States and Canada. The Chinese brand of techno-Orientalism recycles familiar Orientalist stereotypes prevalent in the early days of Chinese immigration to the United States. The Chinese have always been perceived as laborers (or "coolies"—a strictly Western construction), beginning with the railroad workers as instruments of manifest destiny, continuing with the domestic and service industries as repetitive laborers, to the present-day image of vast fields of Chinese factory workers, likened to well-oiled machines in the Western imagination. In 1881, California Senator John Miller described Chinese workers as "machine-like . . . of obtuse nerve, but little affected by heat or cold, wiry, sinewy, with muscles of iron; they are automatic engines of flesh and blood; they are patient, stolid, unemotional . . . [and] herd together like beasts" (qtd. in Chang 130).
6. Forecasts by government and private-sector economists show that China's economy specifically, and Asia's more broadly, will become the top global economy by 2030. The National Intelligence Council projects in a December 2012 report that China's economy is likely to surpass the United States in less than two decades, while Asia will overtake North America and Europe combined in global power by 2030 (Zakaria; National Intelligence Council).
7. In *The Routledge Companion to Science Fiction* (Routledge, 2009), Isiah Lavender notes that "throughout most of its history, SF has reproduced rather than resisted racial stereotypes" (Bould et al. 188); in the same volume, Michelle Reid writes, "Sf imagines encounters with the Other (the alien, the strange newness brought about by change), typically from the perspective of the dominant Self" (257). As Lavender and Reid posit, the genre has a propensity for mapping wide-ranging racial and colonial anxieties upon fictional alien bodies.
8. Takayuki Tatsumi discusses a brief history of Japanese SF in "A Very Soft Time Machine" (250–252).
9. See Renee Tajima and Christine Choy's 1987 documentary *Who Killed Vincent Chin?*
10. Takeo Rivera's in-progress dissertation theorizes Chin's death at length.
11. Orcs, for example, have physical strength but low intelligence, following much of the mythology of orcs, but the game designers inexplicably have the Orcs break dance, racially linking them with African Americans. Goblins are a mercantile race, whose only loyalty is to commerce, which can be read as a Semitic caricature. Humans, of course, are the default Anglo-Saxon warrior race. See Langer.
12. While one could read Japan's embrace of robotics as part of its modernity project, that conveniently elides more complicated racial politics. One might read its investments in robotics as a means of addressing its impending population crisis, and with the labor pool shrinking, it will soon be unable to sustain Japan's economy. While other countries might relax their immigration policies to counterbalance the labor shortfall, Japan sees robotic workers as a means of solving its gerontological problems as well as preserving monoethnicity.

Part I
Iterations and Instantiations

1

Demon Courage and Dread Engines

America's Reaction to the
Russo-Japanese War and
the Genesis of the Japanese
Invasion Sublime

KENNETH HOUGH

In January 1907 Theodore Roosevelt found himself embroiled in a foreign relations crisis with Japan, and San Francisco was the epicenter. The city was still recovering from the great quake and fires of 1906 and was mired in one of the Gilded Age's worst political scandals, with many of its leaders indicted. Within the maelstrom, anti-Japanese labor groups and politicians called for the segregation of the city's schools and a total ban on Japanese immigration. As Americans became consumed with the so-called "Japanese question," the Japanese government cried foul; in the ensuing months, rumors of war spread through both nations (Daniels 34).

Speaking to a hastily assembled gathering of California Congressmen at the White House, an exasperated president warned that they were playing with dynamite: "We are dealing with a nation of proud and brave people. You do not know their resources. War with them would not be anything like war with Spain. The Japanese are not like the Europeans, who will exhaust the resources of diplomacy before going to war. When Japan strikes, she strikes quickly, and without warning" ("Seek to Avert War" 1). The Roosevelt administration had exploited fears of a Japanese attack before. The previous October, Secretary of State Elihu Root had cautioned California legislators that if war erupted, Japanese invaders might seize parts of the West Coast "before we were ready for a real fight" (Challener 244). These bleak assessments triggered a series of war scares that imperiled U.S.-Japanese relations for the remainder of the decade.

Roosevelt willingly deployed the phantasm of a Japanese invasion because he knew it provoked the public's anxieties, especially in the wake of the Russo-Japanese War. The conflict's grandiosity and Japan's apparent command of modern technology made the event unique in an age of Western imperialism. Throughout 1904 and 1905 the West closely followed reports of enormous battles, unimaginable carnage, and unprecedented weaponry. Mass media framed Japan's path to victory as a bewildering combination of Western technology and Eastern *weltanschauung*, somewhat intuiting the Meiji era mindset of *wakon yosai*—"Western science and technology, while resisting Westernization" (Koizumi 30). Roosevelt's 1907 forewarnings of Japanese invasion intentionally evoked the Russo-Japanese War's sensory shocks: surprise attack, savage combat on a vast scale, and Asian conquest of the "technological and futurological imagination," an early techno-Orientalist vision that induced an American identity panic—the *Japanese invasion sublime* (Morley and Robbins 153, 160, 173).

"What the World Has Learned from the Japanese War"

Shortly before midnight on February 8, 1904, Imperial Japanese Navy destroyers launched a surprise torpedo attack on the Russian First Pacific Squadron anchored at Port Arthur, Manchuria. More attacks followed over the next twelve hours, leaving five Russian warships significantly damaged and over one hundred sailors dead or wounded. Japan had struck two days after severing diplomatic ties with Russia and two days before formally declaring war (Wells and Wilson 9). The suddenness of the assault, according to U.S. naval observer Lieutenant Commander Newton A. McCully, left Russian defenders "confused, damaged, and partly disillusioned" (50).

Many early reports excitedly responded to Japan's introducing the torpedo into modern warfare, illustrating the public's interest in war technology. Pervasive was the belief that Japan had suddenly mastered Western weaponry; naval analyst Park Benjamin confidently predicted that Japan's torpedo attack had "determined the command of the sea in the present conflict" (71). The *Boston Daily Globe* found the torpedo's design newsworthy, offering readers a standalone technical illustration, "Death Dealing Whitehead Torpedo, Terror of Modern Warfare, Used by Japanese Navy" (4). "You can bet that the Japs had the very latest and most effective implements for a sea fight at Port Arthur," claimed one American naval authority. "They are progressive, and before they're through may teach all naval persons something" ("Japanese Astonish" 2). The extent to which Western culture came to associate the Japanese with the torpedo could be at times bizarre. A period French postcard caricatured Emperor Meiji and his imperial ambitions by grafting the ruler's head onto a torpedo labeled simply "Japan" (see Figure 1.1).

Despite the hyperbole, Japan's torpedo attack was surprisingly ineffectual. In fact, of the 370 torpedoes used by the Imperial Japanese Navy during the entire war, only 17 found their marks (Kowner, *Historical Dictionary* 381–382). Admiral Tōgō Heihachirō's Port Arthur raid was bold, but failed to eliminate the Russian naval threat in the western Pacific. Instead of gaining control of the seas in the first hours of the war, Japan was forced into a protracted, bloody contest that nearly bankrupted the nation. It eventually seized Port Arthur, but only after months of massive land battles, costing tens of thousands of casualties (Steinberg and Wolff 107–108, 121–123).

FIG. 1.1 A French postcard conflating the emperor with the torpedo, circa 1904.
Source: Author's personal collection.

Yet, like these opening torpedo volleys, the technological aspects of Japan's war ignited the Western imagination, especially as its victories mounted. The Russo-Japanese War was *mechanical*—if not exactly mechanized—and while not as revolutionary as the Great War's airplanes and tanks, its weapons produced a slaughter that prefigured the horrors soon to be unleashed on Europe. Staggering, too, was the sheer array of modern munitions, many being deployed for the first time on an appreciable scale, including contact mines, torpedoes, quick-firing rifles, heavy artillery, machine guns, searchlights, pre-dreadnought battleships, torpedo boats, barbed wire, telephones, wireless radios, aerial observation balloons, transcontinental railroads, and mass media propaganda (Patrikeeff and Shukman 1–4; Kowner, *Impact* 4). Even experimental weapons like submarines and airships, which saw only limited combat, entered the war's imaginary.

Most dramatically, the war's telecommunication technologies collapsed time and space, connecting combatants dispersed over battlefields and linking foreign war correspondents to their home countries. Frequent war reports gave readers a taste of the twentieth century's promise of telepresence, a technological experiential state that mitigated parochialism and increased public investment in a wider world (Sconce 56, 62–63). Instantaneous telegraphy also held new potential dangers. One editorial noted ironically how the same technology that facilitated the Portsmouth peace accords that closed the war also exposed the "thin veneer of civilization that covers the innate savagery of mankind." Peace and understanding might travel telegraph lines instantaneously, but so too could annihilation: "Failure of agreement will mean the awful message to St. Petersburg, and a duplicate to Tokio, 'Let loose the dogs of war.' Again the hands of the clock that indicate the world's enlightenment will be turned back to the mark indicating barbarism" ("Civilization and Savagery" 4).

Death and depravity radiating through telecommunications seemed a point of pride to a modern media basing their integrity squarely on the opening of communication channels to the Manchurian front. Thus supplied by nearly continuous reports, photographs, postcards, and films, Western audiences were able to experience war as no generation had before. They followed the six-week march of General Kuroki Tamemoto's forty thousand troops through frozen Korean wastes to the Chinese border, and thrilled when Japanese howitzers and machine guns shattered the entrenched Russians, forcing them to retreat. Though the fight was strategically indecisive, the psychological impact made by the Battle of Yalu River—"the first time in the modern age that an Asian force crushed a European force in a full-scale clash"—was incalculable (Kowner, *Historical Dictionary* 423–424). Military analysts and casual readers alike came to accept that the combatant best able to fuse high technology with fighting spirit would emerge victorious.

Media use of new communication technologies boosted awareness of the war, but also amplified sensationalism in an age of yellow journalism. Factual reports and sober analysis intermingled with bombastic headlines, rumors, and unabashed editorializing, all tending to inflate Japanese fighting prowess and combat successes, irrespective of battlefield realities. Japan's underdog status and surprising early victories especially excited Westerners, setting the stage for successive depictions of Japanese forces as modern, and the Russians as hopelessly retrograde (Steinberg and Wolff 110–112).

The Japanese juggernaut narrative also consumed popular culture. Advertisers borrowed war imagery to sell everything from medicine to children's toys, often drawing nonsensical connections. A 1904 Ghirardelli's Chocolate ad juxtaposes a Japanese artillery barrage with its alimentative candy, promising to prevent a "war on the system" (3). Even that most American of vendors, the Sears & Roebuck catalogue, sold stereographic photographs of the Japanese army at war for home consumption. Its "Siege of Port Arthur" set bizarrely exoticizes the Japanese as having perfected "scientific and business like warfare," claiming the island nation "could never be invaded except by extermination of every living man" (Sears, Roebuck and Co. and Schroeder 181). Meanwhile, war-themed adventure novels and travel narratives entertained juveniles and adults, suggesting the Russo-Japanese War was but great amusement. In *With Kuroki in Manchuria* (1904), correspondent Frederick Palmer recalls watching the Battle of Yalu, "as if a battle had been arranged for him and he had taken the best position for seeing its theatrical effects" (qtd. in Waller 44–45).

Dramatists could hardly resist such ready-made theater. In 1905 Morosco's Burbank Theater offered the stage play *Prisoner of War*, complete with authentic and elaborate battle scenes ("To Blow Up Ship" 1). Not to be outdone, the nascent movie industry produced silent short films like Selig Polyscope's *Torpedo Attack on Port Arthur* (1904), the Edison Company's *Skirmish between Russian and Japanese Advance Guards* (1904), and Biograph's *Hero of Liao-Yang* (1904). The last, filmed only three months after the battle it depicts, promotes an unambiguously gallant image of "Japanese masculinity, modern warfare and the imperialist contest for control of Korea and China," climaxing with an awe-inspiring Japanese artillery barrage (Waller 53–54).

Japanese propagandists were not oblivious to the power of mass media. Stung by negative publicity over atrocities committed during the Sino-Japanese War, Japan entered this conflict with a deliberate campaign to gain Western respect (Dorwart 109). Statesmen like Prince Itō Hirobumi and Baron Kaneko Kentarō wrote editorials for American periodicals, aligning Japan's war aims with U.S. policies. Simultaneously, strict military censorship kept sensitive information out of the papers and the hands of Russian intelligence. Japan's nationalistic press fielded its own correspondents, who fed patriotic reports to domestic and foreign outlets. Western reporters bristled at the orchestration, but control of the media avoided embarrassing leaks and furthered impressions of Japanese invincibility. Even spies like Colonel Akashi Motojirō manipulated the press to exaggerate Japanese strength, planting rumors about advanced Japanese technology to undermine Russian morale (Sharf 29; Jukes 21).

Japan's careful image management and media repetition of Japanese heroism and technological superiority helped win the war for Western affinity. However, contriving this narrative also stoked apprehensions of a looming Eastern threat to Western civilization.

The Japanese Invasion Sublime

While Japan's march toward world power status was generally celebrated in America, it was also filtered through the West's complex emotional response to race and emergent technologies, and infused with trepidation over an Asian power dominating a white one. Some Americans found this turn of events inspiring. "White supremacy is getting a terrible black eye in and about Manchuria and Mukden," wrote the *Seattle Republican* in March 1905, one of many African American newspapers that saw Japanese victory as a subversively powerful triumph for racial equality in an age of Jim Crow and lynching (qtd. in Kearney 35). Even W.E.B. Du Bois became a "Japanophile" approving the "fear of colored revolt against white exploitation" that Japanese victories produced (Kearney 19, 30, 38, 168).

White Americans' assessment of Japan's rise was more ambivalent. Concerns about "race decadence" bumped against the technological sublime, a state of awe attached to the creations of modern science. Enlightenment thinkers like Immanuel Kant and Edmund Burke had posited that confrontations with terror in the form of great natural forces could elevate observers to a "heightened awareness of reason." With the advent of the Machine Age, some felt that a similar astonishment from encounters with emerging technologies might lead to society's betterment. In fact, David Nye sees American culture's celebration of nature-controlling technologies, in awe-inspiring shared experiences like the completion of the transcontinental railroad, as central to the narrative of American greatness from the nineteenth century onward, forming unities across political, religious, regional, and class divides (3, 6–9, 22, 27).

War was another fraught activity that could potentially unify Americans in purpose, and the experience of modern warfare at the turn of the twentieth century supplanted nature as "the exemplary object or trigger of the sublime" (Ray 134). Likening the horrors of war to the "cunning of nature," Kant acknowledged that "war has something sublime about it" and experiencing its surprises and cruelties might spur humanity toward transcendence. Alleging that both savage and civilized peoples held "superior esteem for the warrior" whose heroism "does not yield to danger but promptly sets to work with vigor and full deliberation," Kant also allowed that the sublime experience of battle could forge national or racial unities as well as strengthen a nation's commitment to moral freedom (Neculau 36–38; Licht 23–25).

The harnessing of the war sublime (which complements and exhibits aspects of the technological sublime) for ideological purposes has been an enduring factor in American history. Looking at the recent war in Iraq, François Debrix notes how Orientalism and confrontation with violent imagery continue in America's "aesthetic imagination" of war as mobilizing factors in the quest for public approval: "This sublime aesthetic of war, relayed by contemporary media and popular cultural forms ... consists of producing spectacular, violent and shocking images of 'others' in distress or harm's way in places where America's wars are being fought.... [I]t is an ideology that postulates that only Americans (even if they are soldiers) are equipped to provide hope, morality, and humanity to the Middle East" (767). Moreover, Debrix sees the imagination of war-borne terror as essential to America's heroic narrative: "An ideology of America at war is enabled through a visual experience that consists of forcing the spectator's imagination not only to go through unbearable and shocking images but also to transcend this initial painful experience by discovering beyond it readily available reasons and larger-than-life truths than can make sense of it all and justify those horrific scenes ... towards some ideas that supposedly can provide solace, understanding, and ultimately pleasure to the spectator" (771).

This ideology epitomized American conflicts waged a century before the Iraq War's technological "shock and awe," and the view that combat with a savage, Orientalized enemy would "help democracy and peace and justice rise in a troubled and violent region" (Bush). Both the Spanish-American War (1898) and the subsequent Philippine-American War (1899–1902) were technology-driven events, fought with Gatling guns, Krag-Jørgensen rifles, steel battleships, and American soldiers, whom Secretary of War Elihu Root appreciated as part of the "great machine which we call military organization" (Simon 47). Beyond proving American ability in battle, and its industrial strength and capacity to make war, proponents felt these wars were essential markers of American modernity. Theodore Roosevelt reasoned their prosecution was "one of the great tasks set modern civilization," bringing blessings of American democracy to the world's backward peoples, and benefiting the domestic sphere by inoculating white manhood against the decline of civilization and alleviating residual sectionalism (Roosevelt 11; Bederman 187; Ninkovich 18–19).

With an ideology that combined technology, war, and race under the banner of civilizing imperialism, the United States entered the twentieth century seeking a "new international identity" (Ninkovich 47, 91–92). New liberating technologies, like wireless transmission and air travel, supported this identity and fostered America's transnational connections. Yet, technology acted as a double-edged sword, increasing encounters with global dangers, and giving rise to a host of new worries about American power. This included the Japanese invasion sublime, a hybrid of the technological and war sublime, and America's agitated view of Asians in the early twentieth century; this fear exaggerated the threat of Japanese militarism and concluded that a conquest of the United States was its ultimate goal. By envisioning Japanese ascendency primarily through a military domination of the Pacific, the Japanese invasion sublime operated as an early form of techno-Orientalism. Embedded within the sublime was also a drive to find a Western technological solution to the menace of Japanese military supremacy.

The Russo-Japanese War was the genesis event because it introduced a modern vision of the East effectively wielding technology against the West. After the war grew a suspicion that Japan, emboldened by its victory over Russia, would strike the United States with a Port Arthur–like sneak attack. The panic was enough to derail the U.S. Navy's plans for a "great western base" in the Philippines, with Japan's hard-won siege of Port Arthur still burning in the minds of American leaders (Challener 182; Edward Miller 79).

Yet, the Japanese invasion sublime was not merely a hopeless resignation to Japanese aggression. Prodded by the outcome of the Russo-Japanese War to confront the unpleasant image of Japanese hegemony, the American military slowly constructed a path around its immobilizing fears: War Plan Orange, America's first and most detailed official imagination of future war prior to World War II. From its genesis in 1907, Plan Orange's many authors "never wavered in their innermost minds" that a complete and utter destruction of Japan was the ultimate goal. Though the plan was endlessly revised, its basic structure yielded the strategy with which the United States triumphed in Pacific War of 1941 to 1945. Yet, no matter how triumphantly it imagined a final victory over Japan, the Orange Plan in each version assumed the Americans would suffer some form of catastrophic defeat to Japan at the conflict's onset (Edward Miller, 347, 363).

The Japanese invasion sublime, fueled by fearful images of Japanese domination powerful enough to undermine American security and triumphalism, shared the yellow peril's "kaleidoscope of apprehensions" that concurrently bedeviled the Western mind (Richard Thompson ii; Sharp 6). Both projected nightmarish images of Asians and fear that "the West could be overpowered and enveloped . . . by the forces of the East" (Marchetti 2). Unique, however, is the origin of the Japanese invasion sublime in a specific context and event. Unlike yellow peril's representation of Asian acrimony toward the West as being ancient, occultish, immortal, and divorced from definite grievances, it was the high-tech modernity exhibited by Japan in the Russo-Japanese War that launched the Japanese invasion sublime and gave it potency (Iriye 7).

Rotem Kowner contends that a "historiographic amnesia" erased Western memories of the Russo-Japanese War within a few years of its conclusion, yet the Japanese invasion sublime served as the West's anamnestic repository for the war—it was mythologized as a prelude to a U.S.-Japanese conflict, and exemplified as a warning of Japanese technological aggression for succeeding generations (*Impact* 2–3). Almost immediately after Russia's defeat, a menacing, technologically adept Japan became the focus of yellow peril media, until the end of World War II (Franklin, *War Stars* 36, 39).

The perception of the Russo-Japanese War as watershed moment was synchronous with the Victorian and Edwardian fixation on race, gender, and national strength. As the United States pondered its vulnerabilities, it developed an incongruous image of Japan: technologically adept, modern, chivalrous, and civilized, yet savage and ultimately an existential threat to the West. This knotty conception largely projected anxieties over decaying white masculinity, through nervous disorders like neurasthenia and declining birth rates, which Roosevelt termed "race suicide" (Bederman 199–200). Such worries underscored "silent invasion" rhetoric about Japanese immigrants; when Los Angeles's Japanese Chrysanthemum Club began raising donations for Japan's war effort, the *Los Angeles Times* accused them (and by implication all Japanese Americans) of being clandestine soldiers disguised as gardeners: "Under this euphonious name, which suggests quaint tea gardens, dancing Geisha girls, and flower bedecked booths and jinrikishas, there creeps the dominant idea of grim visaged War. . . . [U]ntil all the Japanese on the Pacific Coast have been brought within its influence and placed in readiness to respond to any call for aid from their island home" ("War Spirit in Sweet Names" 1). Nourishing these suspicions were reports of Japanese soldiers masquerading as Chinese peasants to elude the Russians in Manchuria ("Plays Waiting Game" 1). Scuttlebutt that secret Japanese armies existed on American soil awaiting instructions from Tokyo gained traction after the war. In 1907 William Randolph Hearst's *San Francisco Examiner* claimed "Japanese troops in the guise of coolies" were covertly maneuvering throughout California (qtd. in Daniels 110). This bogey had a surprising longevity, and suspicions of a Japanese American fifth column undergirded the drive for internment more than three decades later.

Existing apprehensions of white male deterioration coalesced around the Russo-Japanese War's disturbing visuals of modern war and Asian ascendency, giving rise to the Japanese invasion sublime. However, just as Roosevelt and other imperialists believed brutal race wars could strengthen American civilization, the sublime of an exaggerated Japanese menace might also be "a healthy shock, a temporary dislocation of the sensibilities that forced the observer into mental action" (Nye 6). Processed through this perspective, Japan's combination of technology, civilization, and primitive savagery to defeat a decrepit Russia served as a unifying call to arms and a potential solution to perceived American weakness.

"Japan Is Playing Our Game"

To be sure, American fear of Japanese aggression emerged gradually and was just one of many reactions to the Russo-Japanese War. As the fighting commenced, the journal *World's Work* promoted Japanese heroism, patriotism, and possession of "the latest and best devices for both offense and defense" as indications of righteousness (Tison 4699–4700). Throughout the war, the press exhorted Americans to believe Japan's ascendency had begun only after U.S. Commodore Matthew Perry forcibly opened the nation in 1854. Japanese envoy Kaneko similarly stroked the American ego: "To your Perry we owe a debt of gratitude that can never be repaid.... [W]ithout Perry Japan would not have received the blessedness of Western civilization" ("Gives America All of the Credit" 22).

By marking the Japanese with "typical" American ideals and crediting American militarism for their modernity, Americans could invest in Japan's victory as if were their own. U.S.-educated Japanese leaders like Admiral Uryū Sotokichi became honorary Americans fighting for American ideals. The *New York Times* proclaimed Uryū the "Mahan of Japan," and emphasized the admiral's training at the U.S. Naval Academy, marriage to a Vassar graduate, choice of English as his primary language, and conversion to Christianity (Jenkins 7). A Los Angeles doctor went further, explaining, "indeed it is Japan who is fighting the 'white man's battle' . . . for Christian civilization and human liberty, and for all that affects the welfare of the human race, in civil, commercial, industrial, educational and religious liberty" (E. F. Henderson 12). President Roosevelt expressed a similar kinship, marking each Japanese victory on a large map in the White House and contending in private, "Japan is playing our game" (Brands 527; Edmund Morris 312). Roosevelt also claimed that, upon hearing of the Japanese fleet's triumph at the Battle of Tsushima, he became "so excited that I myself became almost like a Japanese, and I could not attend to official duties" (qtd. in LaFeber 82).

Eroding American euphoria, however, were the widening battles and mounting casualties following Japan's quest for that elusive knockout blow. The interminable siege of Port Arthur by General Nogi Maresuke's Third Army between August 1904 and January 1905 was illustrative. While some Western reporters found a "splendid spectacle" in the machine gun fire, heavy artillery, and "human bullet attacks" (*nikudan kōgeki*) by bayonet-wielding Japanese soldiers, the slaughter was disquieting ("First Detailed History" 2). The Russians suffered 33,000 casualties and the Japanese approximately 93,000, with

15,400 killed outright, including Nogi's youngest son. Significantly, one life *was* spared: General Nogi's, when Emperor Meiji rejected his requests to commit suicide in response to the massacre (Kowner, *Historical Dictionary* 266, 290, 299; Steinberg and Wolff 121–123).

The Japanese government, fearing public uproar, sanctified Nogi's suicidal tactics and the troops' self-sacrifice as the ultimate in patriotism. Many Westerners also initially honored Japanese bravery at Port Arthur. Yet, images of Japanese soldiers charging unflinching en masse into the jaws of mechanical death, dying for apparently meaningless objectives like "203 Meter Hill," were as perplexing as they were indelible. Headlines exclaiming Japanese tenacity conjured images of ferocious Asian hordes: "THOUSANDS FALL IN VAIN ATTACKS," "JAPANESE LOSE 22,000 SOLDIERS IN CAPTURE OF HIGH HILL," "LIKE A NEST OF DEMONS." Suggestions of savagery were reinforced by grotesque battlefield descriptions "more infernal than ever dreamt by Dante" with hillsides "literally covered with dead and wounded. The trenches were rivulets of blood" ("No Quarter Asked or Given" 5).

Stories of Russian annihilation and the demonic acumen of Japanese troops formed the seedbed for the Japanese invasion sublime. Popular accounts of the "Japanese Way of Death" with gory artwork titillated and disturbed Western consciences. A surreal illustration from *Cassell's History of the Russo-Japanese War*, for example, shows a "human pyramid" of Japanese soldiers, clambering over the bodies of fallen comrades and rising in an insect-like column to mount a fortress wall (see Figure 1.2). Other accounts implied the Japanese had superhuman, robotic control of emotions and pain, a "clocklike precision" in military organization, and a serene "Japanese calm" with which they greeted war news (McClernand 143; "Japanese Calm" 189).

Characterizations of Asians as automatons in American culture predated the war. In the 1880s politicians sought the exclusion of Chinese immigrant workers on the basis of them being "machine like . . . automatic engines of flesh and blood" unfairly competing with white "human" laborers (Huang, "Premodern Orientalist Science Fictions" 23). Economic dangers from immigration were one thing, but there was sublimity in the Borg-like descriptions *Collier's* offered of the typical Japanese solider as "a perfectly working factor of the great machine-like army in whose pride he is a unit" (qtd. in Waller 59). Similarly, complimentary assessments given by foreign military observers embedded with Japanese troops read as precarious tributes at best. Lieutenant Colonel Edward J. McClernand, military attaché to the Japanese First Army, praised the average soldier's "habit of obedience to superiors [that] is bred to the bone" (22). Yet admiration for blind battlefield fidelity also reinforced a characterization of Japanese roboticism. McClernand further hinted the United States might someday be threatened by a Japan that was "prepared to pass in a day from a peace to a war footing" (143). If such charged expressions

FIG. 1.2 Japanese troops rise in a "human pyramid" to mount a wall at Port Arthur. *Source: Cassell's History of the Russo-Japanese War* (321). Courtesy of the University of California, Santa Barbara, Davidson Library collections.

filled staid military reports, it was little wonder that far more obstreperous assertions about Japan saturated news and popular fiction.

Embedding the Russo-Japanese War in Fiction

The Russo-Japanese War's final battle took place in Portsmouth, New Hampshire, where Japanese and Russian diplomats squared off at the negotiating table. Even here advanced technology was apparent: telegraphs flurried, movie cameras filmed, and while negotiators quibbled, Theodore Roosevelt took a dive in the U.S. Navy's first operational submarine, the USS *Plunger* (Edmund Morris 413). The Treaty of Portsmouth ended the twentieth century's first major war and was Roosevelt's crowning foreign policy achievement, earning him a Nobel Peace Prize (Esthus, *Theodore Roosevelt* 37). Response to the armistice and Japan's victory was enthusiastic, but some critics later charged Roosevelt with enabling despotism in Asia, including one historian who hyperbolically blamed him for the midcentury "dread of destruction of [American] cities in an atomic war" (Beale 456–458).

This sort of apocalypticism emerged soon after the armistice in fiction that distorted memories of the Manchurian conflict. The summer 1909 film *The Japanese Invasion* showed New York moviegoers a Japanese conquest of the American Pacific Coast led by a "General Noki" that the *New York Dramatic Mirror* praised as "vivid action and thrilling realism" (see Figure 1.3). Writer and actress Gene Gauntier recalled the picture caused "almost as great a furor" as the later *Birth of a Nation* (Gauntier 15–16, 132). The 1909 Los Angeles stage production *The Invasion*, a "play of Pacific Coast possibility," had Lieutenant Fulton Lane protect the "Caucasian race" from Kaneko, a "Korean spy and officer of the Muscovite Alliance," who heads an invading army of Koreans, Russians, and Japanese (Harry Carr 15). The play's special effects impressed the *Los Angeles Times*: "The new and scientific warfare, a struggle waged with noiseless guns, smokeless powder . . . wireless telegraphy . . . new and high explosives, and in its culminating moment, a duel between an invading fleet of dreadnoughts and an aëroplane, carrying the Stars and Stripes." A pyrotechnic climax featured a full-size mock-up of a Wright Flyer airplane, with a working engine, bombing enemy warships in San Pedro Harbor (Johnson 1; "Music and the Stage" 5).

In one sense these Japanese invasion dramas operated as the pre–Great War generation's version of the zombie horror film: lurid, entertaining portraits of war and social collapse appealing to viewers unlikely to experience real adventure in daily life. Fictional invasion shocks also reflected lingering fin de siècle anxieties about modernity, and served an important psychological function in allowing audiences to process intangible dangers (Stearns 67–68, 77–78, 144).

Similar scenarios were legion in pulp science fiction novels like Grautoff's *Banzai!* (1908), Fitzpatrick's *The Coming Conflict of Nations; or, The Japanese-American War: A Narrative* (1909), and Norton's *The Vanishing Fleets* (1908). These works also operated as perverse replays of the Russo-Japanese War, once again giving Japan the technological upper hand, but making America the unwitting target. The U.S.-Japanese war imagined in *Banzai!* features a Japanese sneak attack on San Francisco, with Admiral Tōgō delivering the opening blow and motivation: "Let today be the day for the vengeance for Kanagawa. Just as Commodore Perry knocked there with the hilt of his sword on the door of Nippon, let us break in today the Golden Gate of San Francisco" ("Banzai—How Japan Fought" SM5). Though much of this era's future war fiction climaxes with a brilliant American inventor's superweapon overcoming the invaders, H. Bruce Franklin argues that post–Russo-Japanese War invasion narratives tended to be "less sanguine," often dwelling on catastrophic scenes of Japanese victories on American soil (Franklin, *War Stars* 39–40).

FIG. 1.3 Advertisement for the silent film *The Japanese Invasion* (1909). *Source: Moving Picture World* 4.24 (12 Jun. 1909): 863. Courtesy of Media History Digital Library.

Renowned authors like H. G. Wells and Jack London also tried their hand at depicting Japanese invasion and techno-Orientalist nightmares. Both Wells's novel *The War in the Air* (1908) and London's short story "The Unparalleled Invasion" (1907/1910) imagine the rise of a Sino-Japanese superpower (Japanese technology married to Chinese manpower) imperiling Western civilization. In Wells's "macabre vision of a world gone mad," global conflict becomes the opening for the "Asiatic Confederation" to unleash superior aerial technology against Western rivals in an air war fought above the United States (Wohl 91). As with most Japanese invasion sublime literature, Wells's Japan bests the West with its own technology while retaining an Eastern savagery. One sequence in particular has samurai-sword-wielding Japanese airplane pilots—"strange brown men with long bare swords and evil eyes"—destroying German airships and hacking their crews to death (Wells 268) (see Figure 1.4).

FIG. 1.4 Samurai-sword-wielding Japanese pilots slaughter a German airship crew in a battle at Niagara Falls. *Source:* H. G. Wells, *War in the Air* (1908). Courtesy of the University of California, Santa Barbara, Davidson Library collections.

The War in the Air's techno-Orientalist threat ultimately condemns militaristic Western nationalism, which Wells, as a socialist, despised. The techno-Orientalist warning in "The Unparalleled Invasion," penned by fellow socialist Jack London, disturbingly embraces scientific genocide as a bulwark against the threat of Asian ascendency. Though set in the future—pointedly the American bicentennial year 1976—the Russo-Japanese War remains pivotal: "the beginning of the development that . . . was to bring consternation to the whole world." After defeating Russia, Japan turns its dynamism toward technocratic reform of China, whose awakening becomes the war's ultimate repercussion. Once modernized and self-sufficient, China shrugs off Japan, and through an accelerated birthrate threatens to swallow up the world—Roosevelt's fear of race suicide, writ large (London, "Unparalleled Invasion" 308, 311).

Informing this aspect of the story was London's belief that the Japanese and Chinese were merely opposite sides of the same racial coin, evolved from the same "ancient Mongol stock" with "the Japanese a race of mastery and power . . . a race which has always despised commerce and exalted fighting" and the Chinese, a race of dull but willing laborers (London, *Revolution* 274, 279). London's insistence that Japan would eventually be reduced to a race of harmless art makers was retribution for his negative Russo-Japanese War experiences. During the war London collided with Japanese military censors and was arrested on accusations of espionage and assault (Perry 165–167, 173). When freed, London observed Japan's battlefield doggedness and became convinced, "Japanese is the race who can produce real fighting men." However, he interpreted Japan's willingness to suffer massive casualties in pursuit of victory as an Asian devaluing of life (Reesman 99–100). These episodes first inspired a 1904 *San Francisco Examiner* essay "The Yellow Peril," where London decried Japanese superficiality: "There is a weakness inherent in the brown man which will bring his adventure to naught. From the West he has borrowed all of material achievement and passed our ethical achievement by. Our engines of production and destruction he has made his. . . . A marvelous imitator truly, but imitating us only in things material. Things spiritual cannot be imitated . . . and here the Japanese fails" (*Revolution* 283–284). From this essay grew "The Unparalleled Invasion," London's diatribe on the weakness of Japanese modernism and the supreme danger of Chinese primitivism.

After absorbing Japanese modernity, China grows like an amorphous blob through "the fecundity of her loins," enveloping French Indochina and threatening other Western colonies. As part of this "monstrous overspilling flood of life," ten million Chinese immigrants deluge American shores. London eventually unites America and Europe, desperate to stop this devouring yellow peril, in a war of scientific extermination. Waves of "tiny aëroplanes" carrying biological weapons bombard China with glass vials containing cholera, small pox, yellow fever, and bubonic plague. Disease, starvation, and murder quickly spread, and China is consumed by its own savagery. By 1982 China is reduced to a "howling wilderness" (a resonant phrase for Americans, with roots in Puritan history, used also to describe American atrocities during the Philippine-American War in 1901) (Linn 313–316; Johnston 60–63). With the Chinese race exterminated, Westerners are left to occupy the land and husband its natural resources (London, "Unparalleled Invasion" 311–313).

London's vision of "ultra-modern war, twentieth-century war, the war of the scientist and the laboratory" mocked Japan's victory over Russia, in both technology and savagery, when compared with what the West could muster (314). It also turned the tables on the Japanese invasion sublime by prescribing preemptive invasion of Asia (over mere preparedness) as the only defense against Asian aggression. Unlike most Japanese invasion tragedies of a somnolent West caught unprepared by Japanese hostility, this fable is framed as a history lesson from the future, in which Western powers have prevailed by becoming invaders themselves and by pioneering preemptive superweapons. The wedding of technology to racial genocide in response to the Russo-Japanese War illustrates the effect Japan's triumph had on the American psyche. London's genocidal prescriptions echo the Sears & Roebuck catalogue's claim that the only way to defeat Japan was through utter annihilation. And having been originally published in the progressive magazine *McClure's*, his tale similarly targets American middle-class consumers. It is unsettling how the language of ethnic cleansing so easily entered popular culture, and shows just how early Americans began psychologically preparing themselves for the racial animosities that drove the Pacific War and rationalized the use of atomic bombs against Japan.

Though overshadowed by World Wars I and II and the Cold War, the Russo-Japanese War was a transformative event, particularly in Northeast Asia and in terms of U.S.-Asian relations. Japan's victory, though constrained by physical and economic losses, signaled the unhitching of Northeast Asian regional politics from "European tutelage," emboldening Japanese imperialism in China and Korea. While the Portsmouth Treaty helped preserve regional peace until the 1930s, its terms remained a source of Russo-Japanese antagonism, which even Stalin acknowledged in his justification for war against Japan in late 1945 (Yokote 106–109, 112, 121). Moreover, numerous historians suggest that out of the Manchurian conflict came lasting continuities—including "the beginning of century of anti-Americanism" in Northeast Asia—which shaped World War II and the Cold War and continue to influence Asia-Pacific relations in the present (Wolff 126, 138–139, 141; Iriye 1–9).

When, in 1941, war did come between Japan and the United States, newsreels showing the "infamy" of the Pearl Harbor attack fixated on mangled American war machines engulfed in flames and helpless American warriors humbled by the destruction—a more frightening techno-Orientalist image could hardly be conceived. In seeking to understand the origins of the disaster, analysts recalled Japan's surprise attack on Port Arthur thirty-six years before and rechristened it "history's first Pearl Harbor" (Steinberg and Wolff 107–108; "Jap Tactics Highlighted" 12; Krock SM3; Menaugh E8). This linking of 1904 to 1941, while ahistorical, was not altogether in error, for Yamamoto Isoroku, the architect of the Pearl Harbor attack (and Russo-Japanese War veteran), had indeed reflected on the lessons of Port Arthur when planning his Hawaiian assault in 1941: "We must make efforts, based on these success and failures [at Port Arthur], to handle the opening of war with Americans much more successfully" (qtd. in Kiyoshi 81). Both perspectives saw a continuity: Yamamoto summoned Port Arthur as a warning against repeating Japanese mistakes at the beginning of its quest to control Asia. For Americans the nexus of Port Arthur and Pearl Harbor served as proof of an enduring, deep-seated treachery blighting the Japanese character. There was also an implied linearity in transforming the defeat into a desperate and heroic *defense* of Western society, "to secure civilization against barbarous attacks" at its very periphery (Rosenberg, 8, 13). The construction of an invigorating tragedy from the Pearl Harbor disaster shows the longevity of the Japanese invasion sublime and the belief that the clashes of the Russo-Japanese War had been the beginning salvo of a U.S.-Japanese conflict.

Chapter 2

"Out of the Glamorous, Mystic East"

Techno-Orientalism in
Early Twentieth-Century
U.S. Radio Broadcasting

JASON CRUM

Asian subjects abound in early twentieth-century U.S. radio programs. From Fu Manchu and the Dragon Lady to Omar Khayyam and the Indo-Asian Consortium, stories of "yellow peril" and the exotic Orient played on the listening public's cravings for adventure, excitement, and international affairs. Programs such as *Buck Rogers*, *Terry and the Pirates*, *Omar, the Wizard of Persia*, *Fu Manchu*, and dozens of others serialized in fifteen- to thirty-minute time slots performed the affairs of rational, modern U.S. whites against the imagined cultural and technological inferiority of the Asian Other. These and other such programs, concomitant with U.S. global expansion, flatten Near East and Far East subjects into one vast foreign horde that, by being robbed of technological prowess, is both dehumanized and exoticized. The programs play on a U.S. desire to be both modern and, ironically, grounded in a more authentic premodern past. In addition to these serials, for-profit network adult programs and government-sponsored programs further narrated a white, masculine modern U.S. identity. Male characters are almost universally the protagonists of such serialized programs, women being relegated to supporting roles or to domestic spheres. While programs such as *The Goldbergs* and daytime soap operas feature female protagonists, the trend of adventure-based, techno-Orientalist programs reasserts American masculinity and patriarchy, and emphasizes the need to protect American womanhood from Asian hordes. Production companies such as Orson Welles's Mercury Theatre, the Free World Theatre, and the Free Company, though progressive and working on behalf of organized labor or the Roosevelt administration, or working for Depression-relief efforts, nonetheless participate in a flattening of the Asian Other and play on nativist anxieties in a growing U.S. Empire. These different types of programs underscore the breadth and pervasiveness of techno-Orientalism on the radio. For-profit serial programs, aimed at children and young adults, generally include fantastical narratives that play on mystical themes and conflate Asian subjects into one vast horde. Government-sponsored companies, aimed at older teens and adults, employ more realistic narratives that emphasize racial, cultural, and nationalistic differences among Asian subjects. Nonetheless, both varieties posit the United States as the locus of cultural and technological power.

As hobby broadcasting gave way to licensed commercial programs in the mid- to late 1920s, radio broadcasting became an extremely popular form of entertainment and information for millions of Americans. In this era, sports broadcasts, serialized comedy, and drama programs boomed and garnered wide audiences. In addition, the consumerism of radio grew tremendously in the late 1920s and early 1930s, leading critic James Rorty to call U.S. radio advertising "a grotesque, smirking gargoyle set at the very top of America's sky-scraping adventure in acquisition" (Denning 435). The radio itself became more ubiquitous as prices of manufactured sets (as opposed to build-it-yourself hobbyist kits popular in the 1920s) became affordable to middle-class families. By 1940, over 80 percent of U.S. households had at least one radio and over 27 percent of automobiles were equipped (Butch 176).[1]

This chapter, then, addresses U.S. radio broadcast programs from the late 1920s to the late 1940s and shows the staging and configuration of a white U.S. national body against the constructed threat of a technologically and culturally inferior Asian Other. Reading representative broadcast programs such as *Omar, the Wizard of Persia*, *Terry and the Pirates*, Pearl S. Buck's *China to America*, and the Mercury Theatre's *The Garden of Allah*, I argue that techno-Orientalism in early twentieth-century radio programs reveals the racial, technological, and economic anxieties of a growing U.S. Empire. These programs are indicative of "mystery" and "adventure" serial shows, for-profit weekly programs, and government-sponsored programs that stage such places as the Near East, China, and India. Such performances of technological inferiority deny the Asian Other modernity (including the use of radio communications, military equipment, scientific knowledge, and modern cities) and, even as they stress the threat of Asian domination, place the Asian subject in a quaint, fictive past. This disavowal of modernity to the Asian Other establishes the precedent of the United States as the principal agent for twentieth-century global technological prowess.

These and other programs are prime examples of what David Palumbo-Liu calls "enabling fiction[s]"—pop-cultural narrative acts that position the minority as having a "pre-existent positionality" to a Universal. Such "enabling fiction[s]" labor to police the boundaries of whiteness in the United States and assert the threat of Asian-globalism (*Omar*) and Sino-globalism (*Terry*) even as they perform an incipient narrative of U.S. cultural globalism. Palumbo-Liu theorizes the construction of self and group identity as a contradictory movement; the minority subject is allowed to "partake of the unity and authority thought to be enjoyed by the dominant," but "the dominant can withhold such possibilities and place upon the minority subject a set of delimited sites of representation within the supposedly open field of the Universal" (193). Palumbo-Liu suggests that, rather than discard the notion of the Universal, we ought to view the concept as an "enabling fiction" wherein dominant culture is read as a product arising from fictive acts. These fictive acts on radio facilitated the domination of the internal U.S. Other.

Furthermore, if it is true, as Omi and Winant argue, that essentialism entails the "denial, or flattening, of differences within a particular racially defined group" (72), then the broadcast programs this chapter addresses stage the national domination of essentialized Others as a way of justifying the domination of internal ethnic and racial minorities; that is to say, through techno-Orientalism, the production of U.S. whiteness was enabled not only through the racialization and exclusion of nonwhites at home, but also through the domination of Asian Others abroad. For even as national networks performed the boundaries of U.S. whiteness in relation to racialized Others at home, national networks reinscribed U.S. whiteness by staging the inferiority of Asian subjects, the particular individual cultures of which are essentialized and made into a vast foreign horde that is to be both contained and mastered.

At the dawn of the twentieth century, the U.S. Empire encompassed holdings spanning Cuba and Puerto Rico to Hawaii and the Philippines. Theodore Roosevelt's "Big Stick policy," as asserted in his 1904 message to Congress, declared a right to intervene in the national affairs of other countries in the Americas. During this period the United States continued active military operations to establish favorable governments in Latin America (Fejes). Taft's "Dollar Diplomacy" employed military force when, for instance, a U.S.-backed 1909 conservative coup in Nicaragua necessitated U.S. Marines (Ninkovich 121–122).[2] Moreover, completed in 1912, the Panama Canal consolidated U.S. Caribbean influence. By 1918, seeing World War I as a war between antiquated social systems and democratic nations rather than a conflict of dysfunctional capitalism, Woodrow Wilson disavowed Taft's Dollar Diplomacy, which still allowed him the ability to intervene in Mexico and occupy Haiti and the Dominican Republic (Ninkovich 218). Wilson's own racial hierarchy reinstilled essential differences between races; at a meeting in Paris, Wilson tabled a suggestion of racial equality by Japan (Ninkovich 220). It is in this context that techno-Orientalist radio programs took hold of the U.S. consciousness.

The Asian/Sino-Globalist Threat: *Omar, the Wizard of Persia* and *Terry and the Pirates*

There is nothing singular about the racism in the 1931 U.S. network radio serial *Omar, the Wizard of Persia*. Each fifteen-minute program begins with a narrated poem that, like many radio serials of the 1930s, conveniently locates the U.S. listener as the interpreter of an Other ethnic culture:

> Out of the glamorous, mystic east,
> Out of the desert's burning sands,
> The voice of the ancient Persia speaks,
> To the heart of him who understands.

Over the course of thirteen episodes, the program details the adventures of Henry Mason, an American jewel dealer, and his family as they deal with a curse brought on by an emerald Mason purchases in Persia. At the outset, the listener learns that Mason has purchased a cursed emerald in the Middle East and is warned to return it by Marluk, a Persian jewel dealer. The rest of the serial follows Mason as strange things befall his family, including his daughter's fiancé, Jerry, nearly being killed, strange faces appearing in windows, and attacks from traveling Bedouin tribes. Through this, Mason is guided by Omar, the Wizard of Persia, who speaks to him through mystic bells. The series concludes with Mason returning the cursed emerald to a scarred Persian man. Though the shortness of the series run indicates only modest popularity, the program is indicative of numerous other mystery and adventure serial shows that staged American actions such places as the Middle East, China, and India. *Omar* performs a rational and masculine U.S. white national body by staging the intellectual and technological inferiority of a racialized Other. Indeed, within the first thirty seconds of the initial broadcast, Mason proclaims to Marluk, a jewel dealer in Persia, "Nonsense, Marluk. You are superstitious as an old woman. . . . In America we do things differently. There, when the way is dark, the wise man lights a match." In this and other instances, Mason claims a singular voice of reason for American audiences; his suspicion of the

Other implies an intellectual superiority. Indeed, his resistance to coercion is a benchmark of American strength; while searching for an emerald in Persia, Mason resists the attempted mental and physical coercion of Madame Zaire, a Persian merchant, saying, "You know, of course, Madame Zaire, that I am an American citizen! When my country hears of this...." The appeal to citizenship here contrasts with the tribal affiliations of the Persian Other. Mason is a citizen of a modern nation and exhibits intellectual and technological superiority; Madame Zaire and others are antiquated tribal Others who lack intellect and technology.

The conflating of intellectual inferiority, femininity, and the Asian Other is certainly not particular to this show; numerous other radio serials from the late 1920s to the late 1940s such as *Fu Manchu*, *Captain Midnight*, *Jungle Jim*, and *Terry and the Pirates* configured a white national U.S. body in relation to the threat of the Asian Other. *Terry and the Pirates*, a weekday program that ran from 1937 to 1948, narrates the exploits of Terry, a U.S. pilot during World War II, against the threat of Japanese domination. The show was immensely popular, garnering sponsorship from Libby's Puffed Wheat and Quaker Foods, and was also developed for comics and later television. In the radio series, Terry, representing U.S. military power, faces—and conquers—his nemesis, a Japanese "Dragon Lady." At various places in the serial, Terry looks for stolen items such as the "radio device" and the "mechanical eye," a mechanism that detects gold. The program performs a feminized Japanese subject against a hypermasculine Terry. In one particularly telling episode from November 19, 1941, "The Radio Device Is Missing," the Dragon Lady, who is devious yet unable to operate such machines, has stolen a radio transmitter; upon being confronted by Terry and his friend, Pat Ryan, she exclaims, "Terry Lee, you will not live long in this country!" As the Dragon Lady repeatedly pretends that she has no knowledge of the device, Ryan counters her demure, sultry voice with his hypermasculine, "You'll talk to me and you'll like it!" The program thus not only asserts the might of the U.S. military, but feminizes the Asian Other.

In addition to anxieties of empire and racial purity, such programs indicate U.S. unease about the global reach and control of radio as a medium. Broadcasts of Axis propaganda during World War II, for example, complicated national wartime narratives and directly contested American technological superiority. While Ezra Pound's pro-fascist broadcasts from Italy and Axis Sally's broadcasts from Germany affected the European theater, Tokyo Rose's broadcasts from Japan challenged the U.S. denigration of Asian technological prowess. The subsequent 1945 arrest and 1949 trial of Tokyo Rose (Iva Toguri D'Aquino) represents apprehension over an Asian Other who, though a U.S. citizen, exerted control over technology.

These programs further indicate the cultural and social anxieties commonly broadcast on U.S. network programming. In *Omar*, the hyperracialized Asian

Other is responsible for the economic hardships of the Great Depression. Mason, the businessman, acts as a synecdoche for American economic prosperity; his everyman demeanor and rational, nonsuperstitious portrayal contrast with the superstition and greed of the Asian. The cursed emerald, itself, which he sees as symbolic of economic vitality, brings bad luck to Mason. His act then of finding the original owner of the emerald and ending its curse is an act of ridding U.S. economic interests of foreign influence and of restoring economic prosperity.

Such programs further stage anxieties about foreign Asian hordes invading the United States. U.S. concerns regarding immigration were certainly not new. Even as 1.5 million Mexican citizens came to the United States between 1910 and 1920 (Hall and Coerver 126), the Wilson and Hoover administrations sought to restrict and exclude those deemed unfit for the U.S. populace. And though Asian labor played a vital role in the spread of railroads and the development of farming in the U.S. West, Chinese exclusion acts had been passed in 1882, 1892, and 1902. These laws included tax burdens, deportation, and barring of entry. The Immigration Act of 1917 further restricted immigration and established an Asiatic Barred Zone. The Johnson-Reed National Origins Act of 1924 established caps on the number of immigrants from European countries (Meier and Ribera 264–265; Monroy 106). As the Depression entrenched itself into the minds of U.S. residents, nativist arguments placed the blame for economic hardships on nonwhite immigrants. U.S. labor unions, such as the AFL, after attempts to unionize migrant labor in the 1920s, turned to ethnic scapegoating and lobbied for "repatriation" or deportation. Labor, in particular the AFL, believed that "a policy of restriction . . . would enable the United States to face any future emergency with the patriotism resulting from the exclusion of heterogeneous foreign elements" (Lane 363). The perception that immigrants were responsible for white unemployment led to wider legal restrictions against those who even resembled non-European whites. A 1931 California law made it illegal for contractors to employ Mexicans or "aliens"; the term "alien" was perceived to be any nonwhite, regardless of legal status (Monroy 148).

These nativist anxieties of an Oriental invasion and racial inferiority are staged in *Omar, the Wizard of Persia* when, in the seventh episode, Bedouin tribes invade and move quickly through the United States to find Mason and his family at their estate in Chicago. Here, the Bedouins' use of animalistic "wolf calls" to communicate over long distances indicates the inferiority of their language. The animalistic nature of these "wolf calls" contrasts to Mason's use of telephonic and telegram technologies, and positions the Bedouins as technologically inferior animal-exotics. Such nativist tensions of the inferiority of foreign hordes and foreign invasion are further countered by Mason, who hears and understands Omar in addition to using communication technology, thus positioning Mason in a space of technological and cultural superiority. Indeed, while the Bedouins' language skills are inferior—even subhuman—Mason is a technologically savvy American and an interpreter of foreign culture. Early in the series, Omar gives Mason the Mystic Scroll of Persia. This artifact enables Mason to communicate with Omar by listening to "mystic bells" through a trance. In these bells, Mason receives numbers that he then correlates with writings on the Mystic Scroll. In this manner, Omar guides and assists Mason in his quest. Omar transmits such advice as, "The watchful shall not sleep tonight," "Wise men bar the door against the howling wolf," and "Beware! The heart of a woman is weak." Further tempering the nativist paranoia of foreign invasion is the fact that Mason, throughout the series, travels at will through various countries and across the United States on automobile, train, airplane, and ship in order to escape those chasing him. In similar fashion, Terry traverses international borders as he battles foes from Calcutta and China. The point is clear: in the growing U.S. Empire, U.S. citizens may cross national borders as representatives of a benevolent U.S. Empire; non-U.S. citizens, to the contrary, are suspect as animal-exotics who must be contained. Such programs thus illustrate the cultural consciousness and anxieties of a growing empire in economic turmoil.

The Mercury Theatre as Orientalist Discourse

Though best known for their 1938 adaptation of H. G. Wells's *The War of the Worlds*, Orson Welles and his Mercury Theatre Company continued this development of techno-Orientalism. While the aforementioned programs employed science fiction and fantasy tropes, Welles's programs, with their modernist aesthetic of stream of consciousness, assemblage, and vérité, attempt to portray the Orient realistically and authentically. Welles and John Houseman formed the Mercury Theatre in 1937 after working in New York Negro Theatre and Federal Theatre projects on productions such as an all-black *Macbeth* and a *Julius Caesar* set in fascist Italy. Broadcast on CBS, the Mercury Theatre's programs in 1938 and 1939 attempted to use radio for the dissemination of literature and culture. Originally unsponsored, the show aired Sunday evenings from eight to nine o'clock for nine weeks. The company performed renditions of such classic novels as *Dracula*, *A Tale of Two Cities*, *Treasure Island*, and *The Count of Monte Cristo*. Over the next two years, the company staged radio dramas similar to their earlier ones—*Jane Eyre*, *Sherlock Holmes*, *Oliver Twist*, *Heart of Darkness*, and others. Later, Campbell's Soup sponsored the Mercury Theatre, renamed the show *The Campbell Playhouse*, and moved the broadcast to Friday night at nine o'clock. Many of these programs play on techno-Orientalism, exploit foreign stereotypes, and feed the sentiment that foreign lands are inhabited by simpletons and are ripe for the taking.

Unlike the writers behind such serial broadcasts as *Omar* and *Terry*, Welles labors to portray the Orient authoritatively and realistically. *A Passenger to Bali*, *The Garden of Allah*, and *Algiers* are nevertheless fraught with notions of U.S. superiority and create a body of knowledge on the Orient. Welles claims authority on the Orient when he narrates in the introduction to *Algiers*, "Take my word for it, it's authentic. Because, believe it or not, your humble servant has lived in the Casbah. Like Shanghai and Marseille . . . Singapore . . . and all the rest of the wild and wicked cities in the world, where anything can happen—and everything does." He continues by calling the Casbah "a melting pot for all the sins of the earth."

This exoticization and flattening of subjectivity in the Orient is underscored in their November 19, 1939, broadcast adaptation of Robert Hichens's novel *The Garden of Allah*. Here, a British heiress, Domini Enfelden, visits the North African Sahara Desert on a journey of spiritual renewal. She meets with Boris, a Christian monk, who himself is running from his past. Narrated by Father Roubier, a Catholic priest whose omniscience establishes the Westerner in a position of authority over the Orient, the chronicle establishes a Christian god in the Islamic world and makes the Orient into a timeless place where love and renewed faith in Christianity can be found. This narrative, and others, conflates the Orient into one Islamic world of untamed and superstitious people whose identity the listener perceives through such obtuse lines as, "A man who refuses to acknowledge his god is unwise to set foot in the desert." Here, the simple inhabitants of the Orient remind the rational, modern Christian Westerners how to love and have faith.

The authority proffered by the Mercury Theatre and other such programs signifies a superiority complex implicit between broadcaster and listener. Indeed, the lack of subjectivity and technological ability of the Other was deeply entrenched in radio broadcasting not just through legal means but also via instructional manuals. Radio writers' manuals of the time reveal the professional manipulation of identity that minority subjects faced. Offering insight into guidelines on writing for radio programs, many manuals assert that the radio writer should create a universal identity at the expense of a premodern, technologically inferior Other. Written for the aspiring radio writer, Peter Dixon's *Radio Writing* (1931), for example, illustrates the practice of playing to mass national identity rather than local difference: "since you are dealing in averages, you must not dabble too much in things that appeal to the minorities. There is one great average group and there are many minorities. It is safer to please the average—also much more profitable" (61–62). The distinction of the "great average" and "the minorities" underscores the peripheral location of people of color in the United States. Another notable radio writer, Ralph Rogers, writes in *Dos and Don'ts of Radio Writing* (1937), "Think carefully before you select colored characters or rural characters for comedy scripts. These types have been used so often that it takes a veteran writer to put them over" (18). Rogers continues by advising writers that "dumb, slow-thinking characters give the audience a superiority complex that they enjoy" (18). This "superiority complex" indicates the rewards of listening to such programs; faithful listeners perceive their own modernity and technological prowess over inferior Others. This sentiment is found, though, not only in fictional programs, but also in reality-based news reporting. At the dawn of World War II, on October 29, 1938, in *Radio Guide*, a magazine for listeners and trade professionals, William Shirer wrote,

> Wars and war scares require a new technique of coverage these days. The old romantic figure of Richard Harding Davis, the beau ideal of former newspaper days, is gone. In his place is a hard-hitting American news-hunter who mixes sweat and speed and an expert's knowledge of economics into a word-brew and pours it into a microphone. He knows diplomats, prime ministers and cab-drivers. He was born in America—usually in the Middle West. He is tireless, fearless, and sometimes reckless. He was responsible for the most exciting radio week America has known when, three weeks ago, he talked from the frying-pan of Europe.... *Radio Guide* is proud to present in him today's newest hero, the radio war correspondent. (Shirer 1)

Illustrating the power and expectations thrust onto news radio writers and broadcasters, the statement creates a U.S. gaze that is removed from the fray and watching above the action.

Even as the reporter is a "hunter," a rugged, masculine, and modern flaneur who navigates the globe and makes sense of what non-Americans cannot, the listener borrows this sense of superiority and navigates the foreign hordes and their simple, premodern ways.

The Free World Theatre—Staging Enabling Fictions

The techno-Orientalism in United States radio broadcasting was manifest not only in science fiction and fantasy serial shows, but also in government-sponsored broadcast programs. One such collection of programs, the Free World Theatre, written and broadcast for the U.S. national audience in 1943, was an association of progressive writers and actors in wartime Los Angeles, comprising the Hollywood Victory Committee and the Hollywood Writers Mobilization, both local, progressive organizations, that constituted, in Michael Denning's words, "the central cultural apparatus on the west coast" (18). More than simply a writer's collective, the group wrote speeches for organized labor, sponsored cartoonists unions, and created documentary films (Denning 417–418). Funded by the Office of War Information, the artists volunteered their time to create "propaganda—not for war" (Oboler and Longstreet x). Broadcast nationally in 1943 on the American Broadcasting Company, the scripts were collected and published as *The Free World Theatre: Nineteen New Radio Plays* in 1944. In fact, in the ending note to the collected scripts, Robert Rossen, chair of the Hollywood Writers Mobilization, writes that his organization is "a voluntary joining together of the writing guilds on the west coast for the winning of the war and the peace to come."

Though a handful of their broadcasts contest U.S. racial logic, many of the Free Company's broadcasts nonetheless reinscribe the boundaries of U.S. whiteness by way of their essentialist and racialized portrayal of Asian subjects. For instance, *The Last Will and Testament of Tom Smith*, written by Stephen Longstreet and starring James Cagney, takes on the captivity of a U.S. airmen in Japan during World War II. Here, Tom Smith is preparing to be executed by his Japanese captors. Rallying his fellow U.S. captives against their "Jap" captors, Smith urges, "remember all the ads in the slick magazines and all the smiling, slant-eyed faces" (Oboler and Longstreet 152). Later, he describes his Japanese captors as "little hard-looking guys with rat eyes" (159).

Claiming an audience of over five million listeners (Oboler and Longstreet xii), the dramas themselves originated from notable U.S. producers of culture such as Pearl S. Buck and Paul Robeson, and were purported to have been written in response to a statement, question, or issue put forth by someone in the public eye. *Fiesta*, one of the first performances, was "based on a statement by [Mexican] President Avila Camacho" (Oboler and Longstreet 120). *Something About Joe*, one of the last plays, was "based on a statement by Paul Robeson" (170). The dramas ranged from *Fiesta*, in which a man escapes Nazi Germany by fleeing to a small Mexican village, to *China to America*, in which Pearl S. Buck fabricates a broadcast originating in China during the Second Sino-Japanese War asking U.S. citizens for help.

Even as U.S. immigration law excluded Chinese citizens from its national body, Buck's *China to America* stages Chinese inferiority in relation to a white masculine U.S. body. Broadcast on May 2, 1943, at six-thirty on Sunday evening, the broadcast begins with two American radio broadcasters trying to contact China. After they successfully establish contact with a small village radio station (the script does not clarify an exact location), a sampling of Chinese people parade before the microphone to attest to their hard lives during the war with Japan. The Chinese announcer, who can use radio technology to broadcast throughout his village, brings forth a Captain Lin, a soldier; a baker (a male who is castigated for not being a soldier); Mr. Mei, a teacher; Mei's daughter, an eighteen-year-old girl; and Mr. Peng, a Magistrate and "our most important citizen" (141). The play ends with a Japanese air raid killing everyone except Mr. Peng, who urgently asks the U.S. listener for aid. The fact that one Chinese announcer uses radio technology implies agency and a modicum of prowess; nonetheless, the remaining Chinese speakers are not trained in technology, and are portrayed by Buck as rural and simple-minded. Furthermore, the conflating of location and identity to simply "China" flattens the vast linguistic and cultural differences in the Sino region.

The techno-Orientalism employed by Buck establishes a technologically proficient white U.S. body against the inferior Asian subject. Here, speech and accent are markers of difference. In her stage directions, Buck describes the Chinese voice as "rather high and of a distinctly different timbre from the American voice" (141). As if the timbre were not enough to signify difference, Buck writes in dialect with grammatical errors and stilted speech. The first Chinese voice to enter the broadcast is described as follows:

> CHINESE VOICE: China—this is China—Yes, I hear you America! What you say? You want Chinese to speak?

In contrast, both Americans (both male soldiers) speak with forceful, vernacular American English. In the script, Buck writes one American's dialogue, "Hey, whadda yah mean," and "everybody's sayin' this about China and that about China . . . so here's a radio station . . . so why shouldn't I find out for myself?" (140). Though the words are written in slang, one suspects that the listener understands the "American-ness" of the vernacular that the soldiers speak. That the Chinese broadcaster lacks an understanding of English grammar puts U.S. whiteness into a position of cultural dominance. Moreover, continuing to stage the inferiority of the Asian Other at the beginning of the drama, one of the two American broadcasters says, "The radio stations here—the thing you plug into there says 'China'—so why shouldn't I talk to 'em?" (140). Although the play had the political purpose of arousing sympathy for the Chinese victimized by Japanese imperialism, it nevertheless portrayed them as a less advanced people incapable of using modern technology. Buck's conclusion, then, is that China can only respond to U.S. radio broadcasts, while the United States can eavesdrop and impose radio—and technical—superiority over the rural, ethnically flattened Chinese people at will.

Conclusion

Melanie McAlister has recently theorized that U.S. development and "interest" in the Orient was concomitant with cultural production that created a national gaze of superiority. She paraphrases William Leach in *Land of Desire* by arguing, "Orientalism was the cultural logic through which American culture symbolized a break from nineteenth-century Protestant piety and marked the nation's entry into 'modernity'" (McAlister 22). Radio programs between the late 1920s and late 1940s indeed underscore this break and show that the leap into modernity for the United States was accomplished against the supposed technological inferiority of ethnicized and racialized Others. The Asian Other was a prime target for audiences due to immigration history and nativist and economic anxieties. Furthermore, Said writes that Orientalist texts "create not only knowledge but also the very reality they appear to describe" (94). He continues by arguing that "in time such knowledge and reality produce a tradition . . . a discourse, whose material presence or weight, not the originality of the author, is really responsible for the texts produced out of it" (Said 94). As this chapter shows, these discourses or "enabling fictions" broadcast on radio produce a tradition and inscribe a false reality into the U.S. consciousness. Such discourses produced a body of techno-Orientalist thought that became entrenched and naturalized. The amnesia of an imperialist past is made possible by this naturalization process whereby histories of racism, exclusion, and inferiority are effaced or recast as noble endeavors to civilize savages and bring exotics into modernity.

This chapter does not reproach entirely these various producers of culture. Their work toward progressive causes is significant. Indeed, the Free World Theatre advocated for civil rights fifteen years before the civil rights movement took hold in the United States. Orson Welles and his Mercury Theatre actively critiqued the radio's voice of authority and the passivity with which listeners enjoyed their programs. *Omar, the Wizard of Persia* exposed Americans to the writings of Omar Khayyam, a Persian poet and philosopher. Clearly, these producers of culture had benevolent aims. Nonetheless, these representative programs are symptomatic of radio broadcasting in its Golden Age, and indicate the limits of cultural critique during a time of global expansion and incipient global media. For even as they portray the Asian Other as either simple and compliant, or devious and scheming, the narratives provide a backdrop over which U.S. citizens act out their purported modern U.S. identity. Furthermore, they indicate the cultural consciousness of a burgeoning U.S. Empire and create a false reality that robs the Asian subject of modernity, technological prowess, and identity. This chapter concludes that the creation of this false reality must be documented in order for erased histories to be reclaimed.

Notes

1. For an analysis of how radio and household accoutrements affected domesticity, see Ruth Schwartz Cowan's *More Work for Mother* (151–191).
2. For more on Dollar Diplomacy, see Dana Munro's excellent analysis in *Intervention and Dollar Diplomacy*.

Chapter 3

Looking Backward, from 2019 to 1882

Reading the Dystopias of Future Multiculturalism in the Utopias of Asian Exclusion

VICTOR BASCARA

Both technology and Orientalism shared a common investment in realizing a sustainable future. They converged at efforts to turn the problems of difference into nonissues or even perhaps the very rationale for expansion and development. In making cases for or against these futures, utopian/dystopian texts are test balloons for measuring possible destinies for the present.[1] Is that envisioned future one of, say, the orderly liberation of the oppressed and benighted or a chaotic hegemony of inequality and exploitation? The place of Asia in that future becomes an index of success or failure. Is the West's future more Asian or less Asian, and which is preferable?

Both technology and Orientalism have fueled engines of economic growth. A key difference is that technology still tends to be celebrated as innovative and life-saving, and Orientalism is a relic of racist and exploitative imperialism. On the power of technology, Martin Heidegger, for example, in "The Question Concerning Technology," suggestively writes, "Technology is a mode of revealing. Technology comes to presence in the realm where revealing and unconcealment take place, where *aletheia*, truth, happens" (13). Technology has also been the site of profound anxieties about the future, particularly the eclipsing of such quaint notions as discernible reality. Writing in 1936 about the emergent medium of cinema, Walter Benjamin, for example, in "The Work of Art in the Age of Mechanical Reproduction," observes, "The equipment-free aspect of reality has become the height of artifice; the sight of immediate reality has become an orchid in the land of technology." As technology becomes more advanced, it develops a deft capacity to conceal or otherwise normalize its apparatuses, which can ironically be increasingly equipment-laden.

Orientalism can be understood as a once-normalized apparatus for grasping reality. With the rise of decolonization, the ills of Orientalism are now more readily identifiable. What was once a sleek system for civilizing the world is revealed as a clunky ethnocentrism of the so-called West needing an incorporable alterity to be its frontier, materially and ideologically.

This chapter looks to visions of technological futures mapped through the management of Asian difference. By comparing and contrasting two conceptions of the future—in Edward Bellamy's 1887 novel *Looking Backward 2000–1887* and in Ridley Scott's 1982 film *Blade Runner*—we see prognostications that meditate on the chances of realizing a better world than the ones that attended the emergences of these two texts. Through both texts we see efforts to solve the problem of the cost of labor through technology. In Bellamy those efforts are successful, in Scott less so. But both the novel and the film recognize that the viability of the future hinges on the problem of labor exploitation. For Scott's film, the introduction of replicant labor was meant to be the solution to the exploitation of "human" labor, until the replicants turn out to indeed be, as their advertising proclaims, "more human than human" and therefore rise up. For Bellamy's novel, the obviation of racialized and/or immigrant labor is a correlative condition of, if not the implied solution to, the utopia of A.D. 2000. In both instances, readers and viewers are treated to a jump in time to a future point, after these techno-Orientalist answers have come into existence and made their impacts. Both texts use the time travel trope to comment on the possibility or impossibility of solving the problem of labor exploitation, and in both cases the spectacle of Asian difference for the arrival at those futures plays a revealing role: for Scott's ostensibly dystopic vision, Asian difference is pervasive, and for Bellamy's overtly utopic one, it is virtually absent.[2]

"Finally Those Capitalist Pigs Will Pay for Their Crimes . . ."

Time travel has been an effective and entertaining form of social commentary. For example, early in Mike Myers's sharp and highly popular 1997 satire *Austin Powers: International Man of Mystery* (dir. Jay Roach, ninety minutes), Powers is awoken from his 1960s cryogenic sleep to find himself in a 1990s world.³ His handlers debrief him. As he comes to consciousness, he is dismayed to see representatives of both U.S. Strategic Command and Russian Intelligence.

> AUSTIN POWERS (MIKE MYERS): Russian Intelligence? Are you mad?
> BASIL EXPOSITION (MICHAEL YORK): A lot's happened since you were frozen. The Cold War's over.
> AUSTIN: Finally, those capitalist pigs will pay for their crimes. Eh, comrades?
> BASIL: Austin, we won.
> AUSTIN: Groovy. Smashing. Yay, capitalism.

Austin's momentary elation at the downfall of capitalism gives way to a resigned cheer for it instead. An uncertain future for which he fought in the 1960s has apparently reached its conclusion. The joke here is either that 1960s Austin may have actually harbored socialist leanings or that this hirsute covert operative was merely, to borrow Thomas Paine's phrase, "a sunshine patriot," ready to perform alignment with whomever is in power, perhaps the sine qua non of an effective spy. Or perhaps he is both. In either case, a familiar feature of many speculative fiction narratives comes into play: the fish out of water beached through some form of time travel. In such narratives, a dramatic juxtaposition becomes evident between a subject's consciousness and historical change, in this case between a Cold War capitalist lothario and a post–Cold War moviegoing public. The recognized differences, large and small, between that subject's expectations and the changed world can render these changes as radical if not revolutionary, and oftentimes quite humorous. Indeed, many of the pleasures and edifications of these representations occur at such moments of recognition. A drama that can then unfold, whether centrally or implicitly, concerns whether this brave new world has, in the interval, progressed toward a better day or slouched toward apocalypse. These narratives potentially present arguments about what change is needed, how such change may be realized, and what may happen if such change does not occur. The outcomes can mean either utopia or dystopia.⁴

Utopias and dystopias are fundamentally speculative; they extrapolate futures built upon the dreams, or nightmares, of the present. One such well-known coordinate of the not-so-distant future is Los Angeles of 2019, November to be exact. This is a date and location fanboys might sheepishly recognize as the setting of *Blade Runner*, Ridley Scott's 1982 film adaptation of Philip K. Dick's novella about the dreams of insurrectionary androids visiting as nightmares on the minds and bodies of the human world that made them. Yet rather than dwell on that film's conspicuous semiotics of casual, pervasive, and even ominous Asian difference (see Lowe, "Imagining Los Angeles"; Nakamura, *Cybertypes*), this chapter turns instead to an event a century earlier that sought to prevent such a future, the 1882 Chinese Exclusion Act. I argue that from the seeming dystopia of 2019 Los Angeles, we can read a persistent thread of anxieties over labor exploitation and racial heterogeneity, manifested in speculative fiction. I turn then to one of the most influential works of speculative utopian fiction in American literary history: Edward Bellamy's immensely popular novel *Looking Backward 2000–1887*, a text from the tumultuous 1880s that looked forward to a better 2000. Much about this text is progressive, in the narrow and broad senses of the term. Its vision of 2000 is one of a classlessness so appealing *and* plausible that the book momentarily inspired societies to implement the novel's possibilities. By foregrounding the history and cultural politics of Asian exclusion, this chapter considers the extent to which the future possibilities envisioned in *Looking Backward* were doomed by a past and a present in which class and gendered racialization are inextricably bound.

An important intervention of new left social movements has been to critically grasp the depth and complexity of the relationship of race and class in the building and maintenance of modern American civilization. With these conditions appreciated, we see how utopic and dystopic narratives not only extrapolate possible futures but also interpolate occluded pasts that the future can see more clearly than the present seems to be able to. The "color-blindness" that would be reverse engineered into the Constitution by dissenters with the onset of protected racial segregation after *Plessy v. Ferguson* in 1896 would share with *Looking Backward* a common historical blindness fueled by misplaced enlightenment ideals of procedural equality that impeded a more equitable and substantive reckoning with past exploitations.

Yet it should be remembered that this text dramatized the manifestation of progressive ideas. *Looking Backward* is the story of Julian West, a man of leisure who, through a convoluted set of circumstances, inadvertently sleeps undisturbed for 113 years in a sealed chamber in a state of cryogenic preservation in Boston. By having West narrate, the novel views the world of 2000 through the fascinated eyes of West in order to make the book's arguments about the eventual eradication of the social and economic ills that plagued the late nineteenth century. West is repeatedly puzzled at the absence of inequalities, both substantive and procedural. Much of the novel amounts to scenes like the one from *Austin Powers*: the awoken man from the past is told about how things now are. West's main interlocutor is Dr. Leete, his eventual father-in-law, who expounds at great length on the many solutions the world of 2000 has devised to the problems of 1887. There is little conventional action in Bellamy's novel aside from this, not unlike a Platonic dialogue. Between these conversations, West also speaks with and courts Edith Leete, the doctor's daughter. And so the marriage plot functions to formalize the union of the misguided past to the enlightened future, or in this case, present.

Bellamy's text treads a careful middle path between a communistic subsuming of the liberal individual with a Hobbesian world of individuals waging a war of all against all. His novel offers a renegotiation of the social contract where such things as private kitchens and private vehicles are vestiges of an inefficient past that failed to provide "the best for the most for the least," to borrow the phrase of Cold Warriors Charles and Ray Eames. Given the A.D. 2000 setting of *Looking Backward*, the use of the Eames' phrasing may not even really be anachronistic, as Bellamy's world could be seen as realizing the Eames' ideal by 2000.

As an ideal, the realization of this condition in Bellamy's novel means the elimination of fundamental differences about how the world should work and be ordered, which characterizes the terms of the Cold War. The world of 2000 means an arrival at, in other words, the end of history, and one that is the opposite of apocalyptic. The threat of apocalypse under the Cold War, that is, mutually assured destruction (MAD), may prevent wide-scale hot war, but it does not necessarily lead to prosperity. Instead it means indefinitely deferred world war, or apocalypse later. Bellamy presents a way not only of avoiding all-out class war, but of actually achieving "the best for the most for the least" everyone believes in.

The late nineteenth century was no stranger to thinly veiled literary tracts that expounded on utopic visions and/or social critique. This was an era that made best sellers out of William Hope Harvey's *Coin's Financial School* and David Ames Wells's *The Dollar of the Fathers and the Dollar of the Sons*, and later L. Frank Baum's *The Wonderful Wizard of Oz*. What presumably made a book like *Looking Backward* so compelling to readers in the last decade-plus of the nineteenth century was not its fancifulness but rather its plausibility. The appeal of *Looking Backward* is its ability to make something as fanciful as "from each according to need and to each according to necessity"—or even desire—a seemingly realizable destiny, albeit 113 years in the making.

The world that Bellamy envisions is one in which some of the key features of capitalism have been done away with, including competition, the market, individualism, private property, money, and a state apparatus dedicated to the preservation of the aforementioned. Importantly, the disappearance of these social and economic features happens not through a strong state, but rather through a collective realization that these capitalist elements are detrimental to the conditions of production, rather than necessary for such economic activity (see Beard). The time travel conceit of the novel makes it possible for there to be a glossing over of the means by which utopia was realized and for there instead to be a delightfully bewildered enjoyment of the world absent of the past's strife.

Many of these problems are solved through the introduction of new technologies. Dr. Leete's favorite metaphorical illustration of this problem solving is the communal umbrellas that unfurl when rain falls on Boston. Rather than there being the comparatively inefficient system involving individuals' umbrellas and the haphazard awnings we still are cursed with, the steampunk-ish Boston of 2000 has "a continuous waterproof covering" that shelters the sidewalks of that fair city should there be precipitation. Edith remarks, "The private umbrella is father's favorite figure to illustrate the old way when everybody lived for himself and his family" (193). From a twenty-four-hour radio-like musical service to massive communal kitchens, the inhabitants of 2000 are protected from "hunger, cold, and nakedness" rather than "France, England, and Germany." The enemies of these enemies—want and exposure to the elements—have become friends, unifying the nations of the world in a common cause to feed, shelter, and clothe all.

It may come as no great surprise that Bellamy's book does not include Asian American characters, or really any discernible reference to anything Oriental, for better or for worse. The main character of color, West's nineteenth-century African American manservant Sawyer, necessarily falls away from the novel after the slumber. (Sawyer makes a brief return in the psyche-out at the end of the novel, when West dreams that 2000 was a dream only to wake up to find that 2000 is glorious after all.)

For all the book's visions of truly global transformations, it is actually a rather isolationist text, culturally and practically, even if juridically it espouses borderlessness. It presents an interconnected world, in terms of resources and economic networks, but is more or less a snapshot of the demographics that were presumed to exist in late nineteenth-century America. That is, it does not envision a future formed by waves of immigration that would diversify the ethnic and racial composition of the United States. Logically speaking then, this might imply that *Looking Backward* is an anti-immigrant text, imply that this ideal future does not require an industrial reserve army from beyond. But that might not be a fair or really accurate assessment. Rather, *Looking Backward* may be envisioning a world in which mass human movements are unnecessary and people get to stay where they are. And therefore the implicit argument is that people, given the choice, are not inclined to intermix their bodies and gene pools. Unlike the utopic impulses of Gene Roddenberry's *Star Trek*, for example, a multicultural crew is not necessarily the outcome of progressive change. And certainly for a film such as *Blade Runner*, the hyper-visibility of Asian difference in 2019 Los Angeles is a far cry from the bridge of the *Enterprise* or even the racks of the Battlestar Galactica (even if racially ambiguous characters played by Edward James Olmos happen to hail from both Caprica City as well as 2019 Los Angeles). The color-blindness of Galactica and Starfleet is certainly made all the more palatable by enlisting telegenic people like Nichelle Nicols, George Takei, Grace Park, and Kandyse McClure.

Besides, these are worlds where nonhuman characters become allegories of the racialized, whether Cylon or Klingon or Romulan. Or Replicant.

Here questions concerning technology, and the nature of technology, play a central role. We come to understand technology not only as labor-saving machinery but as labor-saving more broadly conceived. Technology, as commentators from Heidegger, Benjamin, and Lyotard to generations of business leaders have extensively noted, is fueled, financed, and defined by forms of speculation. Technology comes into its existence as such through its relationship to the possible problems it emerges to solve and the changed world it will have changed and profited from. Classic versions of these technologies frequently involve the conquest of distance, mortality, pain, and embodiment more generally, resulting in such technologies as flying cars, teleportation, downloadable consciousness, or, for that matter, rolling cars, telephonic communications, as well as various forms of recording thoughts through writing systems.

For Bellamy's text, in a presumed attempt to make its changed world plausibly realizable, the main problem that had to be solved was fundamentally social rather than anything having do with the material infrastructure or natural resources. Changes to the material infrastructure would play a role, but a supporting one to the larger social change that would rechannel resources toward feeding and clothing. Solving the problem of labor gluts and shortages is a matter of not just inventing the next cotton gin but also preventing the labor exploitation that the last cotton gin, or railroad or smartphone, might occasion.

Arguably then, the most substantially plausible problem that Bellamy's 2000 appeared to have solved was not exactly communal protection from rain or food service inefficiency, but the legitimated violences of the business cycle. That is to say, feeding and sheltering were and are widely held priorities that need little strenuous argument to abstractly defend. Yet when providing shelter or food, or medical care, interferes with free trade, free trade is defended. "If you could see how needless were these convulsions of business which I have been speaking of, and how entirely they resulted from leaving industry to private and unorganized management, just consider the working of our system" (250).

When centering the problem of the business cycle as the motivation for technologies, as Bellamy and old left Marxists might, developments such as colonialism and slavery can be seen as technologies that capitalism developed to seek some sort of control over this cyclicality by activating a "safety valve" for overproduction and/or overpopulation (see Turner; Bonacich and Cheng). Industrial (reserve) armies of the enslaved or manufactured or otherwise cheaply gotten and flexibly deployed rely on legitimating technologies of gendered racialization (see, e.g., Ong, *Spirits of Resistance*; Sassen, *Cities in a World Economy*; Parreñas; Rodriguez; McKay). Orientalism can then be paralleled to robotics, in that both are rationales for extracting value by discursively producing objects against which subjecthood is defined (see Said; Huang, "Premodern Orientalist Science Fictions").

The rationales for historical Chinese exclusion up to/after 1882 (see Hune) and the spectacle of racial stasis in *Looking Backward* are congruent manifestations of vastly differing conditions. That is, the former is a condition of Chinese exclusion, one of legislated restriction, while the latter is one of universal choice, including that of the Chinese. Post-Reconstruction America of the 1880s made lynching a means of racial, social, and economic control and saw the effective end of the frontier and of the imperial wars with indigenous populations (see, e.g., White; Wells; Limerick; Blackhawk; Torok). So the matter of managing racial difference is not a small or insignificant one for Bellamy to address. And various institutions, from American literature to world's fairs to pieces of legislation, can be read as clear indices of these dilemmas working themselves out on the terrain of national culture.

The interplay of labor markets and consumer markets from the late nineteenth century to the early twentieth in history is particularly compelling as a counterpoint to the reimagined world of *Looking Backward* where the role of such markets is fundamentally transformed (see Jacobson). That is to say, the blessings of the market—motivation, reward, and punishment for one's compliance with virtuous comportment—persist without the vulnerabilities and unsustainabilities that inevitably come with laissez-faire capitalism.

In Bellamy's 2000 there is a conquest of space, not through teleportation or even flying automobiles, but rather through the trivializing of movement. Julian West, as a man of the late 1880s, is presumably aware of the spectacle if not the importance of immigration in his day: "'Emigration is another point I want to ask you about,' said I. 'With every nation organized as a close industrial partnership, monopolizing all means of production in the country, the emigrant, even if he were permitted to land, would starve. I supposed there is no emigration nowadays'" (187). The answer from Dr. Leete may be surprising. One of the more radical notions of Bellamy's text is its contention that nations will no longer practically or meaningfully exist in the world of 2000.

> "On the contrary, there is constant emigration, by which I suppose you mean removal to foreign countries for permanent residence," replied Dr. Leete. "It is arranged on a simple international arrangement of indemnities. For example, if a man at twenty-one emigrates from England to America, England loses all the expense of his maintenance and education, and America gets a workman for nothing. America accordingly makes England an allowance.... As to imbecile persons, it is deemed best that each nation should be responsible for its own, and the emigration of such must be under full guarantees of support by his own

nation. Subject to these regulations, the right of any man to emigrate at any time is unrestricted." (187)

This vision of a world where migration is precisely not motivated by economics is in stark contrast to the long history of international and intranational migrations. A moment early in the novel, which takes place in the actual 1880s, before West's century-plus mesmeric slumber, ponders the coming workers' revolution vis-à-vis emigration. The assembled gentry fret over the imminent demise of their privileged position.

> "The worst of it," I remember Mrs. Bartlett saying, "is that the working classes all over the world seem to be going crazy at once. In Europe it is far worse even than here. I'm sure I should not dare to live there at all. I asked Mr. Bartlett the other day where we should emigrate to if all the terrible things took place which those socialists threaten. He said he did not know any place now where society could be called stable except Greenland, Patagonia, and the Chinese Empire." "Those Chinamen knew what they were about," someone added, "when they refused to let in our western civilization. They knew what it would lead to better than we did. They saw it was nothing but dynamite in disguise." (103–104)

Knowing what "western civilization" "would lead to" is precisely what *Looking Backward* looks forward to. But this understanding of the relations of East and West in late nineteenth-century geopolitics, held by Mrs. Bartlett and the others disapprovingly depicted in Bellamy's 1880s, is really closer to the exact opposite of actual conditions in the age of empire (see Hobsbawm; Said). Working classes "all over the world" were not really in revolt all at once; Western civilization was indeed penetrating China (see, e.g., Buck; Spence; Schell).

The actual conditions emerging from the age of empire are what we see speculated upon in *Blade Runner* (1982 theatrical release and other years for different cuts, dir. Ridley Scott, ca. 117 minutes). *Blade Runner* is ostensibly a detective story, where Det. Rick Deckard (Harrison Ford) searches for a group of fugitive androids who mounted an uprising and escape and have blended into Los Angeles. It may also be a story of what happens if capitalism proceeds unchecked: namely, the further creation of hyperexploited populations who come to recognize their hyperexploitation, just as populations before them had. The grimy urban trappings of future Los Angeles add to the ambience, but may actually be less a sign of the ravages of capitalism than the social and epistemological crises that the film dramatizes. Given the unpleasant weather, crowding, grime, and violence of 2019 Los Angeles, the label of dystopic may be apt, or at least tempting. Rather than Southern California looking like an image on a postcard or a citrus crate, it looks like an object lesson in poor urban planning, or the lack of any planning aside from the market. It's arguable that if the story had been set in Chicago or New York, the film's status as visually iconic would be considerably lower, as Los Angeles in 1982 still had the status of a city of the future, in a good way. Los Angeles looks instead like a megalopolis of the developing world, which it may be showing itself to be. The air is fouled, litter is everywhere, bandits rove, heterotopic economies proliferate. And yet, it is presumably a functional city where the Tyrell Corporation can design and advance its profitable technologies. Rather than being a racially segregated powder keg that would explode ten years after the film's release, the 2019 Los Angeles that the film shows is a city where diverse populations live together and work, albeit in squalor. A vision of multiculturalism is realized; for example, the racially ambiguous Gaff (played by Edward James Olmos) speaks a pidgin presumably born out of the contact zone that Los Angeles continues to be. And Deckard (played by Harrison Ford),[5] even with all his bluster of disenchantment—which may be an implanted attitude anyway—is a known and functional member of that community, in the classic mold of the noir protagonist. Life in 2019 Los Angeles may not really be so bad, or at least not so different from social and economic realities of its past (see J. K. Lee; Lowe, "Imagining Los Angeles"; Kurashige; Hunt and Yoo). If 2019 Los Angeles is dystopic, that is because it has not changed. The city, by virtue of its being home to the Tyrell Corporation, serves as the background for a failed slave revolt. What they do succeed at is making a lethal pilgrimage of sorts for the Nexus-6 replicants who literally want to meet—and retire—their makers.

    The racial allegory of *Blade Runner* is clearly centered on the Caucasian, even Aryan, bodies of the de facto enslaved replicants. They achieve that social death (see Patterson) by first achieving the abortive possibility of humanity. "More human than human" is the motto of the Tyrell Corporation. "How can it not know what it is?" asks Deckard to Tyrell after administering Voight-Kampff testing on the unenlightened Rachael (Sean Young). And so the crisis that *Blade Runner* brings into visibility is the crisis of visibility itself, as the eyes betray identity through the Voight-Kampff test. Fittingly, in his search for answers to his life's questions, Roy Batty (Rutger Hauer) pays a visit to Hannibal Chew (played by the great character actor James Hong), an Asian American genetic designer for the Tyrell Corporation who specializes in eyes (see Nakamura, *Cybertypes*; Silverman). "I just do eyes," Chew says, pleading his ignorance and perhaps innocence. "If only you could see what I have seen with your eyes," Roy menacingly replies, elliptically referencing a presumed process of radicalization that has taken place in his relatively short life. The replicants emancipate themselves from mental slavery as well as material slavery as they hijack a transport near the Off-World colony. They are able to infiltrate Los Angeles as laborers, such as Leon (played by Brion James) as a sanitation worker or Zhora (played by Joanna Cassidy) as a cabaret performer.

At an early point in the film, Rachael remarks to Deckard, "It seems you feel our work is not a benefit to the public." Deckard replies, "Replicants are like any other machine—they're either a benefit or a hazard. If they're a benefit, it's not my problem." In other words, it is the job of the police to fix the damage that the market has wrought. The Tyrell Corporation attempts to self-regulate by installing a fail-safe: a four-year life span for the replicants. Yet one may wonder if such a provision is practically and even economically viable. Clearly the four-year span proves to be too long, as some replicants are radicalized and rise up, especially through a charismatic leader such as Roy Batty. But four years of service might possibly be too short a term to extract enough labor from replicants to recoup security and R&D and marketing expenses, as well as manufacturing costs. "Do you like our owl?" asks Rachael to Deckard as we see a shot of a majestic example of the species. He asks, "It's artificial?" "Yes," she replies. "Must be expensive." "Very." If a highly convincing "artificial" owl is "very" "expensive," one can only guess how costly a humanoid replicant must be, especially ones that look convincingly like Daryl Hannah or Rutger Hauer or Joanna Cassidy or Sean Young or perhaps even Harrison Ford. The likely high expense of replicant technology is presumably a workable business model with expansion to the Off-World colonies. As the ad slogan we hear repeated in the film states, "A new life awaits you in the Off-World colonies! A chance to begin again in a golden land of opportunity and adventure!" Replace "Off-World" with "California," and it could be 1849 or 1949. Frontiers of speculation yield not only new value but also resistance and revolution, as the world of Bellamy's 2000 have apparently realized.

Across both Bellamy and Scott, the intimate relationship of class exploitation and gendered racialization becomes newly legible and illegitimate through fantasies of what the future might lead to: either the end of value-added differentiation or the creation of new bases for violent revolutionary activity. Both narratives dramatize how capitalism uses technologies in an attempt to cope with the cataclysmic cyclicality of speculation that continues. Asia, whether as specter in Bellamy or spectacle in Scott, serves again as the screen onto which the hopes and fears of the future are projected (see, e.g., Said; Chatterjee; Sohn). Consider the following resonant articulation:

> Walled cities and empires have become unfashionable. The arm of commerce has borne away the gates of the strong city. Intelligence is penetrating the darkest corners of the globe. It makes its pathway over and under the sea, as well as on the earth. Wind, steam, and lightning are its chartered agents. Oceans no longer divide, but link nations together. From Boston to London is now a holiday excursion. Space is comparatively annihilated. Thoughts expressed on one side of the Atlantic are distinctly heard on the other. The far off and fabulous Pacific rolls in grandeur at our feet. The Celestial Empire, the mystery of ages, is being

solved. The fiat of the Almighty, "Let there be Light," has not yet spent its force. No abuse, no outrage whether in taste, sport or avarice, can now hide itself from the all-pervading light.

Those are the words of Frederick Douglass, in his speech called "What to the Slave Is the Fourth of July?"—an oration in Rochester on July 5, 1852. Here, as in the resolution to the Chinese-inflected future envisioned by Joss Whedon's 2005 film *Serenity*, hope is pinned on the notion that the exposure of outrages and deceptions will lead to progressive change, or perhaps at least prosecutions. In Whedon's film, that means broadcasting covered-up evidence of lethal problems at new terraformed Roanoke-esque settlements that wiped out the colonists and created a new scourge, the Reavers, who like zombies and replicants may also constitute the formation of an emergent class entitled to recognition. For Douglass, that means using new technologies for letting the world know—letting even China know—that the United States is to be held materially accountable for the values and practices it has made and was made by.

Notes

Thanks to Uri MacMillan, Eric Estuar Reyes, Victor Hugo Viesca, and Betsy Huang for helpful comments on earlier drafts of this essay. Thanks also to the anonymous readers for their valuable feedback. The shortcomings are of course my own.

1. One may rightly put the U.S. Constitution in that speculative genre, especially the Bill of Rights, as such texts imagine a social formation's capacity to, in the words of the Preamble, "secure the blessings of liberty to ourselves and our posterity" and, in the words of James Madison's *Federalist No. 10*, "break and control the violence of faction."
2. In referring to time travel, I include the idea that the audiences may be the ones taking the temporal leap, even if characters within the narrative do not always make that jump, as is the case with *Blade Runner*.
3. Other satiric examples from mass culture comedies would include *Idiocracy*, *Bill & Ted's Excellent Adventure*, and *Sleeper*.
4. The *Star Trek* franchise, which takes place in the future, is perhaps the most influential effort to envision an ostensibly borderless future. That is, it attempts to strike an ideal balance of having a multiculturalist vision to "boldly go" while nevertheless abiding by an anti-imperialist prime directive.
5. Writing in 1968, Dick speculatively envisioned Deckard being played by Gregory Peck, Richard Widmark, Martin Balsam, or Ben Gazzara (see Dick 156).

Chapter 4

Queer Excavations

————————————◄o►————————————

Technology, Temporality, Race

WARREN LIU

London, circa 1855: Edward "Ned" Mallory, after spending an evening being entertained by Hetty Edwardes, a prostitute, has just walked out onto the streets of Whitechapel, to find the city utterly changed overnight. London's on the verge of a spectacular breakdown, overrun by ne'er-do-wells of all stripes; the skies are clouded over by a miasmatic toxic haze, emanating from the expansion of London's Underground; beneath this (or above it?), time itself stutters—not just a beat or two, but eons—and fitfully collapses. Viewing the scene before him, Mallory sees, in his "mind's eye," the "very sky" that "the Land Leviathans had seen . . . after the earth-shaking shock of the Great Comet . . . and the leaping machineries of Evolution were loosed in chaos."[1] As Mallory, famed discoverer of the brontosaurus (the original "Land Leviathan"), faces the unfolding chaos, his thoughts lead him back to his ancestral home in "peaceful Sussex," with its "clean country air" and its "decent home-cooked food and decent homely drink" (239). He thinks about the impending marriage of his little sister, Madeline, for whom he's already purchased a wedding gift: an expensive clock. He thinks, finally, about that clock, "sitting in its brass-hasped carry-case in the safety box of the Palace of Paleontology" (239).

In fact, it is Mallory's sudden remembrance of Madeline's clock that ultimately spurs him to act, as the following passage makes clear:

> A sudden agony of homesickness struck him, and he wondered what chaotic amalgam of lust and ambition and circumstance had marooned him in this dreadful, vicious place. He wondered what the family were doing at that very moment. What was the time, exactly?
>
> With a jolt, Mallory remembered Madeline's clock.... The lovely fancy clock for dear Madeline, now grotesquely out of his reach.
>
> There must be some way back, some way to cross that distance, surely.... Back to the Palace. Back to his life. (239)

Why, after the long meditation on family and home, is it the question of time ("What was the time, exactly?") that provides Mallory the necessary "jolt" of memory? Why does he seek reunification with the clock, and not the person for whom it's intended? The passage subtly traces the shifting focus of Mallory's desire, progressing from the imaginative reunification with his family, to the seemingly neurotic (although plausibly illogical) reunification with the clock, and finally to the ambiguous, epic-heroic goal of returning "back to his life." What remains unclear is *how* securing the safety of the clock (and not the family it so pastorally evokes) might rescue Mallory from his self-caused metaphysical/physical state of feeling "marooned"—especially given that the feeling itself originates in an "agony of homesickness." Then why not just go *home*?

Readers acquainted with William Gibson and Bruce Sterling's "steampunk" novel *The Difference Engine* will likely recognize the passages described above, as they set the stage for one of the novel's climactic encounters between the forces of good (led by Mallory) and evil (led by one "Captain Swing").[2] Those not familiar with the premise of the novel, which takes place in a past that is dramatically different from our own (thanks to the successful realization of Charles Babbage's analytical engine, which in our reality remains merely theoretical) might well puzzle over a few of the details: when was the London Underground opened? Who discovered the brontosaurus? What is the Palace of Paleontology? Fair questions, given that the novel evokes and references, but tweaks for its own ends, histories both actual and literary.[3] Here, I'd like to sidestep those questions, to begin with an even more basic one: why the clock? Indeed, despite Mallory's remembrance and pursuit of it, Madeline's clock proves ultimately insignificant within the larger narrative of *The Difference Engine*: it's evoked at crucial moments in the plot, pushing Mallory's narrative forward, but is not *in itself* critical to the narrative's resolution.[4]

I do not mean to suggest that the novel somehow "fails" in either its plot ("the clock sub-plot really needs a bit more closure") or its characterization of Mallory ("shouldn't he be more cognizant of the clock's *symbolic* import vis-à-vis the collapse of space-time?"). Instead, my point is that *The Difference Engine*'s thematic, even obsessive focus on time opens up an interpretive frame that foregrounds the multiple ways images of (and references to) time and temporality quite literally structure the text, *despite* the narrative's rather abrupt dismissal of the clock itself, time's most obvious symbol. Perhaps the simplest way to articulate the idea is this: while the significance of Mallory's jolting remembrance (and pursuit) of Madeline's clock is never completely actualized in terms of his character, the anxiety and uncertainty it represents—namely, the novel's subterranean Orientalist-inflected representation of Asian technologies (and Asians *as* technology)—is one of its most central and obsessive concerns.

Indeed, *The Difference Engine* may seem, at first glance, an odd choice of text for a collection devoted to exploring techno-Orientalism.[5] After all, although the text does present readers with a few comically stereotypical Japanese characters and Orientalist tropes, Asia does not figure prominently in any of the novel's three primary narratives, nor does it even seem very invested in complicating or elaborating upon how Asia might fit into the larger scheme of its alternative historical imagination.[6] This (apparent) indifference is precisely what most interests me about the text. In drawing provisional connections among technology, temporality, and race, I hope here to contribute to recent critical theorizations of techno-Orientalism in two key registers: first, by highlighting how temporality *itself* (and not simply the "objects" that measure it) might be understood as a technology, thereby broadening what seems to me an unnecessarily limited view of what constitutes a technology;[7] and second, by suggesting how, if temporality is understood as a form of technology, specific techno-Orientalist tropes (of the type submerged within *The Difference Engine*) might then more generally be understood as themselves premised on a naturalization of a technologically mediated ordering that equates *temporal* with *racial* difference. The racialization of time, I contend, inevitably conditions the novel's science fictional imagination of Asia, even though (or *especially since*) that Asia is not very thoroughly imagined. In this regard, perhaps a third, more implicit goal of this essay is to explore if and how techno-Orientalist discourse might be produced, reproduced, and circulated within and across texts that seem, at first glance, not much concerned with Asia or Asians at all.

Mallory's odd obsession with Madeline's clock, then, is much more than a convenient plot device: it presents an illustrative anchoring point for this essay's central arguments. To preview these points, briefly: in the essay's first section, I argue that Madeline's clock represents both a textual symbol and a contextual sign. Within the narrative, it fulfills a specific diegetic function (although it also slips loose from that function in interesting and productive ways). In a larger context, it reflects the novel's engagement with contemporary debates about temporality, modernity, and the relations between them. Despite *The Difference Engine*'s tongue-in-cheek representations of its Victorian-era characters' hopelessly retrograde attitudes about race (attitudes with which, I submit, the contemporary reader is expected to be familiar, but not *sympathetic*), the novel still relies upon the very *form* of racial difference that its hyperbolically "outdated" representations purportedly upend.

This form is temporal: it visualizes, on the one side, a chaotic, primitive past, and on the other, a rational, perfectible future, thus organizing the *present* as the ongoing act of correctly syncing each side to the other. In this sense, as I will argue, the text's interest in multiplying and displacing time lines cannot be understood as yet another iteration of the all-too-familiar theme of primitive savagery lodged within the heart of civilization. While the text certainly does evoke this trope, more engaging, for the purposes of this discussion at least, is the way it reframes this involute binary in terms of a temporal ordering. This ordering serves as the central motif for the essay's second section: what most concerns *The Difference Engine*, I suggest, is not the threatening savage eternally lurking at the periphery of the civilized, but the threat of an *inappropriate* disordering of the synchronization among past, present, and future.

Like Madeline's clock, however, the technological apparatus that inscribes upon the material world signs of the "natural" must remain invisible, even as it is everywhere evoked. In the essay's third section, then, I explore the associative connections between Madeline's clock and the novel's evocation of excavation, archeology, and "queer" temporalities. My central aim here is both to make an admittedly minor contribution to the influential work already done on queer time/temporalities,[8] and to explore how, in the novel's deployment of both metonymic and metaphoric representations of "natural" (geologic) time, it is precisely temporality itself that becomes the central technology underwriting the novel's subtextual techno-Orientalism that, because most "natural," remains its most unseen.

It is here—in the space of the visible *as* the unseen—that the novel speaks most compellingly to Asian Americanists interested in the discourse of techno-Orientalism. Again, like Madeline's clock, Asia appears in the novel only to disappear, a seemingly minor plot and character diversion that resolves, without being critical to, one of the novel's central story lines. But its apparently trivial invocation is itself a temporal ordering, signifying, on the one hand, the recurrent trope of Asia as a threat to modernity's future,[9] and, on the other, *The Difference Engine*'s own role in the problematic reproduction of the temporalized racial form that underwrites the trope itself.

"What *Was* the Time, Exactly?"

What does the clock mean to Mallory, within the narrative world of *The Difference Engine*? Clearly, the clock represents a romanticized vision of a pastoral, preindustrialized (or, in this case, pre-proto-computerized) England. But more importantly, it represents, for Mallory, a promise of *temporal stability*, premised on the ideology of rational, scientific progress that, as a paleontologist and "savant," informs his character's worldview:[10] "The timepiece ... was an outstanding piece of British precision craftsmanship, though naturally the elegant clock-stand would claim more admiration from the mechanically undiscerning. The stand ... was surmounted by a group of large gilt figures. These represented a young and decidedly attractive Britannia, very lightly robed, admiring the progress made by Time and Science in the civilization and happiness of the people of Britain. This laudable scene was additionally illustrated by a series of graven scenes, revolving weekly on hidden gear-work within the clock's base" (155).

The clock described here is evocatively familiar: it's easy to imagine that you've seen it before, even if you haven't. Upon further inspection, however, the description reveals a series of interesting disjunctions. Note, for example, how the text both reveals and then quickly conceals the clock's initial appeal to Mallory: its "precision craftsmanship," as exemplified by the "hidden gear-work within the clock's base." What displaces Mallory's scientific interest, paradoxically, is an artistic rendering of science-fueled progress that could only "claim more admiration from the mechanically undiscerning." It's precisely for this aesthetic appeal, however, rather than for its "outstanding" (though hidden) technology, that Mallory considers the clock an "apt" gift for his sister (154). It's also, again paradoxically, this aesthetic appeal that separates Mallory from those less "mechanically discerning" people around him—including his sister—for whom the meaning of the clock remains visible, but unseen.

In symbolic terms, then, the clock appears as a manifestation of Mallory's belief in "universal," timeless ideals of rational progress and national destiny, and moreover, grants to Mallory the very god-like powers of Time and Science required to achieve that destiny.[11] This symbolism goes some way in explaining why the clock later becomes suddenly so important to Mallory: it's precisely at this moment that those "timeless ideals" are under attack by the forces of irrationality and self-interest.[12] It's up to Mallory to "rescue" the clock (and more importantly, what it represents) because only he, and other "savants" like him, can see what it truly represents. This also explains why, in the heat of that chaos, Mallory's impulse is to return to the Palace of Paleontology, and not to his home in Sussex: it is science and rationality that will save the nation, not home-cooked food and drink. In this context, it's not entirely surprising that, after this moment, Madeline's clock no longer concerns the text at all.

Indeed, the clock itself is not the real object of Mallory's pursuit, but the temporal stability, and synchrony, the clock represents. But here, the text presents an additional disjunction: notwithstanding the clock's happy allegory, embedded within the gilded triumvirate of Britannia, Time, and Science is an anxious aporia, threatening to collapse the clock's teleological premise. That the people of Britain are watched over by their guardian spirit is not in itself a new conceit. Nor is it very surprising that this spirit is feminine. But it is precisely this image of an originary, mythic, feminine life force that troubles the clock's representational value. While the clock's allegory confirms, for Mallory, the temporal stability of England's great march of progress, it also contains an aporetic kernel of instability that overruns its narrative function, connecting it to a larger historical discourse to which Mallory (and the text itself) anxiously overreacts. It's the clock's evocation of a threatening (feminine, primordial) *asynchrony* that most worries the text, and that proves uncontainable within its diegetic frame.

Primal Scenes

We see hints of this threatening asynchrony early on in Mallory's story, which opens with his winning a life-changing sum at the "steam-gurney" races after placing a sizeable wager on a colleague's radically newfangled gurney, the Zephyr. Right before this, however, we see Mallory among a "herd" of Englishwomen, reflecting on the differences between their dress and the dress of the Cheyenne of North America: "Mallory's eye was still accustomed to a wilder breed, the small brown wolf-women of the Cheyenne, with the greased black braids and beaded leather leggings. The hoop-skirts in the crowd around him seemed some aberrant stunt of evolution; the daughters of Albion had got a regular scaffolding under there now, all steel and whalebone" (74). Ostensibly a reflection of Mallory's "anachronistic" scientific views, the passage also inaugurates a recurring trope centered on the instability of evolutionary forms when placed within the context of human technology. Note, in fact, how the "daughters of Albion," despite their difference from the "wilder breed" of "small brown wolf-women," are also depicted as half animal, half machine ("all steel and whalebone"), suggesting that if this is, indeed, an "aberrant stunt of evolution," it certainly had a technological helping hand.

Later, discussing his steam-gurney's unorthodox design, Godwin (Mallory's colleague from the North American expedition) says, "New forms lead the way. They may look queer at first, but Nature tests them fair and square against the old" (86). He is talking about evolution here, but he may as well be talking about the Zephyr, which not only handily wins the race but also, in so doing, manages to accelerate evolutionary time: "The crowd suddenly burst into astonished outcry—not joy so much as utter disbelief, and even a queer sort of anger.... By the time [the other gurneys] arrived, they seemed to have aged centuries. They were, Mallory realized, relics" (98). As with the example above, the passage here conflates two quite distinct kinds of evolutionary "progress" (or regress): the natural and the artificial, which merge and mix in these cyborgian steam-gurneys capable of aging, and Englishwomen composed of "steel and whalebone." The Zephyr itself is described in such terms, its "queer shape" resembling, at first, a "boat," and then "a teardrop" or "a great tadpole" (78). Careful readers will no doubt also have noticed the trebly repeated association of "queer" with this entangling of "man-made" and "natural" evolutionary time. That same word, as well, is deployed to characterize Collins (aka Captain Swing), whom Mallory has met (and made himself an enemy of) just moments before watching the Zephyr race to the finish: "A queer fellow" (89).

I will return to this fascinating association momentarily. First, it's important to note that the frantic and uncertain temporal disordering begins to proliferate all around Mallory only *after* he purchases Madeline's clock. Warned earlier of Captain Swing's vindictive nature, Mallory stumbles upon proof positive of this right after leaving the shop, clock in hand—not because of anything he himself notices, but because someone asks him the time ("The time? Could this man somehow know that Mallory had just purchased a large clock?" [156]). Without heeding his answer, the man flees, inadvertently cuing Mallory onto the fact that he's being followed (as it turns out, the man does not even want to know the time—he's simply a beggar hoping to earn a few coins). But it's precisely the question of *time* that punctuates the game of cat and mouse consequently played by Mallory and his pursuers, in which Mallory's flight is literally weighed down, and its tempo measured, by Madeline's clock: "Mallory himself took a sudden pretended interest in the clasps of his clock-case. . . . Mallory seized his clock-case in a fierce grip and began to walk quietly down Burlington Gardens. . . . Mallory took another turn, left up Bruton Street, his clock-case growing more awkward by the step. . . . Mallory began to walk more quickly, the case banging painfully against his leg. . . . He trudged ahead with the heavy clock. His hand ached; he was becoming weary" (157–159). What is being "clocked" here, so to speak, is not only Mallory's growing physical weariness, but his sudden *displacement* from the temporal stability that the clock symbolically represents, and his entry into a disordered, asynchronous temporality. More simplistically, as he attempts to lose his pursuers, he turns into an animal: "Mallory felt like a lumbering Wyoming bison"; "he rolled back and snarled—a thick, barking sound, a cry he had never heard from his own throat"; "he sensed somehow that if the bastards smelled his blood they would surely tear him down. Time passed" (160–161).

Time passes, indeed, but it passes *backward*. Or rather, time becomes resynchronized so that Mallory suddenly becomes, like those outdated gurneys, an immediate relic. In fact, to say that Mallory "regresses" is not quite right: he is not physically altered in any way, just as the *form* of the losing gurneys remains the same from start to finish. Rather, he is thrown "out of sync" precisely because he suddenly inhabits the primitive position of the primordial against which the *modern* gains validation and visibility. It's this lack of synchronicity between poles that Mallory notices most: "He propped himself against a wall, hands braced on his knees. A respectable man and woman passed him, and stared in vague distaste.... More Londoners strolled past him, with looks of indifference, curiosity, faint disapproval" (161). Indeed, Mallory's desperate desire to maintain possession of the clock suggests more than economic common sense: the clock, in its very technological might, is the object that guarantees Mallory's modernity, *even as* it inaugurates his temporal dislocation.

Note too that here, as at the racetrack, it is Mallory's experience in the wilds of North America (there, the wolf-women; here, the Wyoming bison) that evocatively returns as the haunting, recurrent threat of a de-evolutionary temporal disorder. North America—the land of "queer improbable names," according to Sybil Gerard, the central character in the novel's opening narrative (65). This opening narrative sets the stage for Mallory by introducing a set of "clacker" (programming) cards that, when run in a government "engine," have the ability to initiate massive systemwide failure—a proto-virus, in other words. More important for our purpose is the sense of "queer" landscapes and disordered time that subtextually connects Sybil's narrative to Mallory's. Sybil asks her lover Mick, for instance, "isn't Texas a frightfully queer place?" (31); watching General Sam Houston speak, Sybil notes that the audience must regard him as "some sort of queer American exhibit" (46); riding the London Underground on the way home from this "queer American exhibit," Sybil thinks, "It was a queer business, the underground, when you thought about it" (48). So let's think about it. What's so queer about the Underground?

Queer Futures

While the operative term used most often in the text to describe, characterize, or evoke temporal asynchrony is "queer," I'm relatively certain that the term is not used self-reflexively, ironically, or in parody.[13] Indeed, the seemingly explosive proliferation of the word suggests to me that, like "time," it's a productively overdetermined term in the text. Note, for instance, how, in the following example, it connects the North American landscape to Asia:

> "They're a queer folk, the Yanks," Mallory said.... "Never saw Americans, just Indians." And the less said about that the better, Mallory thought. "What did you think of India, by the way?"
>
> "It's a dreadful place, India," Brian said readily, "brim-full of queer marvels, but dreadful. There's only one folk in Asia with any sense, and that's the Japanese."
>
> ...
>
> "Oh," said Brian, "when you see some Hindu fakir a-sitting in a temple niche, filthy naked with a flower on his hair, who's to say what goes on in that queer headpiece of his?" (269–270)[14]

Let me suggest at least one central meaning of queer, as the passage above implies: the term signifies the irruption of inappropriate time lines (nonwhite, non-Western) that threaten Western modernity, precisely because it is those inappropriate time lines that Western modernity relies upon, but must disavow, to establish its own exceptional (white, male, heterosexual) universality. It is not the irruption of the primitive itself that disorders time, since the modern necessarily depends upon this evocation (indeed, without the primitive, modernity wouldn't be modern). Instead, it's the way the primitive or primordial past skews the *future*, as a potent threat to modernity's present: the queer future, it turns out, is that which potentially counterfeits the "natural" inevitability of the present, thereby exposing it as the future's *asynchronous past*.

It's worth noting here, however, that the term "queer" is not the only connective thread between these two narratives: by proving the link between Sybil's meditation on the "Underground" and Mallory's archeological digs, *excavation* becomes the associative metaphor intertwining the text's anxious evocation of disordered temporalities and queer time lines. Here, again, is Sybil Gerard thinking about the London subway: "It was a queer business, the underground . . . where the navvies had come upon lead waterpipe of the Romans, and coins, and mosaics, and archways, elephant's teeth a thousand years old. . . . And the digging went on . . . they worked unceasingly, the excavators, boring newer, deeper lines now . . . and soon Lord Babbage's smokeless trains would slide through them silent as eels, though she found the thought of it somehow unclean" (49). As this passage illustrates, when *The Difference Engine* says "excavation," what it means, in fact, is *time travel*: digging into the earth to assemble "newer, deeper lines" connecting and disconnecting nature ("elephant's teeth a thousand years old") to culture ("lead waterpipe . . . and coins, and mosaics, and archways"). Sybil's sense of the uncannily "unclean" thus dovetails with Mallory's fear of de-evolutionary regress. More importantly, in both cases, the ostensible icons representing the triumphant progress of Western technology (the clock, the subway) become, at the same time, sources of deep anxiety over what the archeology of such progress might unearth.

The London Underground, in this sense, is much like Madeline's clock: its symbolism registers a double articulation, on the one hand pointing to the way that technologies of *time* not only support, but render visible, the ideology of "natural" evolutionary progress, even while expressing, on the other, an aporetic uncertainty about the very constitution of the "natural." If Madeline's clock is a metonym for the excavated earth, then excavation *itself* becomes the novel's larger central metaphor for a type of temporal ordering at which Mallory so excels: a *spatial (geologic and geographic)* ordering that *temporalizes race*. Mallory, let us recall, not only sees and understands the "hidden gear-work" of Madeline's clock, but, as an archeologist, literally pierces through and pieces together the jumbled-up, hidden layers of the earth, thereby reconstructing (by reordering) the geologic truth underwriting the triumphal narrative of (white) "man's progress." Here, it is the *earth itself* that becomes the most "natural" clock of all, measuring not only the spatial distance between races (North America, Asia, India), but also their relative positions in a temporal order (North American and Asian "Indians" as *simultaneous* in time—both irrationally "queer"—compared to the Japanese). It's here that the novel's semi-self-reflexive, subtextual Orientalist tropes most revealingly adhere to its representations of technologies of time: the physical, geographic displacement of Asia into North America (and vice versa) suggests a queer, temporal disordering that anxiously rehearses (even as it textually reproduces) nineteenth- and twentieth-century discourses positing Asians as developmentally "in-between" the primitive (Africa, North America) and the modern (Europe).

Let me return, by way of conclusion, to one final example of the text's prolific (or profligate) utilization of the term "queer" to better illustrate—if not neatly, then hopefully provocatively—the multifarious points of contact between that term, temporality, technology, and race. Upon meeting, for the first time, a group of Japanese diplomats associated with Laurence Oliphant, Mallory thinks to himself, "the queer little foreigners seemed so young, so idealistic—intelligent, and above all sincere" (170). What is so "queer" about them, in fact, is not only the uniformity and incongruity of their appearance ("Five Asian men sat about [a table], in cross-legged alien dignity: five sober men in their stocking feet, wearing tailored evening-suits from Savile row" [166]), but their unreasonable expectation of an asynchronous leap into modernity. Thus, despite Oliphant's assertion that "Japan is the Britain of Asia," Mallory remains skeptical that the Japanese can rightfully claim such equivalent status: "It's a bit of a hard slog, though, civilization, building an empire. Takes several centuries, you know. . . . For you, in a few short years, to achieve what we have done" (169). Worth highlighting, however, is that Mallory's skepticism is not directed at the possibility that Japanese could, *eventually*, attain an equal footing with British modernity, but at their desire to do so out of (temporal) order: "But what you propose is simply impossible!" (170).

Most disturbing to Mallory—making the diplomat's sincerity so queer—is his proclamation that Japan will grasp modernity at any cost: "*We will make whatever sacrifice necessary*" (170, emphasis in original). If Mallory fails to grasp the veiled threat behind the diplomat's claim ("perhaps the faint chill in the air was only Mallory's imagination" [170]), he also misunderstands the similarity between their respective positions. Indeed, this similarity is underscored by the presence of another technological object—a whiskey-pouring automaton, in the form of woman with "a look of mask-like composure and a silky black wealth of hair" (166)—that inspired the fraught exchange in the first place. Unlike Mallory's initial encounter with Madeline's clock, however, his encounter with the wooden automaton befuddles his sense of technical mastery. Whereas earlier that clock's representation of an originary feminine life force seems to affirm Mallory's (masculine) rational mastery of time, here that force returns as the troublesome sign of a queer, *racial-temporal* threat, aligning Mallory with what he earlier imaged to be *Madeline's* position, unable to piece the deceptively "natural" surface/skin of the "Japanese" automaton: "the woman had not moved so much as an inch. . . . She made no response. Mallory began to wonder if she were ill, or paralyzed. . . . 'She's a dummy!' Mallory blurted" (168).

One could argue, at this point, that the text here grants the Japanese characters a certain counterdiscursive tinge. After all, Mallory's inability to recognize the automaton for what it is directly supports the diplomat's claim that Japan, like Britain, can achieve prodigious feats of technological superiority. But this claim is immediately checked, I suggest, by the novel's problematic reproduction of the hoary techno-Orientalist trope of Asians as at once inhumanly premodern *and über*-modern. And it is, of course, the automaton that yields this truth: for, if Mallory is not given to see that his misrecognition of "her" humanity places *him* in a queer temporality, then *The Difference Engine* is likewise not given to acknowledge how *its* brief evocation of Japan as an implacably threatening, alternate modernity depends upon its representation of the Japanese, with their "alien dignity," *as* automatons—mechanistic, reproducible, technological, inhuman. What unites the Japanese automaton with Madeline's clock is the way each technological object evokes *and* elides a problematic "origin," at once *past* and *future*, lodged at the heart of any "scientific" technological-temporal ordering. It's not simply that the Japanese are represented as both "later" (already *themselves* automatons) and "earlier" (inappropriately premodern) on the developmental time line that evokes a techno-Orientalist discourse. Rather, it's the way this threatening asynchronicity represents, in the larger text, a technicity originating in a sui generis racial homogeneity, a (past-primordial) homogeneity uncannily mirrored in (and foundational to) Mallory's "scientific" belief in the (future-modern) homogeneity of the perfectly rational "universal" subject. Indeed, what Mallory *cannot* recognize here is also what most troubles and haunts *The Difference Engine's* larger representational matrix: the possibility that race is not *discovered* by, but in fact *constituted through*, the "natural" technologies of time—including, of course, clocks, the earth, and other automata.

Notes

1. Gibson and Sterling (237). Further citations are in parentheses.
2. The definition of steampunk has been the subject of much recent debate; roughly speaking, it's a genre of science fictional novel that merges Victorian or neo-Victorian culture with twentieth-century technologies. *The Difference Engine*

revolves around the intertwined stories of three characters: Sybil Gerard, Edward Mallory, and Laurence Oliphant. Mallory's narrative occupies the largest portion of the text. For more on steampunk, see Nevins, Bowser and Croxall, and Csicsery-Ronay, Jr. (108–109).
3. See Sussman for a review of both.
4. Neither of the novel's two corollary stories rely upon, refer to, or even much mention clocks (and certainly not the one intended for Mallory's sister).
5. As defined by Greta Niu, "a practice of ascribing, erasing, and/or disavowing relationships between technology and Asian peoples and subjects... techno-Orientalism points to the way it ignores the history and constructions of the relationships between Asian people and technology" (74). See also Morley and Robins.
6. Gibson's other work, on the other hand, is much fascinated with "Asian" futures; see, among others, *Neuromancer* (1984), *Mona Lisa Overdrive* (1988), and *Pattern Recognition* (2003).
7. Here, I am thinking of Bruce Braun and Sarah Whatmore's definition of technological objects as both "eventful" and indeterminate: "Things are not just simultaneously material and meaningful; they are also *eventful*.... [W]e wish to underline that things—and especially technological artifacts—carry with them a margin of indeterminacy.... Far from deterministic, technological artifacts temporalize, opening us to a future that we cannot fully appropriate even as they render us subject to a past that is not of our making" (xxi).
8. For more on queer temporalities, see Halberstam, Puar, and Freeman, among others.
9. See the essays by Sohn, Huang, Yu, Niu, and others, collected in the *MELUS* special issue, "Alien/Asian."
10. The novel's alternate history presents an England governed by scientific "savants."
11. Donna Haraway has famously called this the "god trick" (582).
12. Mallory's recall of the clock occurs at the beginning of an insurrection led by Captain Swing; it is both a class war, and a war on the very ideals of science, progress, and rationality that Mallory holds so dear.
13. I find little support for the possibility that the text is an attempt to "queer" science fiction, in the way that queer theorists use the term.
14. More examples from that same section of the narrative: "queer kind of forgery" (275); "a queer sort of talk" (292); "some kind of queer temperance lecture" (297); "these queer objects" (303); "in queer bondage" (304); "sent a queer shiver through him" (304); "queer business" (311); "queer things I saw" (312); "queer leaf" (313).

Chapter 5
I, Stereotype

Detained in the Uncanny Valley

SEO-YOUNG CHU

In an article titled *Bukimi no Tani* (Uncanny Valley; 1970), the Japanese roboticist Masahiro Mori posited a theory to explain how humans react to humanoid artifacts. According to Mori, humans tend to respond with increasing sympathy to a series of increasingly humanlike entities until a certain point (someplace around 85 percent humanlike) whereupon the aesthetic response drops abruptly from sympathy to profound revulsion—before ascending again (toward 100 percent humanlike) to create what looks, when graphically delineated, like a precipitous valley. For this reason, Mori's theory has come to be known as the "uncanny valley."

Mori's theory is usually applied to robots, puppets, and other humanoid figures that elicit what Ernst Jentsch identified in "On the Psychology of the Uncanny" (1906) as "intellectual uncertainty" over whether something is inanimate or alive. In what follows, I apply Mori's theory to a different species of humanoid artifact: stereotypes of the "yellow peril." Through analyses of stories by Sax Rohmer, World War II propaganda, and films from the James Bond franchise, I investigate ways in which the logic of the uncanny valley has interacted with and shaped Orientalist and techno-Orientalist stereotypes. For example, I analyze science-fictional portrayals of Asian bodies that have been dramatically arrested in the midst of being masked or unmasked. Prevented from completing the process of masking/unmasking, stereotypic characters such as the North Korean villain Zao in the Bond film *Die Another Day* (2002) remain detained—stuck—in a state of incomplete "masked-ness" that leaves the stereotypes approximately 85 percent humanlike and entirely disturbing.

In the process of my investigation, I address the following questions: What makes an ethnic stereotype uncanny? Are all stereotypes inherently uncanny? What does it mean to find one's ethnic group detained in the uncanny valley? What does it take for a stereotyped "Other" to transcend the uncanny valley and become recognized as fully human?

According to the *Oxford English Dictionary*, the noun "stereotype," coined in the late eighteenth century by the French printer Firmin Didot, originally denoted the "process of printing in which a solid plate of type-metal, cast from a papier-mâché or plaster mould taken from the surface of a forme of type, is used for printing from instead of the forme itself." Instead of relying on movable type, stereotyping relied on plates wherein the pieces of type corresponding to each page were already fused together, fixed, and consolidated. This technology, which allowed for entire pages of text to be replicated with unprecedented ease, facilitated the mass reproduction of books, magazines, advertisements, and ideas in the nineteenth and early twentieth centuries.

The stereotype-as-a-perceived-type-of-person was invented by the American journalist Walter Lippmann in *Public Opinion* (1922). Like its namesake, the stereotype can be understood as a mold designed to cast a fixed image upon an impressionable substance. In Lippmann's words, a stereotype is "a form of perception" that "precedes the use of reason" and "imposes a certain character on the data of our senses before the data reach the intelligence." The key purpose of this perceptual technology, according to Lippmann, is to enable and automate psychological shortcuts—oversimplified acts of cognition—that relieve the technology's user of the inconvenience of devoting full attention to the irreducibly complex reality of other humans' quirks. "There is economy in this," Lippmann writes of the benefits of stereotyping: "For the attempt to see all things freshly and in detail, rather than as types and generalities, is exhausting, and among busy affairs practically out of the question." Lippmann attributes the growing necessity of stereotyping to "modern life," which "is hurried and multifarious." In Lippmann's view, to live in modern society without using stereotypes—to live in modern society without "economizing attention" to some degree—would be to engage in a disorganized "approach to experience" at once "wholly innocent" of preconceptions and impossibly labor-intensive. Such an approach "would impoverish human life" by leaving us with inadequate time and attention for the people dearest to us, that is, the people who require from us a quality of attention unmediated by stereotypes.

Lippmann's insights helpfully classify stereotyping as a time-saving mechanism. Like any other technology, stereotyping is valuable as long as it is handled with a conscientious mindfulness of its purposes and limits. The dangers of stereotyping lie not in its existence but in the potential for its misapplication. Stereotypes are most dangerous when they are abused as weapons of mass dehumanization targeted against specific groups of people. Moreover, stereotypes are most effective as weapons of mass dehumanization when they result in the aesthetic detention of a targeted group of people in the uncanny valley.

As I mentioned in the opening to this essay, Mori's theory of the uncanny valley can be visualized as a graph. The x-axis corresponds to the humanlikeness of a given entity. The y-axis corresponds to how humans respond emotionally to that entity. The continuum of human responses to a succession of progressively humanoid items can be delineated as a curve that ascends from negative to positive emotions before suddenly descending at roughly 85 percent humanlike and then reascending toward 100 percent humanlike to create what resembles a steep valley. Mori's framework helps to explain why, say, R2-D2 (a droid in the Star Wars universe who is at most 40 percent humanlike in behavior and shape) elicits more sympathy than does the much more recognizably anthropomorphic Showa Hanako (a female robot "patient" who has recently been helping to train dental students in Tokyo and who is at least 80 percent humanlike in behavior and shape).

Yet Mori's formulation of the uncanny valley does not, by itself, explain why a robot such as Showa Hanako elicits such disquiet. Showa Hanako's primary function is to simulate the appearance and actions of someone whose body is obviously in need of repair. As I have argued elsewhere, Mori's formulation of the uncanny valley can be enhanced when it takes into account whether a given humanoid artifact is conspicuously injured and thereby framed as a constructed object "impersonating" a human subject. The uncanniest humanoid artifacts—e.g., damaged robots in the Terminator franchise whose injuries expose mechanical innards—unsettle us because their otherwise perfect "humanity effect" has been violently destabilized.

Like their fellow humanoid artifacts, stereotypes can elicit a spectrum of human responses. Just as not all robots are uncanny, not all stereotypes are uncanny. There is nothing *inherently* uncanny, for example, about stereotypes such as "dog lover," "Sox fan," "vegan," "science fiction enthusiast," and so on. Problems arise, however, when stereotypes are *engineered* to fabricate, automate, and mechanically reproduce uncanny feelings in response to certain "types" of people. An uncanny stereotype elicits intellectual uncertainty over whether a "type" of person is genuinely human and alive. The uncanniest stereotypes elicit revulsion and profound phobia in response to the person(s) stereotyped as uncanny. Often the manufacture of such uncanny stereotypes happens in the context of war and colonialism. Just as individual members of ethnic groups have found themselves detained in prisons and internment camps, ethnic stereotypes have often found themselves aesthetically detained in the uncanny valley.

Indeed, the detention of "yellow peril" stereotypes in the uncanny valley during World War II corresponded to the detention by the U.S. government of thousands of Japanese Americans in the wake of Pearl Harbor. This correspondence is substantiated by an infamous December 1941 article in *LIFE* titled "How to Tell Japs from the Chinese: Angry Citizens Victimize Allies with Emotional Outburst at Enemy." Occupying less than two pages, this article claims the scholarly authority of "physical anthropologists" and "adduces a rule-of-thumb from the anthropometric conformations that distinguish friendly Chinese from enemy alien Japs" (81). Such authority, however, falls apart under scrutiny. Almost all of the article's rhetorical impact is generated not by logical argumentation but by the illogical interaction between the verbal text and the accompanying visual images. While the annotated photographs of Ong Wen-hao and Hideki Tojo might *seem* to convey an aura of scientific fact, in truth the diagrams constitute an exercise in Orientalist physiognomic fantasy. The annotations are riddled with anatomical errors and misinformation. For example, the foremost detail noted in each diagram—"yellow complexion"—is inaccurate, whether such yellowness is specified as "parchment" (upper diagram) or "earthy" (lower diagram). As Michael Keevak demonstrates in *Becoming Yellow: A Short History of Racial Thinking* (2011), the misattribution of yellow skin to East Asians originated in the eighteenth and nineteenth centuries. Moreover, the annotation "epicanthic fold" draws the viewer's attention to the wrong part of the eye. The term actually refers to a fold of skin over the eye's inner angle. (The prefix "epi-" means "upon" or "over," while "canthus" refers to any angle formed by the intersection of the upper and lower eyelids.) In the diagram, however, the phrase "epicanthic fold" is shown as pointing to a crease in the upper eyelid. Perhaps most important, contrary to the article's claims, no individual can be characterized as "representative" of an entire "anthropological group."

As such misannotations suggest, each diagram in the article can be analyzed into two parts that do not necessarily correspond: the visual image and the verbal gloss. Indeed, the verbal gloss, when used as a series of instructions for composing a mental picture, yields an image tellingly different from the image to which the gloss supposedly refers. Below is a "translation" of the first set of annotations/captions into a series of instructions for composing a mental picture. (As I will soon demonstrate, the formula for "imagining" the stereotype in the *LIFE* article originates in Sax Rohmer's influential characterization of Fu Manchu.) "Imagine a man, tall and slender, lanky and lithe, with a parchment yellow complexion, epicanthic fold, a high-bridged nose, cheeks that are never rosy, light facial bones, a scant beard, and a face that is long and narrow. Imagine such a person, and you have a mental picture of the Northern Chinese embodied in one man." Now consider the following translation of the second set of annotations/captions into a series of instructions for composing a mental picture. "Imagine a man, short and squat, with an earthy yellow complexion, no epicanthic fold, a nose that is flat and blob, cheeks that are sometimes rosy, massive cheek and jaw bones, a broad, short face, heavy beard, and a facial expression showing the humorless intensity of ruthless mystics. Imagine such a person, and you have a mental picture of the enemy alien Japs embodied in one man." If one were to compare the two verbal descriptions and then compare the two faces in the photographs, one would realize that the differences between the two verbal descriptions are more dramatic than are the differences between the two faces in the photographs. What the reader skimming the article is likely to visualize, however, is not each face as it appears in each photograph but rather the mental impressions of "yellow" stereotypes generated by the copious verbal annotations. Unfortunately, the inclusion of photographic "evidence" has the effect of granting such mental pictures the illusion of documentary fact.

Meanwhile, the similarities between the two verbal descriptions are more important than are the differences. Both accounts are made of superficial details vacant of human subjectivity. Either account might as well be describing a hollow mask. To don such a mask—to conjugate either verbal description into the first-person singular—serves only to amplify the sound of not-quite-human hollowness. Consider the uncanny effect of the following conjugation: "I am a man, tall and slender, lanky and lithe, with a parchment yellow complexion, epicanthic fold, a high-bridged nose, cheeks that are never rosy, light facial bones, a scant beard, and a face that is long and narrow. I am the Northern Chinese embodied in one man." These words are uncanny because the voice uttering them is the eerie voice of an uncanny stereotype. Recall the context and subject matter of the 1941 *LIFE* article. Would an actual Chinese American human being's first-person contribution to such an article consist of a catalogue of his own body parts punctuated by the claim that such body parts exemplify the body parts of a much broader category of people? To give first-person voice to the catalogue of superficial physiological features is to reveal the article's true end: the assemblage of "yellow" stereotypes empty of inner life or first-person sentience.

The above translations also expose the formulaic syntax implicit in the process through which the article in *LIFE* assembles its stereotypes.

1 Start by positing an individual person (e.g., Ong Wen-hao, Hideki Tojo).

2 Make a list of approximately ten superficial features and ascribe them to this particular individual. (Might ten be the optimal number of features for an "effective" stereotype to possess? Perhaps stereotypes that reduce their subjects to ten or so distinct characteristics are detailed enough to imagine in concrete terms but not so detailed as to preclude easy mechanical reproduction. Just as a stereotype plate is a finite space capable of containing only a limited amount of information, a stereotypical depiction of a "type" of person is a finite space capable of containing only a limited amount of information. In both cases—stereotype plate and stereotypical depiction—the finiteness of the amount of information is what makes possible the convenient mass reproduction of the stereotype.)
3 Identify these characteristics as "representative" of a much larger group of people. In other words, frame the individual person as a personification, an incarnation, a figure of speech. The stereotype is now complete.

This three-step process is not unique to the 1941 *LIFE* article. We see the same process at work in Sax Rohmer's *The Insidious Dr. Fu-Manchu: Being a Somewhat Detailed Account of the Amazing Adventures of Nayland Smith in His Trailing of the Sinister Chinaman* (1913), the opening pages of which contain the most influential instance of the yellow peril stereotype ever synthesized. The introduction of the Fu Manchu stereotype takes place in the context of a dialogue between the novel's two Caucasian British "heroes": Denis Nayland Smith (a police commissioner who travels regularly between England and British colonial Burma) and Doctor Petrie (Smith's friend and the primary narrator throughout the stories). In the following passage, Smith enjoins Petrie—and Rohmer enjoins the reader—to bring to imaginative life what Rohmer elsewhere hyperbolizes as "the ultimate expression of Chinese cunning" (175), an "archangel of evil" (36), "the most malign and formidable personality existing in the known world today" (12), "a superman of incredible genius" (175), the "advance-guard of a cogent Yellow Peril" (157), and "the most elusive being ever born of the land of mystery—China" (193):

> Imagine a person, tall, lean and feline, high-shouldered, with a brow like Shakespeare and a face like Satan, a close-shaven skull, and long, magnetic eyes of the true cat-green. Invest him with all the cruel cunning of an entire Eastern race, accumulated in one giant intellect, with all the resources of science past and present, with all the resources, if you will, of a wealthy government—which, however, already has denied all knowledge of his existence. Imagine that awful being, and you have a mental picture of Dr. Fu-Manchu, the yellow peril incarnate in one man. (13)

To "imagine" Fu Manchu, as the reader is commanded to do in these lurid instructions, is to reenact in one's mind the three-step formula for assembling a stereotype: (1) posit an individual person; (2) make a list of approximately ten features and ascribe them to this particular individual; (3) identify these characteristics as "representative" of a much larger group of people, thereby framing the individual as both an abstract personification and a carnal entity who poses a physical threat. Not only does Rohmer deploy the three-step process of constructing a stereotype in the above passage, but he later refers back to this passage and expands on characteristics such as feline and green-eyed with remarkable frequency. Throughout the novel Rohmer inserts vivid descriptions of the "evil Chinese doctor," and throughout these descriptions a number of arresting epithets tend to recur. The following list contains details that are ascribed to Rohmer's villain over and over again:

- A "brow like Shakespeare" (13, 84, 185), "great" and "domed" in shape (161)
- A "face like Satan" (13, 84, 185) thickly associated with phrases such as "devil" (30, 47)
- A "masklike, intellectual face" (111), "impassive" and "yellow" (113)
- A voice equally "guttural" and "sibilant" (84, 165)
- Eyes that are "narrow and long, very slightly oblique" (36, 85)
- Shimmering green irises (36, 37, 85, 130, 144) possessing the "viridescence" of "the eye of the cat" (84)
- Repulsive surplus eyelids whose "unique horror lay in a certain filminess" reminiscent of "the *membrana nictitans* in a bird" (36, 81, 82, 111, 161)
- A "reptilian" quality (84, 170)
- An "indescribable gait, cat-like yet awkward" (84, 179)
- Long "bony" hands (36, 85) with "clawish fingers" (170)

Each feature has been programmed to sensationalize Fu Manchu while simultaneously repelling the reader's access to Fu Manchu's inner consciousness. The allusion to Shakespeare's brow, for example, invokes the mystique of the Bard's genius. Meanwhile, the extra eyelid, which Fu Manchu can lift or shut at will, has the effect of veiling what is already an opaquely masklike face. Moreover, the ten or so "stereotypical" traits that Rohmer has chosen to illustrate Fu Manchu's inscrutable character are strikingly and alarmingly eclectic. His eyes are not only feline but also birdlike; his inert masklike visage is not only animalistic but also Shakespearean; and so on. Fu Manchu is composed of odd features that come from radically dissimilar contexts—features that the reader does not expect to see coexisting within one another's vicinity, let alone within the same anthropomorphic figure. Rohmer's creation is a humanoid patchwork whose unsettlingly miscellaneous parts vividly evoke a web of seams and stitches. As a humanoid artifact that is always already noticeably damaged, Fu Manchu bears a meaningful resemblance to Frankenstein's uncanny monster. Indeed, it is no coincidence that the actors through whom the Fu Manchu stereotype has most famously been brought to cinematic life—Boris Karloff starred as the fiendish Chinese doctor in *The Mask of Fu Manchu* (1932); Christopher Lee played Fu Manchu in five films, starting with the 1965 film *The Face of Fu Manchu*—are also actors often "typecast" as uncanny humanoid creatures such as Frankenstein's monster (Karloff) and the vampire Count Dracula (Lee).

The final examples of the yellow peril stereotype that I want to discuss are from *Die Another Day* (2002). The twentieth installment of the Bond film franchise, *Die Another Day* seems to be aware, to some extent, of its Orientalist history. Its North Korean villains can be thought of as embellished renditions of such stereotypes as Doctor No (the half-Chinese criminal mastermind in the eponymously named film that inaugurated the series in 1962) and Oddjob (the wordless, brutal Korean henchman in the 1964 film *Goldfinger*). *Die Another Day* even makes an extended allusion to the scenes from *You Only Live Twice* (1967), in which Bond, played by Sean Connery, dons a yellow-face disguise while undercover in Japan. But whereas Bond's disguise in *You Only Live Twice* consists of a wig, costume, and prosthetic eyelids, the disguises in *Die Another Day* are much more elaborate. This time the antagonists are the ones who undergo racial disguise, and the masking occurs at a molecular level in a science-fictional narrative that in many ways is set not on Earth but in the uncanny valley. Unlike Connery's Bond, who as the Caucasian hero of an Anglo-American franchise cannot risk being viewed as uncanny and who is thus portrayed in the film as effortlessly and successfully "passing" as "Asian" with only minimal disguise, the Asian antagonists of *Die Another Day* must endure a medical process that maximizes their camouflage and forces them to risk becoming terminally uncanny in order for them successfully to "pass" as Caucasian.

The main villain in *Die Another Day* is Colonel Tan-Gun Moon, a rogue North Korean army officer who near the opening of the film is supposedly killed by Bond during a chase scene that takes place in the Korean demilitarized zone. We later discover that Moon is alive: cutting-edge gene therapy performed in a clinic in Cuba has completely and permanently replaced his original Korean body (portrayed by the Korean American actor Will Yun Lee) with a Caucasian body masquerading as a wealthy, arrogant, sophisticated philanthropist and fencing champion named Sir Gustav Graves (portrayed by the English actor Toby Stephens). For reasons that will soon become clear, it is important here to note that the "DNA transplant"—the metamorphosis from Moon to Graves—is never shown on screen. The film presents Moon/Graves to us as either "100 percent Asian" or "100 percent Caucasian."

While the villainous behavior of our antihero is frequently on display, Moon/Graves does not reside in the uncanny valley. If anything, the film invites us to view Moon/Graves as a subversive yet aesthetically acceptable version of Pierce Brosnan's 007. As Moon-as-Graves informs his nemesis during a confrontation near the movie's end, "When your intervention forced me to present the world with a new face, I chose to model the disgusting Gustav Graves on you. That unjustifiable swagger. Your crass quips." Deeply critical of Bond's imperiousness and association with British imperialism, Moon has used his own "death" as an opportunity to fashion himself as a stealthy parody of Bond—one with aspirations to out-Bond Bond himself. That Moon/Graves represents a critique of British colonialism is implied earlier on in *Die Another Day*. Moments before his ostensible demise, Colonel Moon expresses to Bond his displeasure that "you British still believe you have the right to police the world"—a sentiment with which Fu Manchu would likely have agreed.

Perhaps the closest Moon/Graves comes to approaching the uncanny valley happens in a scene where Graves is shown using the prismatic "dream machine," a spectacular high-tech mask designed to mitigate what we soon learn is the constant insomnia he suffers as a side effect of the DNA transplant. Yet this shimmering rainbow mask is less uncanny than it is futuristically gorgeous. In its narrative context, moreover, the mask—the luminous dream machine—is intended not to conceal the wearer's identity but to alleviate the suffering that the wearer feels. Accordingly, the mask has the counterstereotypic outcome of calling attention to Graves's inner experiences (rather than to his superficial exterior) and eliciting some amount of the viewer's sympathy. Even if the viewer sees the mask as hideous, the mask is as readily separable from its wearer's face as its own iridescent hues are capable of kaleidoscopic fluctuation. Whereas Fu Manchu's face is described as intrinsically masklike, implying that "face" and "mask" are inextricably the same "immobile" thing, Graves's face does not equal the "dream machine" any more than Bruce Wayne's face equals the mask that Batman wears. Graves's face, in other words, is not an inert object. Instead it is an expressive visage often betraying his subjective emotions. Consequently our aesthetic response to Graves's face is that of one human to another.

Like Moon/Graves, his comrade Zao (played by the Korean American actor Rick Yune) is seriously injured by Bond in the film's opening scenes: an explosion set off by 007 leaves Zao's face scarred and studded with diamonds. Following Moon's suit, Zao undergoes painful gene therapy to replace his original Korean body with the body of a Caucasian man. This time, however, we are given visual access to Zao's DNA transplant. Such access happens in two ways. First, we see—through the eyes of NSA Agent Giacinta "Jinx" Johnson (played by Halle Berry)—computerized medical files detailing Zao's patient status. At this point in the movie's narrative, Zao has finalized the first half—"PHASE ONE"—of his metamorphosis. As the computer screen shows, Zao at this stage of the DNA transplant is suspended in a patently liminal state. He has been mostly drained of his original ethnicity. At the same time, his "target" ethnicity has begun to emerge in the form of extremely pale blue irises. Zao has not yet, however, been thoroughly instilled with the genetic material meant to reconstruct his ethnic identity. Furthermore, the diamond-studded scar tissue on his face has not yet been repaired. As a work of medical artistry, Zao is crude and unfinished. Indeed, the computer screen explicitly labels the second half of Zao's metamorphosis as "PHASE TWO STANDBY" in spectral font, providing us with a glimpse into an alternate future for Zao that will soon be left unrealized and rendered purely hypothetical.

If the first way in which we are given visual access to Zao's DNA transplant is through medical charts and diagrams on a computer screen (specifically, a computer screen where Zao's "original" face and ethnicity are juxtaposed with his never-to-be-completed "target" face and ethnicity), the second way is much more dramatic. Bond, having infiltrated the clinic in Cuba where Zao in undergoing gene therapy, locates the medical chrysalis in which Zao's DNA transplant is in progress. Pointing a gun at Zao's hibernating body, 007 violently interrupts the metamorphosis. Even though Zao manages to survive the surprise attack and escape with his life, his body is left forever "Bonded" in a state of incomplete camouflage.

Unlike Moon/Graves, then, Zao spends much of the movie as a detainee held aesthetically captive in the uncanny valley's depths. Although his eyes are not bright green but ice blue, and although his skin is not yellow but translucent, Zao-post-aborted-DNA-transplant embodies an updated version of Fu Manchu. Vastly disparate elements clash within a single human figure. Zao's eyes look opaque, emphatically artificial, yet the veins and arteries visible beneath the pale raw skin highlight Zao's condition as a creature made of flesh and blood. The diamond-studded scars (Jinx calls them "expensive acne") evoke sharp rigidity, yet the larval complexion implies soft vulnerability. The absence of facial or head hair makes him seem almost like a young child, yet the pronounced brow ridge and Zao's muscularity and imposing height altogether accentuate his masculinity.

What makes Zao particularly uncanny as an incarnation of the yellow peril stereotype is the fact that Zao's body has been visibly detained in the middle of the invisible process of masking itself at a molecular level. The artificiality of the DNA transplant—an artificiality that in Moon's case has been erased by the successful completion of his biological regeneration as Graves—exposes and frames Zao as a humanoid artifact. To look at Zao is to sense layers of synthetic textures animated by a wounded consciousness. So disquieting is Zao's appearance that it apparently triggers a subjective experience of the uncanny valley even in the usually imperturbable NSA agent Jinx. "Why do you want to kill me?" Zao asks. Jinx, unsettled by Zao's uncanniness, responds not by, say, threatening to punish Zao for his criminal activity and terrorist acts, but by suggesting that he ought to be euthanized: "I thought it was the humane thing to do."

Insofar as Zao is a stereotype of North Korea/ns, what does Zao reveal about outsider perceptions of the DPRK? North Korea can be thought of as an uncanny nation that elicits in many observers intellectual uncertainty as to whether its people, its government, its version of communism are alive or dead. Perhaps what is being oversimplified and exaggerated in Zao's features is a mystified sense of North Korea's eerie opacity. The mental shortcut that Zao as a stereotype enables and encourages us to take is a grossly reductive equation: North Korea equals abnormal. By adding a gratuitous aesthetic dimension to this shortcut—by making this shortcut obscenely uncanny for the purpose of entertainment—Zao-as-stereotype obscures the complicated fact that North Korea, while inaccessible to most of the world, remains a lived reality for millions of humans.

Unfortunately, even former North Koreans who now live in South Korea nevertheless reside in a kind of uncanny valley. North Korean refugees, especially those new to the South, are unversed in K-pop, speak Korean with a North Korean accent, use North Korean idioms, find South Korea's hyper-wired culture bewildering, and so on. As a result, many South Koreans negatively view refugees and defectors from the North as almost Korean but not Korean enough. Stereotyped as roughly 85 percent Korean-like, such defectors find themselves detained aesthetically and emotionally in the valley's depths.

If a stereotype is a technology meant to facilitate mental shortcuts, then I have been misusing this technology. More specifically, I have been dwelling on stereotypes of yellow peril—thinking about them at length, spending time with them, treating them as though they were more than two-dimensional, and (unintentionally?) turning them inside out. In doing so, I have come to wonder whether the phenomenon of the stereotype will eventually grow obsolete. A stereotype is a human-shaped technology. Technologies are constantly changing, and they are constantly changing the way humans are shaped—as well as the ways in which human shapes are perceived. (Consider technologies such as Photoshop, cosmetic surgery, and CGI.) What would happen to stereotypes in a world where Zao's face is universally perceived not as uncanny but as aesthetically ideal? Moreover, what would happen to stereotypes in a world where anthropomorphic shapes are obsolete? Would a posthuman world be a post-stereotype world? Or would stereotypes look posthuman?

Insofar as the phenomenon of stereotyping does exist, there need to be ethical principles guiding the conscientious employment and construction of stereotypes. In his science fiction, Isaac Asimov famously devised three Laws of Robotics that govern the behavior of his robot and human characters:

1. A robot may not injure a human being or, through inaction, allow a human being to come to harm.
2. A robot must obey the orders given to it by human beings, except where such orders would conflict with the First Law.
3. A robot must protect its own existence as long as such protection does not conflict with the First or Second Laws. (485)

As a species of humanoid artifact not unlike Asimov's robots, stereotypes can be understood in terms of the three Laws of Robotics. Let me conclude this essay by delineating a corollary to Asimov's laws, namely, three Laws of Stereotypes:

1. A stereotype must not (be constructed or employed to) injure a human being or, through inaction, allow a human being to come to harm. For instance, the technology of stereotyping may be employed, *mindfully and helpfully*, to describe a single facet of an individual person, but a stereotype must never be employed to reduce any individual person to a grotesque racial caricature.
2. A stereotype must (be constructed or employed to) comply with the Universal Declaration of Human Rights.
3. Humans who find themselves harmed by uncanny stereotypes have an obligation to protect themselves from such harm (as long as such protection does not conflict with the First or Second Laws).

This last obligation can be fulfilled in a number of ways, including through education (e.g., in the classroom), through the creation of artwork in which uncanny stereotypes are reworked and reimagined as richly realized human characters, and through the act of refusing to perceive oneself through the lens of a destructive stereotype. To frame the matter in more concrete and practical terms: as long as Asian Americans find themselves—find ourselves—detained in the uncanny valley by harmful stereotypes, Asian American educators have an obligation to teach Asian American literature, history, and culture in ways that are complexly humanizing. Asian American artists have an obligation to create works of art in which uncanny stereotypes are reworked and reimagined as richly realized human characters. (This process of reimagining is already taking place through fictional characters as diverse as the narrator of

Chang-rae Lee's 1995 novel *Native Speaker*, the Guide in Cathy Park Hong's 2006 science-fictional poem "Dance Dance Revolution," and the heroes who populate the lively pages of the 2009 volume *Secret Identities: The Asian American Superhero Anthology*.) Finally, and most important, Asian Americans have an obligation to refuse to perceive ourselves through the lens of destructive stereotypes.

Chapter 6

The Mask of Fu Manchu, *Son of Sinbad,* and *Star Wars IV: A New Hope*

Techno-Orientalist Cinema as a Mnemotechnics of Twentieth-Century U.S.-Asian Conflicts

ABIGAIL DE KOSNIK

Techno-Orientalist cinema is an "mnemotechnics," or "memory technology," of U.S.-Asian relations. I regard techno-Orientalist films as texts that have recorded and transmitted, from the beginning of the twentieth century to the present, the multifaceted ways that Americans have perceived and negotiated the deep, complex interconnections of Asia and America. Technologies that communicate memory from generation to generation are technologies of "cultural memory." Jan Assman states that "cultural memory" comprises memories of events experienced by a community that are "maintained through cultural formation (texts, rites, monuments)" (Assman and Czaplicka 129), such that members of the community who were not alive when the events took place can have some mediated access to those events. Today, we can re-view twentieth-century techno-Orientalist films to gain access to the American perspectives on Asia that the films archived.

In this chapter, I examine three twentieth-century techno-Orientalist films: *The Mask of Fu Manchu* (1932), *Son of Sinbad* (1955), and *Star Wars Episode IV: A New Hope* (1977). I argue that each of these films features techno-Orientalist themes and tropes that represent the state of U.S.-Asian relations at the times that the films were made. *The Mask of Fu Manchu* encodes the "yellow peril" and anti-Asian immigration sentiments that were rampant in the United States in the early decades of the twentieth century, as well as American unease about the rise of Japanese imperialism. *Son of Sinbad* makes both veiled and explicit references to World War II, the Korean War, and the Cold War. *Star Wars IV* is a reaction to the Vietnam War and the 1960s counterculture's interest in Asian philosophies.

I have selected these three films for my analysis in part because they belong to three Orientalist series, two of which (Fu Manchu and Sinbad) began in the nineteenth and early twentieth centuries in book form and then proliferated as film and television texts, and one (the *Star Wars* media franchise) which took the late twentieth century by storm and continues to expand today. Encompassing the arc of the twentieth century, *Mask of Fu Manchu*, *Son of Sinbad*, and *Star Wars IV* link older forms of Orientalist representation with the millennial era of Hollywood techno-Orientalist blockbusters. Orientalism as a phenomenon was not limited to the cultural productions of nineteenth-century European romanticism, and techno-Orientalism did not begin with 1980s cyberpunk cinema. The three films that I analyze illustrate that techno-Orientalist cinema thrived throughout the twentieth century, particularly at moments (the 1930s, 1950s, and 1970s) when the United States was embroiled in crucial conflicts with Asians and Asian nations.

The Mask of Fu Manchu (1932)

As far as I can determine, the earliest techno-Orientalist film produced in the United States was *The Mask of Fu Manchu*. Dr. Fu Manchu, a sinister Chinese mastermind who constantly plots the destruction of the Western world, was created by English novelist Sax Rohmer in 1911. Fu Manchu was the leading antagonist in eleven movies, short-film serials, and television series between 1923 and 1955 (Wong 58); decades of different incarnations across media formats established the wicked doctor as the exemplar of the "Master Oriental Criminal" stereotype (Wong 56).

In *The Mask of Fu Manchu*, Fu Manchu, played by Boris Karloff, is tall and thin, with a long tapered moustache and long sharp fingernails on his index and second fingers. He wears elaborately brocaded silk robes, and he inhabits an expansive lair replete with Asian art and artifacts, including giant Buddha statues. He is a doctor three times over, having earned "a doctor of philosophy from Edinburgh," "a doctor of law from Christ College" and "a doctor of medicine from Harvard." (All quotations in this section are spoken by characters in *The Mask of Fu Manchu* unless otherwise noted.) His lair contains a vast array of scientific and medical equipment. Fu Manchu's background, physicality, and surroundings mark him as brilliant, dangerous, technologically advanced, and eminently Chinese.

Fu Manchu's goal is world domination. His plan is to steal Genghis Khan's golden mask and scimitar from the British archaeological team that has discovered the Khan's lost tomb in the Gobi Desert, and to use the ancient mask and sword to, in the words of British secret service officer Sir Nayland Smith, "declare himself Genghis Khan come to life again," which will allow him to "lead hundreds of millions of men to sweep the world," as all Asians apparently share some kind of belief in the mystical power of Genghis Khan. Fu Manchu almost succeeds, but in the end he is defeated by his own technology, when Nayland Smith turns the ray gun against the Chinese mastermind and his legions of "coolies" (as Smith calls them).

The film's derisive view of the Asian masses is an obvious reference to actual U.S.-Asian relations in the early twentieth century. Fu Manchu and his daughter are depicted as malicious and evil as well as cunning and articulate, but Fu Manchu's followers appear to be nameless, wordless, superstitious beasts of burden who follow Fu Manchu's bidding blindly and are completely interchangeable. It is the number of "coolies" that make them dangerous: both Smith and Fu Manchu state that Fu Manchu's plan to take over the world will be accomplished through his inciting millions of Asians to rise up and, as Fu Manchu puts it, "rain down on the white race and burn them."

White Americans' fear and loathing of Asian peoples as a group that could outnumber and overwhelm them had its roots in the fact that, beginning in the middle of the nineteenth century, waves of Asians entered the United States to fill the rapidly developing nation's vast demand for cheap labor. Lisa Lowe writes, "[T]hroughout the period from 1850 to World War II, the recruitment of Asian immigrant labor was motivated by the imperative to bring cheaper labor into the still developing capitalist economy [of the United States]: Chinese, Japanese, and Filipino laborers were fundamental to the building of the railroads, the agricultural economy, and the textile and service industries" (*Immigrant Acts* 12). Although Asian workers provided value to American industrialists, they were also viewed as threats to the American economy, populace, and nation-state. If Asian workers were allowed to vote and own private property, they could threaten whites' economic hegemony (Lowe, *Immigrant Acts* 13); if Asians were to immigrate without restriction, they could pose serious competition to whites for employment (Lowe, *Immigrant Acts* 13); if Asians were allowed to marry non–Asian American women, they would create a population of racial "hybrids," the prospect of which was repellent to early twentieth-century racists (Palumbo-Liu, *Asian/American* 27–28; Lowe, *Immigrant Acts* 13–14). From the late 1800s through the mid-1930s, to prevent the Asian population in the United States from expanding too greatly or accruing substantial political or economic power, the U.S. Congress passed a series of "exclusion acts" that heavily limited the number of Asians who could immigrate to the United States and constrained the rights of Asians already residing in the country (Lowe, *Immigrant Acts* 19; Palumbo-Liu, *Asian/American* 18–19). In addition, in the early 1920s, the Supreme Court upheld an existing 1790 law that barred Asians from attaining citizenship through naturalization (Lowe, *Immigrant Acts* 19–20), and by 1930 thirty states had passed anti-miscegenation laws ("Legal Map"), making it illegal for Asians to marry non-Asians in most parts of the country. White Americans' dread of the unchecked influx of Asians into their nation and the U.S. anti-Asian measures from this period are remembered in *The Mask of Fu Manchu*, albeit in a heavily coded way.

One reason that Hollywood's techno-Orientalist tradition begins with *The Mask of Fu Manchu* may be the fact that machine metaphors were often employed in public references to Chinese immigration at that time. David Palumbo-Liu cites a number of fiction and nonfiction works published between 1894 and 1929 that refer to Chinese people's "absence of nerves," "special race vitality," and "immun[ity] to stimulants" and their ability to "stand all day in one place without seeming in the least distressed" (36). Betsy Huang quotes California Senator John Miller stating in 1881 that the Chinese were "inhabitants of another planet" and "machine-like," unable to feel heat or cold (Miller was an early proponent of bans on Chinese immigration) ("Premodern Orientalist Science Fictions" 23–24). These late nineteenth- and early twentieth-century discourses characterizing Chinese people as "instruments"—that is, as "exploitable, containable, and inhuman" (Huang, "Premodern Orientalist Science Fictions" 24), and as "the perfect 'laboring machine[s]'" (Palumbo-Liu, *Asian/American* 37)—were transcoded into *The Mask of Fu Manchu* as a swarm of mindless coolies who could be easily "programmed."

However, it is Fu Manchu himself who most clearly embodies techno-Orientalism. Throughout the movie, he is shown to be the inventor and/or master of a diverse array of ancient and advanced technologies, from automatic doors to occult potions to the ray gun that is used against him in the end. And Fu Manchu's evident wealth, aristocratic bearing, and elite education mark him as what James L. Hevia calls an "upper-class 'Mandarin,'" a member of "imperial China's ruling elite" (250). But Fu Manchu also reflects to some degree U.S. suspicions of another rising imperial power in Asia: Japan, which in 1905 defeated Russia and colonized Korea, and whose rapid industrialization in the late nineteenth century had allowed it to fully modernize its armed forces. Fu Manchu is a near personification of the Japan that made many Americans anxious in the first few decades of the twentieth century (an anxiety that only increased in the years leading up to Pearl Harbor and World War II). Fu Manchu, like Japan at that time, was steeped in tradition yet extremely modern, proficient with Western technologies, ingenious at weapons development, and committed to expansionism.

It may seem odd to interpret a character who is manifestly Chinese as representing Japan, but Palumbo-Liu remarks that China and Japan were the two faces, as it were, of the "yellow peril" as perceived by early twentieth-century Americans. "[B]etween the Chinese 'masses' and Japanese military and technological success, we have the instantiation of a fear that Asians might actually hold some superiority over whites," argues Palumbo-Liu (*Asian/American* 36), allowing us to read anti–Asian American sentiment from the period as partly rooted in white Americans' insecurities about their race's ability to triumph against Asia in either armed conflict or in economic and technological competition. *Mask of Fu Manchu* preserves the memory of Americans' simultaneous respect for and worry over China's and Japan's advantages at that historical moment.

Son of Sinbad (1955)

Tales of the daring Persian sailor Sinbad were introduced to Western audiences via eighteenth- and nineteenth-century European translations of *One Thousand and One Nights*, the most famous of which, Sir Richard Burton's *The Book of the Thousand Nights and a Night*, was published in the United Kingdom in 1885. U.S. cinema popularized Sinbad through a hit 1947 Technicolor picture, starring Douglas Fairbanks, Jr., called *Sinbad the Sailor*. Sinbad movies belong to the larger body of Orientalist films that Robert Irwin terms "the *Thousand and One Nights* genre" (224), which includes Thomas Edison's 1902 *Ali Baba and the Forty Thieves*, *The Thief of Baghdad* (1924) starring Douglas Fairbanks, all versions of Aladdin, and other medieval Arab-themed movies.

Son of Sinbad, a 1955 entry in this genre, is described by Turner Classic Movies' Nathaniel Thompson as a "dames-and-desert opus" and a "voluptuous camp exercise" (Thompson). Scores of scantily clad women populate the B movie; Thompson recounts that executive producer Howard Hughes wooed aspiring actresses with promises of parts in motion pictures and then cast them all in *Son of Sinbad* as harem girls. However, I argue that *Son of Sinbad* warrants greater consideration than it has received from cultural critics. Though less famous than *Thief of Baghdad* and *Sinbad the Sailor*, *Son of Sinbad* more directly addresses the technological and geopolitical crises of its times.

Unlike most Arabian fantasy films, *Son of Sinbad* is a techno-Orientalist movie, its plot centering on the question of who will control a weapon of mass destruction—a fearsome ancient weapon called Greek fire. The film takes place in and around the Persian capital, Baghdad, at some time in the distant past (since a figure from Persian history, poet Omar Khayyám, played by Vincent Price, is a main character, perhaps we can guess that the story occurs in the late eleventh or early twelfth century). The narrative turns on the question of whether the secret formula of Greek fire, known only to one young woman, Kristina, will be used to protect Baghdad or will fall into the hands of the invading army of Mongols, led by a dour general named Murad. The hero, Sinbad, and his friend Omar rescue Kristina and take her to the legendary Forty Thieves, who promise to protect her and the secret of Greek fire that she carries. The Forty Thieves are exclusively women, all of them daughters of the original Forty Thieves (their second-generation status matches Sinbad's, who, as the title indicates, is the son of the original Sinbad the Sailor). The Forty Thieves inhabit the caves outside Baghdad and constitute a society of outlaw female raiders. Murad and his army attack the Thieves' caves, but Kristina concocts Greek fire in batches; Sinbad, Omar, and the Forty Thieves are then able to use the powerful weapon to defeat Murad's troops. In the end, Sinbad is made a prince of Baghdad. He crowns his true love, one of the Forty Thieves named Amir, as his princess. Omar and Kristina are a romantic pair. Sinbad appoints the Forty Thieves as the palace guards.

Son of Sinbad is obviously, one might say classically, Orientalist; the costumes, sets, and script all depict what Edward Said describes as "Oriental clichés: harems, princesses, princes, slaves, veils, dancing girls and boys, sherbets, ointments, and so on" (190). Said argues that all of these elements serve, in the European imagination, to facilitate "the escapism of sexual fantasy" (190), and the film certainly offers this same brand of escapism. But *Son of Sinbad* should not be dismissed as unimportant due to its light tone and thin plot. The film's ostensible lightheartedness allowed it to address manifold complex and important foreign and domestic issues of the day. In addition to belonging to the *Arabian Nights* genre, *Son of Sinbad* also fits into a larger genre of historical pictures made in the middle of the twentieth century that, according to John H. Lenihan, played on "Cold-War preoccupations with instruments of destruction" (164). U.S. invention and use of atomic bombs against Japan at the close of World War II, followed by the Soviet Union's development of nuclear arms in 1949 "made the prospect of nuclear devastation frighteningly real" for Americans in the 1950s (Lenihan 164), and Hollywood responded by producing futuristic sci-fi, but also by making "[c]ostume-adventure formulas . . . ancient, medieval, or 19th-century West in setting" (164). Lenihan writes, "From about 1949 through the mid-1950s, film scenarios involving renaissance-Italian canons, frontier-American Gatling guns, Arabian Nights

'Greek fire' [Lenihan is directly referring to *Son of Sinbad* here] and other antique forms of advanced weaponry spoke directly to contemporary concerns about national security and/or the perilous implications of 'the bomb' for the future of civilization" (164–165). In *Son of Sinbad*, Greek fire, whose immense explosive power shocks and amazes all the characters in the film who see the fire deployed, stands in for nuclear weaponry. Knowledge of the formula for Greek fire must be severely restricted "in order that the secret not fall into the hands of the enemy of mankind," as one character says. The notion of safeguarding national security by keeping an important secret about weapons design would have struck a deep chord in 1955, since in 1953 Americans Julius and Ethel Rosenberg were convicted of and executed for passing information about the atomic bomb to the Soviet Union. *Son of Sinbad* dramatizes, in a register that most Americans would have found decidedly unfrightening, the high stakes of Cold War espionage made clear by the Rosenberg case. In the film, a "superweapon" (in Lenihan's terminology) is desperately pursued by a dangerous enemy that is threatening invasion. If the enemy acquires the superweapon, their invasion will succeed and the existing nation will be destroyed. If the enemy fails, then the superweapon can be utilized against the enemy, and the nation will remain whole. In *Son of Sinbad*, as in the Cold War, the rise and fall of empires hinge on the knowledge and possession of a single technology of war. The film defuses the high anxiety of the dire drama that Americans believed they were all playing out, by rendering the tale of military intelligence leaks and nuclear war as a breezy Technicolor romp in a land far away, a time long ago—and offering an ending in which the Persians (representing Americans) use Greek fire (atomic bombs) against the Mongols (Soviets/communists) only to defend themselves, for the sake of protecting their nation, with no negative repercussions. Noteworthy, too, is the fact that midcentury filmmakers apparently had few qualms about depicting Persians as heroes with whom Americans could easily identify, in sharp contrast to U.S. media producers of the late twentieth and early twenty-first centuries, who have often stereotyped Persians, or Iranians, as fundamentalist Islamic terrorists.

Son of Sinbad, despite its unabashed objectification of women, also contains an interesting proposition regarding the role that women could or should play in U.S. national security. In the film, one woman (Kristina) holds and keeps the secret of the superweapon, another woman (Amir) devises the plan that prevents the "leaking" of the superweapon's design to the enemy, and a group of women working together (the Forty Thieves) constitute the majority of the troops who deploy the superweapon against the Mongol army (in fact, Sinbad is the only man who fights with them). For mid-1950s U.S. audiences, the memory of American women entering the workforce in World War II to build munitions and materiel, and to serve in the armed forces in administrative, clerical, intelligence, and operations jobs, would still have been fresh.

Therefore, *Son of Sinbad*'s depiction of women occupying key roles in the war against invading Asians may not have seemed implausible or outlandish to moviegoers of the time; rather, it may have seemed like an homage to women's contributions to the war effort during World War II. To my knowledge, no other films of the "atomic age" feature so many women playing such crucial roles in a fictionalized war effort. I hypothesize that it was precisely *Son of Sinbad*'s Orientalism, and the superabundance of female cast members that this genre enabled, and to some extent required, that led the film's writers to confer such significant military responsibilities on women protagonists.

To contemporary viewers, *Son of Sinbad*'s large female cast may register as typical of the *Thousand and One Nights* genre: white actresses playing dress-up in billowing harem pants, bikini tops, and veils, serving only to satisfy male viewers' prurient interests and female viewers' escapist Orientalist fantasies. But to midcentury moviegoers, the all-women band of Forty Thieves, defending themselves in their stronghold without any men, may have also suggested ultrafeminine versions of iconic female figures from World War II such as Rosie the Riveter, WACs (Women's Army Corps members), and WAVES (Women Accepted for Volunteer Emergency Service—women in the U.S. Naval Reserve). However, lest *Son of Sinbad* be mistaken for a feminist text, we must observe that the film's ending dramatically domesticates all of the female characters: two of them marry the male protagonists, and although the Forty Thieves are still unmarried and fully armed in their new jobs as palace guards, they are under Sinbad's command, and dwell in (and protect) his royal residence, whereas before and during the war against the Mongols, they ruled themselves in the "wilds" outside Baghdad.

Son of Sinbad stands as a cultural memory of how 1950s Americans sought reassurances for their nightmares about the possible outbreak of nuclear war and the possible spread, or even triumph, of Eastern communism. At the same time, the film memorializes the service of women in World War II, perhaps with an eye to the fact that, if President Eisenhower's domino theory, announced in 1954, was to guide foreign policy, the United States would soon be entering war after war in Asia, at which point women might have to once again actively participate in the American war machine (with the expectation that they would happily return to domestic duties in any postwar period). When *Son of Sinbad* was released in 1955, the Korean War was only two years past, and the conflict in Southeast Asia that would escalate into the Vietnam War was already under way. In Howard Hughes's techno-Orientalist fantasy, we find traces of midcentury Americans' need to come to terms with the pattern, then being established, of repeated U.S. military involvement in Asian nations, the possibly apocalyptic stakes of the nuclear arms race, and the continuous involvement of American men and women that might be required by U.S. Eastern "adventures."

Star Wars IV: A New Hope (1977)

"The commercial success of *Star Wars* was certainly astonishing," writes Peter Krämer: the movie accounted for 14 percent of all box office sales in 1977. According to David Cook, *Star Wars* ushered in "the modern-era of super-blockbuster films" (52). Will Brooker writes that "in 1977, *Star Wars* was a phenomenon. For many people now, it is a culture" (xii). But, despite its triumphs, the franchise has not been without its critics. One of the primary faults found with *Star Wars I: The Phantom Menace*, a prequel released in 1999, was its Orientalism: "The evil henchmen in this story seem to be Fu Manchu style Asians," wrote the *Boston Review*'s Alan Stone upon *Star Wars I*'s premiere (Chen); he was not alone in excoriating *Star Wars I* for employing racist tropes (see Chen; Gottlieb).

Star Wars's use of Orientalism actually began in its first installation. *Star Wars IV* contains a legion of Orientalist and techno-Orientalist references that address, in coded ways, the crises of its time. Because of its lasting influence on Hollywood sci-fi filmmaking, the movie established techno-Orientalism as a style of visual representation and storytelling that would become common in sci-fi/fantasy films in subsequent years.

Star Wars IV tells the story of Luke Skywalker, a farm boy on an outer rim desert planet called Tatooine, who finds himself caught up in the clash between the cruel Empire, which rules the galaxy, and the Rebellion, whose mission is to overthrow the Empire. Through accident or destiny, Luke takes ownership of two droids (intelligent robots) who are being hunted by the Empire, one of whom happens to be carrying in its data banks the plans to the Empire's newest, most powerful weapon: a giant spherical space station called the Death Star, which has enough firepower to destroy entire planets. Luke, his droids, his mentor Obi-Wan Kenobi, and their allies, Han Solo and Chewbacca, band together on a mission that leads them first to the Death Star itself (where they rescue one of the Rebel leaders, Princess Leia, and Obi-Wan sacrifices himself in a duel with the evil Imperial commander Darth Vader to save the rest of the group), then to the secret Rebel base. At the base, the Rebels analyze the Death Star plans carried by the droid and find one weakness in the space station's defenses. Luke joins up with the Rebel fighters who head out in single-pilot fighters to destroy the Death Star, and it is Luke who manages to squeeze off the blasts that cause the Death Star's reactor to explode, demolishing the entire station.

Star Wars is saturated with Orientalist references. Several key characters and plot elements are borrowed from Japanese director Akira Kurosawa's samurai film *The Hidden Fortress* (1958). Darth Vader's helmet is based on the *kabuto* helmets worn by samurai lords (Mary Henderson 189). The wide shots of desert on Luke's home planet Tatooine are reminiscent of David Lean's majestic *Lawrence of Arabia* (1962). Luke's white workaday clothes closely resemble a *karategi*, or karate training uniform. Obi-Wan wears long robes, possesses an aura of calm, delivers wise utterances, and has obviously mastered the ancient mystical ways of the now-extinct Jedi Knights, all of which makes him an exemplar of what Jane Iwamura calls "the icon of the Oriental Monk" (6). "The Force," which Jedis believe "is an energy field created by all living things" that "surrounds us," "penetrates us," and "binds the galaxy together," as Obi-Wan instructs Luke, is reminiscent of the Chinese concepts of the Dao and Qi (or Chi). Jedi light sabers look like *katana*, or samurai swords, in laser form, and Vader and Obi-Wan's style of sword fighting closely matches a dueling scene in *The Hidden Fortress*. The names Obi-Wan, Han, and Leia all sound Asian or Pacific.

But *Star Wars*'s techno-Orientalism can be primarily found in the opposition between the Rebellion and the Empire, the clash of two war strategies and two uses of military technology. *Star Wars* is a parable about the Vietnam War, in which the Rebellion plays the part of the North Vietnamese, and the Empire takes the role of the United States. In the Vietnam War, the North Vietnamese forces had only a small fraction of the armaments and funds of the American military, and yet they triumphed over the United States by relentlessly using guerrilla and low-tech tactics that harassed, surprised, subverted, and demoralized the Americans sufficiently to make them withdraw their troops after a ten-year engagement. George Lucas, the auteur behind *Star Wars*, stated in 2005 that he made *Star Wars* "during the Vietnam War and the Nixon era" ("Star Wars"), and in 2010 Lucas's friend and sometime collaborator, sound designer Walter Murch, gave his view on how *Star Wars* constituted Lucas's response to Vietnam. Murch said that after Lucas's movie *American Graffiti* became a box-office hit in 1973, the director wanted to make a film explicitly about the Vietnam conflict, "but it was still too hot a topic, the war was still going on, and nobody wanted to finance something like that. So George . . . decided, 'I'll put the essence of the story in outer space and make it happen in a galaxy long ago and far away.' The rebel group were the North Vietnamese, and the Empire was the United States. And if you have the force, no matter how small you are, you can defeat an overwhelming big power" (Hogg). In *Star Wars*, the Imperial space ships are many times the size of any of the Rebel's fleet; the Empire's black-and-white weapons, uniforms, and spatial environments are sleek, modernist, standardized, and sophisticated. In contrast, most of the Rebels' technological objects, from the Millennium Falcon to the X-wing fighter ships to Luke's droids, appear worn, vulnerable, and prone to breakdowns. The Rebellion also simply lacks the Empire's firepower. In repeatedly drawing a sharp contrast between the Empire's advanced weaponry and infrastructure and the Rebellion's inferior technologies, the film echoes the differences between the technological assets of the United States and North Vietnam throughout their armed conflict.

In *The Closed World*, Paul N. Edwards describes how, during the Vietnam War, the extremely technologically advanced U.S. sensor detection system, which ran from 1967 to 1972 at a cost of nearly $1 billion per year, was rendered almost useless by the North Vietnamese's "confus[ing] the American sensors with tape-recorded truck noises, bags of urine, and other decoys, provoking the release of countless tons of bombs onto empty jungle corridors which they then traversed at their leisure" (4). General Vo Nguyen Giap, the North Vietnamese military's commander-in-chief, stated in a 1996 interview that his troops believed "it was a myth that we could not fight and win [against American combat forces] because they were so powerful. . . . We had to resort to different measures, some of which are quite simple" (2), such as deception, hiding, evacuating, and using small arms against U.S. aircraft. Similarly, in *Star Wars*, a handful of dedicated individuals, using "quite simple" tactics and technologies, are able to overcome the powerful weapons and troops of the Empire.

Star Wars also encodes a different sort of encounter between the United States and Asia that took place in the 1960s and 1970s: the discovery of ancient Asian philosophies, especially Zen and Daoism, by Americans seeking alternatives to corporatized and commodified culture and the domino-theory interventionism of the U.S. military-industrial complex. Betsy Huang points out that the sixties and seventies works of renowned science fiction authors Philip K. Dick and Ursula Le Guin "look to Daoist thought as a means of cognitive revision and spiritual transformation for the West" ("Premodern Orientalist Science Fictions" 25). *Star Wars* provides the ultimate example of "technologizing the Orient" (Huang 25)—that is, turning the Dao into an instrument that Westerners can use to critique or escape their own society's "imperialistic agendas" and "rhetoric of progress" (Huang 27). In *Star Wars*, Luke successfully draws on the Force (the Dao) to precisely target the Death Star's single weakness, thus eliminating the world-destroying weapon (the nuclear bomb). Daoism is instrumentalized as the only weapon that can defeat nuclear arms. To be sure, there is a colonizing aspect to *Star Wars*'s appropriating Daoism and other Asian signifiers. The film offers a fantasy of white culture employing and enacting Asian-derived philosophies and aesthetics without any hint that a translation or borrowing is taking place. By eliding the geographic, historical, and sociocultural differences between West and East, *Star Wars*, like all Orientalist texts, makes the incorporation of select elements of Asianness into Westernness seem natural. U.S. sixties and seventies counterculture, along with more recent American "new age" movements, can be accused of similarly (mis)appropriating Asian cultural tropes while effacing references to the actualities of Asian nations and peoples and U.S.-Asian strife. At the same time, it must be acknowledged that *Star Wars* inverts the West's traditional hierarchy of civilizations by privileging premodern Eastern Daoism over hypermodern Western war technologies.

Star Wars thus records 1960s countercultural Americans' belief and hope that, if Western modernity was so insistently on a path of unjustifiable warmongering, then perhaps the low tech of Asia—simple weaponry and decoys, and philosophies such as Zen and Daoism—could constitute an appropriate countermeasure to Western modernity's most dangerous product, the nuclear bomb.

Conclusion

Traces of *Star Wars IV*'s techno-Orientalism are evident in its sequels and prequels, and also numerous U.S. sci-fi movies and television programs of the 1980s to 2000s. Futuristic combat that incorporates Asian martial arts, Asian-inspired costume design, and low-tech idealistic revolutionaries battling high-tech fascistic empires can be found in films such as *Mortal Kombat* (1995), the *Matrix* film trilogy (1999–2003), and *Equilibrium* (2002) and in the television series *Firefly* (2002). While cyberpunk novels and Japanese sci-fi also clearly influenced millennial Hollywood techno-Orientalism, it cannot be denied that *Star Wars IV*, an economic juggernaut and cultural touchstone, served as a model for the cinematic texts produced in its wake. Other millennial films, however, seem to have been more informed by earlier twentieth-century techno-Orientalist movies than by *Star Wars IV*: links between *The Mask of Fu Manchu* and *Blade Runner* (1982), and between *Son of Sinbad* (and other *Thousand and One Nights* movies) and the *Indiana Jones* films (1981–2008), appear especially strong.

The fact that we can discern chains of influence connecting earlier techno-Orientalist texts to later ones shows that the techno-Orientalist elements of a given text are not confined to that text. Rather, techno-Orientalist metaphors, visual themes, plots, and character stereotypes readily travel from one text to another, even between texts separated by decades. U.S. filmmakers from different eras draw various elements from the well of techno-Orientalist tropes as they wish, so we may encounter similar techno-Orientalisms in any number of films across U.S. history. Techno-Orientalism has proved a persistently valuable resource to be repeatedly mined by American cinema for a reason: for as long as the United States has been producing cinema, it has been engaged in both economic and military conflicts with Asia and Asians, conflicts in which questions concerning technology have loomed large.

Chapter 7
Racial Speculations

(Bio)technology, *Battlestar Galactica*, and a Mixed-Race Imagining

JINNY HUH

Today, you can choose the race of your child. Of course, one may argue that we have always been able to choose our children's race via geographic, religious, economic, and cultural sanctions to determine with whom one is willing (and not willing) to have sexual relations. But, with advancements in reproductive technology, a woman today can not only choose the race of her child but also gestate a baby not of her (or her partner's) racial background. As much as these advancements may evidence the progress of our growing multicultural and multiracial world, the reality of the new reproductive choices and practices reveals otherwise. At a historical juncture where color-blind ideology shields our cultural as well as our own individual racisms, reproduction and the baby industry remain racially coded and determined. A recent telling example includes an advertisement from MIT's newspaper, *The Tech*, described below in full:

> GENIUS ASIAN EGG DONOR
> wanted to help us build our family
> $20,000 compensation

Email [ ]@alumni.caltech.edu for more information.

We are a couple seeking an Asian egg donor to help build our family. You should be near top of your class, and preferably have some outstanding achievements and awards. We prefer Asian race, such as Chinese, Japanese, Korean, Vietnamese.

You should be between 18–35 years old.

An example of our ideal egg donor: 21 year old Chinese MIT student, top in her class, several awards in high school and university. She wants to be an egg donor in order to help bring a child into the world with the same special gifts she has.

Your eggs will be fertilized with sperm from the man, and the resulting embryos used to impregnate the woman, or possibly a surrogate mother.

About us: we are a highly educated couple, but we are unable to have children due to infertility of the woman. The man is a highly accomplished scientist/mathematician and businessman, the woman has a good PhD-level university degree. The man is of European race, woman is Chinese.

We value education, and we live in one of the best school districts in the world. We hope that our child will be gifted, as each of us is, and that he/she will have a positive impact on the world. (*The Tech*, November 20, 2012)

As evidenced in this couple's search for an egg donor, race is a central factor in reproduction, one that not only determines the selection of our intimate partners but also equates "hereditary" traits to certain groups in a process of reproductive racialization. The ad is particularly alarming because it delineates certain parallels in the configuration of a "super race." From the maintenance of the model minority myth and the assumption that Asians have "genius" traits to the economic differentiation between potential parents and donors, what is perhaps most alarming is the implicit conclusion of this configuration: the reproductive future of the human race is centrally determined by those with economic means and specific racial desires.

This essay argues that anxieties of racial mixings are evident in the intersection between biotechnology and race. In contemporary popular culture, this anxiety is evidenced in speculative narratives such as the recently reimagined *Battlestar Galactica* series (2003–2009; hereinafter *BSG*). In the miniseries pilot of *BSG*, the robotic Cylons have attacked their human "masters" after a forty-year armistice, resulting in about fifty thousand human survivors. Subsequently, in order for the human species to survive, Commander Adama, the unofficially elected leader of the fleet of human survivors and the flagship Galactica, declares, "They [the survivors] better start having babies" (Miniseries Pilot). This edict—the urgency to procreate—will become one of the driving objectives of the Galactica mission. Reproduction is an immediate priority for the human race threatened with extinction and, accordingly, *BSG*'s narrative arc is framed by "baby talk" from beginning to end. It turns out, however, that although recognized as an award-winning series applauded for its color-blind casting and story lines, *BSG*'s racial blindness, in fact, belies the black versus Asian racial reinscription upon female bodies. Eve Bennett, Juliana Hu Pegues, and Christopher Deis have previously explored the racialization of blackness and Asianness/Orientalism in *BSG*; this essay builds upon their work by elaborating upon the intersections of techno-Orientalism, biotechnology, reproductive technology, and racial mixing to highlight *BSG*'s anxieties about race, reproduction, and ancestry. *BSG* reveals that although historical racial contaminations, particularly the "taint" of blackness, still resonate today, Asian-white mixings are not only acceptable but highly desirable. But this desire comes with a caveat: the pairing is desirable only when the Asian partner is female and ultimately conforms to the submissive Asian woman stereotype. This is strikingly evidenced by Athena's (played by Asian Canadian Grace Park) transformation from threatening Cylon Eight sleeper agent to loyal wife and mother. These anxieties and desires are also reflected in the reality of our own reproductive spheres as aided by assisted reproductive technology (hereinafter ART). I begin by contextualizing our current technological moment and the relationship between race (particularly Asianness) and reproduction through biotechnology and reproductive practices. I will then conclude with a close reading of Cylon Eight, who embodies both technological and reproductive anxieties and possibilities.

Race-ing (Bio)technology

On November 29, 2012, the Dear Prudence advice column on Slate.com published a query from "Want to Be a Dad." The father-to-be, who is white, wonders how to approach his infertile Asian wife about wanting all-white babies. He writes, "Her race isn't a problem for me and I would have had no difficulty raising mixed race children, but frankly, now that I have the choice, I'd prefer my kids to be white. We live in a fairly homogeneously white area and at the end of the day I want my kids to look like me, their cousins, and the kids they'll go to school with. I don't think my wife has ever experienced racism, but I think she might understand my point of view" (Yoffe). Like many couples who prefer (at least initially) genetic children (or the semblance of) to adopted ones, this couple chooses ART. Through egg donation (and other fertility treatments such as sperm and embryo donation), they demonstrate that today we can *choose* the race of our babies. Aside from the potentially disturbing outcome in the above scenario in which the Asian woman becomes an incubator for whiteness, this man's query also reflects an anxiety of detection not uncommon in reproduction, particularly in ART. The desire for a genetic connection to one's child is a strong and powerful force, one that is desperately sought despite financial, emotional, and physical difficulties.[1] The strong desire for a biological connection is also the main reason why many couples opt for ART rather than adoption. In the case of "Want to Be a Dad," the man's desire for his children to "look like me, their cousins, and the kids they'll go to school with" also reflects what Prudie (aka journalist Emily Yoffe) writes as the parents' wish to keep secret their use of ART.[2] Whether due to the shame of infertility or for cultural and religious reasons, the need for secrecy is a central component of today's reproductive practices.

In many respects, ART has become the new racial science, one that foregrounds race as a determinant in the policing of reproduction, inheritance, and the future *look* of race. According to the Centers for Disease Control and Prevention, the percentage of infertile women between fifteen and forty-four in the United States is 10.9 (6.7 million); as a result, over 1 percent of all infants born in the country every year (about 47,090 babies in 2010) are conceived using ART. ART not only offers individuals the possibility of becoming parents via technological advancements, but also offers potential parents the ability to "design" their babies, ensuring everything from the embryo's sex to genetic screening (preimplantation genetic diagnosis) in which DNA can be scanned for certain diseases like Tay-Sachs and Down syndrome. Reminiscent of the science fiction film *Gattaca* (1997), advances in ART and the completion of the Human Genome Project in 2003 have now made possible techniques of genetic detection. Furthermore, many argue that ART has created a new form of eugenics in which hair, eye, and skin color can also be selected to create the new super race.

This is the outcome that may result if the reproductive desires like those of "Want to Be a Dad" are met—that our current state of color-blind ideology is one that may boast of multiculturalism but is still engrained with racist beliefs and desires. At a time when headlines include "The End of White America" (Hsu), perhaps it is not too surprising that the emergence of designer babies and reproductive technologies is a growing trend. In this light, we are currently witnessing the scientific and technological manipulation of the face of race.

I introduce the implications of ART here in order to illustrate how race oftentimes produces a power differentiation between technology and reproduction. In 2013, not only are the rates of nonwhite babies rising,[3] but the parallel increase of biracial and multiracial birthrates has fostered an atmosphere of what author Danzy Senna has satirically referred to as the "Mulatto Millennium." Alongside this change in demographics is our growing reliance on biotechnology through which a parent can now select not only a child's skin/hair/eye color but also gender, athletic abilities, weight, height, and susceptibility to certain diseases. In terms of race selection, then, a white couple can have either their genetic white baby (via a white or nonwhite gestational carrier) or a nonwhite baby using an embryo adopted from a domestic or international agency. Despite not sharing any genetic link, a white woman can birth a nonwhite baby and nonwhite women can birth white babies.

Parents-to-be as well as ART practitioners place restrictions upon certain mixings that mirror centuries-old racial paradigms. For example, during her ethnographic research in the San Francisco Bay area, Gillian Goslinga-Roy uncovered racist ideologies where white surrogates refused to gestate a black baby but welcomed an Asian baby. As "Julie," a white surrogate, explains, "It feels foreign to me. Different. I could carry a Japanese baby or a Chinese baby because they are white to me. Society sees them as white. But a Black child is more difficult. I'm already surrounded by controversy: I married a man thirty-two years older than me. I work in a late-term, problem-pregnancy abortion facility. And I'm a surrogate. To give birth to a Black child would add one more controversial aspect to my life and I'm not ready to be on the front page of the *National Enquirer*" (116). Here, gestating blackness is a contamination too taboo to warrant consideration. As Goslinga-Roy points out, what is telling is "how carrying *someone else's* (white) child provoked no gut reaction in her whatsoever. . . . But the mere thought of carrying someone else's *Black* child immediately made her experience the surrogacy as a very intimate and at once very public violation of her bodily and moral boundaries" (116). In contrast, it is important to point out that gestating a Japanese or Chinese baby is not considered *National Enquirer* material. In other words, Asian-white mixes have overcome societal prohibition, symptomatic of broader perceptions of Asians as the model minority.

The fear of racial contamination is illustrated throughout the fertility treatment process in what Foucault would call the "biopower" of ART or the "techniques [used] for achieving the subjugations of bodies and the control of populations" (140), such as population control and selective reproduction. By managing and manipulating racial mixings, ART practitioners become arbiters of heredity and the future look of race. In her study of fertility technology, Seline Szkupinski Quiroga reveals how racial borders are policed and maintained during each step of the fertility treatment process. For example, in describing the matching process between sperm donor and recipient, she writes, "The goal of matching is threefold: (1) to increase the probability that the child's physical characteristics will be similar enough to suggest that the social parent could have contributed his own genetic material; (2) to mimic the physical attributes of what white Americans perceive as a biological family; and (3) to maintain secrecy about the use of a donor by ensuring that the child could 'pass' as a genetic child and not be mistaken as a product of the mother's sexual infidelity" (150). Szkupinski Quiroga explains that while the first two goals are reflective of biologism or the need to "look" like a natural family, the last goal reflects the "raced and gendered nature of the heteropatriarchal family model" (150). In other words, the child cannot be interpreted as the visual evidence of the mother's infidelity. Here, the child's racial visibility/decipherability is the physical evidence of his/her mother's loyalty not only to her husband but to the family's genetics via the erasure of (her) infertility.[4] In the ART process, the mother's infidelity is achieved only hypothetically via a mixed-race sexual union. In order to prevent this, donor semen is "categorized racially, and sperm banks rely on donor self-identification and physiognomy to assess the validity of a donor's claim to whiteness" (150). Oftentimes, sperm vials are, in fact, color-coded to match the donor's racial identification (black/brown caps for African Americans, yellow caps for Asians, white caps for Caucasians, and red caps for those with "unique ancestry" such as East Indians, American Indians, Latinos, and mixed race individuals). Sperm banks play race managers through careful cataloguing of various physical characteristics in order to choose the "appropriate" donor. This catalogue serves "as a proxy for proof of a donor's racial pedigree" (150).

In contrast to the racist taboos and anxieties that black bodies, blood, and genes still signify in ART, it is interesting to note that Asian genetics and bodies are in high demand in both ART and adoption. With all factors being equal (health of infant, age, the adoption budget, the type of agency employed, etc.), white babies demand higher costs and longer wait periods in domestic adoption because they are the most desired. In contrast, black or multiracial babies are the least in demand, thus the cost and waiting period for them are considerably lower, especially if one adopts via the foster care program. One adoption agency, Wide Horizons for Children, states on their website that "[f]amilies are especially needed for children of African American heritage and children who may have a health risk or concern." Here, blackness and disease and/or disability are on par. On the contrary, Asian adoptions compose about 60 percent of all international adoptions according to the Department of Health and Human Services. Domestically, Asian American adoption composes such a small number that reliable estimates could not be generated; this disparity may be explained by the fact that very few Asian American babies are placed in adoptions due to cultural or religious taboos. Interestingly, however, Asian eggs are a hot commodity and demand as much as two or three times the price of other eggs (and, as noted in a recent *Los Angeles Times* article, up to a hundred thousand dollars). "ASIAN EGG DONORS NEEDED" signs can be found all over Ivy League college campuses, for if the donor boasts an Ivy League pedigree with high SAT scores, she can command a higher price. Demand is so high that some egg donor agencies, such as the Asian Egg Donor Agency in New Jersey, specialize in Asian eggs. As Stanford bioethics professor David Magnus writes, "What we have is the beginnings of the specter of eugenics... the makings of a super-race and a slippery slope. What we have is an actual egg selling, not egg donation" ("Eggs from Young Asian Women in High Demand").

Techno-Orientalism, Cylons, and Racial Reproductions

As speculative science fiction, *BSG* offers the possibilities of the what-if scenario by transforming the "specter of eugenics" into a speculation of racial mixing via biotechnology. Mirroring the current popularity of genealogical research such as PBS's *African American Lives 1 and 2* (2006 and 2008, respectively) and *Race: The Power of an Illusion* (2003), *BSG*'s conclusion narrates the origins of humanity's heritage and genetic material. In *BSG*'s genealogical analysis, however, blackness is erased out of our evolutionary history. This is unsurprising since all the black characters tend to either die or disappear upon arrival onto the New Earth; indeed, much has already been written (both critically and informally) about *BSG*'s problematic representation of blackness.[5] In terms of the human characters, one has only to look at Dee, Bulldog, Phelan, Elosha, and Sue-Shaun to witness the disappearance of black characters into the inevitable "black hole." Dee commits suicide, Bulldog is literally abandoned to the Cylons by Adama only to return to be abandoned again, Phelan is a criminal (aka "felon") who is killed off by Apollo for being the immoral leader of, yes, the Black Market, the priest Elosha dies after triggering a Cylon landmine on Kobol, and Sue-Shaun begs Starbuck for death while hooked up to the Cylon fertility machine. An online commenter notes, "Every single black character was killed, murdered and mutilated in the *BSG* Universe. Adolf Hitler could not have dreamed up a more inspirational script" (Levinson). The conscious erasure of blackness is further evidenced when the Galactica fleet lands on what looks like the African continent during the series finale. But, instead of seeing dark-skinned natives, the fleet witnesses a group of pale-skinned, spear-yielding humans wandering the plains. Although our glimpse of the natives is very brief, the only recognizable codes of blackness are the paint marks covering their bodies. Dr. Cottle, Galactica's medical officer, tellingly reveals, "Their DNA is compatible with ours" ("Daybreak, Part 2"), emphasizing the culmination of their procreative mission. In other words, the light-skinned natives are genetically (and ideologically) compatible with the humans for breeding purposes. This final episode emphasizes ways in which *BSG*'s erasure of (and ART's containment of) blacks and blackness reflects a form of narrative genocide in which blacks are eliminated from visions of what the Cylons foretell to be "the shape of things to come."

The creative possibilities of being able to select a baby's race are reconfigured via the various possibilities of racialized couplings in *BSG*'s call to procreate. At the end of the miniseries pilot when the human race is threatened with extinction, President Roslin says to Commander Adama, "If we are going to survive as a species, we need to get the hell out of here and start having babies" (Miniseries Pilot).[6] Looking at white Billy (President Roslin's assistant) and black Petty Officer Dualla/Dee, Commander Adama concurs, declaring, "They better start having babies" (Miniseries Pilot). This desperate need to reproduce becomes a gentle reminder with each episode via the fluctuating numbers of the survivor count posted on Colonial Fleet One. This call to breed, then, creates an interesting dilemma between humanity's survival and the policing of procreation. While Adama's initial reaction to Billy and Dualla's blossoming romance is to call for babies, white-black unions are not the intended or desired solution.

If *BSG* shows that Asian-white mixing is acceptable (via the revelation of Cylon-human hybrid Hera as our common ancestor), it also reveals the unrelenting fear of black-white miscegenation in existence since American slavery. Initially created as slave labor, the Cylons are perhaps best embodied by its only black instantiation, Simon.[7] In "The Farm," Simon is a doctor attending an injured Starbuck, the Galactica fleet's blond-haired and blue-eyed gifted Viper pilot. In this sense, Simon's blackness is signified multiple times (as Cylon slave, as visibly black, and as black sexual threat). It is under his care that Starbuck discovers she is a prisoner at a Cylon hospital, and that the Farm is a breeding ground where human women are used as "baby machines" in the Cylons' plan to create human-Cylon hybrids. Simon, who stands over a half-dressed, vulnerable Starbuck, declares,

> Gotta keep that reproductive system in great shape. It's the most valuable asset these days.... Finding healthy childbearing women your age is a top priority for the Resistance and you'll be happy to know that you're a very precious commodity to us.... You do realize that you're one of the handful of women on this planet actually capable of having children. That is your most valuable skill right now.... The human race is on the verge of extinction. And to be quite frank with you, potential mothers are a lot more valuable right now than a whole squadron of viper pilots. ("The Farm")

The symbolism of this scene is clear, as Christopher Deis notes: "While Starbuck is not penetrated by Simon sexually, she is symbolically raped, penetrated surgically in her abdomen (and, likely, also penetrated medically through vaginal examinations while unconscious)" (165). The haunting of slavery reinforces the fears of black male–white female relations when Starbuck encounters Sue-Shaun, a black female resistance fighter, hooked up to machines that are harvesting her eggs. The stark image of Sue-Shaun's lifted and separated legs, with metal instruments attached to her womb, brutally echoes the subjugation of black women's bodies as enslaved reproduction delivery systems during slavery. Rather than live as a breeder, Sue-Shaun begs Starbuck to kill her, which reinforces not only the "unnaturalness" of the Cylon's dependence on reproductive technology but the horror of black women as reproducers. After Starbuck escapes, Athena tells her that the Cylons are "conducting research into human-Cylon breeding programs" because Cylons cannot reproduce biologically, and that they believe procreation is one of God's commandments. While Starbuck kills both Simon and Sue-Shaun, albeit for very different reasons, the message here is unmistakable: any suggestion of black-white procreation results in death. This is further emphasized when another variation of the Simon Cylon is literally shackled like a slave, perhaps as punishment for his role in cross-racial/species breeding, later in the season ("A Measure of Salvation"). Arguments against black-white mixing are again underscored when black female officer Dualla's relationship to two white men (Billy and Apollo) ends with the death of the one who proposes to her and her own suicide in the middle of season 4.[8] *BSG*'s limited visions of black-white mixings reveal a fear of blackness that continues to prevail today.

If black-white mixing is the utterly unmentionable, Asian-white mixing is the "shape of things to come" as mixed-race Hera is often identified as throughout the show. The parallel story lines of the two main Eight model clones, Boomer and Athena, are significant because as visibly Asian cylon models, they simultaneously evoke the fear of yellow peril paranoia within a story line already centered on Orientalized terrorism (see Hu-Pegues; Bennett, "Techno-butterfly"). The Eight's embodiment of both fear and seduction is illustrated when multiple copies of nude Eights confront Boomer in "Kobol's Last Gleaming, Part II." This is the only time multiple clones of Cylon model are revealed to the audience on such a large scale, not only implying the threat of the never-ending horde of Asians but also fixating Asians (especially Asian women) with their sexuality. This allusion to Asian female sexuality continues with the parallel Athena story line in which she not only seduces her victim and becomes pregnant, but her pregnancy becomes the literal and symbolic future of humanity. When Messenger Six reveals the baby to Baltar, strongly implied to be Athena and Helo's yet unborn daughter, Hera, she declares that the baby is "the guardian and protector of the new generation of God's children. The first member of our family will be with us soon, Gaius.... Come... see the face of the shape of things to come." The "face" and "shape" is mixed-raced on multiple levels: Asian-white, Cylon-human, alien-earthling. Of Greek mythological fame, Hera was the goddess of marriage, emphasizing *BSG*'s acceptable delineation of racial mixings and couplings. The racialization of this scene is significant because it outlines Baltar and Six as exemplars of the white, heteronormative couple who simultaneously welcomes and concedes the future to an Asian-white mixed raced baby. Interestingly, while Athena's name invokes the Greek goddess of wisdom and war, she is revealed to be quite the opposite when her initial Cylon threats become domesticated and contained throughout the series, transforming Athena from temptress and sleeper agent to loyal wife, soldier, and subject. It is also important to note here that the Asian-white mixing is acceptable only when the Asian partner is female, highlighting the invisibility and silencing of Asian male sexuality in *BSG* as well as ART practices.[9]

Thus, whereas Asian male sexuality is invisible and the biotechnology of black ART practices via Sue-Shaun is portrayed as "unnatural" and horrific, the biotechnology of Athena's procreation is celebratory, medically revolutionary (as described below), and unifying. Athena, in fact, embodies biotechnology itself (with an Orientalist twist). For as humanoid robots, don't all Cylons personify the intersection of living organism with technological application? We witness the simultaneous repulsion/attraction of this dualism when, upon learning of a Cylon computer virus attack, Adama requests Boomer's help to contain it ("Flight of the Phoenix"). Within moments of the attack, Boomer plugs herself into the network by inserting a fiber optic cable into her hand while a horrified crew watches in stunned silence. Boomer erases the virus and sends a virus of her own onto the Cylon ships, disabling and leaving them vulnerable to fleet assault. Here, the Orientalized figure of feared technology is at once appalling and appealing for both her capabilities as well as her complete disregard for her own kind.

The simultaneous awe and terror of techno-Orientalism are perhaps best exemplified by *BSG*'s rhetoric of blood. From our historical classification of the "one-drop" rule to the current policing of blood quantum levels in Native American communities to the popularization of DNA and ancestry testing, blood has been a central marker of racial differentiation since the commencement of U.S. racial formations. Blood also plays a central part in *BSG*'s message of ancestry and race. One of the dilemmas running throughout the show is President Roslin's unpublicized cancer; in an episode titled "Epiphanies," Roslin's cancer returns and threatens her life and, subsequently, the survival of the fleet. Parallel to Roslin's cancer story line is the dilemma of Athena's pregnancy. Early on in the episode, Roslin orders the destruction of the human-Cylon hybrid, the unborn Hera, arguing that "[a]llowing this thing to be born can have frightening consequences" ("Epiphanies"). But, when Hera's fetal blood is discovered to be a cure for cancer and injected into an ailing Roslin, Roslin declares a ban on all abortions. This is a significant moment in which Cylon blood is transformed from contaminant to cure, a metamorphic moment that also mirrors Boomer/Athena's conversion from threat to cure. Most significantly, it is also the crucial moment when yellow peril is domesticated and contained by civic technologies, represented by President Roslin's body.

Unintended Conclusions?

I conclude with some observations on *BSG*'s final message. The central anxiety running throughout the show is the anxiety of detection: Who is Cylon? Who is human? How can we tell the difference? This anxiety of not knowing is intimately related to questions of racial mixing: What does the mixed-race individual look like? How does racial mixing (and oftentimes the racially ambiguous embodiment of that mixing) force us to redefine boundaries of race (or, within the specific dynamics of the show, the definition of human)? In today's reproductive field, these questions become complicated by the limitless racial possibilities offered by ART practices. *BSG*'s revelation that we are all part Cylon (and, hence, passing for human), while having the potential to destabilize our need to define boundaries, is weakened by the racial restrictions and delineations it places on Asianness and blackness. For if *BSG*'s intent with its climactic disclosure of our Cylon genes is to force us to question our common human ancestry, the impact of our species/racial self-reflection is weakened by the very racialized restrictions placed upon its supposed color-blind characters and plot.

Notes

1. The desperate struggle for a genetic child is perhaps best illustrated in the reproductive journey of Will and Mo, two self-described health care professionals who have endured seven IVF (in-vitro fertilization) treatments, six miscarriages, and finally a baby girl born in 2012. Their journey can be followed on lifeandloveinthepetridish.blogspot.com.
2. It is important to note here that "Want to be a Dad" dismisses the probability that despite the racial background of the egg donor, the child will probably look like him in some way since his sperm is being used. The real fear here is that an Asian "taint" will automatically erase any evidence of whiteness. For this future father, tainted whiteness is not whiteness at all.
3. In May 2012, the Census Bureau announced that white births are no longer the majority in the United States. Subsequent headlines declared "Fewer White Babies Being Born" (Siek and Sterling) and "Whites Account for Under Half of Births in U.S." (Tavernise).
4. It is important to note here that although this study is centered around a sperm donor and, therefore, the infertility of the father, the onus of reproduction and heritage is solely relegated to the mother figure. Thus, while the father may be the infertile one, it is the mother who will bear the burden of her child's racial ambiguity.
5. In addition to Christopher Deis, several blogs have queried *BSG*'s antiblack racism including Uneven Steven, Uncle Sam's Cabin, and SyFy.com's forum titled "Is *Battlestar Galactica* Racist?"
6. The urgency to procreate is so desperate that President Roslin even declares an executive order to ban abortion (see season 2.5, episode 7).
7. "They were created to make lives easier for humans," reads the miniseries' opening lines.

8. We see another version of the Simon/Four Cylon model in *The Plan* (2009), a film released after the series' finale but set during the time period of *BSG*'s miniseries to season 2. *The Plan* is told from the Cylon perspective, and as such we observe Simon, now married with an adopted stepdaughter, as a medic onboard Cybele. This version of Simon is telling because it furthers the antiblack/white mixing of "The Farm" with a slight twist. Simon's wife, Gianna O'Neill, is played by Lymari Nadal (an American actress of Puerto Rican descent and wife of actor Edward James Olmos, who plays Commander Adama). In a show without racial distinction, Gianna is obviously "Othered" in that her speech is strongly accented, although visibly she can pass for white. Either way, Simon's black threat is again eliminated when after a scene of lovemaking, he releases himself out of the airlock while he declares his love for family. As Simon is out of range of any Resurrection Ship, his death is permanent.
9. We have to think of only Gaeta's character to support the reading of Asian men being silenced. Played by biracial (Asian-white) actor Alessandro Juliani, Gaeta is portrayed as the ultimate traitor to humanity when he sides with the Cylons. As a result, he is executed by firing squad for mutiny and treason by series' end. In the webisodes revealingly titled "The Face of the Enemy," Gaeta's character is disclosed to be in a relationship with Louis Hoshi, whose Japanese-sounding surname translates to "star" in Japanese according to battlestarwiki.org. Interestingly, the Asian homosexual relationship is doomed to failure, one that is further supported by Gaeta's weakness in character. For while the threat of the Asian (Cylon) woman is contained and domesticated, the Asian male is not offered the same opportunity and ends in a shameful death. As a side note, it is also important to point out that the "shape of things to come" is embodied by a containable female, rather than perhaps a more threatening male, progenitor.

Chapter 8

Never Stop Playing

---◄○►---

StarCraft and Asian
Gamer Death

STEVE CHOE AND SE YOUNG KIM

A 2012 television advertisement for the handheld Sony PlayStation Vita depicts a young white hipster playing his PlayStation 3 console in his apartment. He has just hit a home run in the video game *MLB: The Show*. Hard rock music plays in the background of the commercial while a male voice-over intones, "It's a problem as old as gaming itself: Stay home and just keep playing or get to work on time so your coffee breath boss doesn't ride you like a rented scooter." The music swells as the man picks up his Vita and continues playing baseball while walking out the door. Standing at a busy city intersection with his eyes looking down at the screen of his handheld gaming device, the voice continues, "Who says you have to choose? Your PS3 stays home but the game goes with you. Never stop playing." The ad cuts to another medium shot of the trendy man, walking toward the camera through a fenced tunnel, eyes still glued to his Vita. The crack of a baseball bat signals that he has just hit another home run on his ongoing *MLB* game.

This image stands in stark contrast to that featured in a February 3, 2012, news article, published in the U.K.-based website sky.com under the title "Gamer Dies at Web Café—But No-One Notices." The article reports that a twenty-three-year-old Taiwanese man was found slumped in a chair in an

Internet café in Taipei. He had been playing the online real-time strategy game (RTS) *League of Legends*. Police reported, "He was rigid on a chair with his hands stretched out towards the keyboard and mouse." The young man had been playing for at least twenty-three hours straight. Others were oblivious to the condition of their fellow gamer for another ten hours. The police were disgusted to hear that patrons wanted to continue playing instead of answering questions for the investigation. The *LoL* player had a preexisting heart condition, and the combination of fatigue and lack of physical movement led to blood clots and finally cardiac arrest. He "never stopped playing"—at least, until his physical body gave out.

For the young, healthy white male, gaming without end is made into something desirable. Rising from the couch with his Vita in hand, he can continue playing and never has to stop being hip. The commercial glorifies life as a gamer, one that need not be interrupted by the demands of work or by a boss who will ride him "like a rented scooter." The death of the Taiwanese gamer on the other hand invokes anxiety, highlighting not the fun of gaming without end, but the deleterious effects and fatal consequences of prolonged physical inactivity. His race marks him as other to the Caucasian man, and his self-destructive obsessiveness as deviant from the self-possessed, seemingly reasonable gamer. In this, the characterization of the Taiwanese player overlaps with already existing Orientalist stereotypes of Asians males circulating in the West: immature, disaffected, asexual, physically weak, socially inept, and definitely not hip. Compared to the healthy body of the white gamer, the Asian player plays ostensibly in order to compensate for his physical impotence.

Moreover, the news report evokes the culture of video gaming in Asia, of *World of Warcraft* gold farmers and virtuoso *StarCraft* players dominating the global virtual space: these are Asians who treat gaming as a form of work. Those images have their parallel within the Orientalist imagination, namely in anxieties surrounding outsourced jobs that once belonged to Western workers and in yellow peril fears of millions of Chinese laborers working "without end." The rhetoric of gamer death eerily resembles that concerning *karōshi*, or "death by overwork," in Japan and other East Asian contexts. Referring to Japan's "high-tech enchantment," David Morley and Kevin Robins argue that techno-Orientalism consolidates anxieties around technology with the exotic Asian Other: "The association of technology and Japaneseness now serves to reinforce the image of a culture that is cold, impersonal and machine-like, an authoritarian culture lacking emotional connection to the rest of the world" (169). This Orientalist projection stands in contrast to the fantasy of the Western subject characterized as humanistic and possessing free will and soul. These are properly autonomous subjects who know how to exercise their freedoms and pleasures responsibly, unlike the "soulless" Asian.

In this essay, we show how the Asian gamer may be understood within the discursive powers of techno-Orientalism that make the Asian Other knowable and controllable. This understanding reveals Western fantasies of virtual escapism, while the death of the Asian gamer ruptures precisely these fantasies—of never working while video gaming constantly, and of eternal life without death. In order to put forward this argument, we will look closely at the popular sci-fi RTS game *StarCraft*, released in 1998, and the cultural trends surrounding it. Our reading of *StarCraft* gestures toward attitudes around video gaming that do not celebrate playing without end, while challenging the sacredness of life and guaranteed leisure time in capitalism.

The first reported instance of online gamer death in Asia was in October 2002, when twenty-four-year-old Kim Kyung-jae played nonstop for eighty-six hours until he collapsed and died in an Internet café in Kwangju, South Korea (Gluck). Just ten days later, Lien Wen-cheng died in a café in Fengyuan, Taiwan. The twenty-seven-year-old had been playing for thirty-two hours straight; he was found in the restroom bleeding from the nose and foaming at the mouth (Farrell). On August 5, 2005, Lee Seungseob went into cardiac arrest following a fifty-hour marathon session of *StarCraft* in Taegu, South Korea (Zimbardo). According to the psychiatrist at the hospital where Lee was taken, he had neglected to eat and sleep while playing. In 2005, *Xinhua Online* reported that a young woman, identified only as "Snowly," died after playing *World of Warcraft* "for several continuous days during the national day holiday." An online, in-game funeral was held in her memory by fellow gamers ("Death of Net Addict"). A twenty-six-year-old man identified only by his surname "Zhang" died in the Liaoning province of China on February 24, 2007. During the Spring Festival, Zhang had spent most of the seven-day holiday playing online computer games (Yong Wu). Also in 2007, a thirty-year-old man died of exhaustion after gaming for three days straight in Guangzhou, China ("Chinese Man Drops Dead"). On December 27, 2010, a nineteen-year-old college student, identified by his surname "Moon," collapsed in a café in Ulsan, South Korea, after playing first-person shooter (FPS) games for twelve hours (Cho). A thirty-year-old man died in a cybercafé outside of Beijing, China, on February 22, 2011, after playing online games for three days (Goswami).

A *Kotaku* article from 2007 opens with the headline "Another Chinese Man Dies from Gaming" and comments on this proliferation of gamer death in Asia. Referring to the player from Guangzhou, journalist Mike Fahey begins with a glib suggestion: "Someone really needs to tell the people in East Asian countries to stop gaming before they die." He wryly notes, "Watching a person die from lack of common sense always makes me thirsty," and proposes "a free latte policy" to encourage gamers to stop playing. Fahey then concludes, "I know the loss of a human life is not a laughing matter, but I just cannot fathom gaming to death. Back in 2001, there were weeks when I would spend every waking hour playing EQ, but I at least took chair naps and tried my very best not to die. Worked for me. *sigh*" (Fahey). Fahey characterizes Asian gamers as obsessive, easily manipulated, and lacking in "common sense," while his own gaming experience worked for him. His position of healthy self-control draws a hard line between himself and the inferior Other, allowing the Western journalist, as Edward Said writes, "a whole series of possible relationships with the Orient without ever losing him the relative upper hand" (7). Reinstating the difference between reality and simulation, Fahey knows that he must not lose himself to the game. But the assertion of difference betrays anxieties around the fantasy of excessive gaming and the fine line between excessive fun and death, anxieties that are quickly projected back onto the seemingly less grievable other. The Asian gamer dies because of his immaturity and inability to moderate his own pleasures. Meanwhile, Fahey discursively constructs himself as self-possessed much like the Vita player from the Sony commercial, while the possibility of his own potential death is deflected and disavowed.

The small sampling of gamer casualties listed above suggests a number of patterns. Most are male and under the age of thirty. Reportage on gamer death is generally limited to a number of areas, namely South Korea, China, and Taiwan. Moreover, most have died in public spaces, generally Internet cafés that contain dozens of networked computers where one is charged an hourly rate, for use as long as one likes. During the day, these twenty-four-hour cafés are occupied by casual users who need to check email or their Facebook page. At night they are populated by young men who play online games such as *StarCraft*, *World of Warcraft*, and *League of Legends* into the early morning hours. While Internet access in the home remains inexpensive, it is cheaper to play in public, away from the judgmental gaze of family members. In these Asian contexts, where class stratification remains rigid, all gamers feel the desire to escape the hypercompetitiveness of the school system into the digital worlds found in cheap and readily available Internet cafés.

Of the East Asian countries where cybercafé culture thrives, perhaps none have legitimated and institutionalized this online culture as much as South Korea. Indeed, without the rapid expansion of high-speed Internet (over 90 percent of South Korean households have a broadband connection) and the proliferation of Internet cafés (*PC bang* or "PC rooms"), the incredible popularity of *StarCraft* would not have been possible. Meanwhile, its wide dissemination is enabled by its low system requirements, as *StarCraft* can be played on most PCs at roughly the same level of performance, regardless of whether one's computer is new or old. The popularity of online video gaming is further legitimized through the professionalization in Korea of eSports, which raises the stakes by underwriting *StarCraft* competitions with venture capital, while extremely skilled players are promoted and made into national heroes.

In September 1999, Internet provider Kornet, a branch of Korea Telecom, launched a TV commercial featuring professional *StarCraft* player Lee Gi-seok. Lee had won the grand prize at the second season of Blizzard's *StarCraft* ladder tournament in June of that year. In the commercial, he is introduced with his Battle.net ID, *Ssamjang*, also the name of a fermented bean paste sauce. Before the international recognition of Korea's national team in the 2002 World Cup, Lee proved that Koreans could be world champions, even if only in video gaming. His dominance and the dominance of other players such as Lim Yo-hwan were key in further legitimizing gaming as a national endeavor through their success on the international gaming circuit. The World Cyber Games was established in Korea in 2000, and the first World Cyber Games Challenge opened on October 7, 2000, with sponsorship by the Ministry of Culture and Tourism, the Ministry of Information and Communications, and Samsung Group.

Because this level of engagement with *StarCraft* does not exist in the United States or Europe, it has elicited fascination and even mild incredulity in the English-language coverage of eSports. This fascination often imposes national and cultural stereotypes. In an article called "The Country That Loves PC Gaming So Damn Much," journalist Brian Ashcraft writes that "just the mention of South Korea conjures up images of net cafes and online gaming" (Ashcraft, "The Country"). Fascinated, he continues, "The entire nation of South Korea seems fixated on the game—with tournaments and TV programs. You could say it's the country's national (digital) pastime!" (Ashcraft, "Why Is StarCraft"). Detailing the "nature" of Koreans' interest in *StarCraft*, Ashcraft's language describes not an engagement but an obsession with gaming. In another article titled "Why Is StarCraft So Popular in Korea?" he cites Rick Rumas, a filmmaker/writer based in South Korea, who speculates on Koreans' obsession with competitive activity. "This can range from math to science to Rubik's Cubes, and while StarCraft generally is not a 'recommended' pursuit, it falls under a similar obsessive mindset" (Ashcraft, "Why Is StarCraft"). The Korea that Ashcraft and Rumas discuss is one where excelling in competition is valid in and of itself, and the areas where Koreans excel are those that are stereotypically associated with Asianness: math, science, and now *StarCraft*.

This is the general movement of the English-language discourse surrounding *StarCraft* in Korea: it gestures toward the existence of a phenomenon that needs to be comprehended, but the resulting "comprehension" moves along preexisting lines of Orientalism. Operating under the premise of understanding the Other, Ashcraft's inquiries ultimately perpetuate an idea of essential difference in Korean video game culture. And to this extent, he remarks that the obsession with *StarCraft* remains beyond him: "Interesting, but what is it with Korea and *StarCraft?* I mean, seriously, what's with the default setting?" (Ashcraft, "Stink at StarCraft?"). That gaming may constitute a form of spectator sport is, for Ashcraft, senseless, entertainment without a point. "Perhaps I haven't played the game enough and perhaps it's actually riveting entertainment, but viewing it as a spectator sport is beyond me. What's Korean for boring?" (Ashcraft, "StarCraft on Korean").

Through the 2000s, as the visibility of Korean gaming culture spread throughout the world in articles such as those published in *Kotaku*, authorities in Korea raised the issue of video game addiction. While video game addiction is not spoken of to the same degree in the West, this problem cannot be reduced to an absolute difference between the West and Asia. Rather, there are historical specificities in the gaming culture of Asia that are not present in the American and European contexts. For the addictive tendencies that Ashcraft clumsily interrogates, the troubling phenomenon of gamer death as well as the broad legitimization and professionalization of gaming must be thought of in relation to South Korea's rapid modernization. According to a study conducted in 2006, about 210,000 Korean children aged six to nineteen were addicted to video games (Y. H. Choi 20), and exhibited classic symptoms such as mild to severe depression, restlessness, and anxiety when away from the computer. Four years later, a study conducted by the National Information Society Agency identified approximately 8 percent of the population between nine and thirty-nine as Internet addicts (Jiyeon Lee). These reports point to the rise of a discourse of crisis around Internet addiction. According to another study, nearly 30 percent of children and teenagers under eighteen may be considered addicted to the Internet, spending at least fourteen hours a week online (Fackler). Reflecting the increase in web usage, these statistical discourses also reify the category of the Internet addict. Although the American *Diagnostic and Statistical Manual of Mental Disorders* (*DSM*) does not include Internet and video game addiction in its latest edition (*DSM-5*), the condition is treated as such in Korea. The government has been actively involved with Internet addiction in youths, ranging from 11.5 billion won annually spent on treatment centers to surveys distributed in schools to help teachers identify potentially addicted children (Sutter). As of June 2007, 1,043 counselors have been employed at over 190 hospitals and treatment centers to treat what is considered a national problem. In late 2011 the government implemented a controversial system called the "shutdown law," also referred to as the "Cinderella law." This system bars children and teenagers under the age of sixteen from access to video game websites after midnight (Jiyeon Lee).

This anxiety finds its allegorical form in the sci-fi genre elements that circulate in *StarCraft* itself. The narrative is driven by dread surrounding assimilation and/or domination by an inhuman Other, a familiar trope of the genre. While the player can play any of the modes as one of the three races, it is clear that the player is meant to identify most fully with the human Terrans. Through the single-player campaign, the player must fend off both the Zergs (the buglike aliens) and the Protoss (the technologically advanced aliens). Becoming infested by the Zerghive mind is the worst outcome for the player and the human race because, like the addicted gamer, the Terrans lose their humanity. One of the central characters of the franchise, the human Sarah Kerrigan, is abducted by the Zerg and through metamorphosis is turned into "The Queen of the Blades." Her transformation into an evil alien conforms to common sci-fi conventions, bringing together anxieties around alien others with male anxieties surrounding female sexuality. In this, *StarCraft* delineates the human by setting it over and against that which has been deemed inhuman. This issue of abjection and abnormality permeates South Korea's ambivalent relationship with *StarCraft*. On one hand, the nation has enjoyed a thriving, highly competitive, and thus exciting culture of video gaming, whether through eSports or the industry itself, yet simultaneously it has found itself at odds with its young people spending hours on end on their computers like so many infested Terrans.

Video gaming culture in South Korea constantly oscillates between two contradictory tendencies. Gaming enjoys a level of legitimacy unheard of in America and Europe: fast broadband Internet, cable channels that treat gaming as a spectator sport, and corporate sponsorship. Top *StarCraft* players are celebrated for their APM (actions per minute) and featured on television commercials selling soft drinks. However, this culture also enables and perhaps creates highly addictive tendencies in young players. These players then are disparaged for their supposed inability to work through emotional problems and chastised for what is taken as an escape into a virtual world inhabited by Terrans, Zergs, and the Protoss.

In an essay called "Angels in Digital Armor: Technoculture and Terror Management" (2010), media scholar Marcel O'Gorman argues that notions of heroism in contemporary technoculture aim to satisfy two primary existential needs: the desire for recognition and the denial of death. Most video games interpellate players by reinforcing ideologies that underpin the sovereign subject, who believes herself to be immortal and master of the world represented on the computer screen. Gaming is one part of a broadly conceived digital technoculture for O'Gorman. Appropriating Bernard Stiegler's thesis that the technologization of culture is linked to profound malaise and ontological indifference, O'Gorman argues that online heroism, constituted through attention garnered on Facebook, YouTube, and the news media, goes hand in hand with the disavowal of mortality and finitude. Toward this O'Gorman analyzes cases of gamer death in China and Korea, the Columbine High School shootings, and Cho Seung-Hui, the Virginia Tech shooter, as "explicitly technological, or even 'cyber,' because they involve the perpetrators' use of media to rehearse or to promote their exploits in a desperate plea for recognition" (O'Gorman). He does not discuss race explicitly but implies that all users of digital media are somehow implicated.

While we agree with O'Gorman's diagnosis of the culture of online celebrity and the proliferation of technically induced malaise, his analysis runs the danger of overgeneralization with the blanket term "technoculture." We would like to attend to the specificity of video gaming and its Orientalist figuration by isolating a mechanic of *StarCraft* that is common to most video games: the acquisition of capital. More specifically, for the remainder of the essay we further interrogate the relationship between work and play. While drawing from McKenzie Wark's *Gamer Theory* and key game play mechanics from *StarCraft*, we argue that extreme video gaming may be read to challenge the presuppositions that deem it "unproductive" labor. In doing so, we argue that extreme gaming upends notions of capitalist time, pointing to ontological aporias that blur the distinction between Occidental and Oriental.

Playing *StarCraft* teaches its players about life outside of the game, a testament perhaps to its broader relevance, training them to become better capitalists. Because of the cutthroat level of competition and the constant influx of new talent, professional gamers in Korea mostly enjoy short careers that are abbreviated by mandatory military service. After being discharged from the military, pro gamer Lee Joong Heon was employed at a video game company. But after a five-year retirement, Lee, formerly a *Warcraft III* player, decided to return to eSports and made the transition to *StarCraft II*. In a 2009 interview, Lee relates that his return is temporary and that he will retire again in three years. A job in a trading company is lined up for him once he is done gaming professionally (Yong-woo Kim). In a parallel career move, pro gamer Seo Ji-hoon found a position as a sports marketer with the Korean conglomerate CJ Group once he retired from *StarCraft*. A book published in 2000 in the wake of the financial crisis called *Starcnomics* connects *StarCraft* and its game play mechanics to the business world (Tae-heung Kim; Hee-jong Kang). The parallel between the logic of gaming and business may be evidenced in the United States as well. The University of Florida has offered a class on "21st Century Skills in StarCraft," while the University of California, Berkeley campus has competitive *StarCraft* courses. Playing *StarCraft* teaches one to become better at life within capitalism.

These examples illustrate that *StarCraft* is not merely a form of play; instead, much of the "play" within the game could be considered a form of work. Unlike many video games, the player does not control an avatar or an in-game virtual representative (usually the main character of a narrative). In *StarCraft* and many RTS games, the player assumes a godlike overseer/manager position with an isometric view of the battlefield. At the start of a session, the player can see and control his or her base, with the rest of the map, in the bottom-left corner of the screen, obscured by a "fog of war." If the player clicks on parts of the map past his or her base, the view is hidden in blackness until it is traversed by one of the player's military units. The player knows only two things: how large the map is and that an enemy is located somewhere. As in cognitive mapping, the player wishes to lift the fog of war to chart out the playing area and master the space. The player does not engage the enemy immediately, for he or she must first build up forces in preparation for it. And in order to prepare, the player must acquire and manage resources, like the capitalist in life outside the game.

Thus despite its twenty-fifth-century settings, game play in *StarCraft* proceeds with twentieth-century late capitalistic assumptions. At the start of each game, the player is given a central base, four worker units, and start-up capital. With these resources, the player constructs more buildings such as barracks, factories, gateways, and spawning pools in order to recruit more workers, build new structures, and produce new military units. The worker units acquire vespene gas (a resource only found in the game) from geysers and harvest minerals from the environment. The barracks train an array of offensive and defensive military units, each with particular modes of movement and attack patterns. Oftentimes preparation for battle—and the battle itself—can take only minutes or an hour and more, and the player is forced to make most of these crucial moments by planning ahead, making quick decisions, and moving rapidly. The thrill of engaging the enemy must be preceded by this tedious labor, which is squandered when the player's units are destroyed in combat. As such, the aim of producing only in order to destroy and be destroyed aligns *StarCraft* with something akin to building a sand castle. The pleasure of constructing a sand castle is embodied in the labor utilized to build something ephemeral. Within capitalism, this ephemerality is obscured by the ideological belief that tedious labor is productive labor, yet management within *StarCraft* brings the basic ephemerality of capital itself to the fore.

In *Gamer Theory*, McKenzie Wark breaks down the distinction between the real world and the illusory world of the video game. He coins the term "gamespace" to signify not the virtual realm depicted on a screen, but a physically placeless realm where the logic of gaming, including quantitative modes of human valuation such as the "lifebar," indicated underneath each unit, underpins lived existence. In contrast to Johan Huizinga's famous definition of play as "a stepping out of 'real' life into a temporary sphere of activity with a disposition all of its own," for Wark playing video games is coextensive with the human operation of hardware and software in our contemporary post-Fordist economy (26). "Games are not representations of this world," Wark writes, "they are more like allegories of a world made over as gamespace. They encode the abstract principles upon which decisions about the realness of this or that world are now decided" (20). Considered within the logic of late capitalism, gamespace quickly takes on a holistic aspect, for it also describes the total administration of human activity outside the video game, while perpetuating the ideology that the game is nevertheless predicated on the "fair fight" and the maintenance of a "level playing field." Gamespace overlaps with the space of the neoliberal, global economy. For Wark, a critical theory of video games begins by taking outside reality not as the model to which games should aspire, but itself as "a gamespace that appears as an imperfect form of the computer game" (22).

As Wark dismantles the binary between reality and game, other distinctions are implicated. Specifically, if gamespace describes an existential condition in late capitalism, and if the mechanics of reward and punishment operative in video games allegorizes an identical mechanics in contemporary lived life, then Wark's deconstruction necessarily carries similar implications for the distinction between work and play. While in an earlier era of capitalist development such a distinction structured what Marx called "species-being," as well as productive and unproductive activity, in the age of video games work becomes another form of play, and vice versa. Gaming is a form of work, but as of yet not everyone is paid to play.

The rules of fair play in video games and the ideology of neoliberalism intersect: if the player works hard, the player's efforts will be acknowledged and the work compensated. Most video games are motivated by this reward dynamic through the achievement of a high score or the acquisition of coveted items and money, both of which correspond to the acquisition of capital in the nonvirtual space. Endless acquisition in gamespace is particularly pronounced in the practice of "gold farming," widespread in China. Gold farmers play for hours acquiring virtual capital in MMORPG games such as *World of Warcraft* in order to sell it for real capital (Vincent). Yet through this, traditional ontological distinctions between gaming and the actual world are radically confused. Approaching online RPGs as an economist, Edward Castronova describes the relatively banal "economics of fun" that underpin the synthetic world of games. "The economy is in fact an integral part of the fantasy," Castronova writes. "Nothing makes a world feel more alive than an active market system" (172). Gold farming, the most laborious form of contemporary video gaming in the neoliberal economy, troubles Western capitalist notions of work and play by bringing tedium into play. It is thus perhaps not a surprise that certain journalists express disdain for professional video gaming and with the idea of eSports: for them, video games belong to the realm of leisure, sitting for hours being unproductive, and are not supposed to be laborious.

Yet in this, *StarCraft* offers peculiar problems. *StarCraft* provides abundant financial reward, especially for professional gamers, who are among the highest paid in Korean eSports, but its game play does not depend on conventional systems of reward. In-game capital provides player satisfaction in most games. However in *StarCraft*, since in-game capital is ephemeral, the player has only his or her professional record. This is contrary to other games where gamers have something "to show," such as a powerful avatar with the capital, commodities, and experience to signify the labor and time put into the game. In *StarCraft* the only record of total labor time is the players' IDs with their career wins and losses. The point of *StarCraft* is not to accumulate resources, but to use them as efficiently as possible before the match is over. In-game resources such as minerals and vespene gas imitate the exchange value of money in order to produce more buildings and units, but there is no long-term merit to the production of surplus value beyond the length of the individual match. Unlike in gold farming, accumulated capital retains no exchange value. Instead, resources have use value insofar as they become mobilized to defeat the enemy. Seen from the perspective of gamespace, the conditions of the professional *StarCraft* player imitate those of temporary capitalist labor, but the player's activity also reveals the virtual ontology and short-term orientation of capital itself. The management of minerals and vespene gas in many ways allegorizes the management of virtual funds for short-term, liquid markets in the shadow banking system.

If games create environments where gamers, regardless of their identity, compete in "fair play," then extreme gamers push its limits by playing harder than everyone else. The morbid fascination in gamers who play themselves to death then threatens to expose an older ideological assumption that underpins this very interest: that human activity may be divided cleanly between unproductive leisure and productive labor. Despite the claim that postindustrial economies have unilaterally dissolved the boundary between leisure and labor, within techno-Orientalism this ideological remnant of the industrial economy reinscribes the division. Asian gamer death then remains ambivalent, for it blurs the discursive boundaries that underpin the gamespace of contemporary capitalism while taking the logic of life in neoliberalism to its limit. The threatened subject of the neoliberal economy must subsequently underscore the real historical specificities that persist between cultures and reconstitute them on the level of ontology. The Western gamer then, like that depicted in Sony's commercial, believes that he or she can stay on top without having to compete with the rising Asian economies. Such differences are all too often understood within the tropes of racism and technology: Asians are chained to their computers through their addiction to *StarCraft*, while the West remains essentially free, having a much more "healthy" relationship to video games. However, our analysis of gaming and capital suggests that all users are implicated in the logic of gamespace.

The dream of "never stop playing," like the mystifications of Orientalism, reflects not the truth of the exotic Other, or the transgressive possibilities opened up by purchasing a PlayStation Vita, but the narcissism of the capitalist subject. The dream of gaming endlessly reflects the dream of the hip gamer who never has to work, while the Asian gamer, who dies from playing, points to a fundamental aporia that subtends the binary between work and play, and between self and exotic other. As Alexander R. Galloway puts it in his book *The Interface Effect*, "We are all gold farmers" (136). This thought troubles binaries of life in industrial capitalism by which we understand value and productivity in modernity. In this, the Asian gamer may be thought of as "ahead" of the West in terms of the development of the neoliberal economy. Reinstating racial binaries functions as a bulwark against the deconstruction of life (which should be productive in capitalism) and death (which is often considered unproductive), as well as against the anxiety this deconstruction produces. Fetishizing Asian gamer death and the Asian work ethic performs the work of disavowal, disavowal of the fundamental differences that persist between self and other, while attempting to mediate non-Western modes of capitalist productivity.

When Blizzard released *StarCraft II* in 2010, eAthletes immediately embraced the new installment. Professional leagues sprouted up, and in May 2012 both OnGameNet (the most prestigious *StarCraft* league) and the Korean eSports Association announced that they would be making the official transition to *StarCraft II* (TeamLiquid). Lim Yo-hwan, the player most synonymous with *StarCraft*, also retired from *StarCraft: Brood War* to begin playing *StarCraft II*, a move so significant that a documentary titled *Lim Yo-hwan's Wings* was produced (Ho-kyung Choi). The industry was able to migrate quickly because of the similarity of the mechanics between *StarCraft* and *StarCraft II*. And thus like its predecessor, *StarCraft II* may be read to problematize the binary between work and play outside the game, as well as imaginations of Occident and Orient. It also makes apparent the quick turns in the cutthroat Internet gaming milieu that characterizes much of East Asia and brings to the fore the culmination of capitalist logic. This is the very same mechanism that cycles eAthletes, while leaving young men, and the occasional young woman, dead in *PC bangs* just as quickly as it promotes them to national heroes. While these gamers perish in their quest to never stop playing, the death of the Asian gamer will be appropriated within the geopolitics of labor in Asia—unless, of course, video gaming is allowed to transcend reified notions of play.

Chapter 9

"Home Is Where the War Is"

Remaking Techno-Orientalist
Militarism on the Homefront

DYLAN YEATS

Against the backdrop of some of the largest ever joint U.S.-South Korean military exercises in the spring of 2011, Kaos Studios released *Homefront*, a first-person shooter video game set in the near future where players fight North Korean occupation forces on the West Coast of America. The game's tagline is "Home Is Where the War Is." The game opens with a fake history of the Korean invasion that starts with Secretary of State Hillary Clinton's real press conference accusing North Korea of sinking South Korea's *Cheonan* corvette in March 2010. This event is framed as the beginning of a movement to unify North and South Korea and then all of Asia against U.S. interests, culminating with an all-out invasion. The uncanny use of Clinton's speech made *Homefront* something of a promotional tie-in to rhetoric about North Korea's threat to global security that U.S. policy makers were trying to sell. On the day of the game's U.S. release, Kaos even staged a fake march across the Golden Gate Bridge (the site of the game's climactic final battle) protesting real North Korean human rights abuses (Jamison).

Homefront illustrates the ongoing mass-market cultural work of reproducing and repackaging aggressive U.S. policy objectives into feel-good defenses of the "American Way." Many analysts claim that wealthy, industrialized, and technologically innovative South Korea can protect itself, but that tensions with the North provide a convenient rationale for permanently stationing fifty thousand U.S. troops there (Cumings). Aggressive American war games in the Yellow Sea use the supposed threat of North Korea as a stand-in for China, the true target of such military posturing in the region. *Homefront*'s developers initially sought to cast China as its invading force (Totilo, "China Is Both Too Scary and Not Scary Enough"), but also found in North Korea an easy enemy against which players can justly, and safely, act out their aggression. However, *Homefront* is also a remake of the 1984 film *Red Dawn*, where a patriotic band of American teenagers rebel against an occupying Soviet army. MGM Studios literally remade *Red Dawn* in 2010 with the Chinese in place of the Soviets—but studio executives decided to shelve the project after it was filmed in order to digitally remake the Chinese invaders into North Koreans (Fritz and Horn), releasing a heavily reedited version in November 2012. The "original" *Red Dawn* was itself something of a remake as part of a broader campaign to fancifully revive the Cold War hysteria of the 1950s. By hailing the perpetual war-(re)making at the heart of the "America" they seem to celebrate, this family of texts expresses a deep ambivalence about the role of screen enemies in this process. Rather than distract from this ideological work, such ambivalence animates their cultural power and political resonance.

Excavating the genealogy of *Homefront* and its imaginative reworking of U.S. foreign policy rhetoric can help elucidate the "techno" in the term "techno-Orientalism." Techno-Orientalism describes texts that produce visions of the purportedly technologically sophisticated economies and peoples of East Asia as foils for Western anxieties about the digital or information age. *Homefront* and the 2012 remake of *Red Dawn* register these anxieties quite precisely. In both texts North Koreans use an electromagnetic pulse to disable the communication systems upon which the U.S. military depends, and the invaders quickly take much of America. This techno-Orientalist peril is reminiscent of James Hevia's reading of the early twentieth-century Dr. Fu Manchu novels. Hevia argues that the "Devil Doctor's" ability to repurpose the knowledge infrastructure underpinning the British Empire for his own nefarious plots is what makes the character so scary. *Homefront* and *Red Dawn* continue this tradition of reworking anxieties about the reliance on a fetishized notion of information dominance by fixating on Oriental villains who upset the fantasy of Western technological supremacy.

In the context of mounting media fixation on cyber-security, driven in part by political projects to depict China (I mean, North Korea) as trying to hack America out of its role as military-technology leader (Singel), the fears expressed in the 2012 *Red Dawn* in particular illustrate the anxious stakes of techno-dominance. The occupying North Koreans have their own communications network, and the film's plot is driven by a hunt to retrieve one of the invaders' radios, so the forces regrouping in Free America can reverse engineer it. However, the film explores the ramifications of this technological upset through the ambivalent specter of the U.S. war in Iraq. Without computer guidance systems or satellite telecommunications, the occupied Americans are reduced to the status of Iraqis, dependent upon a technologically superior invading force that claims to be their friend. The invading North Koreans tout that they have come to liberate Americans from their own failed leaders, but they will not tolerate insurrection. This won't do for the Wolverines who launch the resistance using the moniker of their high school mascot. Jed, a veteran who has just returned from Iraq, convinces his budding guerrilla troops that they have an advantage. The occupiers, he knows from experience, don't really want to be there, whereas the Wolverines are fighting for their home and freedom. Jed claims that both the Viet Cong and America's Founding Fathers knew that guerrilla tactics could drive imperialists away by wearing them down. In this way, the 2012 *Red Dawn* seems to suggest a deeply ambivalent circular logic. The North Koreans serve as a harbinger for America. Should American military technology fail, America will be occupied the way it has occupied others. But in the hands of the film's enemy Orientals, America's own strategy is revealed to be terrifying and immoral; and given the U.S. experience in Iraq (and Vietnam) we know that this occupying technology cannot succeed.

The overlapping and contradictory identifications expressed in *Red Dawn* and *Homefront* between Iraqis, North Koreans, Chinese, Vietnamese, and Russians (and the list could, and does, go on) illustrate the polymorphous Orientalism at play in these texts. This displacement of enmity reflects a broader tradition of American war-gaming. *Red Dawn* (2012) producer Tripp Vinson stated he was interested in remaking the 1984 original because he had enjoyed it as a kid and thought "the idea of an invading army is something that speaks to the American psyche" (Hasan). However, the American psyche is not static, but continually reproduced, remade, and cultivated by image makers backed by the power of the state. Since World War II, politicians and pundits have used the specter of "Oriental" enemy invasions to scare Americans into defending themselves against a succession of intractable foes by embracing the emancipatory promise of military technology. Defenders and definers of America have replaced Soviet communism with new archenemies across East Asia and the Middle East. Cyberwar has replaced the Space Race. The ease of this transition suggests how the shifting goals of U.S. policy, not any overarching immutable cultural or geostrategic affinity across the "Orient," shape how Americans understand the implicit "Eastern" threats to an imagined "West." This complements Edward Said's central contention that the Orient is not a real place that experts in the West analyze: the Orient is a fantasy, produced by analysts with the power to assert its existence. Adding "techno" to Orientalism registers the embeddedness of such civilizational logic within the sixty-year American struggle for military industrial techno-dominance in the supposedly epic contest over the fate of the world.

As remakes, *Red Dawn* and *Homefront* hint at their participation in the ongoing reproduction of techno-Orientalist militarism at the heart of the U.S. political culture. These texts hail a tradition of attacking Americans in order to convince them they are, or could be, under attack from so-called Orientals. Key to this tradition of making and remaking techno-Orientalist militarism were a succession of groups named the Committee on the Present Danger (CPD). In 1950, a group of establishment elites founded the first CPD to promote the military to foster an "American Century" rooted in free trade by challenging Soviet attempts to close off global markets. To do so, this CPD depicted the Soviet threat to America as a zero-sum game. Behind closed doors in Washington, the CPD stewarded the adoption of the secret NSC-68 memoranda shortly before the Korean War. NSC-68 was the ultimate techno-Orientalist document, describing the Soviet Union as a "fanatical," "intractable," "inescapably militant" enemy "antithetical" to the existence of freedom and Western "civilization" (Pietz). NSC-68 advocated removing Cold War strategy from congressional oversight and placing it squarely in the charge of a vastly expanded military to develop a technological supremacy that could bolster freedom and counter communism any- and everywhere. Under the banner of anticommunism Americans launched a program of mutually assured destruction and the development of brutal countersubversive campaigns at home and abroad (Sanders 23–50).

But by the 1970s this techno-Orientalist vision began to crumble under its own weight (Englehardt). All the sophisticated surveillance and targeting seemed unable to win in Vietnam or America. Revelations about the existence of NSC-68 and the extra-legal activities it fostered provoked widespread distrust in the military establishment. The growing sense at that time that the desperate pursuit of anticommunism was neither possible nor healthy for American society led to the embrace of détente with first China and then the Soviet Union. However, hawkish politicians and defense analysts who were being pushed out of the military establishment founded a second CPD in 1976 to remake Orientalist fears, and revive the promise that technology could defend against them, in order to reassert their declining influence (Cahn). This is the all-too-real backstory to *Homefront* and the *Red Dawns*.

The second CPD sought to pathologize the movement away from techno-Orientalist militarism by helping popularize a term supposedly coined by Henry Kissinger: the "Vietnam Syndrome." In the fallout following the retreat from Vietnam, mainstream commenters began to argue that the zealous assault on communism had led analysts to misunderstand the situation in Vietnam and to wrongly imagine that ever escalating carpet bombing and computer-aided strategy could defeat a popular insurgency united against a foreign occupying power (Edwards 113–145). But advocates of the "Vietnam Syndrome" countered that this critique of techno-Orientalist truisms was naïve and even dangerous. Neoconservatives sought to refocus American fears on the Soviet Union to revive the imagined political and moral clarity of the anticommunist and militaristic 1950s. To this end, the second CPD argued that Soviet overtures for détente and arms reduction were in fact strategic deceptions. They claimed that by focusing on the Soviets' "capabilities rather than his intentions, his weapons rather than his ideas, motives, and aspirations," even the CIA vastly underestimated the Soviet threat to America (qtd. in Cahn 163). CPD Sovietologist Richard Pipes argued that the American tendency to "mirror image" blinded analysts and the public from realizing that the Soviet "totalitarian mindset" was not "guided merely by self-serving motives," but instead dedicated to world domination by any means (6–7). Such rhetoric suggested that American obliviousness to the fundamental *difference* of their Eastern foes left the United States vulnerable to a surprise attack.

The second CPD's remade Cold War sought to not only rollback Soviet communism but also challenge the various "countercultures" that emerged in response to the Vietnam War. The CPD argued that it was not flawed techno-Orientalist policies that left sixty thousand American soldiers and one-fifth of the Vietnamese population dead with no strategic gain, but a fundamental weakness in American resolve. To this end the second CPD celebrated emerging presidential contender (and former CPD member) Ronald Reagan's campaign pledge to "rearm America." Reagan and the CPD relentlessly criticized President Jimmy Carter's embrace of détente and arms reduction as epitomizing the dangerous malaise at the heart of the "Vietnam Syndrome," and handily won the presidency in 1980. Once president, Reagan installed nearly fifty fellow CPD members into the White House. Reagan appointed Pipes to a staff position on the National Security Council where he argued that revolutionaries from Northern Ireland, Iran, Palestine, and across Africa and Latin America were not the products of local conflicts exacerbated by American and Soviet intervention but were instead all agents of a global conspiracy directed by Moscow. The renewed embrace of proxy wars and nuclear buildup that followed led to some of Reagan's lowest approval ratings, but CPD-allied advisors encouraged Reagan to whip up excitement for a renewed Cold War (Sanders 277–342). To do so, Reagan delved even further into policies rooted in techno-Orientalist fantasy.

Reagan's background as an actor and anticommunist crusader gave his administration a perceptive sensitivity to narrative that allowed him to revive the oppositional civilizational logic of Orientalism and the redeeming promise of military technology (Rogin). Speaking at Disney World's future-oriented EPCOT theme park on March 8, 1983, the president stated, "[W]atch a

12-year-old take evasive action and score multiple hits while playing 'Space Invaders,' and you will appreciate the skills of tomorrow's pilot." That night, Reagan sought to paint the arms race as a moral act in an address to the National Association of Evangelicals. The president asserted that the world was divided between good and evil and that American disarmament would abandon Christianity to the threat of communism and reward "the aggressive impulses of an evil empire." Two weeks later Reagan sought to make the revived prospect of nuclear war less terrifying by announcing on television, and without consulting the Defense Department, a billion-dollar Strategic Defense Initiative (SDI) to build a computerized shield to protect Americans from Soviet missiles that might be launched in response to Reagan's renewal of the arms race. The fantastic technology of the SDI would allow the United States to assert global military dominance without risking nuclear annihilation. Most analysts and academics considered SDI (or "Star Wars" as it was termed in the media) scientifically impossible. Many commentators noted that Reagan's SDI proposals were eerily similar to the plot of one of the president's earliest films, *Murder in the Air* (1940), about a weapon that "not only makes the United States invincible in war, but in so doing promises to be the greatest force for world peace ever discovered" (Boyer 205). But this did not stop the administration from opening nearly unlimited funding channels for developing the proposed military technology.

The resonance between the 1984 *Red Dawn*, released during Reagan's reelection campaign, and this remade techno-Orientalist militarism should not surprise us. Reagan's first secretary of state, Alexander Haig, produced the film. In 1982 Haig retired to the Board of Directors at MGM Studios, which had long ties to the military and anticommunism, and *Red Dawn* was his first project. He was also no stranger to fiction. Haig had served as Nixon's chief of staff during the Watergate crisis, and as secretary of state he sought to convince Congress and the American people that Nicaragua was a staging ground for a Soviet assault on U.S. territory. According to MGM vice president Peter Bart, the studio and Haig sought to make a "jingoistic" film following the success of *Rambo: First Blood* (1982)—the irony of course being that John Rambo, a disaffected Native American veteran trained in guerrilla tactics, fights U.S. authorities who betrayed him, not agents of the "Evil Empire."

The exaggerated camp violence of the first *Red Dawn* (prompting the MPAA's first PG-13 rating) hypnotically lulls the viewer into accepting the film's central fantasy that patriotic carnage can regenerate the moral clarity and manly resolve necessary to protect America. The film opens with a montage of classic small town American vistas before pausing at a statue of a "Rough Rider" on the Colorado town green. The inscription on the pedestal reads, "[B]etter to win or lose than be mediocre or timid," attributed (inaccurately) to Theodore Roosevelt. At the local high school a teacher lectures about the Mongol invasions of Europe in the eighth century as Soviet paratroopers land in the background. Such framing immediately prepares the audience for a battle between East and West—a battle this opening sequence suggests would not have been necessary if the United States hadn't forgotten its imperial roots and the perpetual threat from Asian hordes.

Despite the seemingly patriotic overtone of *Red Dawn*, the film provocatively reverses the historical allusions it exploits. In their resistance to the invading Soviets, the Wolverines symbolically transform into Indians. Jed leads his friends into the Arapaho National Forest where he claims the Blackfeet launched their last stand against his white pioneer ancestors. There the Wolverines learn to hunt and live in the woods undetected, ritualistically drink the blood of deer to symbolize their brotherhood, and even ambush unsuspecting Soviet wagon trains from the camouflaged cliffs above. *Red Dawn* writes this vexed identification with Indians onto the geopolitics of the late Cold War. When the Wolverines find a soldier from Free America, the soldier places their local struggle in a global context: "I've seen this before in Nicaragua, El Salvador, Angola . . . it's the same as Afghanistan." The visual logic of the Wolverines scrambling across rock faces away from Soviet airships like their Afghani freedom-fighter brethren helps reimagine the U.S.-backed insurrections in Nicaragua, El Salvador, and Angola as part of a heroic indigenous defense strategy against aggressive and unjust communist "invasions"—it brings the war home.

However, the invading forces in the 1984 *Red Dawn*, while purportedly Soviet, seem eerily American—for after all if the Wolverines are Indians, the Soviets are cowboys. The opening paratrooper sequence reinforces this view by replicating the real images of the U.S. paratrooper invasion of Grenada just a year before *Red Dawn*'s release. The Soviet invasion depicted in *Red Dawn*, with its overwhelming force and minimal local resistance, mirrors Operation Urgent Fury (the official name of the Grenada invasion) far more than a Manichean showdown between the two largest militaries on earth. The Wolverine's embrace of low-tech guerrilla tactics suggests that they, like Rambo, are justly defending their land from invading American troops. Like Rambo, they have become the Viet Cong.

These ideologically rich masochistic fantasies reveal *Red Dawn* as both a weapon in and (perhaps unconscious) analysis of America's war against itself. Like Reagan's policies more generally, the film relishes in rolling back a decadent and fracturing culture into a more normative, patriotic, and simpler time. Through the fence of a reeducation camp, Jed's father appeals to the soon-to-be Wolverines, "I was tough on you, and I did things that made you hate me, but you understand now, don't you?" In Reagan's America, the stagnating economy and "Evil Empire" justified shock therapies of financial deregulation and the slashing of social programs alongside the largest military buildup in human history. These policies sought to toughen up America at the cultural level and punish those who abandoned the moral clarity of the early Cold War.

While *Red Dawn* was not an immediate financial success, it has grown in popularity over the years (the *National Review* named *Red Dawn* the fifteenth "best conservative film" in 2009) in part because the Reagan administration launched a public relations campaign with enough influence to redraw the contours of American politics. Neoconservatives deftly used the cultural fallout surrounding the failure of the Cold War techno-Orientalist vision to reanimate support for regenerative war. However, this project has been haunted by the ambivalence it exploits. In the 1984 *Red Dawn* a Soviet commander cautions his Cuban protégé not to make the same mistake the United States did in Vietnam by trying to win the "hearts and minds" of locals instead of employing brute force. This reference suggests that the U.S. failure in Vietnam was due to the soft touch of effete occupiers, not the inability of technological brutality to engender popular support, but it also equates those immune to the "Vietnam Syndrome" with agents of the "Evil Empire." In 1985, as Reagan waited for word about negotiations to free thirty-nine American hostages held by Hezbollah in Lebanon, his press secretary made clear the president was watching the new *Rambo: First Blood Part II*. In that popular sequel the army allows Rambo out of prison in order to return to Vietnam and rescue prisoners of war left behind there. Rambo's only question is, "Do we get to win this time?" They respond, "Sir, that's up to you." Reagan similarly sought to let America's military might out of its cage. The next morning at the press conference announcing the hostages' release, Reagan joked, "Boy, I saw Rambo last night. Now, I know what to do next time this happens" (qtd. in Jeffords 28). Embracing the film in this way suggested it was Rambo's domestic jailers, not foreign enemies, who held Americans prisoners of war. While Rambo proved America could "win this time," the Vietnamese guards he killed were proxies for his U.S. government captors.

This ambivalent pop militarism helped solidify the emerging POW/MIA movement, which Reagan had supported in his campaign against Carter. While by the mid-1980s the Vietnamese government insisted there were no POWs and none have surfaced since, such political theater mobilized a generation of Americans to express their fury about the "Vietnam Syndrome" at an annual Memorial Day motorcycle parade founded in 1988 under the name Rolling Thunder. This name is a play on Operation Rolling Thunder, the massive U.S. campaign that dropped three-quarters of a million tons of explosives on Vietnam from 1965 to 1968 with an estimated eight to one civilian to combatant kill ratio (Franklin, *Vietnam and Other American Fantasies* 173–202). Such naming suggests enraged patriots can commemorate apocryphal American prisoners of war by bombarding the America that betrayed them just like that America bombed the innocent Vietnamese civilians. This is the domestic corollary to the unnamed U.S. Army major's famous quote about his assault on Ben Tre in Vietnam: "It became necessary to destroy the town to save it" ("Major Describes Moves"). Rey Chow has argued that the Cold War promoted a culture of "targeting" and destruction as proper responses to vexing problems. When neoconservatives sought to rehabilitate techno-Orientalist militarism, they depicted America as its own worst enemy. Tragically, Timothy McVeigh embraced an extreme version of this when he tried to try to save America from itself by bombing federal employees in Oklahoma City in 1994. McVeigh claimed *Red Dawn* was his favorite film (Bart).

The defense of techno-Orientalist militarism has become literally hardwired into American political institutions. The cultivated need for enemies for Americans to define themselves against was complicated when the supposedly intractable Soviet Union crumbled under its own weight to everyone's surprise in 1991. Think tanks such as the Center for Security Policy, founded by Reagan's former Deputy Assistant Secretary of Defense (and CPD member) Frank Gaffney in 1988, and the Middle East Forum, founded in 1990 by Pipes's son Daniel Pipes, scrambled to find new spectral enemies endangering the world's largest military in order to maintain their political influence. These think tanks repurposed and remade security discourse rooted in the idea of an intractable civilizational clash between the West and communism into one between the West and the rest—simply recasting new actors into the well-established roles of American strategic drama (Little 226–266). The neoconservative Project for a New American Century (PNAC) outlined the necessity for a more aggressive stance against China and Iraq under the title *Present Dangers*, edited by Robert Kagan and William Kristol (vii) in its bid to revive a "Reaganite policy of military strength and moral clarity." When PNAC-supported George W. Bush assumed the presidency later that year, his advisors (including former CPD member Paul Wolfowitz) immediately began strategizing about how to scare the American people and Congress into another round of war against intractable Oriental enemies. However, even the pursuit of this techno-Orientalist fantasy betrayed its own ambivalence. The U.S. military named the December 2003 hunt for deposed Iraqi leader (and former U.S. ally) Saddam Hussein "Operation Red Dawn," and code named his two suspected hiding places "Wolverine 1" and "Wolverine 2"—as if to suggest that the United States was the overpowering evil occupying force in "Indian country," and Hussein an Iraqi hiding in the hills to lead a patriotic resistance (Sirota 139–169). Nonetheless, as Americans increasingly equated the mounting failures in Iraq to the failures in Vietnam three decades before, hawkish politicians sought to remake and refocus the war's goals by founding a short-lived third CPD in 2004 dedicated to channeling American fears of government manipulation toward the threat radical Islamic terrorists pose to the safety of the world (Barry).

The rise of first-person shooter video games such as *Homefront* (now one of the most popular genres of game, even if *Homefront* itself was not a huge financial success) stems directly from this relaunching of techno-Orientalist militarism. Reagan's SDI reinitiated collaboration between the military and commercial computer research, which had ceased following the Vietnam War (Edwards 275–319). In 1999, the Department of Defense founded the Institute for Creative Technologies at the University of Southern California to bring the academy, Hollywood, and military together to create the next generation of military video games—including 1984 *Red Dawn* writer/director John Milius, who also wrote the story line for *Homefront* (McNary). Pandemic Studios collaborated with the ICT to build a hugely expensive officer training simulator titled *Full Spectrum Command*. At the same time, West Point and the Naval Academy began developing a digital training program later turned into the *America's Army* video game made available for free at recruitment events and online. To promote this game the military staged a mock "invasion" of a gaming convention in Los Angeles, two months after the U.S. invasion of Iraq. And if such stunts weren't evidence enough of an unconscious recognition of the nefarious invasion of military needs into civilian life, the joint Army-Navy project that created *America's Army* was named Operation Star Fighter, a reference to the 1984 film *The Last Starfighter* in which aliens use arcade games to recruit gifted teenagers to fly their warcraft (Halter 176–236).

Military-produced video games do not portray specific enemies, but their commercial offshoots do (Allen). Destineer Studios released *Close Combat: First to Fight* (2005), where U.S. Marines invade Beirut to root out Iranian and Syrian terrorists using a simulation platform they had developed for the Marines. Pandemic Studios released a commercial version of *Full Spectrum Command* as *Full Spectrum Warrior* (2004) with a regime-change story line set in fictional Zekistan—where U.S. army officers hunt Taliban and al-Qaeda terrorists driven out of Afghanistan and Iraq (Höglund; Halter 230–233). The studio then used the government-funded platform to release telling sequels: *Mercenaries: Playground of Destruction* (2005), set during a police action in North Korea and immediately banned in South Korea, as was *Homefront* (Brooke; Gaudiosi); and *Mercenaries 2: World in Flames* (2006), where the United States invades Venezuela, prompting the legislature there to ban all "violent" video games (Toothaker, "Venezuela to Outlaw"). These games were all distributed by THQ, which hired actors playing North Korean troops to promote *Homefront* by invading the same gaming convention the real U.S. Army did seven years prior (de Matos).

Milius's *Homefront* represents the culmination of this sort of genre, its website stating, "Join the Resistance, stand united and fight for freedom against an overwhelming military force . . . set in a terrifyingly plausible near-future world." While I focus more on *Homefront*'s premise than its game play, the player's experience is important and suggestive. Following the optional backstory film referenced in the opening paragraph, players are born into the game with the ability to move freely about the virtual environment, until North Koreans barge in and arrest them. Unable to move, the player is forced to watch the daily sufferings of a Korean-occupied suburb which includes American children themselves forced to watch their parents' executions. When resistance fighters attack the prison bus players are trapped in, they grant players re-birth into the freedom of movement. In the first gun fight that follows, in a bombed-out White Castle restaurant, players must fight for freedom having already experienced the meaning of bondage within the game itself. Game reviewer Stephen Totilo felt the unique emotional impact of these features, stating, "For the first time in a war game, I wanted to make the bad guys pay" ("A Video Game That Dares").

But again, just who are the "bad guys" players want to make pay? In *Homefront*, the North Koreans have irradiated the Mississippi, dividing the United States into West and East, in an eerie play on the division of Korea in 1952. Like the real Americans in Vietnam, the fake Koreans in the game have concentrated Americans into horrible camps supposedly for their own protection. American players are reborn into the role of occupied Vietnamese or Iraqis launching a low-tech moral war against a techno-dominant evil foe. The enemy invaders, while purportedly Korean, are in effect the blowback of a half century of U.S. foreign policy. In this way *Homefront* betrays a pervasive but often repressed anger about the role of war in American society.

Far from illustrating that America "kicked the Vietnam Syndrome" (a claim made by CPD ally President George H. W. Bush after the first Gulf War), *Homefront* suggests another syndrome that might animate some of the current interest in this sort of virtual warplay. Psychologist Chaim Shatan first diagnosed "post-Vietnam syndrome" in the early 1970s, which was later renamed post-traumatic stress disorder. Shatan went on to argue that young military recruits in boot camp, mercilessly hazed by officers against whom they had no recourse and whom they were led to idolize, brutally redirected their suppressed homicidal anger and outrage either against themselves through drug use or against real or imagined Vietnamese enemies. Cultural critics have suggested that releasing such violence within the safe space of a video game can actually help players gain control of their own aggression and fears (Power). The sheer volume and popularity of military games suggest the pervasive desire to play through America's traumatic war-making past, present, and possible future. Kuma Games has produced numerous titles where players can inhabit real soldiers in real scenarios, ranging from Vietnam to the 1980 failed rescue of American hostages in Iran to the 2004 U.S. assault on Fallujah (Stahl). These games are popular with the enlisted and therapists have even used *Full Spectrum Command* to help traumatized veterans gain control of their war experiences by reliving them in a virtual environment (Halpern). Before the team who developed *Homefront* joined THQ, they worked on award-winning games depicting battles from World War II and the First Gulf War under the banner of Trauma Studios (Alexander).

Like *Homefront*, the popular *Call of Duty* gaming franchise also helps players transpose themselves into the victims, rather than the perpetrators, of techno-Orientalist trickery, and lets them unleash untempered aggression on their screen enemies. *Call of Duty: Modern Warfare* echoes the 2012 *Red Dawn*'s ambivalent celebration of war. In the game, players inhabit U.S. troops invading a fantasy Middle Eastern country to suppress a Russian-backed revolution there. However, the game reveals the revolution is a trap. Islamic rebels detonate a nuclear bomb in their own city in order to kill thirty thousand U.S. Marines—which is in fact the opening salvo of a Russian invasion of the United States. The chapter of this video game sequence is titled "Shock and Awe," the U.S. military's name for the strategy of rapid dominance through spectacular destruction used to open Operation Iraqi Freedom. While players of *Modern Warfare* get to enjoy shooting and bombing America's enemies, such enjoyment is enhanced by the "Shock and Awe" over the Russian plot to make the United States a suicidal victim of its own violent aggression. In the 2012 *Red Dawn*, the Wolverines sit around a campfire discussing what they miss from before the North Korean invasion. One yells "playing *Call of Duty*," to which another retorts, "but we're living it!" The characters in *Red Dawn* 2012 have become American Viet Cong and Iraqi guerrillas because of America's overreliance on the promise of aggressive techno-superiority. In the video game they are living they get to fight for their freedom against the failures of techno-Orientalist militarism to protect them, but also against the insistent invasion of techno-Orientalist fear mongering into their lives. These characters might not be entirely conscious of it, but they enjoy the relief that comes with finally fighting at home, where the war is.

Part II
Reappropriations and Recuperations

Chapter 10
Thinking about Bodies, Souls, and Race in Gibson's Bridge Trilogy

JULIE HA TRAN

At first glance, William Gibson's Bridge trilogy of *Virtual Light*, *Idoru*, and *All Tomorrow's Parties* seems to employ the typical stereotypes about Asians and race that the genre of cyberpunk has often been criticized for. Gibson's trilogy features Tokyo or other Japanese cities as dystopic future worlds that are exotic, enticing, and cognitively estranging, as well as eccentric Japanese characters alien in their foreignness, and thus irrefutably Other. These rather techno-Orientalist details resound strongly with literary critiques of Gibson's work, which position the cyberpunk texts as reductive renderings of Asian subjects and virtual technology. For instance, writing about Gibson's earlier Sprawl trilogy (*Neuromancer*, *Count Zero*, *Mona Lisa Overdrive*), Wendy Hui Kyong Chun accuses Gibson of high-tech Orientalism, which she describes as "[that which] seeks to orient the reader to a technology-overloaded present/future (which is portrayed as belonging to Japan or other Far East Countries) through the promise of readable difference, and through the conflation of information networks with an exotic urban landscape" (*Control and Freedom* 177). She goes on to explain that "[t]he Japanese Orient is a privileged example of the virtual. It orients the reader/viewer, enabling him or her to envision the world as data. This twinning sustains—barely—the dream of self-erasure and pure subjectivity. Most simply, others must be reduced to information in order for the console cowboy to emerge and penetrate" (Chun, *Control and Freedom* 195). In Chun's reading of the cyberpunk author, she argues that Gibson's texts present the techno-Orientalist gaze of a Western author imagining the East. Greta Niu defines techno-Orientalist figurations more broadly as those that force us to question and examine critically the relationships among Asian subject, virtual technology, and desire. Given this definition, we might imagine new types of critical analysis positing something more than the unidirectional techno-Orientalist gaze of the West upon the East. Japanese literary critic Takayuki Tatsumi, for instance, envisions the transactions between Japan and the United States as more akin to a "revolutionary paradigm (gear) shift mechanism," which "replaces the outmoded 'o(rientalist)/o(ccidentalist)' paradigm" (*Full Metal Apache* xiv). In Tatsumi's formulation, techno-Orientalist constructions—about Asian people and Asian places and their relationships to technology, digital media, the future, and so forth—traverse back and forth across the Pacific, much like the shifting mechanism of a manual car. One clear example that Tatsumi offers of this "paradigm shift" is that of the American cyberpunks and the Japanese reaction to such literature: "Anglo-American writers, through their own logic of mimicry, imitated and reappropriated 'Japanesque' images, that is images that at once draw on and distort Japanese culture. At the same time their Japanese counterparts came to realize that writing subversive fiction in the wake of cyberpunk meant gaining insight into the radically science-fictional 'Japan'" (xv). In Tatsumi's example, Japanese authors find in the U.S. cyberpunks' techno-Orientalist visions of future Japan a literary representation of present-day Japan that is strangely accurate. For the Japanese authors, these Americans' distorted mimicries capture confusing postmodern Japan better than literary realism, which results in mutual borrowings and mimicries from both sides.

Building upon Tatsumi's model of transcultural interaction, I argue that Gibson's Bridge trilogy both explicitly highlights traditional techno-Orientalist discourse and complicates it. The texts fall in line with traditional techno-Orientalist figurations via their exoticized representations of both Asian subjects and spaces. At the same time, these representations are complicated in the trilogy by the increasingly permeable boundaries between (1) virtual space and material space and (2) interiority and exteriority. My reading disrupts the representations of racial embodiment that are dependent on the aforementioned binarisms, and Asian persons and spaces as passive and thus penetrable objects for Western subjects. While Gibson's earlier work displays a strongly Western-centric rendering of Asian subjects and virtual technology, his subsequent Bridge trilogy reveals a more sophisticated techno-Orientalist construction in which Western and Asian portraitures cross-pollinate, ultimately undermining the racial and ethnic hierarchies implicit in traditional techno-Orientalist readings of Gibson's work.

The Virtual and the Orient

William Gibson's first novel, *Neuromancer*—a landmark text for cyberpunk and the winner of both Nebula and Hugo Awards—opens in Chiba City, an urban landscape filled with coffin hotels, Yakuza, and street samurai. Japan serves as little more than an exotic backdrop for this narrative about cyber cowboys, cyborg assassins, and sentient machines. Gibson's second trilogy—consisting of the novels *Virtual Light, Idoru,* and *All Tomorrow's Parties*—seems very similar to his Sprawl trilogy at first glance and might appear to merit the techno-Orientalist criticisms leveled at Gibson's earlier work. Colin Laney, the protagonist of *Idoru* and *All Tomorrow's Parties*, is the stand-in for *Neuromancer*'s console cowboy Case: both are white males skilled in computer hacking. Both prefer spending time in the virtual realm and neglect their physical bodies. All three novels in the trilogy either have Tokyo as a prominent futuristic urban backdrop and/or minor Japanese characters displaying eccentric social behavior. While these texts could ostensibly be read as examples of techno-Orientalism, I argue that something different occurs in them: representations of otherness in the text resemble techno-Orientalism on the surface but ultimately prove to be disruptive of such stereotypes.

Asian markers and characters proliferate in Gibson's trilogy. For instance, Lucky Dragon is a chain convenience store which links exotic ideas of Asianness ("the smiling Lucky Dragon [logo] [was] blowing smoke from its nostrils" [*Idoru* 135]) with the dull and unimaginative multinational corporation: rigid binders of rules and protocols, lack of empathy or concern for customers or employees. Mr. Park, the manager of the Los Angeles Lucky Dragon in *All Tomorrow's Parties*, is a caricature of the foreign Asian Other—unfeeling, profit-driven, broken English. From these two examples, it would seem that larger anxieties about globalization and cultural homogenization become aligned with the exotic and foreign Orient. Paradoxically, the alien Asian becomes associated not just with the dizzily changing world order, but with archaic and dying rituals of the past. Present in all three books is Yamazaki, the Japanese "student of existential sociology," who "record[s] ephemera of popular culture" (Gibson, *Idoru* 6, 9)—in other words, a passive observer of the external world rather than an actor with agency like the console cowboy hero. In a dramatic fight scene in a nightclub, Yamazaki is shown carefully safety-pinning the ripped sleeve of his coat back in place, suggesting an absurd and impractical need to preserve external appearances in the midst of real physical danger. While most of the Western characters are preoccupied with realistic and pressing concerns, the eccentric Japanese character is concerned only about saving face. His rigidity and conformity to stale cultural customs make him seem out of place in the quick-moving, digitally mediated world of Gibson's books.

Among the instances of techno-Orientalism in Gibson's texts, there is one salient example from *All Tomorrow's Parties* that largely complicates the assumed relationship between the Asian subject and the advanced technological future:[1] Cardboard City, a slum in a Japanese railway station consisting of cardboard carton homes pushed together. The novel opens with the following scene in the railway station: "Through this evening's tide of faces unregistered, unrecognized, amid hurrying black shoes, furled umbrellas, the crowd descending like a single organism into the station's airless heart. . . . [D]erelict shipping cartons huddle in a ragged train, improvised shelters constructed by the city's homeless" (*All Tomorrow's Parties* 1). This passage is reminiscent of Ezra Pound's "In a Station of the Metro," a short poem based on the Japanese haiku form that reads, "The apparition of these faces in the crowd; / Petals on a wet, black bough." Pound's modernist work and its anxieties about urbanism are echoed in Gibson's passage with its deindividuated and faceless Japanese crowd, seemingly dehumanized (like Pound's "apparition[s]"), but at the same time, this city scene is likened to natural tropes like "single organism" and the description of the railway station possessing a "heart." This mixing of urbanism with the organic again recalls Pound's combining of the city metro and "Petals on a wet, black bough" in the same sentence, the turn between artificial and natural resting upon a single semicolon. This pattern of relating the man-made to the organic continues when we are informed that this "labyrinth of cardboard" (2) has sprung up organically—"improvised"—it is an artificial human habitat that is simultaneously natural. Its material is likewise more organic than conventional architectural urban structures of steel or concrete. Blurring the boundaries between artificial and natural in this passage about the Japanese subway station serves to denaturalize the association that is often made between Asians and urban futures hypersaturated with advanced technology and efficiency. As if in further testimony to this point, within one of the cardboard residences, an old man in traditional Japanese garb works painstakingly on a toy model figurine, a "robot or military exoskeleton" (3). In his anachronistic garment, the old man is a cultural stereotype, the antiquated Asian artist armed with his set of sharp tools and slender paint brushes. At the same time, this character, an artisan who emphasizes skill and craft, disrupts other techno-Orientalist representations disseminated in Gibson's postnational world of franchises and mass-produced items, such as the corporate Lucky Dragon, or techno-Orientalist narratives about technology represented by the "robot or military exoskeleton" in the old man's hands. Last, the old man lives adjacent to the American data analyst Colin Laney, which invites a comparison between the Asian subject who can adapt and survive in a world of shifting technologies and global information, and the white console cowboy who, by this point in the trilogy, has sickened and deteriorated physically, spending all of his hours in the virtual realm, while his physical body rots (and eventually dies) in a cardboard box.

Laney's death could be interpreted as the typical cyberpunk trope of privileging the virtual realm over the "meat" or flesh of the body, but this reading overlooks the significant relationship constructed here between cyberspace and real urban locations. As Thomas Foster points out in his literary analysis of *Neuromancer*, critics who laud cyberpunk urban landscapes as sites of creativity and freedom often neglect "the ideological and often specifically racist subtext that informs the language of urban 'ruin,' 'decay,' or 'blight,' language more often used to describe racialized 'inner-city' ghettoes than cities in general" (206). The fact that Laney can deliberately choose to live in Cardboard City reflects his position of privilege: he takes for granted and overlooks the social conditions of its actual inhabitants, the Japanese slum dwellers. He can escape embodiment and his material surroundings by accessing cyberspace. Such details align with Foster's assertion that the console cowboy uses locales of urban decay as his creative playgrounds. At the same time, however, it is important to note that Laney's decision to reside alongside the other Japanese slum dwellers is a cosmopolitan way of living in proximity to difference. This, in addition to the organic quality of the slum and the traditional artisan inhabitant, is a means of rewriting and denaturalizing racial stereotypes about which groups tend to live in urban slums.

Another eccentric Japanese character in Gibson's trilogy is *Idoru*'s Masahiko, one of the denizens of the virtual Walled City. Masahiko is clearly a stereotype or stock character representing the technologically brilliant *otaku*. Similar to white male console cowboy protagonists like Case or Colin Laney, Masahiko spends much of his waking time (and his dreams, we are told) in the virtual realm: as a result, his physical appearance is characteristically sloppy and his culinary tastes are unhealthy: at first mistaken by another character "to be an older girl, side-parted hair falling past her shoulders," he wears "old gray sweatpants bagging at the knees. Grubby-looking white paper slippers" (128). His hair is "long and glossy and smoothly brushed, but . . . there was a bit of noodle caught in it, the thin kinky kind that came in instant ramen bowls" (129). His room smells "of boy, of ramen, of coffee." It could be argued that Masahiko might be read as yet another Western version of a technophilic stereotype of the Orient. Indeed, his character is rather flat and lacks the depth of some of the more central characters. This flatness and the techno-otaku stereotype that is Masahiko, however, is no simple unidirectional techno-Orientalism on Gibson's part. The techno-otaku is actually a common stock character in many popular Japanese mangas, animes, and films.[2] In fact, Masahiko is an amalgamation of multiple stock characters from Japanese popular culture: in addition to being a techno-otaku, he is the aloof older brother, the slovenly or lazy genius, the *bishōnen* (or male who is beautiful enough to be mistaken for a female character). In such a case, Japanese popular culture has directed a lens of techno-Orientalism at itself in creating these stock character tropes, and Gibson in creating Masahiko (and Yamazaki and Mr. Park) has translated these tropes into American science fiction. Gibson's mimicry of Japan's mimicry of the Western techno-Orientalist gaze destabilizes the notion that the East is the passive object of the West's gaze; here the gaze traverses dynamically in both directions, a dialectic that forces the reader to critically examine such cultural stereotypes. I interpret Gibson's self-conscious translation of such stock types as one of the beneficial and multicultural outcomes of the very global digital technologies that Gibson is writing about. As Takayuki Tatsumi has pointed out, the act of translation itself is "made possible by the effect of the cyberpunklike development of a global communication system—a system that endorses the synchronic nature of cyberpunk" (107). Rather than merely settling on the initial idea that the West is only objectifying the East, this sychronicity that Tatsumi speaks of allows us to ask these questions: How does the same cultural stereotype of the otaku emerge on both sides of the Pacific? How does this figure change during its transcultural crossing and become reappropriated?

Incorporeality, Virtuality, and Race

In the 1990s both popular culture and academic theorists promised freedom from the constraints of race, gender, sexual preference, and class via the Internet. This optimism was short-lived: in the twenty-first century, we know that bodies matter and that narratives about virtual disembodiment or equality often depend upon the very racial or gendered stereotypes that they purport to be eradicating.[3] Technoculture studies scholar Lisa Nakamura sets up a key question about race and the Internet: "Can the Internet propagate genuinely new and nonracist (and nonsexist and nonclassist) ways of being," or is "online discourse ... woven of stereotypical cultural narratives that reinstall [the] conditions of gender, race, and class as conditions of social interaction?" (*Digitizing Race* xii). Gibson's Bridge trilogy investigates this very problem, ultimately demonstrating that discourses of race, gender, and class are reliant on the binary opposition between physical and virtual, as well as interiority and exteriority. Gibson destabilizes these easy binary distinctions through the creation of an alternative space, Walled City, and a character, Rei Toei, who is both real and virtual.

In the future universe of Gibson's trilogy, the Internet has become as highly regulated and policed as actual physical spaces. In reaction to this, radicals create a digital city located outside of the restrictions of the mainstream Internet: Walled City has "no laws ... just agreements," and therefore houses an eclectic population who have founded a new space outside of, and resistant to, the dominant digital culture (*Idoru* 209). As Masahiko puts it, it is "of the Net, but not on it." Gibson's "Walled City" much resembles the "City of Bits" described by the late William J. Mitchell, who was dean of the school of architecture at MIT and a prescient urban and media theorist: "This will be a city unrooted to any definite spot on the surface of the earth, shaped by connectivity and bandwidth constraints rather than by accessibility and land values, largely asynchronous in its operation, and inhabited by disembodied and fragmented subjects who exist as collections of aliases and agents. Its places will be constructed virtually by software instead of physically from stones and timbers, and they will be connected by logical linkages rather than by doors, passageways, and streets" (William J. Mitchell 24).[4] The emphasis on virtual "logical linkages" over physical barriers like "doors and passageways" suggests that the virtual city does not share the same social inequities that are represented by the architectural enclosures of material cities, meant to keep locals in and invaders out. At the same time, it would be inaccurate to maintain that Gibson's Walled City is "unrooted to any definite spot . . . on earth" because we learn that Walled City is a reproduction of the real city of Kowloon (also known as Kowloon Walled City). A largely ungoverned settlement in Hong Kong, when it was a British colony, Kowloon functioned as an autonomous zone that had been without laws or police because of a mistake in the possession agreement with China. As described in Gibson's novel *Idoru*, it was a tiny space but extremely densely populated, which housed "drugs and whores and gambling. But people living, too. Factories, restaurants. A city. No laws" (221).

Gibson's allusion to the historical Kowloon Walled City goes beyond merely exoticizing the city for its criminality and otherness. Rather, I argue that the historical allusion grounds Gibson's virtual Walled City in real, inhabited space, thus disrupting the taken for granted binary between digital and physical spaces. This linking together of virtual and material space continues in the first lengthy description of the city:

> Something at the core of things moved simultaneously in mutually impossible directions. It wasn't even like porting. Software conflict? Faint impression of light through a fluttering of rags. And then the thing before her: building or biomass or cliff face looming there, in countless unplanned strata, nothing about it even or regular. Accreted patchwork of shallow random balconies, thousands of small windows throwing back blank silver rectangles of fog. Stretching to the periphery of vision, and on the high, uneven crest of that ragged façade, a black fur of twisted pipe, antennas sagging under vine growth of cable. And past this scribbled border a sky where colors crawled like gasoline on water. Hak Nam . . . City of Darkness. Between the walls of the world. (*Idoru* 195)

Most salient in this passage about Gibson's Walled City are the architectural structures that abound—buildings, balconies, windows, and façades. Even though these appear as man-made structures, Gibson weaves natural or organic imagery into their descriptions: Chia, the young protagonist of Gibson's second text of the trilogy, can't tell if what she first sees is a "building" or "cliff face," windows become "silver rectangles of fog," pipes are described as "black fur," cables are dense as "vine growth," and the sky is a combination of gasoline and water. Similarly, diction such as "countless unplanned strata, nothing about it even or regular," "accreted patchwork," "uneven crest of that ragged façade," and "scribbled border" repeat the notion of improvisation over orderliness. This blurring of boundaries between natural and artificial, material and virtual is what composes this ideal city of Gibson's. It is a different virtual experience from the cyberspace of *Neuromancer*, with its abstract, jewel-colored geometric forms and its clean dualism of "meat" and virtuality. Bodies and the spaces they inhabit—Laney's deteriorating body in Cardboard City; Zona's disabled, brown body in Mexico; Masahiko's unconscious body sprawled in a love hotel in Tokyo—simply can't be obscured under the Internet's optimistic rhetoric of universal freedom and the disappearance of space and distance. The ideal city must combine the material and the virtual; it must use the new digital order to restructure and reconfigure our inhabited spaces.

There is a long philosophical tradition of theorizing the virtual in a way that suggests that the virtual is consistently tied to the real. I will briefly survey some of the dominant critical approaches here, before turning specifically to Brian Massumi's theoretical model that links new modes of bodily sensation to virtual experience—of particular importance to our discussion of digital technologies, race, and embodiment. In *Matter and Memory*, Henri Bergson aligns the virtual with memories and dreams: "Whenever we are trying to recover a recollection, to call up some period of our history, we become conscious of an act *sui generis* by which we detach ourselves from the present in order to replace ourselves, first, in the past in general, then in a certain region of the past—a *work of adjustment, something like the focusing of a camera*. But our recollection still remains virtual" (143). For Bergson, the virtual (dreams, memories, imaginations, pure qualities) is real insofar as it has an effect on us; in other words, the virtual insists on the real. It is not accidental that Bergson uses the analogy of a technological apparatus—the "focusing of a camera"—to ground his notion of the virtual in material reality. Building on Bergson's ideas, Gilles Deleuze writes that both the actual and the virtual are real, but not everything that is virtual is or becomes actual. Similarly, science philosopher Pierre Levy maintains: "The virtual is that which has potential rather than actual existence. The virtual *tends* toward actualization. . . . The tree is virtually present in the seed" (23).

Political philosopher and social theorist Brian Massumi describes the virtual as being akin to unused, potential energy. As he puts it, "One way of starting to get a grasp on the real-material-but-incorporeal is to say it is to the body, as a positioned thing, as energy is to matter. Energy and matter are mutually convertible modes of the same reality. This would make the incorporeal something like a phase-shift of the body in the usual sense, but not one that comes after it in time. It would be a conversion or unfolding of the body *contemporary* to its every move. Always accompanying. Fellow-traveling dimension of the same reality" (5). Most helpful about Massumi's theory is the manner in which he describes the virtual in relation to the body's sense of affect and sensation. Rather than existing as abstract information, for Massumi, the virtual consists of processes that operate on multiple registers of sensation. He sums this phenomenon up as the "'real but abstract' incorporeality of the body" (21).

Massumi's notion of the virtual sensations of the body finds an illustrative example in Gibson's *Idoru*. Returning again to the passage that details Chia McKenzie's first experience of virtual Walled City, we encounter multiple references to movement and affect in cyberspace: "They were inside now, smoothly accelerating, and the squirming density of the thing was continual visual impact, an optical drumming.... A sharp turn. Another. Then they were ascending a maze of twisting stairwells, still accelerating, and Chia took a deep breath and closed her eyes. Retinal fireworks bursting there, but the pressure was gone" (195–196). The primary sensory quality evident in this passage is that of sight or vision. On the surface, this dominance of vision aligns with our typical experience of interacting with the computer or laptop: viewing a virtual two-dimensional image (or sometimes three-dimensional, as Internet connectivity and bandwidth constraints evolve) on a screen and pointing and clicking simultaneously with one's fingers on an electronic mouse. However, Gibson's depiction of Walled City exceeds these purely physical, bodily sensations. The visual sensation described occurs on another register beyond merely seeing, given the diction of "impact," "drumming," and "fireworks bursting" in conjunction with the eyes. In terms of the tactile, we are informed of Chia's experience of a "squirming density" and "pressure" that appears alien and estranging to our regular body's resistance against gravity. The pressure and density that Chia experiences most likely come in conjunction with the intense speeds at which she is traveling in cyberspace. Gibson's portrayal of her movement in the cyber plane mostly resembles flight, particularly in conjunction with the pressure that Chia describes (g-force, per chance?). The way that Chia is able to navigate her virtual body with sharp turns and accelerations around Walled City's immaterial architecture, its labyrinth of stairwells and buildings, constitutes an affective experience that exceed the regular sensations perceived by the body's sensory organs; Chia's online venture into Walled City can be accurately described only as sensations of Massumi's "real-material-but-incorporeal" body. Chia's navigation of her virtual urban space becomes an experience that augments, supplements, and cross-hatches her material urban inhabited space.

In creating an alternate space that straddles the incorporeal and the material, Gibson is perhaps offering us his vision of "genuinely new and nonracist (and nonsexist and nonclassist) ways of being" (to borrow Nakamura's earlier phrasing). It is a virtual experience that does not negate the physical. Put another way, Thomas Foster reminds us that discourses of race have long been constructed within realms of the virtual and incorporeal, even before the advent of digital technologies. He points out "there is a specific racial history of the expropriability of the 'soul'" (xxiii) and that "white power to represent blackness . . . takes the form of 'miscegenated texts,' in which African-Americans figure as black bodies with white souls, that is, with an interiority comprehensible to white readers" (xxiii). Given this history, we might conclude that discourses of race have been reliant on the binary opposition between incorporeal and material, as well as interiority and exteriority. Gibson's *Idoru*, Rei Toei, proves to be a thought experiment that challenges and disrupts such oppositions.

Gibson's *Idoru*: Cybertype or Multicultural Cyborg?

Rei Toei, the idoru or idol singer of the second text of Gibson's trilogy, is a world-famous pop star, an ideal beauty, an icon of sexual desire, and an artificially created avatar that disrupts the boundary between the completely virtual and the completely real. We are told she is "a personality-construct, a congeries of software agents, the creation of information-designers" (55). Rei is basically an exotic, virtual pinup girl, her immateriality inspiring physical male lust. When she first appears before Rydell—a rent-a-cop who appears in all three books of the trilogy—she is first naked, and then seen wearing clothes identical to his own. The detail of mirroring Rydell's clothing suggests that Rei has no subjectivity of her own, but is only a reflection of Rydell's masculine, Western desire. Her digital perfection creates an unrealistic ideal of beauty, which is most likely Gibson's commentary on media stardom with the fan club that chases Rei and her "lover" Rez in *Idoru*.[5]

Eventually, however, the idoru evolves beyond this simulation of exotic Asian feminine beauty. At the end of *All Tomorrow's Parties*, multiple physical Rei Toeis emerge from nanofax assemblers (a device utilizing nanotechnology to replicate items in various locations) across the world, a far cry from her original form as ephemeral hologram. In a fateful twist of irony, the nanofax assemblers are stationed at Lucky Dragon franchises. The stores, stereotypes of impersonal Asian global commodity culture, and their nanotechnology are subversively reappropriated by Rei. Rather than the goal of virtual disembodiment and "jacking in" to cyberspace that characterized Gibson's earlier Sprawl novels, the idoru achieves the opposite objective of moving away from her original status as digital code toward literal corporeality and physical embodiment. We are told that she becomes "an emergent system, a self continually being iterated from experiential input . . . that river in to which one can never step twice. As she became more herself, through the inputting of experience, through human interaction, she grew and changed" (163). Rei Toei herself comments, "I'm so much more . . . I could go anywhere." Here, while the idoru does not move entirely from being the sexual object of the male gaze (the multiple Reis emerge naked from the assemblers), Rei does appear to emerge as sentient subject, capable of independent thought and mobility. Her nakedness, in contrast to her earlier propensity to reflect others' clothing appearances, may suggest a rebirth of sorts, in which Rei is now a blank slate ready to learn and acclimate to her external environment according to her own choices and will. The multiple Reis, however, also work to destabilize the notion of independent subjectivity and free will: we are left wondering which is the true Rei, or if there never was a true originary Rei in the first place since she was artificially constructed as a virtual, hologram idol.

The idoru shifts from object to subject, along with the resultant potential destabilizing of such subjectivity. As mere software, code, and programmed sexual desire at her inception, Rei Toei literally cements the notion of the Orient as an object devoid of subjectivity. Later, as she emerges naked from every Lucky Dragon nanofax kiosk on earth, the exoticized desire that she inspires has an uneasy and anxious merger with her status as autonomous subject. The bystanders watch her materialize from the assemblers first on television screens (every Lucky Dragon franchise has television displays of video surveillance of other Lucky Dragon franchises, all across the world), and then turn in shock to see Rei, not in the digitally mediated form of the TV screen, but directly before them in the flesh. This part in the narrative has a surprising effect of breaking the fourth wall for the reader of Gibson's text as well: we, like the bystanders outside of the Lucky Dragon, are accessing Rei virtually (albeit in literary form), but the multiple Reis that pop out all over the world suggest that she can turn up anywhere, pushing the reader to not grow too comfortable with passively and pleasurably absorbing Rei and her story.

In challenging assumed notions regarding virtuality/reality, interiority/exteriority, and subjectivity/objectification, Gibson's Bridge trilogy destabilizes certain binary oppositions and preconceptions that consistently undergird techno-Orientalist stereotypes and narratives about Asian peoples and places. His texts demonstrate that techno-Orientalist discourses depend upon these oversimplified and neat binarisms. For instance, Gibson's earlier Sprawl trilogy was contingent upon oppositions between "meat" and cyberspace, while the Bridge trilogy challenges us to think about the slippage and permeable boundaries between the virtual and the real. Such speculation allows for heterotopias like Gibson's Walled City, where new modes of bodily sensation are introduced, and perhaps if we speculate further, new modes of thinking about racial embodiment beyond fantasies of Western penetration of the East. This is not to say that there is a symmetry between Western projections of the East and Eastern imaginings of the West; the West's techno-Orientalist representations of the East are quite powerful and pervasive. While it is important to critique representations of virtual Orientalism, I argue that such critiques are incomplete if they do not move beyond the unidirectional gaze that the West focuses on the East. We can do such work by examining the potential for dynamic crosscurrents or transactions that move in both directions (for instance, the East's projections of the West, or even of itself), and by examining the potential for techno-Orientalist discourse to adapt and disrupt its own stereotypes and representations.

Notes

1. I borrow this formulation—the assumed relationship between the Asian subject and advanced technology—from Greta Niu's definition of techno-Orientalism.
2. One particular character from the highly popular manga and anime *Death Note* (serialized in the Japanese manga magazine *Weekly Shōnen Jump* from December 2003 to May 2006), L, could serve as a virtual doppelgänger for Gibson's Masahiko. Known only as L, the prodigy and brilliant detective mentally duels (and bests) serial killer Light Yagami, all while sitting casually in front of a computer screen, hair disheveled and donning baggy clothes.
3. On the other hand, feminist scholars have long argued the importance of the body. For instance, see Judith Butler's *Gender Trouble*.
4. *City of Bits* (1995) is the first of a trilogy by Mitchell: the ensuing texts are *E-topia* (1999) and *Me++: The Cyborg Self and the Networked City* (2003).
5. One of the delightful twists of Gibson's novel is the ensuing union and marriage between the virtually programmed Rei and Rez, a human pop star and thus himself somewhat of a digital, virtual projection rather than actual human.

Chapter 11

Reimagining Asian Women in Feminist Post-Cyberpunk Science Fiction

KATHRYN ALLAN

Much has been written about cyberpunk's depiction of the gendered, sexualized, and, to a lesser extent, raced body. Wendy Hui Kyong Chun, in "Race and Software," points out the use of "high-tech orientalism" in "foundational cyberpunk previsions, from William Gibson's 1984 *Neuromancer* to Neal Stephenson's 1993 *Snow Crash*, [that] use 'Asian,' 'African,' and 'half-breed' characters to create seductively dystopian near futures" (306). The "high-tech orientalism" of which Chun writes has often been located in female bodies. While the female characters in classic cyberpunk are imbued with high-tech gadgetry—like *Neuromancer*'s Molly's mirror shades and nail blades—they are also "Orientalized," rendered as "meat" and objects of white, Western male desire. Chun argues that, as a way to know and make the Other accessible and open to the user/reader, "high-tech orientalism offers the pleasure of exploring, the pleasure of being somewhat overwhelmed but ultimately 'jacked-in'" (306–307). In this chapter, I take up two feminist revisions of techno-Orientalist cyberpunk tropes (the "pleasure" and real-world consequences of technological exploration) in Tricia Sullivan's *Maul* (first published in 2003) and Larissa Lai's *Salt Fish Girl* (first published in 2002).

Feminist Post-cyberpunk and the Raced Body

Before I discuss *Maul* and *Salt Fish Girl*, it is important to situate these texts in their generic context: cyberpunk and feminist speculative fiction (SF). In *Rewired*, James Patrick Kelly and John Kessel trace the ways in which 1980s cyberpunk has matured into today's post-cyberpunk: "Originally 'the street' in CP [cyberpunk] meant the shadowy world of those who had set themselves against the norms of the dominant culture, hackers, thieves, spies, scam artists, and drug users. But for PCP [post-cyberpunk] writers the street leads to other parts of the world. Their futures have become more diverse, and richer for it. Asians and Africans and Latinos are no longer just sprinkled into stories as supporting characters, as if they are some sort of exotic seasoning. PCP writers attempt to bring them and their unique concerns to the centre of their stories" (xi). Post-cyberpunk retains the original "adversarial relationship to consensus reality" (xii), but opens up the ranks of its characters (and writers) to include all of those who make up the global underclass. Feminist SF, following a similar generic trajectory, began moving away from its utopian-centric narratives of the 1960s and 1970s into stories that incorporated substantial technological themes and tropes (many of which were reminiscent of those characteristic of the cyberpunk movement) during the 1980s and the 1990s.

One of the great sticking points for feminist scholars when reading cyberpunk has been the centrality of the cyberspace (or console) cowboy, usually a young man who plugs into the feminized cyberspace matrix to become the idealized hacker-hero. Focusing on the foundational work of William Gibson's *Neuromancer* series, Nicola Nixon argues, "The political (or even revolutionary) potential for SF, realized so strongly in '70s feminist SF, is relegated in Gibson's cyberpunk to a form of scary feminized software; his fiction creates an alternative, attractive, but hallucinatory world which allows not only a reassertion of male mastery but a virtual celebration of a kind of primal masculinity" (204). A good deal of this "primal masculinity" relies on techno-Orientalist tropes to provide the settings and peoples that support this hallucinatory world of male mastery for Western white men and their technological toys (e.g., *Neuromancer*'s Case and his Japanese-made "Ono-Sendai Cyberspace 7" cyberdeck and goggles).

With their critiques of capitalism and globalization, the latest generation of feminist SF novels echo cyberpunk's concerns with commerce and power as they continue to address issues of gender and racialized identity. I classify this coming together of the two subgenres as *feminist post-cyberpunk*, exemplified by texts such as Sullivan's *Maul* and Lai's *Salt Fish Girl*. I suggest that feminist post-cyberpunk takes the most intriguing parts of cyberpunk—cyberspace, biotechnological engagement, urban dystopia, and global networks—while rejecting its white (heterosexual) masculine claims on both the subject and technology. Feminist post-cyberpunk takes in a broader consideration of what it means to be gendered and raced in an age when technology transcends geopolitical borders and exists both outside and inside of the body. Lai's *Salt Fish Girl* and Sullivan's *Maul* are populated with the marginalized characters of cyberpunk's past: women of color, clones, lesbians, children, the poor, and the disabled. In each text, these once sidelined figures take center stage as they directly interact with or literally embody technology.

In "After/Images of Identity," Lisa Nakamura states, "Rather than being left behind, bracketed, or 'radically questioned,' the body—the raced, gendered, classed body—gets 'outed' in cyberspace just as soon as commerce and power come into play" (329). To borrow Nakamura's use of "outing" here, feminist post-cyberpunk texts tend to explicitly "out" the gendered and raced body, especially in terms of its role in networks of commerce and power (often highlighting situations of exploitation). In a novel like *Salt Fish Girl*, where the "outing" is wholly intentional, Lai wants the reader to know exactly who is at the center of her novel (a young queer Asian woman) in order to fully empower that identity position despite attempts to control and diminish it. In Sullivan's *Maul*, however, the "outing" of the female Korean American protagonist Sun is not as empowering as she is revealed to be a technological product (i.e., a computer generated avatar). In the rest of this chapter, I articulate the ways in which these feminist post-cyberpunk novels give voice to Asian women in high-tech future worlds, but, at times, still struggle to completely reject the techno-Orientalism of classic cyberpunk.

Virtual Agency in Sullivan's *Maul*

Maul is set in a world not totally unlike that of Gibson's Sprawl series: the boundaries between bodies and technology blur, humanity struggles for survival, corporations control reproduction, and everyday violence is the norm. Sullivan draws attention to the precariousness of human agency, specifically by looking at an immune system brought to "life" by virtual technologies. As *Maul* unfolds, the reader follows two narratives: that of Meniscus and the women who experiment on him, and that of Sun, Suk Hee, and Keri (teenagers of Korean and Jewish descent), who are virtually mediated avatars of Meniscus's immune system. Cooped up in a viewable laboratory cage in the middle of an amusement park (which resides at the center of a mall), Meniscus is a "Y-autistic" (15) cloned male. Central to the plot of *Maul* is the virtual space that soothes Meniscus and enables the microbes to communicate with him. Mimicking traditional cyberpunk, Sullivan uses technology to enable his transformation. Through the virtual (and expensive) game No Systems Mall 7 (or Mall), Meniscus literally conjures up people and events as a way to cope with the experiments he is forced to undergo. The Korean American Sun and her friends are the avatars of Meniscus's immune system and 10Esha and her crew—the "villains"—represent the emasculating virus thriving inside of him. Meniscus becomes a virtual battle ground between the tools of technology and the human body.

Noting the fluidity between flesh and computer in cyberpunk, Sabine Heuser states that the genre "offers a uniquely fluid capacity to change gender, name, age, culture, race, role, and personality in the process of moving from one world into another. Both spaces, urban and virtual, are presented as complex domains with difficult borders, fractal geometries, and a multiplicity of cultures" (64). Following traditional feminist SF narratives, I propose that Sullivan attempts to demonstrate the fluidity of gender by taking gender roles to an extreme in both the "real-world" and virtual narratives. While the "real-world" plot line of *Maul* offers up numerous instances of gender boundary crossings and reiterations of heteronormativity, I find the virtual narrative of the game Mall far more critically productive. The gendered bodies with whom Meniscus physically interacts are simple parodies: muscles, moustaches, and aggression equal masculinity, while emotional instability, soft features, and a flair for fashion equal femininity. Without an equal balance of both sexes (as a sex-specific plague decimated the male population), the gender relations in the world of *Maul* have gone awry. Subverting traditional gendered hierarchy, Sullivan places women in the masculinized roles of overseer and tormentor. Unable to challenge the threatening female masculinity of his oppressors, Meniscus uses Mall to experiment with, and eventually subvert, this gendered hierarchy. As avatars of his immune system, Sun, Suk Hee, and Keri are reflections of the fleshy women Meniscus encounters—but whereas Maddie (the doctor in charge of his "care") and the other women are selfish, incompetent, and overly emotional, the avatar teenagers are aggressive, resourceful, intelligent, and team-oriented. By exploring gendered identities through virtual reality, Meniscus attempts to understand and modify his own embodied sense of gender.

Through the avatars of Sun, Suk Hee, and Keri, Meniscus's subconscious struggles to reconcile itself with his state of powerlessness and subjection. The gender-power exploration begins with Sun and Suk Hee's insistence that women are not passive victims, but perpetrators of action (e.g., "the engines of life"; 5). Using the image of wolves, Suk Hee details how "the alpha female fights the other females to compete for who gets to mate with the alpha male. The alpha males sometimes fend off other males who want to mate the females, but not as ferociously as females fight" (19). The avatars' refusal to identify with ascribed female weakness reflects Meniscus's desire to become autonomous and powerful; he too aspires to attain "alpha" status. Through Suk Hee and Sun, Meniscus utilizes the virtual space of Mall in order to challenge the boundaries of gender norms. His exploration of gender can occur within Mall as it is a safer place wherein alternate forms of embodiment exist without threatening real-world gendered constructs.

In addition to problematizing the cultural assignment of gender in *Maul*, race undergoes similar processes of dislocation from the body, but, unfortunately, with less success.[1] "While telecommunications and medical technologies can challenge some gender and racial stereotypes, they produce and reflect them as well," Nakamura tells readers ("After/Images of Identity" 325). Sullivan "produces and reflects" racialized stereotypes through the "bugs" inhabiting Meniscus's body. I read *Maul* as a work that sets out to problematize race as connected to the vulnerable, physical body, but ultimately ends up "outing" the raced body as a commodity, reaffirming the racial stereotypes of the techno-Orientalized female as a body who enacts her (limited) agency for the benefit of the white male user in virtual environments and is rendered invisible in the "real" world.

The real-world scenario in *Maul* is predominantly a "white" space while the narrative of virtual Mall is populated primarily by Korean American, Latina, and black teenagers. Although it is understandable that Meniscus identifies with female avatars (as he has few male role models to emulate), the fact that Sullivan characterizes them as racially minoritized Others, and, moreover, as engaged in urban gang warfare, is highly problematic. Nakamura describes the taking on of racialized personae as "identity tourism." She states, "Tourism is a particularly apt metaphor to describe the activity of racial appropriation, or 'passing' in cyberspace" ("Race In/For Cyberspace" 714). In the virtual space of Mall, Meniscus is engaging in this form of passing as his avatars are represented as Asian. Speaking directly about the appropriation of Asian personae, Nakamura argues that they "reveal that attractions lie not only in being able to 'go' to exotic places, but to co-opt the exotic and attach it to oneself. The appropriation of racial identity becomes a form of recreation, a vacation from fixed identities and locales" (715). For Meniscus, immersing himself in virtual reality is not only a form of recreation, but a needed "vacation" from bodily suffering. Through Sun and the other racialized avatars, Meniscus escapes his own fixed identity as a white male test subject. Echoing the same contentions as Nakamura, Anne Balsamo posits that "[c]yberspace offers white men an enticing retreat from the burdens of their *cultural* identities. In this sense, it is apparent that although cyberspace seems to represent a territory free from the burdens of history, it will, in effect, serve as another site for the technological and no less conventional inscription of the gendered, race-marked body" (131). Interpreting the Mall narrative generously in the context of a feminist revision of a classic cyberpunk trope, I suggest that Sullivan establishes virtual reality as a site wherein Meniscus can free himself of his cultural identity—an identity that, in his female-dominated world, is marginalized and exploited (mirroring the reality of race relations in our modern world).

Sullivan structures the fictional virtual world of *Maul* in a way that seemingly allows for such racial appropriation. While Sullivan provides her characters an "out" when they engage in racial stereotyping (e.g., "Remember, I'm allowed to say this shit, I'm half-Jewish"; 81), she nevertheless engages in identity tourism throughout the novel. Despite the supposed progressiveness of the avatars' gendered identities, Sullivan relies on racialized stereotypes to flesh out her characters. Sun's racialized otherness is emphasized repeatedly throughout the text. For example, Sun questions her correct use of English: "Grammar, like I said before, I wasn't born here and I can never be totally sure" (123). This stereotyping of the Korean immigrant with a poor grasp of the English language is carried throughout the novel with the figure of Sun's mom, who speaks with "dropped articles & shitty grammar" (3). Sullivan also reinforces Suk Hee's racialized "Asianness" throughout the text. For instance, when Suk Hee sees a pair of shoes that she likes, "[s]he runs with tiny, cute little steps as if her feet are still bound in some kind of race-memory thing" (20). Even more problematic than Sun and Suk Hee's pronounced stereotypical "Asianness"—as they are the "heroes" of the story—is the characterization of the other female avatars that represent the Y-plague microbes. The "bugs" infecting Meniscus manifest themselves in virtual Mall as the Bugaboo gang, which comprises violent, racially minoritized teens. Watching the Bugaboo gang arrive, Sun observes, "Look at those Latina chix with their big tits, and that Swedish-looking emaciated blonde.... And the fat one—of course, the obligatory fat one who is all attitude and Heavy Style" (22). The 10E virus strain manifests itself as the dark-skinned 10Esha, and all of the Bugaboos are marked by racial otherness, characterized by a propensity for violence. During his initial exposure to 10E, Meniscus feels "scared. 10E likes it. 10E takes his fear and turns it into poison. He turns to Mall in hope of exerting some control, but 10E knows about Mall. It's there, waiting for him.... Want[s] to own him, enfold him" (15). The Bugaboo gang, an expression of the 10E microbes, is clearly characterized as a threat to the white male body. Even though Sun and Suk Hee represent the "good" side (i.e., the immune system fighting off a viral invasion), they nevertheless are reduced to technological tools in service to a white body.

Nakamura also theorizes that identity tourism in virtual spaces allows for the participant to reenact familiar power relations: "As Said puts it, the tourist who passes as the marginalized Other during his travels partakes of a fantasy of social control, one which depends upon and fixes the familiar contours of racial power relations" ("Race In/For Cyberspace" 715). In the case of *Maul*, the "familiar contours of racial power relations" are played out in two ways: first, Sullivan merely replicates the stereotypes of racialized violence for sensational effect, and, second, she does so in order to emphasize the disjuncture between the body deemed unfavorably marked by gender and race (the Asian female) and the social body proper (the white male). The techno-Orientalized bodies of Sun and Suk Hee, as well as those of Bugaboos who are marked by skin tone as others, are thereby set apart from the technologically advanced "white" space of the laboratory that confines Meniscus. While Meniscus may arguably find identification with the avatar bodies with which he populates Mall, the fact that they are young Asian women with no real agency (and are, essentially, products for his use) recuperates the racial tension inherent in identity tourism. Sullivan reduces race to an issue of corporeal embodiment in *Maul* rather than positioning it as belonging to the same set of arbitrary normative social constructions that define gender. Sun and Suk Hee are ultimately playing pieces in someone else's game.

Human 2.0: Lai's *Salt Fish Girl*

Larissa Lai's *Salt Fish Girl* is also a novel with two main narrative lines: that of Nu Wa (the ancient Chinese creator goddess) and the salt fish girl in nineteenth-century China, and that of Miranda and the clone Evie in a future Canadian Pacific Northwest. Just as I focused on the "virtual" world in *Maul*, my discussion of *Salt Fish Girl* addresses the narrative of Miranda and Evie as their story line most obviously exemplifies the text's cyberpunk inheritance. I show how Lai's feminist post-cyberpunk book establishes a new critical literature for the techno-Orientalized body with its exploration of cloning and biotechnology in a world perishing under rampant globalized capitalism. Robyn Morris writes, "Lai's fiction functions as a contestation and complication of the literary and filmic perpetuation of an ideology of a pure, ordinary and unmarked 'humanness,' a definition which has historically accorded the white, western, heterosexual male with a universal and centred subject positioning" ("What Does it Mean to be Human" 81). I propose that Lai's move to denaturalize normative constructions of identity and "humanness" speaks to the novel's cyberpunk inheritance. Like *Maul*, *Salt Fish Girl* re-imagines classic cyberpunk concerns (with technological embodiment, globalization, and corporate control over bodies) with a feminist perspective. Lai approaches genetic engineering, for instance, from multiple angles: first, following in the footsteps of cyberpunk, she criticizes the corporate greed and capitalist amorality that creates factory-floors full of expendable cloned Asian female workers (the clone becomes metaphor for the new "disposable Asian worker" in the era of globalization); second, exemplifying the best of feminist SF, Lai explores what cloning means for gendered and racialized constructions of identity, in particular for Asian women. These techno-Orientalized characters are not part of the exotic backdrop in some Westernized cyber-fantasy; they are at the center of the novel, leading the narrative.

In *Salt Fish Girl*, Lai attempts to answer what humanity might look like if technology and capitalism continue their current courses of progress. Central to the novel is Miranda's durian-odor and the ways it is linked to the transformative "sleeping disease" affecting those in the Unregulated Zone. Miranda learns that: "The symptoms [of the disease] are so peculiar, and so unlike any other known disease—foul odours of various sorts that follow the person without actually emanating from the body, psoriasis, sleep apnea, terrible dreams usually with historical content, and a compulsive drive to commit suicide by drowning" (100). There is no real understanding of the source of the "sleeping disease" though some "theorized that it might be the product of mass industrial genetic alteration practices" (102). Its lack of containment—and visible effect on the bodies of the afflicted—marks already marginalized bodies as threats to the "public good." Through the figure of the durian-scented Miranda, Lai plays off of long-used Western racist attacks against people of Asian descent as "smelling funny," as if their bodies are inherently different when compared with the contained and "scentless" white body (of course, an utter illusion). From the outset of the novel, then, Miranda's otherness is an aura that permeates every aspect of her daily life.

As Lai's narrative of the "sleeping disease" and Miranda's corporeal difference indicates, the misuse of (bio)technology is a great source of anxiety. One of Miranda's first encounters with "technology-out-of-control" occurs while visiting the house of a school friend. Visiting the notably white-skinned Ian's house, she meets his parents, both of whom have unnaturally gleaming white teeth; his father has "arm muscles [that] rippled unnaturally," and his mother's "eyes were both prosthetic and had a terrible piercing intelligence to them. She was immaculately dressed in a stiff, shiny metallic dress. But she had an awful smell about her, like rusting iron only much more intense" (64). Like the high-tech nonsensical wallpaper of Ian's home (64), his parents are also dressed in biotechnology as fashion. The "stiff, shiny metallic" corporeal embracements displayed by Ian's parents suggest attempts at fortifying the boundaries of, and blocking access to, the body (from their obvious symptoms of the "sleeping disease"), but ones that ultimately fail. Whereas Meniscus uses technology to successfully liberate himself from the control of others in *Maul*, both Miranda and Ian's mother are unable to contain their shared difference (i.e., strong bodily odor) through technological draping.

Salt Fish Girl is certainly not a utopia and Lai denies her characters any solace in technology. Even the seemingly safe escapist technology of virtual reality—so celebrated as freeing in *Maul*—becomes another capitalist tool of domination and exploitation. Clad in his "Business Suit" ("a large black suit made of some shiny synthetic material, elastic and tight fitting" 25), Miranda's father navigates the virtual "Real World" as a glorified tax collector for the government. While in the virtual environment, Miranda's bookish father appears on a view screen as "tall and strong and solitary. . . . It was my father, but a much younger, stronger, more heroic version of him, both like the man I knew and entirely without the soft, gentle, bookish demeanour with which he carried himself through family life" (26–27). Transformed on-line, Miranda's father appears "better than" himself as he "helped the helpless and swallowed increasingly long streams of razor disc birds that turned into numbers when he opened his mouth. The Business Suit made tax collecting into a marvellous adventure" (27). The "Real World," like the Internet of today, claims to change the mundane (e.g. tax collecting) into the extraordinary, when in actuality, it is a reflection of the physical world. Instead of offering a reliable escape from economic exploitation, the virtual "Real World" further substantiates reliance on existing power structures.

While virtual space often allows the user to transcend the body in traditional cyberpunk, "Real World" denies that corporeal escape to its virtual denizens. In *Maul*, Meniscus achieves corporeal freedom through his virtual interactions, but Lai denies her characters this fantasy of escape. During a work day, Miranda finds her father retching into the "Business Suit" while writhing on the floor in pain as the General Receivers (the tax bosses) "extract taxes" from his avatar (27–28). Not only are beatings a routine aspect of virtual tax collecting, but "Real World" is rife with thieves and their attacks also result in actual physical consequences. In response to such scenes of brutality, Robyn Morris argues that "Lai exposes the technological as a paternal and profit-driven process; a process that, in this future city called Serendipity commodifies identity and complicates our past conceptions of humanness as realness" (85). The experiences of Miranda's father in "Real World" complicate traditional notions of "humanness as realness" and embodiment. Since the virtual beatings translate into real bodily suffering, the boundaries between the real self and the virtual self are therefore revealed as extremely permeable, just as they are for those afflicted by the "sleeping disease." In addition, Lai underscores the "realness" of the Asian body: Miranda and her father are real physical bodies that exist in the real world and don't have some kind of special inherent mastery over technological space.

Throughout *Salt Fish Girl*, Lai is careful to reject the traditional cyberpunk use of the passive techno-Orientalized female body as she articulates the consequences of nonnormative reproduction for racially minoritized bodies. Writing in the late 1990s as the emerging issue of cloning fueled Western imaginations, Marlene Barr speculates that "the most dangerous issue is not duplication but, rather, the lack of mass production of certain humans: gays, Jews, people of color, women" (203). Going against Barr's particular dystopian fear of the erasure of sexual and racial minorities, however, Lai imagines a world wherein the cloned bodies are *only* women of color. Lai explores the very scenario that Barr does not predict: what would happen if mass-produced clones are those of bodies already exploited by the global capitalist system? Lai's critique of the Western marginalization (and exploitation) of the Asian body is strongly evident through Miranda's apprehension and horror over cloning. On entering Dr. Flower's experimental laboratory hideaway in the mountains, Miranda follows the escaped clone Evie and sees "the fridges where all the DNA was kept, the vials of fertilized and unfertilized eggs, the cold steel tables upon which the act of creation took place. All these tidy attempts to control the mud and muck of origin upset me" (268). Dr. Flower's experiments with cloning translate literally into attempts at controlling paternity and maternity of the Asian body—a way to either contain or erase racialized otherness that is seen as threatening, or contaminating (just like the sleeping disease), to the white male body.

In Lai's dystopian scenario, it is a small leap to make from the exploitation of racialized women's labor in the present world to the one of 2044 where women of color are mass produced solely for the exploitation of their labor. Evie believes that her cloned genes might have originated from a Chinese woman named Ai who married a Japanese man and was interned in the Rockies during World War II, but most likely, the clones—all named Sonia, as another measure to strip them of individuality and agency—are genetic composites pulled from the "Diverse Genome Project" which "focused on the peoples of the so-called Third World, Aboriginal peoples, and peoples in danger of extinction" (160). The bodies of the Sonia clones are treated as tools of production: Evie tells Miranda that she is one of "at least a hundred thousand" (158) clones bred and forced to work for Nextcorp, a corporation that produces Pallas shoes (157). The worker clones are controlled by an implanted mechanical device, their "Guardian Angel," which "looks after us, monitors our body temperature, notes the presence of disease, helps rescuers find us if we get lost" (159). The Sonias are neither autonomous beings nor human—they are literally manufactured bodies, *products*, to be used and thrown away. Clones, just like real Eastern world factory workers, are ultimately deemed lesser beings as the whims of the marketplace determine their value. In *Salt Fish Girl*, Lai exposes the harsh reality of cyberpunk's techno-Orientalized body—technology does not free it from suffering or erase the moral failings of those who seek to exploit it.

Further deepening the perceived otherness of the Sonia clones is the indeterminacy of their origins. Miranda is shocked by Evie's admission of her illegal nonhuman status (158), as she explains that her "genes are point zero three percent *Cyprinuscarpio* freshwater carp. I'm a patented new fucking life form" (158). Taken out of the realm of the human, Evie and the other Sonia clones are reduced to their patented genes—they become nothing more than tools for production. Addressing the clones' indeterminate humanity, Robyn Morris argues, "The figure of Evie, and her human/fish genes, exists in a liminal state, neither fully human nor non-human. This ambiguity surrounding her identity is one way that Lai complicated conceptions of humanness as whole, centered, complete; 'the real thing'" (92). Despite recognizing her own corporeal difference, Miranda's discomfort with Evie reflects current anxieties surrounding cloning as a technology that challenges normative definitions of what constitutes a human being and brings into question who (or what) is ultimately responsible for human agency and creation.

Lai emphasizes that the clone body, the techno-Orientalized body, is nevertheless an active one. Owning their right to reproduce, the escaped Sonias use genetically engineered durian fruits (the same fruit that brought Miranda into being) to bear children. Living and creating families outside of the factories, the clone Sonias reject subjection and control by those who deny them their humanity and insist on creating new lives, literally, for themselves. While Lai warns against the exploitive use of cloning and genetic modification, she also proposes that when taken up outside of dominant power structures, such technologies can be enabling for marginalized bodies by offering them novel modes of replication. "It is through Evie and the Sonias' quest for independence that Lai rejects the narrativizing of women, and more particularly, women of Asian descent, as passive and silent under white, Western, patriarchal scrutiny" (Robyn Morris 89), effectively refiguring the central hacker-hero of classic cyberpunk. While global capitalism seeks to turn Asian bodies into expendable workers for the pleasure and use of an insatiable Westernized market, Lai situates her Asian female characters as operating competently and creatively within society, within the real world, despite its exclusionary cultural constructions of their identity.

In feminist post-cyberpunk texts like *Salt Fish Girl*, Tara Lee argues that the multinational network of a global market "is premised on the breaking apart of bodies and a blurring of boundaries that were previously considered stable. Late capitalism imposes itself on the globe by fragmenting the body until it is nothing more than pieces for power dispersal" (2). The fragmentation of the Asian female body is represented in both *Salt Fish Girl* and *Maul* (as expendable clones or coded avatars), and both novels give voice to a competent female agent. But where Lai allows her protagonists the freedom to find their way in the (dangerous) world, Sullivan replicates aspects of classic cyberpunk's techno-Orientalism, such as limiting the sphere of action for Asian bodies to virtual environments. While Sun and Suk Hee are central to the narrative, and, in doing so, are engaging and capable figures, they have no real-world relevance, serving only as technological tools for the personal exploration of Meniscus. Lai, on the other hand, fleshes out her Asian women, both figuratively and literally. Asian bodies have no special mastery over virtual environments (as demonstrated with the "business suit"), but they do have real-world presence—a presence that involves suffering and adaptation. The techno-Orientalized body in *Salt Fish Girl* is not a static one; like all bodies, it is capable of transformation and agency. As a genre, feminist post-cyberpunk still has some work to do in imagining high-tech futures without reinscribing techno-Orientalist tropes. But regardless of its limitations, it nevertheless opens up a space for Asian women to use the technological tools once reserved for the Western white cyberspace cowboy and direct their own (physical and virtual) futures.

Note

1. To her credit, Sullivan, having read several critiques of her work (including my own on *Maul*), as well as through her own self-reflection, has written about her unintentional recuperation of racist stereotypes on her LiveJournal blog, in the post "when autobiography turns bad & shows your cottage-cheesy ass" (see http://triciasullivan.livejournal.com/140128.html).

Chapter 12
The Cruel Optimism of Asian Futurity and the Reparative Practices of Sonny Liew's *Malinky Robot*

◆◊▶

AIMEE BAHNG

> The really good news is that few Asians have lost their optimism about the future. They have no illusions about the crisis but are confident that they remain on the right trajectory to deliver the Asian century.
> —Kishore Mahbubani, "Why Asia Stays Calm in the Storm"

The cover of Kishore Mahbubani's 2008 publication *The New Asian Hemisphere: The Irresistible Shift of Global Power to the East* presents readers with what seems to be the global sign for financial growth: skyscrapers under construction. Cranes perch atop every tower, suggestive of the "all-at-once-ness" of growth in Asia. The illuminated construction site stretching into the night sky highlights the unrelenting pace of growth, which proceeds even as the rest of the world sleeps. The scene is a familiar one, prefigured by the race for the tallest building that ran across parts of Asia (Singapore, Malaysia, Taiwan) in the early 2000s.¹ But the unpainted, all white structures feel eerily hollow and decontextualized. There's no sign of the human laborers who welded and wired these structures. The lot is all but empty, with the exception of one nondescript car parked in the foreground. This scene of speculative building—construction predicted but not contracted to sell—feels like an already haunted future, in which "New Asia" has become an empty lot, evacuated of its denizens and prepared to signify the sheer potential of capital.

Published amid the financial crisis of 2008, Mahbubani's book, as well as his *Financial Times* declaration of a realizable Asian Century that serves as this essay's epigraph, excite what Alan Greenspan once called "irrational exuberance." Uttered in a speech Greenspan gave in 1996, in his capacity as chairman of the U.S. Federal Reserve, the phrase characterized the "unduly escalated asset values" of Japan's economic bubble. The next day, Tokyo's stock market fell sharply, closing 3 percent down, and Greenspan's speech largely presaged the Asian financial crash a year later. The extent to which economic projections hang on the words of figureheads like Alan Greenspan demonstrates how such speculations work as performative speech acts that call the future into being. Similarly, the optimism Mahbubani announces in forward-looking, prophetic tones ("optimism will deliver the Asian Century"), affectively structures speculative investment in Asian futures. This vision of the new Asian hemisphere, colonized by empty high-rises reaching toward limitless horizons and built by deterritorialized workers, projects a future of automated speculative building, fueled by investment hungry banks. If Greenspan and Mahbubani both grasp how their respective declarations of pessimism and optimism will affect the global economy, they do so with two different Asias in mind: Japan of the late 1990s and Singapore at the dawn of a "new Asia" in 2008.[2] The so-called Asian Century, toward which Mahbubani's optimism strains, functions as a large-scale speculative fiction spawned from neoliberal fantasies that capitalize on a literary genre's already problematic investments in techno-Orientalism.

In their 1995 examination of techno-Orientalism, David Morley and Kevin Robins call attention to U.S. and European fantasies of Japan and its shift in those imaginaries in the 1980s from an exotic playground to a land of emotionless automatons. Perhaps epitomized by Western dystopian cyberpunk such as Ridley Scott's *Blade Runner* (1982) and William Gibson's *Neuromancer* (1984), techno-Orientalism figures the Japanese as "unfeeling aliens; they are cyborgs and replicants. But there is also the sense that these mutants are now better adapted to survive in the future" (170). While Morley and Robins understand techno-Orientalism as primarily born out of Western anxieties about Japan's challenge to U.S. economic hegemony, they also suggest more specifically how techno-Orientalism arises just as Japan emerges as "the largest creditor and the largest net investor in the world" (153). What Morley and Robins never fully develop, and what I want to explore in more depth here, is this coordinated turn toward Asian futures in both financial and cultural forms of speculation.

Mathematical models of probability and investment strategies based on extrapolation are forms of speculative fiction that project finance capitalism's visions of futurity onto the world. Interdisciplinary scholarship from the past two decades has pointed to the performative aspects of economic speculation (MacKenzie, Muniesa, and Siu), the sociological systems of financial markets (Knorr-Cetina and Bruegger), the impact on subjectivity of financial instruments such as derivatives and debt bundling (LiPuma and Lee), and the "financialization of daily life" (Martin). Because speculative economies rely ever more on rhetorical tools and narrative strategies to explain and market the practice of trading on futures and securities, financial speculation and speculative fiction both participate in the cultural production of futurity, and futurity becomes the arena in which new subject formations emerge. Does techno-Orientalism register anxieties about finance capitalism, or does finance capitalism use techno-Orientalism as a basis for its extrapolations of futurity? I emphasize the co-constitutive relationship between the cultural production and financial worlding of Asian futurity.

A peculiar question arises then, when Asian economic and political architects themselves participate in the projection of Asian futurity, all the while drawing on a techno-Orientalist toolkit. I argue that critical analysis of the discursive site of Asian futurity reveals points of contradiction in American neoliberalism as it travels that have to do with earlier forms of racial and colonial subjugation providing the scaffolding for the architecture of neoliberalism itself.[3] As Asia develops its own neoliberal rhetoric, articulating its own futurity poses certain problems that necessitate a disavowal of the racism of techno-Orientalism. What stands in to "smooth" that difficulty is the heteronormativity techno-Orientalism always espoused that Asian futurity posits anew as part of its road map, capitalizing on aspirational teleologies, valuations of privatized worth, and nationalisms consolidated through processes of racialization.

I focus my investigation on techno-Orientalism's role in the production of a global neoliberal subject in contemporary Singapore, where a tech economy adopts and adapts localized versions of seemingly universalized notions of "the good life." Building on Lauren Berlant's theorization of "cruel optimism," this essay levies a critique of "the Asian Century" as imagined by economists around the world. It argues that a revisionist Asian futurity needs to intervene in the neoliberal orientations of "the good life" and, in the face of foreclosed futures, open possibilities of what Eve Sedgwick has called "reparative practices."

For an inspiring glimpse of what reparative practices in the context of techno-Orientalism might look like, I turn to Sonny Liew's graphic story collection

Malinky Robot (Figure 12.1), which fabulates an alternative imagining of Asian futurity, as told from the perspective of the global South. *Malinky Robot*, a title that translated serendipitously from Russian as "odd jobs," or "little work" (Villarica), depicts a multiethnic Asian futurity burdened with precarious living conditions, precipitous divides in wealth, and ecological as well as economic fallout propagated by global capitalist greed. Liew, born in Malaysia but working mostly out of Singapore, offers gritty, agitated aesthetics and sparse storylines that restore texture, abrasion, and friction to the slick, polished surfaces and epic narrative scales of techno-Orientalist futures. Liew's personal trajectories map a complex history of Singapore as a site of multiple layers of European (Portuguese, Dutch, British) and Japanese imperialism. In its turn toward self-governance, Singapore has also been the scene of ethnic- and class-based tensions among exploited Malaysian workers and a predominantly Chinese ethnic majority population who constitute the managerial class. With particular attention to Singapore's own aspirations to become a "technopreneurial" city-state of the future (Ong, *Neoliberalism* 181), this essay looks to *Malinky Robot* as a crucial counternarrative to techno-Orientalism as it is deployed not only by Western fantasies of a docile East but also by Asian aspirations to challenge U.S. global hegemony.

FIG. 12.1 Cover of *Malinky Robot* (France). *Credit:* Sonny Liew.

Future • Singapore

Since the 1997–1998 and 2007–2008 financial crises, Singapore has emerged for the moment as probably the most "triumphant" Asian economy, cited as the fastest growing in the world with one of the highest GDP per capita—an accomplishment often attributed to its aggressive and perhaps desperate turn toward financial liberalization after the 1997–1998 crash. A key part of engineering this turn toward a radically more neoliberal economic policy involved the state reimagining itself as a "New Singapore"—an international hub of financial speculation, engineering, and biotechnology: a city-state of the future. "Future • Singapore" and its more recent attenuation "Future-Ready Singapore" name two initiatives sponsored over the past five years by the state's Economic Development Board (EDB) and clearly instantiate Singapore's active reinvention into a neoliberal platform, "designed to develop and test bed new ideas and solutions in the areas of urban living, wellness, ageing and healthcare, and lifestyle products and services."[4] The "Western" fantasy of Asia as supplementary and disposable plays out here in state policy and ideology, wherein "Singapore" stands to profit from such complicity. Future • Singapore solicits international investments by positioning itself as a speculative geography: "Companies need somewhere to hatch ideas, a laboratory to test concepts, a facility where prototypes can be test-driven. We offer Singapore as that partner-location, as a living laboratory for innovative companies to experiment and develop world-class solutions."[5] Following Bruno Latour's injunction to examine the dirty underbelly of the laboratory—all the monstrous discards of experimentation—let us pursue those anarchic variables that interfere with the EDB's smooth projections of futurity.

The self-fashioning of a "worldly Singaporean" as the idealized inhabitant of this Asian future involves the figurative disavowal as well as the actual evacuation of undesirable populations in Singapore that has occurred since the turn toward neoliberalism. Singapore's investments in cosmopolitanism depend on carefully state-controlled movements of migrant laborers from other countries around Southeast Asia, including the Philippines, Indonesia, Sri Lanka, and Bangladesh. In addition to the disparities in flexibility afforded foreign care workers via the stringent work permit system, which segregates workers into high-skill and low-skill groups, Singapore also marginalizes its ethnic Malaysian population, which makes only half the monthly income of Chinese Singaporeans and constitutes only 2 percent of the nation's university graduates. In these ways, the promises of meritocracy and technofuturity touted by state officials and reiterated internationally fissure along national, ethnic, and class lines.

Future • Singapore culls its "flexible citizens" not only by integrating foreign professionals through intermarriage and streamlining their paths to citizenship, but also by pointing existing Singaporeans to "upgrade and upskill" towards professional, managerial, executive and technical (PMET) jobs ("Sustainable Population").[6] Feeling the booming population's strain on infrastructure and national identity, the state released a white paper in January 2013 titled "Sustainable Population for a Dynamic Singapore," which reveals an unsustainable tension between the need to "support a dynamic economy . . . to meet Singaporeans' *hopes* and aspirations," on the one hand, and to "keep Singapore a good *home*" with a "strong Singaporean core" on the other (1–2, emphases in original). Witness here the state's neoliberal fantasies bumping up against a nationalist imaginary sustained by a (racially? ethnically? "proto-Singaporean"?) consolidated "core." Two demographic visions for future Singapore—of global business elites, on the one hand, and of a more homogeneous national body politic on the other—compete without much regard for those whom both would readily displace. What would an alternative fabulation of a Singaporean future—one that doesn't step even deeper into neoliberal fantasies that produce unsustainable, uneven, and unethical systems—entail?

Reparative Practices: Life in the Gutter with *Malinky Robot*

Sonny Liew's *Malinky Robot* intervenes in neoliberal discourses of constantly upgradeable lives. The five short stories in the collection, published by Image Comics in 2011, feature a motley crew of characters. Atari is a chain-smoking kid with a trenchant understanding of harsh realities. "[S]treetwise, with a world-weary air . . . [he] spends his time busking, shoplifting, stealing bicycles and reading comics" (Liew, boxed set character card). His slightly more optimistic and notably alien—or at least nonhuman—companion, Oliver, is "as uncertain as anyone else where he came from or what he is" (Liew, boxed set, character card). Atari and Oliver's middle-class friend Misha lives on the fancier side of the tracks, buys them lunch, and passes along his games when he moves away. Finally, there is Little Robot, originally discounted by Atari as "more of an appliance," whose perspective nonetheless shapes the narrative arc of "New Year's Day," the fourth short story in the collection. Though the narrative voices are many, the reader primarily encounters the world of *Malinky Robot* through this interspecies assemblage of human, alien, and robot. Cultivating bonds of affiliation that cut across conventional categories of human and nonhuman, these life forms illustrate a practice living in common against a terrain jagged with joblessness, the apparent implosion of public education, and ecological devastation. Cast aside along with other discarded bits of a neoliberalized economy, they embody the fallout of Singaporean "reengineering" of its citizens (Ong, *Neoliberalism* 185). The reader follows the protagonists as they make their way through their everyday encounters with poverty, despair, and boredom. Even amid severe conditions, though, Atari, Oliver, and friends enliven worlds of possibility in everyday practices of care. They help each other relocate, pool resources and hatch plans to make money in unsanctioned ways, and perhaps most significantly, they speculate together: pondering alternative histories and dreaming themselves into imaginative worlds that look, smell, and feel different from their immediate surroundings.

Set in a dilapidated urban landscape, *Malinky Robot* revisits the primal scene of techno-Orientalist fantasy: Tokyo. However, by focusing on Tokyo's day laboring district of Sanya (Taito-ku), which remains home to Tokyo's dispossessed, Liew shifts the origin point of Japan's economic success and underscores the vulnerability of those who were not folded into the prosperity of global capitalism.[7] Like the denizens of Tokyo's Sanya, Oliver and Atari "eke out a life" in a geopolitical context that works hard to eliminate them from the picture (Liew, boxed set, character cards). Together they scrape together bits and pieces of culture, currency, and materials from the discarded matter of the city. "Eking out a life"—one of Liew's most favored characterizations of Oliver and Atari's mode of engaging the world around them—resonates profoundly with Sedgwick's formulation of reparative practices, which illuminate "the many ways selves and communities succeed in extracting sustenance from the objects of a culture—even of a culture whose avowed desire has often been not to sustain them" (150–151).

Sedgwick's formulations of reparative versus paranoid modalities distinguish between ways of experiencing time—within and beyond narrative forms. Distinct from *paranoid* reading, which is motivated by an attempt to inure oneself to potentially horrible futures, reparative reading stays open and vulnerable to the radical possibilities of surprise (Sedgwick 146). Though called sequential art, comics as a literary form have a propensity for bending time across the page, wherein the space between panels—"the gutter"—could represent a fleeting moment or eons of time passing, not necessarily in chronological order. *Malinky Robot* flexes the possibilities of its graphic form to capture play and adventure in slow time at a moment when blockbuster films profit from ever more accelerated pacing. With sparse, unspectacularized storylines like "a robot walks home," or "two kids borrow bikes to visit a friend," Liew's utopian visions—ephemeral and provisional—unfurl across the daily exploits and mundane, communal acts of these unlikely heroes of the future. *Malinky Robot* ruminates on forms of idleness that upend perceptions of "wasted" time, while simultaneously highlighting the waste of capitalist overproduction. Whereas the dystopian tenor of techno-Orientalist cyberpunk and the breakneck ambition of Future • Singapore both engender a paranoid relation to futurity by manifesting either foreboding or securitization against it, *Malinky Robot* remains remarkably open to surprise and radical uncertainty. In this way, it articulates a reparative form of speculation—one that revels in the play of chance rather than the taming of it (Hacking).

The comic opens in 2024 atop a skyscraper, where sunrise finds the protagonists on top of the world, not because they own or dominate it, but because they have made the rooftop their makeshift shelter. Atari and Oliver are homeless, making do with life in urban decay. Here, "Mornings are . . . STINKY!!" (11). This is the surprising pronouncement that begins "Stinky Fish Blues," the first story of the collection. At dawn, Oliver encounters not the optimistic vista of sunlit horizons but the smell of a stagnant city, littered with signs of broken technological promises. And yet, the morning does bring surprising, if fleeting, moments of hope and unexpected opportunity. Oliver and Atari go fishing down at the docks and discover rare life in the toxic waters—the nearly extinct *Foetidus Piscis* (the stinky fish), persisting despite barrels of industrial sludge polluting its home. Their fortuitous catch fosters the hope of cashing it in for reward, but the fish ultimately falls prey to a friend's more pressing need to eat it. The kids are bummed, but not dejected, as prospects of cashing in recede to make allowances for the sharing of life in this contingent community. The stinky fish, living beyond all probability in pernicious conditions, serves as a fitting compatriot for Oliver and Atari, who manage to do more than just survive in a hostile environment. They dare to have dreams, foster friendships, and have adventures that actively extend the possibilities of the living conditions allotted them, even if their dreams remain decidedly out of reach. The view from the top of Oliver's transient skyscraper haven differs from what Michel de Certeau describes in "Walking in the City." From the summit of the World Trade Center, de Certeau experiences being "lifted out of

FIG. 12.2 "Oliver atop Skyscraper." *Source: Malinky Robot* 22. *Credit:* Sonny Liew.

the city's grasp.... When one goes up there, he leaves behind the mass.... His elevation transfigures him into a voyeur" (92). But Oliver's prospects remain decidedly unchanged by this perspectival shift. He remains untransfigured, looking up like a homeless alien, not "looking down like a god" (92). This difference reverberates profoundly across the context of Atari and Oliver's likely futures working the construction sites that emblematize "New Asia" and its speculative building frenzy.

Indeed, when the two look upon a construction site (Figure 12.3), they consider their curtailed set of opportunities, and even Oliver's moment of ebullience ("I wanna fly a plane!") seems squelched as the frame zooms out to capture the dwarfing effects of the world around him.

The tops of skyscrapers yield only visions of unattainable aspirations and failed promises for Atari and Oliver, but they pursue adventure nonetheless and find in an arcade a virtual realization of Oliver's hopes to pilot a plane (Figure 12.4). In this closing frame of the story, Liew leaves us with a stunning display of reparative practice, of engaging in fleeting acts of pleasure to carve out alternative ways of looking forward.

Together, Atari and Oliver explore alternative economies of exchange: they "borrow" bicycles that allow them to visit their friend Misha across town. Their mundane push toward collective ownership stands in stark contrast to the stealing-for-profit story their friend shares with them over lunch at "McDonnell's" about Obiyashi Takamashuru, an unscrupulous man who stole the design for cantilevered gears on bikes from their mentor, Mr. Bon Bon. This short vignette about bicycle thievery turns sideways when it's revealed that bicycles themselves carry with them another story of stolen property.

The bicycle, as we learn from Misha's tale of Obiyashi Takamashuru, is always already stolen, as concept, as design, as vehicle when the very mechanism that facilitates its locomotion turns out to be a lifted idea. Framed as the first in a series of comics within a comic, Misha's *Ingrown Nale* reveals the history of the bicycle as property privatized and patented in the shadiest of circumstances, throwing the world of propriety into ethical question. Drawn in the heavily cross-grained and stridently scraggy pen and ink style of graphic mavericks such as Robert Crumb, *Ingrown Nale* (ostensibly produced from Misha's hand but also a testament to Liew's creative range) takes the reader into Obiyashi's demented world of ruthless corporate competition, greed, and dishonesty. We follow Obiyashi to work on the day of his death and descent to a Dante-inspired hell, where he confesses how he stole the design of the cantilevered gear system. Though certainly incentivized to villainous action, Obiyashi turns out to be a dupe, trapped in the promise of a better future (Figure 12.5). Before his fateful cardiac arrest, he reflects on his situation: "30 years! My life, a series of dwindling offices. I long for: the ocean, the trees, the breath of my children as yet unborn. Today, though, will be a day different

FIG. 12.3 "I Wanna Fly a Plane!" *Source: Malinky Robot* 21. *Credit:* Sonny Liew.

FIG. 12.4 "Flights of Fancy." *Source: Malinky Robot* 29. *Credit:* Sonny Liew.

from days before" (45). We witness this corporate wonk's perpetually fruitless drive toward upward mobility in several key details. Obiyashi's namesake might ironically be Obayashi Global, the Japanese multinational construction corporation behind the building of Tokyo Sky Tree, the world's tallest broadcasting tower. Obiyashi's ascent in the corporate elevator leads him to a dead-end cube of an office; in his futile attempt to climb out of hell, he maniacally exclaims: "They gave me an office! They gave me a car! And a hat to wear for when it got windy!" (48). In these exclamations we hear the despair wrought by this subject's investments in "aspirational normativity" (Berlant 164): a constantly upgradeable life, heteronormative reproductive futurity, and a drive toward individualistic achievement. Obiyashi has spent years subjected to the "good life" logics of neoliberal capitalism—the logics that rationalize financial and social speculations privileging profit for the few over more disposable lives that don't fit or aspire to the same narrative.

The astonishing and inspiring element of the *Malinky Robot* stories is their commitment to disarming the seduction of neoliberal ascension and individualism in favor of cultivating extended practices of care and more inclusive notions of family and collective responsibility. In Figure 12.6, we see Oliver's comic strip embedded within the larger comic world of *Malinky Robot*. "Hi-Life" features two construction workers on their lunch break, sitting on a beam high up in a skyscraper, evocative of the famous *Lunchtime atop a Skyscraper* photograph shot at Rockefeller Center in 1932. In both examples, the drama revolves around the precariousness of high-rise construction work. Without harnesses, the workers seem alarmingly casual with their safety. Unlike the New York City Depression photo, though, the display of risk in Oliver's

FIG. 12.5 "A Series of Dwindling Offices." *Source: Malinky Robot* 45. *Credit:* Sonny Liew.

version has not been staged by corporate interest to promote the building of another Rockefeller skyscraper. Neither is the uncertainty of a man's future contained by a narrative about the importance of saving. Liew opts, instead, to stay with the awkwardness of uncertainty, as one of the workers admits that he spends all his money on alcohol. In *Malinky Robot*, a postfinancial crash story, putting money in a savings or interest-bearing retirement account might actually be more foolish than "squandering" one's earnings on the pleasure of daily drink. The snippet demonstrates Liew's purposive undercutting of "the good life" promise—a promise of better futures that the act of building skyscrapers would seem to deliver. In *Malinky Robot*, though, technological inventions—whether in the form of skyscrapers or cantilevered bike gears—fail to deliver on their promises. Oliver's "Hi-Life" points to the irrelevance of whether these workers invest in the future or not; it recasts the tale of opportunity as a farce for those whom capitalism has deemed disposable, replaceable, and ultimately without future.

Liew sabotages reproductive futurity in a similar comic within a comic that plays on the popular children's magazine activity of "spotting the difference." Whereas a smiling child secures the happiness of the family portrait in the first panel, a tombstone supplants the child in the second and shatters the sunny disposition of reproductive futurity. Also shattered is the very exercise of spotting differences. These images make no pretense to similitude; with starkly contrasting color palettes—the first in bright, mostly primary colors and the second in macabre grayscale—their differences hardly require

FIG. 12.6 "Hi-Life." *Source: Malinky Robot* 54. *Credit:* Sonny Liew.

practiced sleuthing or careful management of propriety. Instead, Liew revels in impropriety, putting pressure on *Highlights* magazine's tagline, "Fun with a Purpose." Oliver's morbid rendering of spotting differences interrogates and dramatically halts the instrumentalization of fun.

The critique of instrumentalized fun stands in direct contrast to Oliver's own preference for "irrational exuberance" over edutainment's developmental games, designed to put kids on the dubious cutting edge of competitively tracked educational systems governed by quantitative evaluation and technopositivist entrepreneurs. In this way, Oliver's "Spot the Difference" comic registers a complaint against what Lee Edelman has termed "reproductive futurity," a holding up of the figure of the child as the naturalized site of political incitement. The fraught case of imagining who shall inherit future Singapore, though, charts how capitalist development and ecological sustainability hold the question of reproduction and futurity in tension. Whereas a pronatalist movement in the 1980s led to a "baby bonus" program with financial incentives for couples considering second and third children, 1999 (on the heels of the financial crash of 1997–1998) marked the launch of Singapore's international headhunting program to recruit students and professionals primarily from India and China (Ong, *Neoliberalism* 185–186). In 2001, the baby bonus program was reinstated, awarding mothers $4,000 for each of the first two children born and $6,000 for the next two. More recently, at Singapore's 2008 National Day, Prime Minister Lee Hsien Loong dedicated more than 5,000 words of his speech to discussing the falling birthrate (Mahtani). Singapore's concern over its low birthrate (among the lowest in the world) was perhaps most overtly broadcast when a 2012 Mentos ad went viral, calling for a "National Night" wherein Singaporeans would enact their "civic duty" to make babies.[8] Set to a song in which a male vocalist raps, "It's National Night and I want a baby, boo, I know you want it, so duz the SDU," the commercial references the Social Development Unit (renamed the Social Development Network), a governmental body devoted to addressing the birthrate issue and housed under the broader reaching Ministry of Social and Family

Development. That state development includes such calls to reproduction as civic duty situates Singaporean futurity not in the figure of the child, but in actual children. The Mentos commercial, in its unapologetic overture to heterosexual baby-making, makes clear the connections between reproductive futurity and other speculative futures. National Night, according to the video, also means getting aroused by the potential of buying a $900 stroller and taking a stroll through the Gardens by the Bay park—a billion dollar, 103 acre public construction project that resembles a giant bubble of speculative financing with all the aesthetic trappings of speculative futurity. It is against these financial forms of irrational exuberance that Atari and Oliver's flights of fancy and moments of ebullience stand in contrast.

In another sidebar comic within a comic, Atari's imagined superhero Doctor Midnight (Mr. Bon Bon in disguise) administers punishment to his foes even as he spouts after-school specials' canned statements about health and fitness. With each POW! KRAK! BIF! blow to the thugs who have come to claim the stolen bicycles, the Doctor administers "medicine" (60): "FLOSS after every meal!" "ALWAYS wear your seat-belt!" and "Maintain an ACTIVE lifestyle!" Doctor Midnight's recitation of sound-bite self-improvement and healthy living as civic virtue is decidedly ironic. For all of modern science's promises of its beneficial effects on the population, these pledged benefits have passed over Oliver and Atari, who seem wholly unmoved by overtures to longevity and prosperity. As the sworn defender of street urchins, Dr. Midnight interrogates for whom these logics of prolonging life are designed. After dispatching his adversaries, he rebukes the thin assurances of better tomorrows: "Who builds the *cities*? By whose sweat, by whose blood?? And in return to ask nothing but a *roof* over their heads.... Seeking merely to manage from day to day ... in these times of *unending* change ... and in the bitter end to shuffle into the darkness of this mortal coil that *binds* us all. What is it that *awaits* us beyond that final frontier? What *indignities*, what *sorrows*? What semblance of this *hell* that we have already tasted on this *cruel* earth?" (61, emphases in original).

The city of the future does not provide a roof over the heads of those who built it. Oliver and Atari "manage from day to day" by squatting in makeshift shelters either on rooftops or in abandoned "McDonnell's" sites, making do with the materials of dilapidated futurity. Midnight's closing monologue alludes to the oscillatory quality of Hamlet's considerations "to be or not to be." The allusion helps illuminate the relationship between life and futurity ("perchance to dream") and insists on the importance of regarding the future as contested and critical terrain.

If they were to buy into the aspirations of upward mobility and the gleaming promises of Asian futurity, Oliver and Atari would partake in what Lauren Berlant has called "cruel optimism." Berlant's project investigates "what happens to fantasies of the good life when the ordinary becomes a landfill for

FIG. 12.7 "Dr. Midnight's Soliloquy." *Source: Malinky Robot* 61. *Credit:* Sonny Liew.

overwhelming and impending crises of life-building and expectation whose sheer volume so threatens what it has meant to 'have a life' that adjustment seems like an accomplishment" (3). In many ways, *Malinky Robot* sketches out in haunting beauty the condition of "living in crisis" (Berlant 63), wherein we encounter Atari and Oliver negotiating "the impasse" of everyday crisis in their temporary shelters and tender socialities. In Atari and Oliver's daily exploits, we find a sustained rumination on the productive relationship between two truant geeks who aspire "toward and beyond survival" (Berlant 9), but in ways that move "toward an opening that does not involve rehabituation, the invention of new normativities, or working through and beyond trauma" (Berlant 17).

Rather than eschewing Asian futurity in the face of techno-Orientalism, *Malinky Robot* follows Berlant's injunction "to imagine better economies of intimacy and labor" (Berlant, "On Her Book Cruel Optimism"). Launched from within a McDonnell's where Atari and Oliver have scored a free lunch from their friend Misha, this series of embedded comics, which include Misha's story of the theft of Mr. Bon Bon's intellectual property, Oliver's Sunday funnies about joblessness and curtailed futures, and Atari's Doctor Midnight superhero comic, allow incredible artistry and imaginative storytelling to unfurl against the backdrop of super-sized French fries and the multinational reach of corporations like McDonald's. As the friends return to their neighborhood on their borrowed bicycles, they run into Mr. Bon Bon, whose backstory they've just learned over lunch. In the closing full-page panel of "Bicycles," we see Bon Bon crouch to inspect the cantilevered gear, the sign of all that could have been. But, as the ordinary hero, Mr. Bon Bon simply asks if the kids are hungry and suggests a new noodle place where they can eat, "his treat." In the cruel world of foreclosed opportunities, where Mr. Bon Bon works construction even though his invention could have gained him access to a life of financial security and relative comfort, Liew's story bears witness to the startling willingness to cultivate tender ties in precarious times. *Malinky Robot* posits an alternative to cruel optimism—call it a queer exuberance—that persists not only in the queer kinships Misha, Atari, Oliver, and Mr. Bon Bon form amid conditions of contingency and precarity, but also in Sonny Liew's ekphrastic exercise that restores texture to Asian futurity when techno-Orientalism works to smooth over the vicissitudes of neoliberalism. As Singapore relies increasingly on temporary migrant workers, its flexible accumulation trades on the cruelly optimistic drive toward a "good life" and the promise of an Asian futurity that will never arrive for the vast majority of the workers who sustain the wealth of the few. *Malinky Robot* imagines otherwise.

Notes

1. See *The New Asian City* (Kim Watson) and *Worlding Cities* (Roy and Ong), in which Ong quotes Rem Koolhaas's 2004 statement, "the skyline rises in the East."
2. It's particularly important to remember Japan's occupation of Singapore (1942–1945), which marks Singapore as not only a former British colony but also a city-state with multiple imperialisms in its history. As this chapter takes particular interest in a Singaporean text's relationship to techno-Orientalism, which is most conventionally associated with Japan, one must consider the postcolonial context of Singapore, even as we witness neoliberal ideology and policy take shape in that context.
3. In this way, the special issue of *American Quarterly* on "Race, Empire, and the Crisis of the Subprime," 64.3 (Sep. 2012), coedited by Paula Chakravartty and Denise Ferreira da Silva, has been helpful.
4. Singapore Economic Development Board, "About Singapore—Singapore's Fundamentals—About Business Opportunities in Singapore—Singapore's Fundamentals—Trust," *Future Ready Singapore,* http://www.edb.gov.sg/content/edb/en/why-singapore/about-singapore/values/trust.html.
5. Singapore, Singapore Economic Development Board, *Annual Report 2007–2008* 19 Aug. 2008, http://www.edb.gov.sg/content/dam/edb/en/resources/pdfs/publications/Annual%20Reports/Annual-Report-2007-2008.pdf.
6. "Upgrading" and "upskilling" are iconic neoliberal concepts, the counterpoints to the mobility of global elites who exercise what Ong has called "flexible citizenship."
7. Liew learned about San'ya from Edward Fowler's *San'ya Blues*, which he picked up from a bargain book bin at Brown University. Fowler's ethnography of day laborers in Tokyo offers an alternative narrative to the history of the Japanese economic boom from 1989 to 1991.
8. Thanks to Catherine Fung for calling my attention to the Mentos "National Night" and "National Day Proposal" ads.

Chapter 13
Palimpsestic Orientalisms and Antiblackness

―――――――――――◂○▸―――――――――――

or, Joss Whedon's *Grand Vision of an Asian/American Tomorrow*

DOUGLAS ISHII

Firefly, a cult hit television series that ran on FOX from 2002 to 2003, marked a departure from the Buffyverse, the 1990s and 2000s Californian settings of Joss Whedon's first series, *Buffy the Vampire Slayer* (1997–2003) and its spin-off *Angel* (1999–2004). Set in the postapocalyptic 'Verse, *Firefly* expanded the Buffyverse to the Whedonverse—a term that denotes beloved Whedon's growing oeuvre across television, film, comics, and online content. *Firefly*'s 'Verse is decorated with English-to-Mandarin code switching, English/Chinese bilingual signs, and, as Rebecca M. Brown catalogues, material objects, costumes, and customs from all around a past-turning Orient. I use "past-turning Orient" to refer to the durable geopolitical tropes, identified in Edward Said's *Orientalism* (1979), of an amorphous East that exists in a decadent, unchanging past against the West's modernity. Despite *Firefly*'s Oriental atmosphere, only a handful of phenotypically Asian characters appear on-screen, and only one has a minor speaking role. Nonetheless, *Firefly* features notable black actors Gina Torres and Ron Glass as central crew members.

Their inclusion seemingly responds to Kent A. Ono's critique of antiblack racism in *Buffy*, but their race is never addressed directly. Racial difference in the 'Verse is simultaneously hypervisible yet invisible.

These contradictions of racial inclusion and disappearance draw my attention to *Firefly*. The show marked its tenth anniversary in 2012 and celebrated at the San Diego Comic-Con with a panel that reunited cast and crew to answer audience questions. There, Mike Le, Media Liaison for media advocacy organization Racebending, asked Whedon, "One of the things I loved about *Firefly* was the exploration of the fusion of Asian and American cultures. Many Asian Americans go through a similar journey. I was wondering, if you were to explore that again in the future, if you would be willing to include Asian or Asian American performers?" Le's question takes *Firefly*'s Orientalism to symbolize racial identity, and asks where the Asian American subject fits among these Asian objects. Joss Whedon answered, "Yeah, absolutely. It's not a mission statement, in terms of who I'm casting for a particular thing. It was a mission statement of the show to say that cultures inevitably blend, even if it happens through conquest and violence." Le, unsatisfied with Whedon's reply, wrote a July 17, 2012, rebuttal at Racebending.com, "Frustrations of an Asian American Whedonite." Le explains, "[I]t was clear that the notion of cultural integration was more important than the practice. That the grand vision of an Asian/American tomorrow was more important than the inclusion of Asian faces and voices today." Le's "Asian/American tomorrow," a future of "Asian" cultures evacuated of the people, addresses *Firefly*'s deployment of techno-Orientalism alongside a past-turning Orientalism. As Greta A. Niu explains, techno-Orientalist tropes envision technological development as an exceptionally American enterprise, in spite of Japanese and Chinese contributions, while using Asian signs and bodies to symbolize technology's pervasiveness in a futuristic world gone wrong (Niu 74). I refer to Le's "Asian/American tomorrow," a techno-Oriental future laid onto a past-turning Oriental yesterday, as *palimpsestic Orientalisms*.

Commenters on Le's article claim that the prominent creative role of Maurissa Tancharoen, Whedon's Asian American sister-in-law, in his later FOX series *Dollhouse* (2009–2010) corrects *Firefly*'s Orientalism emptied of Asian people. Tancharoen is credited with incorporating Sierra, played by biracial Asian Australian Dichen Lachman, as a key supporting character; black American actor Harry Lennix plays central character Boyd Langton, further indicating the racial diversity of the cast. However, I focus on this diversity to complicate Le's assumption, one shared by many, that inclusion would remediate racism. Through close readings of episode settings, dialogue, material objects, and characters of color in *Firefly*, its follow-up feature film *Serenity* (2005), and *Dollhouse*, I examine across these two franchises the ideological relationship of Asian and black American inclusion to racialized tropes of palimpsestic Orientalisms and blackness. Their (white) protagonists' promise of freedom from dominant power—the colonial state in *Firefly* and unregulated corporate greed in *Dollhouse*—is achieved through racialized and indeed racist fantasies of palimpsestic Orientalisms, blackness, and whiteness. What does this triangulation reveal about the imagined future of racial difference in the Whedonverse specifically, and in speculative fiction more generally?

Framed by comparative and postcolonial approaches to Asian American studies, my approach to techno-Orientalism destabilizes the false universality of the "human," that animating figure of speculative fiction. In "The Intimacies of Four Continents" (2006), Lisa Lowe locates the modern "human" subject's nineteenth-century emergence, which normalized freedom, liberty, rights, and progress, within the material conditions produced through slavery, genocide, and indenture. Critical analyses that affirm liberal categories like freedom, rights, and progress forget that they arise from the exclusions, occlusions, and deathliness of race. Race thus temporally marks an ontological difference from the modern subject of liberal humanism; to be nonwhite is to be out of sync with modernity. Within this chronotopic definition of the "human," the postmodern future of techno-Orientalism has left the "human" and its modern present of mercy and community behind to become a technocentric dystopia, while the decadent premodernity of past-turning Orientalism leads "humanity" astray from its modern values of discipline and order. Moreover, outside of these time zones of the "human" is the subjection of blackness. In Lisa Nakamura's analysis, blackness in the digital age signifies techno-primitivism, primitive spirituality, and laboring exchange value. Reading depictions of technology in multiracial futures, Nakamura shows how white heroism takes on moral power through projections of Asianness and blackness: Asianness symbolizes a tool for white success, while blackness—stuck in an unmodern irrationality—legitimizes but never equals white valor (*Digitizing Race*, 109, 116, 127–128). These figurations of time racialize liberal humanism's promise of freedom as whiteness; the category of the "human" and its appearance of universality disguise these structuring exclusions.

To be clear, I love Joss Whedon and his dedication to human rights, seen on-screen in the Whedonverse's thematic preoccupations and off-screen in his support of international feminist organization Equality Now. However, as Mimi Thi Nguyen contends, the "human" of human rights structurally depends on the inhuman violence spread in delivering its promises of freedom. First, by naming race as this inhuman remainder, I intervene in the field of Whedon studies. The incredulous tone with which Eric Hung reviews this literature in "The Meaning of 'World Music' in *Firefly*" suggests how these aca-fan analyses forgive representational color-blindness, whitewashing, and racism beyond the screen to praise the auteur; the *Dollhouse* special issue of *Slayage: The Journal of the Whedon Studies Association* does not include race in its vocabulary. Focusing on race in the narratives of the Whedonverse introduces the inhumanity of the "human" as an unresolved problematic of minoritized groups' struggle for representation. Second, I take up techno-Orientalism as a relationally racializing trope in speculative fiction to illustrate the nonequivalent co-construction of anti-Asian and antiblack racisms. These palimpsestic Orientalisms are not a fiction to be proven false, but characterize the twenty-first-century anxieties of difference in the white supremacist culture from which Whedon writes; Asian American expression or presence alone cannot correct these interconnected racializations.

No Power in the 'Verse Can Stop Me: *Firefly* and the Racialization of "Civilization"

Set in A.D. 2517 after the fall of Earth, the fourteen episodes of *Firefly* and their continuation in *Serenity* follow Captain Malcolm "Mal" Reynolds (Nathan Fillion), war hero of the Independents, the losing side of the War of Independence. Whedon explains in a *Serenity* special feature that the *Firefly* 'Verse takes the United States and China as "the two great superpowers" that "merged into the beginning of the Alliance"—thus, the Orientalia that decorates the 'Verse. Created at the turn of the twenty-first century, *Firefly* in this way indexes U.S.-centric globalization and "China rising" xenophobia. Inspired by the Battle of Gettysburg, Whedon imagined the Independents as the Confederates—though he jokes that the Independents "[weren't] fighting for slavery." *Firefly* reconstructs the frontier in space by borrowing the Wild West genre's iconic heists, gunfights, and saloon brawls, and highlighting worlds at the edge of civilization. Whedon notes that these outer planets are actually more "diverse" than the U.S./Chinese amalgam of the Alliance's central planets, suggesting his contention that *Firefly* explores the oppressive "ugliness" underneath the Alliance's utopic civilization. *Firefly*'s joining of the Oriental East, the Wild West, and the Confederate South builds this ugliness that threatens the white protagonist around anti-Asian and antiblack fantasies.

Mal is joined by the loyal crew of his Firefly-class ship, the *Serenity*; Zoe Washburn (Gina Torres), his steadfast second in command in the war and on the ship; Hoban "Wash" Washburn (Alan Tudyk), the plucky and eccentric pilot; Jayne Cobb (Adam Baldwin), the mercenary combat expert with an eye for payday; and Kaylee Frye (Jewel Staite), the innocent but gifted mechanic. Renting a shuttle aboard *Serenity* is Inara Serra (Morena Baccarin), a Companion, part of a recognized sexual/spiritual order of courtesans. In the pilot episode "Serenity," the crew picks up Shepherd Darriel Book (Ron Glass), a man of the cloth with a mysterious past, and Dr. Simon Tam (Sean Maher). Simon smuggles onboard his sister River (Summer Glau), whom he has rescued from Alliance laboratories. Simon and River become fugitives, and given this chance to subvert the Alliance, Mal keeps them. *Firefly* follows two main story arcs: first, to find work, both legitimate and illicit, that will sustain the crew and the ship; and second, to outpace both the Alliance and the Reavers, nomadic raiders whose name evokes the setting's constant threat of destruction, rape, and murder.

Palimpsestic Orientalisms, which appear in *Firefly*'s scenes of "civilization," symbolically racialize the Alliance to construct a moral boundary between the Western self and the Oriental Other. Episodes like "Shindig" (episode 4), "Safe" (5), "Ariel" (9), and "Trash" (11), as well as *Serenity*, dress characters of the Alliance, such as doctors, scientists, dignitaries, and government personnel, in attire influenced by prior eras of Chinese clothing—a nostalgic stylization Betsy Huang references as premodern Orientalism (Huang, "Premodern Orientalist Science Fictions" 24). This past-turning Orientalism measures the crew's proximity to Alliance "civilization" through its opulence. However, *Serenity*'s touch-screens display Chinese characters, and the film's plot to uncover the Alliance secrets River holds begins with a subliminal message in the Fruity Oaty Bar commercial—an animated parade of absurd images against Chinese hanzi and Japanese katakana, what Whedon calls on the DVD Easter egg "the idea of a Japanese commercial on steroids." These scenes of techno-Orientalism suggest the underlying affluence of high-tech interfaces. Both high society and technological access signify class privilege; these are both inscribed as Asian to render them foreign to the Wild West of *Firefly*'s intergalactic frontier. This rejection of class marks the East as the progenitor of an empire that must be escaped through another Westward Expansion.

Firefly uses these racialized geographies to envision freedom in space, opposing the foreignness of "civilization" to the *Serenity* crew's Wild West "authenticity." In "Shindig," Mal, reacting to the disrespect Inara's client, Atherton Wing (Edward Atterton), shows Inara, unknowingly challenges him to a swordfight. Though this duel mixes fencing with the decorum of pistols at dawn, Mal prepares the night before, locked in Atherton's estate, by swinging a scimitar—an Oriental object of the Middle East. He is coached by Inara, whose education and comportment embodies *Firefly*'s high-class premodern Orientalism. Inara evades Mal's oncoming strikes; her instructions to make concentrated thrusts instead of powerful shoulder swings make evident that Mal's formless strength is out of place in Inara's "civilized" art form of swordplay. Mal then tells Inara about her Companion contract with Atherton: "You think following the rules will buy you a nice life, even if the rules make you a slave." Mal equates Inara's contracted labor to slavery, mobilizing the moral association of slavery with evil to implicate her classed location within the Alliance's "civilization" as unfreedom. In Whedon's geopolitical commentary, the memory of black slavery moves from the white South to the Oriental

East—a mythical elsewhere written onto the North, a place built on the rules. This rhetorical move disavows the racism of *Firefly*'s Civil War nostalgia by occluding the material base for this scripting: the South's dehumanizing plantation regimes. "Shindig" reaches its climax the next day as the viewer witnesses Mal struggling in the duel against Wing. Inara breaks the proverbial rules; she distracts Wing by agreeing to make her Companion contract permanent, which enables Mal to disarm him. With the crowd looking on, Mal refuses custom and spares Wing's life in a final critique of high society—but not without twice stabbing Wing nonfatally for comic relief. The triumph of Mal's unruly white South is a contradictory imagining of freedom that as Mal's "authentic" white masculinity paradoxically reaffirms whiteness as freedom from white supremacy.

The recurrence of the fictional warrior/poet Shan Yu in the tenth episode, "War Stories," as a symbol of spiritual Oriental sadism suggests that the depraved torture of psychopathic syndicate leader Adelai Niska (Michael Fairman) is the same violence of the Alliance's "civilization." "War Stories" begins as Shepherd Book watches Simon, who is trying to determine what experiments the Alliance performed on River. Book asks Simon if he knows of Shan Yu, who "[w]rote volumes on war, torture, the limits of human endurance." Book recites Shan Yu's proverb about torture and truth, and speculates that the Alliance experimented on River's brain "[t]o truly meet her, as Shan Yu would have said." The scene cuts to Niska, prefacing a torture by quoting the same Shan Yu sentiments. Niska later captures Mal and Wash, and grins as his torture expert electrocutes them; he forces Zoe, who attempts to buy them back, to choose only one; he smiles as he cuts off Mal's ear while she helps a wounded Wash back to the ship. Though Fairman's Niska takes on an Eastern European air, Eric Hung addresses how Niska's leitmotif, sounded by the Armenian duduk, associates him with Western Asia. Niska's excessive, extralegal violence in *Firefly*'s immediately post-9/11 context evokes Oriental terrorism. However, using tropes of spiritual Oriental sadism to connect the Alliance's experimentation to Niska's torture, *Firefly* implicates the Alliance's imperial state and its "civilization" as terror's true source.

Book's familiarity with the symbolic text of Niska's insanity illustrates how the depraved violence of Oriental "civilization" articulates with blackness. Shepherd Book's backstory, depicted in the comic book prequel *Serenity: The Shepherd's Tale* (2010), was one of violence that led to religious awakening. This nexus of violence and religion also characterizes the Operative (played by black Briton Chiwetel Ejiofor), the film *Serenity*'s antagonist. The Operative, who wields a sword over a firearm and understands his pursuit through honor, symbolizes a dogmatism akin to Book's antiquated spirituality, one that manifests the Alliance's Orientalized violence through blackness. The Operative, who sees assassinating River as inaugurating "a world without sin" and designates the deaths he metes out as "good deaths," does not question his racialized primitive spirituality until Mal causes his belief to crumble. Facing off at *Serenity*'s climax, the Operative performs a martial art move to debilitate Mal by inducing a full-body spasm; as Mal explains, it does not work because of nerve damage he sustained in the War of Independence. Indeed, the War of Independence enables white Mal to triumph against this notably black dogmatist, and, as in "Shindig," Mal's victory reaffirms that the white South he represents will rise again.

Against the freedom symbolized by Mal's whiteness, blackness cannot be free. Dee Amy-Chinn suggests that *Firefly*'s interactions between white and black bodies reflect the sexuality of the white subject: Jubal Early, portrayed by black actor Richard Brooks, who threatens to rape Kaylee in the final episode, "Objects in Space," highlights her purity; by contrast, Zoe's marriage to goofy Wash sutures virility to his nonnormative masculinity. The racism of Jubal's depiction as a psychopath who attacks the crew and threatens the three nonblack women is evident; Zoe's inclusion appears to displace that racism, yet both tend toward violence as a means to their ends. However, Zoe is the Captain's faithful right-hand (wo)man and Wash's faithful wife, while Jubal Early is a bounty hunter whose occupation suggests the predominance of lawlessness. Zoe's blackness disciplined by multiple white men contrasts Early's blackness that is not even disciplined by law. As per *Firefly*'s Civil War nostalgia, blackness possessed by white masculinity tames its danger, while undisciplined blackness threatens white death. If a risen China brought about the "civilization" that cheats (southern) whites of freedom, blackness then signifies the violence that must be tempered through a racializing discipline.

Sign a Contract to Be a Slave: *Dollhouse* and the Freedom of Sexuality

Perhaps the significant presence of actors of Asian descent in *Dollhouse* corrects their absence in *Firefly:* Sierra is a primary supporting character; Topher's assistant Ivy (Liza Lapira) and the doll-turned-"tech head" Kilo (played by Tancharoen) recur throughout the series; and numerous Asian/American extras speak, like one-time character Jack (Ian Anthony Dale) of season 1's "Hauntings." However, *Dollhouse*'s pilot begins with Echo (played by white actor Eliza Dushku) in a motorcycle race through the electric streets of Los Angeles's Chinatown—one that ends with a crash into a nightclub, where she dances the night away. Her opponent, also her lover, is revealed to be her client; Echo is a "doll," one who has a set of memories and skills—an "imprint"—uploaded to her brain by the Dollhouse to be anyone for the right price. Her client references *Cinderella* to explain Echo's departure to an onlooker, but this fairytale is haunted by the techno-Oriental decadence of the faux-futuristic Chinatown setting. The camera's first glimpse inside the L.A. Dollhouse lingers on its reflective hardwood floors and zen gardens, as dolls perform Tai Chi and tend to bonsai trees. This spiritual Orientalism, described by secondary antagonist Alpha (Alan Tudyk) as "feng shui up the yin yang," accommodates the child-like state of inactive dolls. Thus, despite the inclusion of characters of Asian descent, palimpsestic Orientalisms persist in the background. *Dollhouse*'s strategic inclusion of Asian characters illustrates how palimpsestic Orientalisms work through these racialized bodies to construct a moral narrative about technological development.

Dollhouse ran for two abbreviated seasons, totaling twenty-six episodes. The first season focuses on Echo's dollhood, while hinting at her life as activist Caroline Farrell. Echo befriends fellow dolls Sierra and Victor (Enver Gjokaj), which surprises scientific mastermind Topher Brink (Fran Kranz) and her handler, Boyd Langton (Harry Lennix); dolls are supposedly unable to form attachments autonomously. Season 1 unveils the power of the L.A. Dollhouse, run by the ruthless Adelle DeWitt (Olivia Williams), as FBI agent Paul Ballard (Tahmoh Penikett) investigates Caroline's disappearance and eventually finds his way to the Dollhouse. In season 2, Echo develops self-awareness with the help of Paul, her new handler, and Boyd, promoted to Adelle's chief of security. Adelle confronts the Rossum Corporation, the pharmaceutical research company that runs the global network of Dollhouses, as Rossum begins to put dolls in seats of government power in its schemes to end free will. Facing series cancellation at the end of the season, *Dollhouse*'s acceleration to conclusion sees Echo, Paul, Sierra, and Victor joining forces with Adelle, Topher, and Boyd to take Rossum down. The final episodes of both seasons reveal that the world, ten years later in 2019, has been reduced to a wasteland after Rossum unleashes the mind-erasing Dollhouse technology in an event called "The Wipe."

Though Orientalia does not decorate the post-"thought-pocalypse," *Dollhouse*'s palimpsestic Orientalisms locate the hubristic origins of "The Wipe" in Asia. In "The Attic" (season 2, episode 10), Echo, placed in the Dollhouse's psychic torture chamber of the episode's title, bests the system and escapes her nightmare. A katana-wielding figure in a black bodysuit attacks her; she fights it off and follows it, revealed as Arcane, through a network of other Attic-induced personal nightmares. In one, Echo finds herself seated on the floor of a Japanese teahouse, served by a geisha in full dramatic makeup as the sounds of bunraku and shamisen fill the scene; Echo, confused, speaks to a man eating with chopsticks a brimming plate of meat. This affable man of the Tokyo Dollhouse shares that he discovered vulnerability in the Dollhouse programming. She sees that his legs have been cut off, and wanders to the kitchen to witness zombie-like chefs in Kabuki makeup carving and cooking his dismembered legs. Echo picks at Rossum's secret in an Oriental hellscape; the Dollhouse fantasy materializes as the man's nightmare of finding pleasure by eating himself. If *Firefly* is shaped by Civil War nostalgia and "China rising," the Japanese man's self-cannibalism illustrates *Dollhouse*'s Cold War anxieties about twenty-first-century technological corporatism—the Asian threat to American exceptionalism. To manage this threat, Asia must always be shown as the victim of its own inhumanity, but must also be seen as threatening to spread its cruelty.

Sierra as a figure makes Asian difference manageable through the negotiations of race and sexuality that Wendy Hui Kyong Chun argues make total control feel like freedom in the digital age. "Belonging" (season 2, episode 4) explains that Sierra's original identity is Priya Tsetsang ("Real Tibetan name, by the way," Maurissa Tancharoen shares, to reflect Lachman's multiracial identity), an Asian Australian artist in America sent to the Dollhouse against her will by Nolan Kennard (Vincent Ventresca), the Dollhouse's medical consultant. Topher allows Sierra to confront Kennard as Priya, who kills Kennard in self-defense and returns to the Dollhouse to erase this memory. Tancharoen explains in the commentary that Sierra/Priya has "been victimized a lot, and in many, many ways," such as her repeated rape in season 1. Cowriter and co-story editor Jed Whedon chimes in, "But you feel bad for her, and you're rooting for her." Tancharoen muses, "And she finds the one thing that all of us are looking for": her love for Victor (whose past as veteran Tony has not yet been revealed), one that she feels but cannot remember. Priya's freedom over her sexuality—her pursuit of love even in the Dollhouse's servitude—designates her "humanity" and, as Tancharoen and Whedon explain, makes her the show's sympathetic moral center.

Sierra's role as *Dollhouse*'s moral center attempts to abate the racism of how the show mitigates its violent premise. In "Meet Jane Doe" (season 2, episode 7), as part of Rossum's hostile takeover of the L.A. Dollhouse, three men in turbans come to discuss a Dollhouse in Dubai. Thomas Harding, Adelle's supervisor since Rossum's usurpation, suggests, "The girl would be perfect for Dubai." Harding endangers Sierra's freedom to love by separating her from Victor. The threat of a Middle Eastern Dollhouse, the sight of turbaned men, overlays this threat to love, recalling post-9/11 xenophobia and registering American exceptionalist anxieties about weaponized technology going elsewhere through the local site of her romance. While Sierra's service in the L.A. Dollhouse presents the viewer with questions of ethics and agency, her compulsory transfer to Dubai symptomatizes Harding's abuses of power that must be stopped. These racialized men evoke and reinforce terror as despotic Orientals who do not respect "humanity," in distinction to the predominantly white clientele and multiracial staff of the L.A. Dollhouse.

Dollhouse visualizes its future of freedom by using Lachman's multiracial Asian body as a screen for racial projections. *Dollhouse*'s final episode, "Epitaph Two: Return," jumps to the post-"thought-pocalypse" of 2019. Though Priya now scorns Tony, they have had a child, Tony Jr., portrayed by a multiracial child actor. Priya lives at Safe Haven, a low-tech commune of survivors, including Caroline and much of the cast save for Tony. The group discusses a plan to release a pulse that would reset everyone's memories and identities to before "The Wipe," but would force the former dolls to forget everything—including Priya's multiracial child. This discussion is interrupted by the arrival of Tony and his "tech heads," a band of soldiers who use the imprinting technology to upload superior skill sets. Tattooed, leather-clad, with facial implants for imprint uploads, the tech heads' cyberpunk appearance contrasts Safe Haven's pastoral influence. Priya opposes working with them and argues with Caroline; in this scene, the camera glances at Kilo, the Asian American tech head, as Priya says, "They're freaks." White Caroline's body mediates between the bleach-highlighted Priya in a prairie dress and the raven-haired cyberpunk Kilo in leather, posing the dark and technologized (and, as suggested later, queer) "bad Asian" against the bright "model minority" mother in a visual allegory of the world's fate. The series' final montage after "The Wipe" has been reset, in which the former dolls avoid the pulse in the ruins of the L.A. Dollhouse, includes a shot of Tony Jr. reading with Priya and Tony. Reading paper books by candlelight, their prison made a home, heterosexual family reunited, the effects of world-ending technology disappear alongside racial difference; this safe space is cleansed of the palimpsestic Orientalisms of "tech" and "feng shui up the yin yang." Through this imagery, *Dollhouse* rewinds to a domestic intimacy lost to technological development, but also fast-forwards to a future in which the dilution of racial difference by whiteness signifies freedom.

While multiracial intimacy implies freedom from Asian technological corporatism and post-9/11 terrorism, blackness structures *Dollhouse*'s moral premise, in which the Dollhouse exchanges wealth for human agency. "Man on the Street" (season 1, episode 6) begins with a news segment in which a black reporter interviews pedestrians for their thoughts on the urban legend of the Dollhouse. This framing narrative includes a black woman's perspective on the Dollhouse that articulates this unfreedom through race and morality:

WOMAN: Oh, it's happening. There's one thing people will always need: it's slaves.
REPORTER: Well, some of the versions of the story say that the dolls themselves are volunteers.
WOMAN: There's only one reason that people would volunteer to be a slave, and that's if they *is* one already. Volunteer. You must be out of your [bleep] mind.

The loud black woman and her large body give the analogy of slavery its racial legitimacy. However, the black woman's scripting through "sassy realness" delegitimizes her voice because of her perceived technological underclass status: she is unable to see the Dollhouse's possibilities. The black man, who through the classed contrast of his eloquence and professionalism maintains "human" universality in spite of his race, subordinates the black woman's analysis of slavery's afterlife to a paranoid suspicion born of her own disposability.

This racialized and classed "human" universality thus enables race's centrality and invisibility in *Dollhouse*'s analysis of freedom. In "Omega" (season 1, episode 12), Echo confronts Caroline, her original personality uploaded to the body of a kidnapped woman. Responding to Caroline's explanation that she signed a contract with the Dollhouse, Echo says, "I have thirty-eight brains. Not one of them thinks you sign a contract to be a slave. Especially now that we have a Black President." Indeed, *Dollhouse* makes visible the bodies robbed of agency in the pursuit of pleasure; however, the black voice that said this earlier is ignored. Slavery and its systemic erasure of a group's humanity remains associated with blackness in *Dollhouse*, which, as in *Firefly*, invokes black slavery as a symbol of unfree labor. However, for Echo, President Obama's first election, true to neoliberal "postracial" schemes, indicates that systemic racism no longer exists—reducing race to surface appearances. In *Dollhouse*, black slavery matters because it underwrites the inhumanity of forced subjection, but the white doll who experiences unfreedom after equality's "postracial" arrival becomes the figure of victimhood.

That's Chinese for Petty: Speculating Otherwise in the Racial 'Verse

Through the palimpsestic Orientalisms of *Firefly* and *Dollhouse*, this analysis has focused on the racialization of class, technology, and spirituality in "multicultural" narratives that nonetheless deploy difference in a possessive investment to keep freedom white. But, as Lisa Lowe argues in *Critical Terrains: French and British Orientalisms* (1994), Orientalist discourses are internally unstable. Such instability occurs in Maurissa Tancharoen's "Nobody's Asian in the Movies" from *Commentary! The Musical* (2008), a collection of metacritical songs in the DVD special features of Joss Whedon's *Dr. Horrible's Sing-along Blog* (2008). Tancharoen's lyrics explain why she wrote the female lead, but placed herself in the background: "Nobody's Asian in the movies / Nobody's Asian on TV / If there is a part there for us / It's a ninja or physician or a goofy mathematician / or a groupie in the chorus: that's me." She likens being an Asian American actor to being told, "It isn't Viet Cong / it's comic relief"; she connects the unevenness of Asian Americans' limited visibility to cultural legacies of anti-Asian violence. However, to answer "Who do they want before they want an Asian?" Tancharoen lists racial and ethnic designations, locating Asian American representation within a competitive economy.

Yet "Nobody's Asian in the Movies" simultaneously critiques the systemic exclusion that makes this competition for inclusion matter. A repeating refrain throughout Tancharoen's song riffs on the "Oriental riff." Long a part of the European and North American racial repertoire to sound Oriental otherness, the Oriental riff moves down and back up the pentatonic scale in staccato tones, usually doubled at the fourth and always in even time: the Orient is jarring and could repeat indefinitely. Tancharoen instead swings the beat and begins with a major third instead of a perfect fourth, rendering the riff both familiar yet alien through its stylization. Upon repeating the riff once, Tancharoen's second descent down the pentatonic does not return up the scale; she continues down, breaking the cycle of the Oriental riff by refusing its symmetrical construction. Tancharoen's song thus tangles lyrics of Asian American multicultural inclusion with a score that interrogates the Oriental otherness that excludes Asian Americans from inclusion as "human." Her riff on the Oriental riff gestures to what Lisa Lowe calls "those other humanities" that fall away from the white modern subject of freedom, sovereignty, and rights ("Intimacies of Four Continents" 208).

Tancharoen's example points to these instabilities within the Whedonverse's imagining of "humanity" and its racial inhumans. For example, a humorous moment in "Trash" from *Firefly* plays with palimpsestic Orientalisms' claims to representation. Mal and Inara argue over what Inara perceives as Mal's obstruction of her Companion contracts and what Mal sees as Inara's disrespect for the crew's work—what she has just referred to as "petty theft":

INARA: I didn't mean petty.
MAL: What did you mean?
INARA: Suoxi?
MAL: That's Chinese for petty.

The 'Verse's Oriental hybridity slips: Mal reflexively reveals how "Chinese" has been imposed and remains externalized: centuries after the merging of the United States and China, Chinese is still recognizable as foreign. The label "Chinese" flattens the difference between Mandarin and Cantonese dialects and understands "Chinese" through the normative grammar of singular language. This goof illustrates the nonreferentiality of *Firefly*'s palimpsestic Orientalisms, which masquerade as the ethnographic "truth" of Asian difference. *Firefly*'s vision of a risen China spins racial fantasies, not to explore cultural fusions, but to buttress American exceptionalism and white selfhood.

Thus, rather than attempting to find ourselves within the Whedonverse, one site of the desire for inclusion in the "human," my readings of *Firefly* and

Dollhouse have shown that such "humanity" is impossible for people of color because it is a racial project. As "Nobody's Asian in the Movies" suggests, Asian Americans and other minoritized groups might consider how inclusion signifies only when contrasted by legible difference. Notably, Tancharoen's song about finding Asian Americans within the "humanity" of media representation while remarking on its contradictions is a joke. We can understand this as speculating otherwise: taking pleasure in recognizing that we want what disenfranchises us in the first place. Perhaps speculating otherwise may start to liberate us from the "human" and its limited freedom.

Chapter 14

"How Does It Not Know What It Is?"

———————————◄o►———————————

The Techno-Orientalized Body in Ridley Scott's *Blade Runner* and Larissa Lai's *Automaton Biographies*

TZARINA T. PRATER AND
CATHERINE FUNG

Much of the criticism engaging with "race" in *Blade Runner* (1982), directed by Ridley Scott, examines the film's racial politics within the black and white binary that is the axis of U.S. race relations. The character of Rachael, a replicant, has been read as a mulatto, a passing figure and as symbolically "black" (Nishime, "The Mulatto Cyborg"; Silverman; B. Carr; Locke). Larissa Lai, a U.S.-born Canadian writer, has been one of the very few to imagine Rachael as Asian (Reid; Park). In her short story "Rachel," Lai makes an explicit critique of the logic of race and production undergirding the film. A father figure, assumed to be Eldon Tyrell, the head of the corporation that produces the replicants, explains to the policeman, assumed to be Deckard, "Her mother is Chinese, and very circumspect" (53). While reading Rachael in the context of a racial politics rooted in a discourse of black and white cannot be dismissed,

Lai's interpretation of Rachael as embodying articulations of "otherness" is more complex than reading her within a strictly U.S. taxonomy of race. Lai also recontextualizes the film in the long poem "rachel," from her collection *Automaton Biographies* (2009). Lai's reimagining of Scott's cinematic cyberpunk progenitor enables us to expand the reading of the raced body as mediated by overlapping notions of "Asianness" and "blackness" constructed by both U.S.-Canadian and British Orientalist discourses.

It is precisely Lai's poetic engagement in *Automaton Biographies* that facilitates our reading of the film's complex constructions of race. In moving from novel to film to short story to poetry, Lai raises the questions of how race is made representable in each genre and of what happens when creative writers take up the cinematic to invoke the apparatus of film as thematic thread. Our analysis of Lai's engagement with *Blade Runner* reveals the much larger problematic facing the marginalized subject, that of the tyranny of the lens. How does one contend with the history of image making in which one is the abject object?

Rachael is particularly interesting within the range of other racialized figures in Scott's film and its source material, Philip K. Dick's novel *Do Androids Dream of Electric Sheep?* In Dick's novel, which explicitly constructs identity within U.S. topographies of race, personhood is determined by one's ability to move to off-world colonies advertised with explicit allusions to U.S. slavery: "The TV set shouted, '—duplicates the halcyon days of the pre–Civil War Southern states!'" (17). Within this black/white racial topography, Dick curiously inserts an Asiatic body in the form of Roy Baty (Batty in the film), an "Andy" (a lifelike android), who is described as having "intelligent eyes but flat Mongolian features" (152). The film recodes Roy's otherness by presenting him as Aryan; the character is portrayed by bleached blonde and blue-eyed actor Rutger Hauer. Thus the film displaces the "Asiatic" from the male body and projects it onto the female characters in his cinematic landscape. Lai, in explicitly rendering Rachael as the inscrutable Asian, highlights how the film's Orientalist vision, metaphorized as a literal and racial landscape, attempts to enslave or contain the visible subject. Asianness, as a signifier that moves from text to text, from body to body, resists being "known." It is precisely in not knowing what they are that Lai's bodies offer a critique of the modes through which race is identified and constructed.

Retrofitted World: *Blade Runner*'s U.S. Topography of Race

The "bodies" populating the urban landscape of *Blade Runner*'s Los Angeles are cordoned off by a digital divide metaphorized in the film's "retrofitted" environments. This dystopia is strewn with trash and surplus bodies equated with global refuse.[1] "Asians," in coolie hats harkening back to late nineteenth- and early twentieth-century iconography, crowd sidewalks and ride bicycles through dimly lit wet streets. Remarkably, as noted by the few critics who address race in this film, there is almost no "black" presence in this futuristic urban landscape. Brian Locke's "White and 'Black' versus Yellow: Metaphor and *Blade Runner*'s Racial Politics" considers the absence of the black body in the Los Angeles imagined in the film and concludes that "blackness" is not literally but symbolically present in implicit gestures to narratives of enslavement, escape, and capture that come out of an explicitly African American literary tradition (114–115). For Locke, this absence is evidence of a "sentimental logic" that casts white men as victims. Locke thus reads *Blade Runner* as a neo–slave narrative that attempts to "recuperate the power of whiteness" (133). Similarly, Jane Chi Hyun Park reads the film through a strictly Americanist lens, arguing that the film uses "Asian" signifiers as "an unsettling backdrop that ambivalently reflects and responds to national anxieties about the rising economic power of Japan abroad and the increasing number of Asian immigrants at home" (xii). Because Park contextualizes the film within a U.S.-centered genealogy of Hollywood film noir, she does not account for British constructions of race that proliferate in the film's diegesis.

Our analysis, facilitated by our dual pronged critique of Scott's *Blade Runner* and Lai's *Automaton Biographies*, is one that contributes to the ongoing discussion in the work of scholars like Locke and Park. We read this film as invoking symbolic blackness through its "skinjobs," its "slaves," which we agree it does, and also argue that the "black" and "Asian" bodies in the film are readable within not only U.S.-Canadian constructions of race but also British constructions of race. Through an analysis of Lai's "rachel," we are able to read the film's intersections of U.S.-Canadian and British Orientalisms, and reconsider contexts of production and corporeal topographies that heretofore have not been visible.

In *Blade Runner*, several people work for Tyrell, including J. F. Sebastian, a geneticist. His home is Los Angeles's historic Bradbury Building,[2] with its deteriorating façade and interior, wrought iron work, exposed elevators, and eighteenth-century French-inspired rooms, constitutes a living tomb of colonialism and narratives of conquest. The Bradbury, and the Los Angeles depicted in this film, are, according to Syd Mead, one of the film's set designers, "retrofitted," which he defines as "upgrading old machinery or structures by slapping new add-ons to them" (Bukatman 21).

Sebastian is a "doll maker" who has participated in the creation of the replicant "slave race." He gleefully announces that there is "a little bit of him" in Roy and Pris, two replicants who have sought him. Yet, Sebastian is only one of many creators, a mere cog in the larger mechanism of colonial production (Hicks). If there is any character in this film that can be located in an exclusively U.S. colonial taxonomy of race, it is J. F. Sebastian. He suffers from

"Methuselah Syndrome," a disease that prematurely ages him and makes him identifiable within an American southern vernacular. His skin, with its yellowish/tan tint, and overalls with caliper-looking instruments in the front pockets invoke a cobbled-together image of phrenologist, eugenicist, and Old American South. Prior to this role, William Sanderson played southern "hicks" and "moonshiners" (Sammon 141). Sebastian becomes readable in the genealogy of "tinkerers" who created and sustained a network of relations of colonial capital and the discourses of race, sex, sexuality, and gender that undergird the institutions of slavery and imperialism.

Sebastian's manufactured "friends," living toys, are the kith and kin to violent intrusions of the nation state. One "toy" wears a kaiser helmet and possesses a long nose. A second figure is a teddy bear dressed as Napoleon. These two figures, the kaiser Pinocchio and Napoleonic teddy bear, signify colonial projects and quests for "adventure" without thought to the consequences of entering "dark continents," Opium Wars, and claiming "jewels" for the Crown. Sebastian and his home are signifiers of both the "Old South" and the "Old World." He and his friends are deemed unsuitable for emigrating to the off-world colonies. At the same time, he represents the corruption, deterioration, and obsolescence of fabricators. His body, diseased and decrepit, simultaneously young and old, signifies time out of time. He is master and slave, white and black, collapsed in one: the degenerate mulatto with no place in the new colonies.³

The film constructs a world that is as anxious about race as it is about technology. One of the most telling aspects of the film's racial logic is the absence of the technological reveal; there are no moments when we see the internal mechanics of replicants' bodies. We do, however, see blood. When replicants are "retired," the kineticism is inhuman, but the blood is not. In national contexts where blood and blood admixture are preoccupations, where racial identity is quantifiable by way of percentages, blood remains at the core of race logic. That her death is mechanized is consistent with representations of the techno-Orientalized body. The replicant, as a technologically produced body, performs "human" to a frightening degree of accuracy. The need to eradicate the threatening body is commensurate with twentieth-century anxieties about "blood" as a way to discern "race" and therefore humanity. While these anxieties are fears of miscegenation, they are also fears of the "Orient's" takeover of Western capital and the mutability of whiteness.

The fear of racial and technological takeover manifests in the film's rendering of female bodies as at once Orientalized and incapable of reproduction. The female replicants, Rachael, Zhora, and Pris (Sean Young, Joanna Cassidy, and Daryl Hannah, respectively), are "pleasure models," designed for nonreproductive sexual labor. As sexual laborer of "off-world colonies," Pris embodies locales of sexual tourism: Thailand, Vietnam, Korea, the Philippines, and

Japan. Her body, generated from "sexless" scientific production, has been created to satisfy the needs of both sexual tourists and labor camps. She, along with what Lai reads as her "sisters," become territory to be repeatedly conquered. Deckard conquers Pris's body by shooting her in the abdomen, leaving a gaping bloody wound complemented by her visible open mouth and hanging tongue. When he "retires" Pris, it is an oversexed end, the tragic result of a life of sexual servitude and labor.

Rach(a)el's Broken Syntax

Larissa Lai's *Automaton Biographies* (2009) is a collection of poems, the first of which, "rachel," is a rewriting of Lai's own short story "Rachel," published in the collection *So Long Been Dreaming: Postcolonial Science Fiction and Fantasy* (2004). Lai's move to poetic form enables her to play with language in a way that links one's self-understanding and self-determination to linguistic expression that was not possible in the short story (and, arguably, not in the film either). Lai's poetic play with the character's name, the omission of the indefinite article "a," affects a determinate subject, one that challenges the overdetermined filmic "Rachael." Lai deemphasizes the "circumspect" Chinese mother in her short story and instead focuses on the paternal. In shifting to the paternal, Lai troubles genealogy in a way that allows superfecundation, making Rachel the locus of multiple genealogies of production.

The poem begins with Rachel referring to her father, who, with his mathematical talents, is able to create replicas of human beings: "2019 and all is well / i tower my mythic birth / my father's a doll maker / his algorithms spill life / more human than human" (13). In the film, the doll maker is J. F. Sebastian, but the line *"more human than human"* is spoken by Tyrell. The poem also opens with the scene from Tyrell's boardroom, where the film first introduces Rachael: "we manage our doric columns / even the sun / the way light tumbles / through our boardroom / rues our mumbly owl" (13). Lai highlights the film's allusion to the "mythic birth" of Athena, the goddess who springs from Zeus's head. In the film, replicants pass as humans by showing evidence of having mothers (and Lai quotes the filmic Rachael when she shows Deckard a childhood photograph, *"Look, it's me with my mother,"* in an epigraph). The poem establishes Rachel's genesis as paternal. Furthermore, Lai makes ambiguous the identity of Rachel's father—he could be the doll maker who built her or the corporate head who conceived her existence.

Lai introduces a third father: "i athena my own sprouting / this knowledge colds me / in my ice-fringed room / my asian fits this frost" (16). The "icefringed room" refers to the laboratory of Chew, a Cantonese-speaking Asian man (Chinese American actor James Hong in the film) who specializes in crafting eyeballs for Tyrell. Lai writes, "i owl my blink / slow stare i thought was mine / father given" (16). The broken syntax suggests a disruption in her understanding of her genealogy. She inherited her eyes from Chew, not Tyrell. Rachel regains some syntactical coherence when she says, "my heart exudes a kind of love / a kind of mourning" (16). The repetition of the word "kind" evokes the words "kin" and "kindred," as Rachel expresses a sentimental attachment to the idea of having a father. The film does not establish any relationship between Chew and Rachael; Lai, however, positions Chew as a figure that mediates Rachel's recognition of her own identity. Lai gives Rachel an explicitly Asian genealogy that we don't see in the film.

Rachel recognizes Chew's submissive position relative to Tyrell. Lai writes, "i hang memory on icy lines / tedious laundry / someone else's dirt" (17). The word "icy" again refers to Chew, and the reference to laundry invokes the nineteenth-century Chinese American laundryman. In spite of his expertise, Chew is treated as nothing more than a line worker who never interacts with the boss, yet bears the brunt of his transgressions. He is further marked linguistically when he responds in heavily accented English while being interrogated by the replicants in search of their father: "I don't know such stuff. I just do eyes." Lai's references to Chew, however oblique, highlight his racialization. Rachel says, "my eyes fine as china / man could make them" (25). The enjambment between these two lines form the racial epithet "chinaman," hearkening to the history of Asian laborers seen as low-skilled laborers and treated as threats to white American labor.

In establishing this racial kinship between Rachel and Chew, Lai offers a reading of the replicant as product and perpetuation of Asian labor, a new form of "yellow peril," an image that, as Gina Marchetti, argues, has roots traceable to the medieval threat of Genghis Khan and Mongolian invasions of Europe.[4] Rachel refers to wars between human and replicant races that result in a new world order: "our century jades terror / knowledge my athena / wars for us / the blunt rapes / the mass racial graves" (31).[5] Lai's use of the phrase "mass racial graves" addresses the history of wars the United States has waged in Asia and the Pacific Rim and foregrounds a reading of the wars between humans and replicants as an allegory for those between the West and the East. The character's full name, Hannibal Chew, alludes to the Carthaginian military commander from the second century B.C. who almost defeated the Roman Republic.[6] The representation of Chew is consistent with ambivalent characterizations of Asians as variously aggressive masterminds (Fu Manchu/Hannibal types) or passive instruments of intellectual and physical labor. His surname denotes consumption; he is at once the laborer consumed by voracious modern corporatist interests and the threat that consumes.

In rendering Rachel as Asian, Lai highlights the xenophobic undercurrent that some argue is already in Scott's film, which, released in 1982, can be read in the context of a political climate resulting from the economic "threat" of

Japan and so-called Asian tigers: Hong Kong, Singapore, South Korea, and Taiwan (Yu; Niu; Bukatman; B. Carr; Silverman; Park). Lai highlights how Asian engineering is characterized by its inscrutability and precision:

> our racial differences mechanic
> eyes limbs secret
> parts design-soaked
> and calculated in advance
> superior strength
> minds sharp as
> haystack needles
> unpredictable and algorithmic
> death is our only weakness (34)

Lai's Rachel offers a flip side to "yellow peril," which is the "model minority."[7] Just as replicants' ability to master skills and pass for human positions them as a threat, the notion that Asians have exceeded whites in education and earning power casts them as threats to white hegemonic rule.[8] Rachael's story line primarily entails her being taught, first by Tyrell and then by Deckard. In Scott's film, the police discern between replicants and humans by viewing their irises through a machine called the Voight Kampff while asking them a series of questions. Replicants are revealed when their answers betray a gap in cultural knowledge or when they show an abnormal physiological response to a question. When Deckard interviews Rachael, he offers the following hypothetical: "You're watching an old movie. It shows a banquet in progress. The guests are enjoying raw oysters." The needles on the Voight Kampff machine swing swiftly, indicating a possible aversion. Deckard continues, "The entrée consists of boiled dog stuffed with rice." The question that reveals Rachael to be a replicant invokes the Western perception of Asians as dog eaters (Frank Wu). In *Blade Runner*, this is the marker of the nonhuman.[9] In order to pass, Rachael must not only assimilate to a culture in which raw oysters are acceptable dinner banquet food, but also adopt a cultural bias that reproduces anti-Asian rhetoric. In this respect, Rachael becomes the immigrant being schooled. She must be converted from the foreign threat to the assimilated model minority.

Lai highlights the ways in which Rachel's ability to pass as human relies on her ability to speak: "i marvel my limbs' articulation / warmth my heart makes from nothing / for no one but the hand / that winds me" (17). Though referring to her body, "articulation" also refers to her speech. The repeated labial sounds in these lines signal a prelinguistic humming, suggesting that the hand that instructs Rachel on how to behave also teaches her how to speak. As if to draw attention to the violence of that instruction, Lai's Rachel expresses an anger that the film's Rachael never does: "this rage i told you / i toy my own mind / quick computation brings ugly feelings / terror the old man / is not my father / is god in his heaven / and what's right with the world?" (18) Unlike filmic Rachael, who runs to Deckard for confirmation of her suspected replicant status, Lai portrays Rachel as the schooled subject that begins to resist her instruction.[10] With its vague syntax, this verse expresses a disavowal of four possible "fathers": the Chinese father, through whose eyes she sees, the white father who socialized her, the "mulatto" father, and finally "god in his heaven," an allusion to the role Christianity serves in "civilizing" colonized subjects and assimilating immigrants. Rachel's speech becomes a mishmash of sound bites; her ability to assimilate rests on an ability to imitate, which falters: "pretty policeman's seen the letter / the law of my birth / four years line my fibre / his rib? or any other part / belonging to a man / i search my memory's lineage / for signs of suture / a kiss is just a sigh / a scar / lipping the star of midwife" (20). She alludes to Eve's genesis from Adam's rib, the song "As Time Goes By" from the film *Casablanca*, as well as Shakespeare's *Romeo and Juliet*. Her cultural references are assembled from multiple sources like Frankenstein's monster, and "sutured" together like sound and visual text in film. Her loss of speech allows Deckard, the man who stripped her of her ability to speak, to step in as a new teacher.

The film represents Deckard as refuge; Lai represents Deckard as rapist. In Scott's film, when Rachael attempts to leave Deckard's apartment, Deckard pounds the door shut, pushes her against the window, glares, and then kisses her. He orders, "Say, 'Kiss me,'" to which Rachael acquiesces. Deckard says, "Say, 'I want you,'" to which Rachael repeats, "I want you." Deckard orders, "Again," and Rachael obeys. Rachael then says, "Put your hands on me," and they embrace. Deckard's seduction is coercive and operates via replacing Rachael's speech with his. For the rest of the film, Rachael says nothing until she parrots Deckard, "Do you love me?" and she answers, "I love you." He asks, "Do you trust me?" and she answers, "I trust you." In Lai's poem, it is precisely this robbing of language that equates with rape. Lai collapses two scenes in which Rachael seeks Deckard—the first when she goes to his apartment and tells him about a childhood memory, the second which concludes with the love scene—into one:

> this secret thread and tendril
> he knows
> this intimate doctor
> sailor, policeman, chief
> i auto every memory
> mimetic someone else's
> dead mother spider
> someone else's curious brother

policeman's hands are hot
as tears my ducts
manufacture this dribble
i salt   i water (21)

Rachel, in testifying to her childhood sexual explorations with her brother, resembles a penitent confessing to a priest. This conflation of Deckard as paternal figure and priest enables us to understand Rachel as submitting not to a lover and protector, but to an assailant: "a kiss is just a bullet wound" (22). Rachel cries at Deckard's touch, and her tears are "manufactured" expressions of alienation. The gap between "i salt" and "i water" suggests a silencing or inability to protest. The film represents this scene as seduction; Rachael is a willing participant. Lai's Rachel is unambiguously violated and conquered.

Zhora: "Watch Her Take Pleasure from the Snake"

Although the filmic Rachael never appears in the same scene with her Nexus 6 "sisters," Lai's poetic reading of the film's characters enables us to see the links among Rachael, Pris, and Zhora. All the female replicants in this film, to one degree or another, signify "racial otherness" commensurate with both U.S.-Canadian and British stereotypes of "Oriental" and "Black" bodies. In the case of British configurations of race, anything not white is "black," if not "blackish," with blackness as a categorical catchall for sub-Saharan African, African, North African, Arab, Middle Eastern, and South Asian. Zhora is readable within an explicitly British system of racialization. At the same time, she also signifies U.S. constructions of blackness. Zhora is a dancer at Taffey Lewis's club, a site reminiscent of speakeasies or "black and tan" clubs of the Prohibition or Harlem Renaissance eras but also located within an ethnic enclave that is equal parts Chinatown and "Middle Eastern" marketplace.[11]

This club is configured as a site of racial and sexual transgression (Chauncy; Huggins). Deckard enters pretending to represent the "Confidential Committee on Moral Abuses." Zhora responds to his queries as to whether or not she has felt exploited with "I don't know nothin' 'bout it." The language she uses is grammatically and syntactically "black," or at the very least classed. Tone, inflection, and idiom mark her in ways that exceed the "tanning" pigments used to color her skin. Framed as Orientalized Other, Zhora "takes pleasure from the snake" in a dance we never see. She is either unaware of and unconcerned with exploitation, or incapable of being subjected to sexualized violence because she is incapable of saying "no." Similar to Rachael's, Zhora's body is caught up in analogous networks of ambivalent stereotypes, but they are of darker caste "Oriental" *and* "Black" bodies. In the eyes of the state, filmically represented by Deckard's boss Bryant, Zhora is a conflation of "Beauty and the

Beast—she's both." She, like Rachael, is at once sexual object and sexual threat, but unlike Rachael, Zhora is darker, literally and figuratively, and as such she is unteachable and untamable.[12]

The representation of Zhora, Pris, and Rachael as "Oriental" is consistent with Ella Shohat's discussion of the Orientalist gaze in film that represents non-European lands as "awaiting the touch of the colonizer," with the implication that "whole continents—Africa, America, Asia, and Australia—could only benefit from the emanation of colonial praxis" (20). Shohat further posits that the Orientalist image "is best epitomized by an iconography of papyruses, sphinxes, and mummies, whose existence and revival depend on the 'look' and 'reading' of the Westerner" (26). In the case of *Blade Runner*, Rachael, Zhora, and Pris are "Oriental" by virtue of their proximity to each other and signifiers of the "Orient." In Zhora's case, she is the dancer, the harem girl, the Egyptian artifact "discovered" and on display. Zhora, in Lai's interpretation, is "chinatown's best snake dancer / exotic limbs / art of face" (24).[13] Her body is a canvas, painted to look like a statue with images of "snakes" tattooed along her face and neck, aligning her with the iconography of a plundered Ancient Egypt and "geopolitical maneuvers of Western powers" (26).

Pris: The Deadly Double/Kabuki Doll

If Rachael signifies the Orient in U.S.-Canadian terms, and Zhora does so in British terms, then Pris represents the collapse of multiple racial constructs. As Shohat argues, "discovery" is the primary metaphor of engagement for the Westerner with the "Orient" (27). Deckard metaphorizes the "West" through his uncovering "skinjobs." He reveals Zhora's mark—her tattoo; he undoes Rachael with his "taking" and "teaching," and literally unveils Pris prior to "retiring" her. After Zhora and Leon have been retired, Pris lies in wait for Deckard in Sebastian's home. She, in Kabuki makeup and veil, sits perfectly still, among Sebastian's other life-size dolls and toys. Visually, Pris is flanked by a mechanical "laughing Chinaman" doll on one side and a fez-wearing minstrel with teapot in hand on the other. The laughing Chinaman conflates Western appropriations of folk and religious figures, rendering not just the Chinese male but "Asian" culture and "Eastern" religions ridiculous. The befezzed black figure with red lips, black lacquered skin, and rolling eyes collapses iconographic images of African American minstrelsy, northern Africans, Arabs, with trade routes and commodities in the intensely British "tea service." All of these "bodies" are part of an iconographic landscape of colonial racism.

Pris is the dangerous doll, the mail-order bride, veiled and shipped throughout the colonies to provide pleasure. Her "return" to the site of her creation is untenable and uncanny. As a doll, Pris's body is an entity unto itself and disturbingly so—the more lifelike the doll, the more inescapable the crisis of humanity.[14] The Tyrell Corporation's motto is "More human than human," and it has successfully fabricated replicants that are more human, and arguably more humane, than the humans who occupy the same landscape. In Lai's interpretive framework, Pris's body is localizable within networks of production, exchange, and capital. Taking Pris's dialogue from the film, Lai writes, "i'm not lost / it's the city," and then in the following quatrain links production to a history of violence and its contemporary incarnations: "under assembly-line eyes / fresh as new bruises / that is, dilapidated ancient / nothing's new under the gun" (25). These lines link modern technological production to the violence of old technologies of race and aesthetics. With the line "olympia curses vision," Lai alludes to Manet's 1863 painting *Olympia*, which scandalized the French public with its representation of an unrepentant nude courtesan and her black servant. Lai's allusion cements Pris's sexual labor with the production of knowledge.[15] Like the courtesan, Pris is a "pleasure model," the embodiment of beauty and sexual labor. The second line of the couplet, "*spin about, wooden doll*" (25), is an explicit reference to a scene in the film set in J. F. Sebastian's home in which Pris, folded up in a chair like human origami, spins a broken doll, a miniaturized version of herself. The doll is cut off at the waist, a symbolic link to Pris's function in and with (a)sexual production. Outside of biological production, "she handles hot eggs / menaces our genetics," yet, by virtue of her "birth," as the child of men and technology, she is more hybrid, more mixed, more fecund, and more raced (36). She is bride and whore, camouflaged in whiteness and femininity, a broken doll and "atomic bride / among other sad girl / manikins waiting too long / in white" (36).

The "other sad girl[s]," Rachael and Zhora, are both kin to dolls and "man." Later, Rachel describes Pris as "her deadly double" (36), her "quick twin" (37), describing J. F. Sebastian's home as Pris's "dilapidated carnival palace," a space where she "barnums her daily seductions / on Cartesian logic" (36). In the film, Pris declares, "I think, Sebastian, therefore I am," and through Lai we hear the collective declaration of the Nexus 6 daughters who recognize their "degenerate kin." Pris, like her "darker" sister Zhora, is a murderer and entertainer. She is atavistic, a howling wolf, a nutcracker (37). We understand Pris, her body and the context in which it is placed, as localizing multiple, aggregated, and excessive genealogies of racial construction: black, white, Asian, U.S.-Canadian, British, post- and neocolonial.

Gaff: Problematic Hybrid Masculinity and Racial Cartography

The excessive genealogies of racial construction are embodied most prominently in Gaff, the ambiguously raced police officer who gives Deckard his assignment. In a turn that suspends Gaff's allegiances, Lai suggests that Gaff is Rachel's brother, inserting a reference to origami when Rachel recalls a childhood memory: "i dream insect hatching / my brother's incest / curious as logic / of folded paper" (17). The play between "insect" and "incest" reinforces webs of reproduction that pervert familial paradigms. This play on words also invokes "incept," meaning "to begin" and "to ingest," signaling the generative and consumptive aspects of this reproduction. In so doing, Lai reinforces her critique of presumptions of genealogical certitude.

Gaff's genealogical incertitude is reinforced by his vexed relationship to racial categories.[16] He is the sole "Latino-like" presence in the film's imagining of Los Angeles, which is curiously devoid of Latino bodies. In spite of this, his body is not locatable in any one praxis. A floating signifier, his body is containable within recognizable discourses, yet simultaneously resists them. His eyes, ice blue in color, are also lined to affect Asianness. His facial hair evokes images of Fu Manchu, Charlie Chan, as well as stereotypical "cholos." Gaff speaks Cityspeak, a language Deckard refuses to speak or acknowledge he understands, which is a combination of English, German, Chinese, French, Hungarian, and Japanese. According to Scott, Edward James Olmos went to the Berlitz school to create "Cityspeak," and for all intents and purposes, Gaff is the only figure literate in this language. It was also, according to Scott, Olmos's choice to play the character as "multi-ethnic, multi-national, and as multi-lingual" (*Dangerous Days*). Gaff's racial and linguistic hybridity makes his genealogy impossible to locate or identify.

In this inscrutability, Gaff is outside heteronormative and homoerotic desire, subtextually present in the erotically charged relationship between hero and antihero, Deckard and Roy. Lai reframes the film's sexual politics, placing heterosexuality outside Gaff's purview but allowing him to retain the ability to read it: "your human / subject's broken star / our crossed wires clutch ever bigger / guns they hold / our 'i' / this certainty" (40). One cannot read the second and third lines without seeing "star crossed lovers" and the subsequent lines "death bottle / corks this fountain / our elevators seal breath / moment's crumpled aware," without seeing direct allusions to Shakespeare's *Romeo and Juliet* (40). Gaff does not participate in this romance, but watches from outside. Gaff's erotic energy is contained in a closed circuit, as reflected in his kineticism, with limbs held tightly to his body and his mechanistic gait aided by a cane. Similar to Rachael, Gaff's clothing fits his body like a glove, but unlike Rachael, Gaff never lets his hair down. He is never unveiled in the same manner as Zhora, Pris, or Rachael. He remains unreadable.

At the same time that Gaff is an unruly body, he is also a functionary, a cog in the disciplinary machine. He blends with the background, the unobtrusive observer that is everywhere and knows everything. Unlike the film's patriarchs and their prodigal sons, Gaff has no loyalty to the machine itself. Somewhat omniscient, Gaff leaves evidence of his knowledge in the form of an origami unicorn in Deckard's apartment, suggesting that he not only knows that Deckard is concealing Rachael within, but also confirms that Deckard is, in fact, a replicant. As a functionary of the state, Gaff is obligated to "retire" Rachael and doesn't. Instead, he leaves clues of his knowledge through his manual dexterity. Gaff folds matchsticks into men and paper into fantasy much like the "fathers" in this narrative fold genetics, biomechanics, and robotics to create bodies of and for fantasy.

Gaff represents a far more threatening erotic formation; he is the "impossible / beast" (40), the one who can discern the beast in Deckard and knows his dreams. He is the "passing" figure who doesn't know that he is passing. In the penultimate scene of the 1982 theatrical release of the film Gaff shows his hand when he yells, in perfect English over the rooftop, "You've done a man's job, sir. I guess you're through, huh?" As Deckard and Rachael speed though a utopic/edenic lush green landscape, Gaff's words conclude the film: "It's too bad she won't live. But then again, who does?" Given that Gaff does let Rachael live, this line can be read as disingenuous. In the poem's penultimate section, Lai repeats this line in Rachel's voice, allowing Gaff and Rachel to occupy the same ontological space. Ambiguity emerges with the words, "gotcha, deckard" uttered by either Rachel or Gaff (40). This section concludes with the disambiguating lines: "all along / you were one of us" (40). With these lines, Gaff, Rachel, and Deckard function in the same circuits of production.

"The Tyranny of an Object"

Turning once again to the question of genealogy, Lai's poem ends with a letter from Rachel to her mother, who is figured in both the poem and the film as an absence. The film represents the mother via a photograph, reminding us that Rachael has no "real" genealogy. As if to obscure the maternal even further, Lai represents this connection via a letter written primarily in binary code. That a reader must turn to a piece of software to translate the letter reinforces the notion that a process, in this case a virtual cartographer, is required to turn the text and body into a conceptual map that can be understood. Translated, the letter reads, "*dear mother /* return to languish *that is to say* anguish of foreigner's fodder *otherwise* the boarder pictures a *mixture of* canada wild enough to retrack railway *cn to cnn and rpms to dna* the bend in my corner / love rachel" (41, our translation, italicized words originally in English). With the rhyming words "languish" and "anguish" (which also invoke "language"), the letter expresses pain, distress, and degeneration, and attributes those feelings to the experience of being a foreigner, immigrant, laborer, and manufactured product. This is reinforced by the invocation of "father" through "fodder," thus collapsing paternal lineage with accessible, inferior, disposable material used first in colonial capital (as in "canon fodder") then first-world corporatist interest. These interests have destabilized national borders. Lai deploys the word "boarder," a homonym for "border," gesturing toward the representation of immigrants as guests and interlopers within national boundaries. The phrase, "boarder (border) the pictures" refers to visual representation, while the overlapping phrase, "pictures a mixture," evokes a hybridity that challenges the notion of a nation based on homogeneity. Specifically, it is the "mixture of canada wild enough to retrack railway" that not only asserts a hybrid nation, but does so by invoking the Chinese laborer, the "fodder" used for transcontinental and transnational railway production. Such industrial infrastructure is then connected to technologies of media production, "cn to cnn," Canadian National to Cable News Network; all represent the formation of national identity and the conduits through which bodies, capital, and information move. This movement, this circulation, is expressed in "rpms," revolutions per minute, referring to the centrifugal force associated with the technology of discs, records, wheels, and cogs. The inclusion of "dna" links this range of technologies to a biological production manipulated by "science." DNA signifies a map of how the human body can be atomized and broken down to its constitutive parts. The "bend in my corner," not only evokes origami, but also corner markets, thus suggesting how genetic material becomes a product of commerce; first- and third-world economies are collapsed as the Hong Kong street markets, Middle Eastern bazaars, and third-world higglers become the connecting agents of a counter capital formation.[17] As an automaton, Rachel's body, with its rebellious "corners" and edges, is "cornered," or contained and disciplined, in order to maintain these circuits of production and exchange. Finally, this letter contains no commas after "mother" or between "love" and "rachel," creating a syntactical ambiguity that blurs the line between address and command. Collapsing biological reproduction and mechanical production, the letter suggests that the code itself *is* Rachel's mother, thus blurring the borders between familial and national romance. On the whole, this letter contemplates how the racialized laboring body is constructed in order to function within colonial and neocolonial figurations of power.

Lai combines DNA and binary code to expose the processes of encoding bodies and the labor on which neocolonial forces depend. In terms of its visual coding, *Blade Runner* is wedded to a system of overdetermination: the tyranny of the visible. Together, the women in the film, Rachael, Zhora, and Pris, are the geisha, harem girl, tragic mulatta, Native informant and conspirator, Egyptian jewel, immigrant daughter. Because these women are played by Caucasian actors at the same time that they are represented through reductive stereotypes of blackness and Asianness, their racial otherness assumes a stability of signifiers at the same time those signifiers move between bodies and discourses. As spectators, we are expected to identify and disidentify with the positionalities presented in the film's diegesis. Scott's production of a "real," the process of suturing the body to discourses, seeks to stabilize the signifiers of race, humanity, and embodiment. Lai makes the processes of identifying and disidentifying explicit and self-conscious; her poetic form enables us to see the fissures, the suture sites, and scars.

In 2013, *Blade Runner 2*, also to be directed by Ridley Scott, was in preproduction. Thirty years after the release of the original, China has emerged as a global power, North Korea has become posited as a military threat, and U.S.-Vietnam relations have normalized. Asia continues to be a space of anxiety. In both *Red Dawn* (2012) and *Olympus Has Fallen* (2013), North Korea is depicted as terrorizing the United States, with the latter film channeling anxieties about a United States weakened by "blackness." *Pacific Rim* (2013) is about the invasion of an alien species incubating in the Pacific. In *Iron Man 3* (2013), the enemy is "The Mandarin." Over the past thirty years, fear of the Cold War enemy (as in the 1984 film *Red Dawn*) and fear of the Japanese corporation (the 1993 film *Rising Sun* and the 1995 film *Johnny Mnemonic*) have been transferred to the techno-Oriental subject. Given the contexts of post-9/11 and the great recession of 2008, the techno-Orientalized body mediates anxieties about terrorism and U.S. economic fragility. The question now is what enemy the sequel to *Blade Runner* will generate, what automatons will occupy this ever-present topography of futurity and decayed capital, and what fantasies they will mobilize.

Notes

1. In the documentary *Dangerous Days: Making Blade Runner* (2007), Lawrence G. Paull, production designer, claims that the film's producers "were able to create the look based on what goes on in various cities all over the world: whether it be Tokyo, Kyoto, or Beijing or Hong Kong or whatever."
2. Paul M. Sammon describes the Bradbury as "an early utopian novel set in the year 2000 and featuring descriptions of numerous futuristic commercial buildings" (139).
3. Our reading of J. F. Sebastian pushes against readings of him (such as Park's) as solely "white" or "classed." We read this figure in conversation with eugenics discourse, in which the passing and mulatto figures are inherently degenerate.
4. See John Laffey, Timothy P. Fong, and Doobo Shim for contemporary incarnations of the "yellow peril."
5. Lai's use of "jades" as a verb denotes "to abuse" or "to overwork," but also alludes to the Asian gemstone.
6. It goes without saying that the name "Hannibal," referring to the son of Hamilcar Barca, the Moor, invokes an anxiety over blackness.
7. For the conflation of "model minority" and "yellow peril," see Gary Okihiro and Yuko Kawai.
8. See Lucie Cheng and Philip Yang's "The 'Model Minority' Deconstructed."
9. In Dick's novel, Luba Luft, from which Zhora is crafted, tells Deckard, "They used to eat boiled dog stuffed with rice in the Philippines. I remember reading that" (103).

10. Because Park reads Rachael as a femme fatale figure within the tradition of Hollywood film noir, she reads this scene as a moment of heteronormative sadomasochistic desire (78).
11. Scott conflates both British and American notions of "Blackness" via colonialist topographies, exemplifying Edward Said's formulation of the Orient as a shifting signifier. Lai's aesthetic enacts the Saidian critique of the Cartesian dualism that produced the "Orient." The West, according to Said, defined itself as "not East" and therefore created an ontological certitude for itself through the production of knowledge; they articulated subjectivity through the objectification of the East/Orient (17).
12. The representation of these female figures we read in a continuum of femininity and sexual labor not unlike British painter Edwin Long's 1875 *Babylonian Marriage Market*, which, taking its inspiration from a passage in *Histories* by Herodotus, depicts women being auctioned off in "marriage."
13. Since Ludwig Borchardt's infamous 1912 "discovery" and 1924 "official unveiling," the limestone bust of Nefertiti has become a signifier of German nationalism and Egypt has been petitioning for its repatriation. In one of the test shots, Joanna Cassidy is shown wearing the "cap-crown."
14. The obvious colonial narrative interlocutor here is Joseph Conrad's *Heart of Darkness*, specifically the text's interrogation of the "humanity" of the raced body. The female Nexus 6 models Zhora and Pris both howl, leap, and spin in one way or another upon their death, and these deaths, like their bodies, are linked to racial fetishism.
15. See Sander L. Gilman's critique of this iconography.
16. A gaff is a long stick with a hook on it (the cane that Gaff carries in the film) that is synonymous with a harpoon or butcher's hook. In addition, a gaffe is defined as a social faux pas and a deception. More telling, in the context of sexual identities, a "panty gaff" is used by cross-dressers to hide their penises. A "gaffer" also refers to the chief electrician on a movie set.
17. See Saskia Sassen's concepts of the "global city" and "survival circuits."

Chapter 15

A Poor Man from a Poor Country

―――――――――――◄○►―――――――――――

Nam June Paik,
TV-Buddha, and the
Techno-Orientalist Lens

CHARLES PARK

When Nam June Paik passed away in his Miami Beach winter house in early 2006, numerous galleries, museums, and art organizations throughout the globe memorialized him with tributes worthy of someone of his stature. His obituary in the *New York Times* (January 31, 2006) celebrated him as the inventor of video art, and the *Times* of London (January 31, 2006) lauded him as "one of the very few artists who single-handedly changed the course and tone of art in the 20th century." As the first artist to experiment with and use video as a legitimate medium, Paik was influential in altering the relationship between art and electrical engineering. Paik's collaboration with the Japanese engineer Shuya Abe, for instance, resulted in the Paik-Abe video synthesizer as well as the incorporation of robotics into art with *Robot K-456*. At the vanguard of the use of video and televisual technologies as an artistic medium, Paik was always conscious of technological development and its impact on postindustrial societies; Paik predicted the development of satellite and cable TV and, in 1974, coined the term "electronic superhighway."

The global scale of his memorials attests to the fact that Paik was a global artist. His works were accessible to a general international audience, and a few were actually transnational in scale. In fact, his interests in televisual technologies naturally led Paik to utilize telecommunication technology to reach a wide audience. His works *Good Morning, Mr. Orwell* (1984) and *Bye Bye Kipling* (1986) were simulcast—although not without their technical difficulties—over several cities on different continents. Paik's sculptural pieces, likewise, engage the audiences with their whimsy, as well as quickly flashing, colorful images that are familiar to anyone now in the post-MTV era. With these techniques, Paik's art speaks a language that is easily understandable and relatable for audiences in the developed world whose lives are surrounded by quickly shifting technological advances that make communications easier, compress distances, and make certain images recognizable across cultures.

Paik is also global in a sense that he is a figure who is cosmopolitan with homes in many different places. He could effectively call New York and Düsseldorf home, and his upbringing in Korea and education in Japan and Munich also influenced the trajectory of his career. Thus his *Bye Bye Kipling* directly addresses Rudyard Kipling's "The Ballad of East and West," which begins "Oh, East is East, and West is West, and never the twain shall meet." It is worth noting that the quatrain that begins and ends the poem reads in full,

> Oh, East is East and West is West, and never the twain shall meet,
> Till Earth and Sky stand presently at God's great Judgment Seat;
> But there is neither East nor West, Border, nor Breed, nor Birth,
> When two strong men stand face to face, though they come from the ends of the earth!

In this sense, it is ironic that Paik chooses to bid farewell to Kipling since Paik himself represents the two sides of the border facing each other. Thus Paik traverses the seeming differences between the "East" and the "West." Yet he also used his status as an Asian in the Western European/American art world to his advantage, providing his work with an "Asian sensibility" that was different from the works of other artists in the postwar avant-garde Fluxus movement, of which he was a member.

The fact that Paik is of Korean descent made him susceptible to this categorization as an "Asian" artist even as his mentor, John Cage, who was heavily influenced by Zen Buddhism, was not. Whereas for Cage his Buddhist sensibility is learned after studying under various monks and teachers, Paik's is deemed to be a part of his genetic code so that everything he does is "naturally" Buddhist in nature. Paik's "Asianness" made his art equally Asian to his Western colleagues and audiences. Indeed critics often talk about Paik as an artist who is bridging the "gap" between "the East" and "the West." Paik certainly realized the commercial implications of this role and did not shy away from it, as the titles of some of his works (*Bye Bye Kipling*, for instance) suggest. Rather, throughout his career he has repeatedly said of himself, "I am a poor man from a poor country, therefore I have to be entertaining all the time" (qtd. in Hanzal). Carla Hanzal sees this as an ironic self parody and a strategy "to engage the audience and to traverse cultural boundaries." While I agree with this assessment, the self-designation as a "poor man from a poor country" underscores his awareness of his precarious position as an Asian-born artist in a Western art world that too often excludes non-Western artists. Furthermore, Paik's desire to be "entertaining" often led him to present his art as standing on both sides of the border between East and West. Consequently, his work in general—and, as I will argue, his *TV-Buddha*, in particular—has often been viewed as culturally paradoxical and even antithetical.[1] My argument is that this is a gross misreading that desires an essentialized "East" and "West" in Paik's work. Instead, one must read Paik's art as demonstrating the fluidity with which cultural and technological exchanges occur, and just how quickly these exchanges can be absorbed to generate hybrid identities and cultures. In order to explicate these readings fully, however, a bit of context is necessary.

Through the course of the second half of the twentieth century, Japan became synonymous with technological advancements, manifesting in the West in the form of consumer electronics and automotive manufacturing. The development of the transistor, coinciding with the end of World War II and the start of an economic boom in the United States, allowed Japanese corporate conglomerations to turn the Japanese economy toward the development of consumer goods for sale in the United States and Western Europe. Within a generation, Japan transformed itself from military/colonial power to a manufacturing/economic power, with a focus on gaining market shares in the booming American consumer market of the 1950s and 1960s. It was also at this time that Nam June Paik came into his own as an artist and gained international acclaim for his use of consumer electronic technology in his works.

Paik was born to an affluent family in Seoul, Korea, in 1932 during the Japanese occupation. His family left Korea in 1949, a year before the Korean War started, eventually settling in Japan by way of Hong Kong; Paik later graduated from the University of Tokyo in 1956 with a degree in aesthetics and music history and a thesis on the modernist composer Arnold Schoenberg. Realizing that in order to study modern composition he needed to be in Europe, Paik moved to Germany to study at the University of Munich and the Academy of Music in Freiberg. In the early 1960s, he became involved with the Fluxus movement, performing at various "happenings" throughout Germany. Paik eventually began utilizing used TV sets as art objects, exhibiting them first in 1963 at the Exposition of Music-Electronic Television in Wuppertal, Germany. The fact that he became involved with Fluxus, which took its cue from the Dadaists, is fortuitous since his musical composition skills were mediocre at best. Besides, his performance pieces, many of which called for violently attacking musical instruments, took Paik away from composition and moved him toward a form of expressionism. He eventually became the first video artist when he purchased Sony's first portable video camera at New York's Liberty Music Store in 1965. On the same day, he was delayed on his way home by Pope Paul VI's procession through the city, which Paik recorded with his new camera and screened that same night to an audience in a Greenwich Village cafe. Thus began video art.

In telling the story of the first video art piece, Patricia Mellencamp finds that "[t]he irony of Japanese consumer technology in the hands of a Korean in New York filming the Pope and triggering an art movement funded by the NEA and the Rockefeller Foundation is delightful indeed" (41). More than ironic, however, that video art began with the confluence of an Asian-born artist utilizing Japanese technology in the West has merely added credence to techno-Orientalist readings of Paik's work. As David Morley and Kevin Robins explain in their discussion of techno-Orientalism, Japan's technological rise since the 1960s has caused a sense of "cultural emasculation" in the West, and, as a result, "these postmodern technologies [became] structured in the discourse of Orientalism" (169). In this sense, Paik's use of cutting-edge technology since the late 1950s represents, on the one hand, a postmodern sensibility brought upon by these televisual technologies, while, on the other hand, it presents the avenue through which his works are "misread" from a techno-Orientalist perspective in a way that works by Bruce Nauman, Bill Viola, or Gary Hill are not.[2]

For the casual art patron, however, Paik's TV and video sculptures will be most familiar. Whether it be his large TV flags or the massive video walls or sculptures made from vintage TV sets, the viewer is drawn to the scale of the pieces and then to their accessibility. On one level, it seems clear that Paik is making a political or a social commentary about the state of modern societies through these pieces, even if they do not know exactly what that commentary is. This accessibility, not to mention his prolific production, makes his work perfect for public spaces, and his works can be seen in lobbies of corporate buildings, city squares, and sports venues throughout the world. Of all his work, however, arguably his most popular piece is *TV-Buddha*.

The fact that *TV-Buddha* has become so popular is itself almost ironic since this piece was an afterthought. This is a story that is now almost legendary for video art scholars: Paik needed to fill an empty wall at an exhibition at New York's Gallery Bonino in 1974. In order to do so, he set up a TV with a closed-circuit camera behind it and placed a statue of a monk (he apparently thought the statue, which he purchased as an investment, was that of a Buddha) opposite the TV so that the statue is facing its own image displayed on the screen. It became one of Paik's more well-known pieces and has been remade in a number of different variations between 1974 and throughout the 1980s, incorporating different statues, different TV sets, and different overall configurations, while maintaining the same general concept.

And just as there are different versions of this piece, there are different critical assessments of what this piece means, none of which are entirely satisfactory. For instance, Jon Kessler writes in *Artforum* that some critics have considered *TV-Buddha* Paik's "interpretation of a Zen parable, but it also reveals his familiarity with Western media theory. So, while representing an unanswerable koan, it simultaneously comments on Marshall McLuhan's notion of a 'global village,' as well as [Guy Debord's] undoing of the self through accumulated representation. I think of TV Buddha [*sic*] as the first reality television show, portraying a self-affirming condition—'I exist because I'm on television'—happening in real time." Through this analysis, Kessler makes a distinction—by his use of the "but . . . also"—between "Zen" and "Western media theory" that makes it clear that these are distinctive and mutually exclusive philosophies and theories. Likewise, Edith Decker-Phillips, states, "The goal of [the Buddha's] meditation was absolute emptiness, beyond time and space, but the picture which appeared on the monitor returns him to his physicality which he cannot escape. Buddha, the symbol of Oriental wisdom, was thus forced to become a modern Narcissus" (75), thereby positing the totality of "Oriental wisdom" on the person of the Buddha.

Furthermore, Walter Smith believes that *TV-Buddha* should be viewed as Buddhist art. He feels that the current criticism sees this piece from a privileged Western perspective that wants to explain it from the tradition of Western art history and criticism. Smith, being a scholar of South Asian art, is familiar with Buddhist themes and motifs as well as iconography and is able to examine it from the vantage point of other Buddhist art, tracing its precedent through the story of Buddhas Gautama and Prabhutaratna, wherein just as Gautama was teaching his followers about the transcendental nature of the Buddha, Prabhutaratna, a Buddha from a previous world age who had been in enlightenment for hundreds of thousands of years, appeared to illustrate this point. Face to face, then, the two Buddhas discussed philosophy, much as Paik's TV-Buddha faces itself—one a present physicality and the other, through the delay in the camera-TV loop, an image of the past.

Of course, the fact that Paik made this piece quickly in fact could buttress the Buddhist motif of the piece. More specifically, the quickly made work of art, apparently without forethought or planning, is perfectly in line with Zen philosophy, which, taking its cue from Daoist aesthetics, stressed spontaneity. Zen (Ch'anin Chinese) monks during China's Sung Dynasty "composed poetry using a Taoist aesthetics that valued spontaneity and concrete visual imagery" (Robinson and Johnson 206). Once Zen Buddhism became popular in Japan, the relationship between religious practice and aesthetics became even more entwined. According to Richard Robinson and Willard Johnson, Zen aesthetics stressed "total sincerity to one's present activities, however minor, for the sake of one's spiritual development" (243). This spontaneity and the emphasis on aesthetics are some of the reasons that Zen Buddhism appealed to the composer and Fluxus contributor John Cage as well as to Beat writers such as Gary Snyder, Jack Kerouac, and Allen Ginsberg, who preached "first thought, best thought."

In addition, Zen Buddhism believes in the intuitive understanding of one's buddhahood. Although originally it emphasized meditation as the central way to discover this inner self, later Zen Buddhism also allowed for spontaneous awakening without the rigors of meditation. Because Paik has often used "Zen" in the title of his works, such as *Zen for Walking* (1961), *Zen for TV* (1963), and *Zen for Film* (1964), and because of his relationship to Cage—a practicing Zen Buddhist, although not a meditating one—many art critics often wonder whether Paik himself was a Zen Buddhist. Performance pieces such as *Zen for Head* have only added to this question of Paik's religious leanings. In this piece, performed at the Fluxus International Festival of New Music in 1962, Paik dipped his head in a bucket of black paint mixed with tomato juice and dragged it like a brush down a long roll of white paper. Depending on the critic, this piece references either the eighth-century master calligrapher Zhang Xu, the eighth-century painter Wang-hsia, and/or the Japanese artist Hokusai, all of whom are said to have painted with their heads on different occasions (Doris). Some critics have also pointed out that *Zen for Head* is also a performance of the avant-garde composer LaMonte Young's *Composition 1960 #10*, which directed the performer to "[d]raw a straight line and follow it" (Rhee 48). Yet at the same time, Paik's performance is also in line with the outrageously antiestablishment and performative nature of the Fluxus movement and of the works of abstract expressionist painter Franz Kline. (It is worth noting that some critics thought Kline borrowed heavily from Japanese calligraphy and brushwork, a claim that Kline denied throughout his career.) Despite the references to Buddhism, however, in an interview with Otto Hahn, who asked him whether he was a Buddhist, Paik responded in the negative, adding simply that he was an artist, thus adding to his complexity.

But the fact is that Paik does utilize Asian and Buddhist themes and motifs. Consequently, Paik's frequent juxtaposition of Western and Asian images has also simply been attributed to his being Korean by critics and reviewers. Jieun Rhee, citing Abdul JanMohamed, argues that Paik is someone who exists in a "specular border." According to JanMohamed, a "specular border intellectual [is] someone one who is 'familiar with two cultures, [and] finds himself or herself unable or unwilling to be "at home" in these societies.'" Instead, these intellectuals "subject the cultures to 'analytic scrutiny rather than combining them'" with the hopes of defining "utopian possibilities of group formation" (qtd. in Rhee 47). Rhee's main contention is that Paik's "Asian diasporal body" inhabits a liminal space of the specular border. Rhee sees Paik's works, then, as producing "a hinge function showing how ideas and meanings are transformed when they cross 'imaginary' borders of East and West." But despite the "imaginary" nature of the border, Rhee quickly argues that Paik's negotiation of "both worlds... opens up the interface between East and West" (Rhee 50). Furthermore, Jacquelyn Serwer says in her critique of Paik's cathedral-like sculpture *My Faust: Technology*, but also of his works in general, "Relationship between East and West, past and present, seriousness and whimsy show Paik maintaining his Zen-like equilibrium" (90). (Here she confuses Zen with Daoism, further underscoring the notion that Eastern philosophies are interchangeable and without identifiable distinctiveness for the Western critic.) Consequently, Paik not only becomes a conduit through which East and West interface but also acts as an equalizing force between the two.

Indeed, this expectation is not uncommon for artists who are of Asian descent working in the West. In her discussion of the Asian American artist Yun Gee, Elaine Kim explains how Gee was regarded as an "exotic novelty" by the European art community in the 1920s. Unable to be taken seriously as an artist in the United States, Gee went to Europe, where he received a warmer reception. Nonetheless, this reception was contingent upon his satisfying the Orientalist expectations of his European critics. In particular, according to Kim, Gee was expected to blend Eastern and the Western artistic sensibilities in his work (7). In other words, Gee was expected to incorporate "Asian" images or themes into his paintings rather than merely "copying" or reproducing Western themes or styles. This blending of the East and the West is an attribute that is seen as a given when the Western art/literary establishments formulate the artist and/or writer of Asian descent working in the West.

TV-Buddha is a popular piece precisely because it seemingly positions two incongruous cultures against each other. The Buddha, with its disavowal of materiality, sits opposite the video camera and its image on a TV screen—TV, of course, representing banality and the penultimate lowbrow culture. They seem at odds with each other, and this incongruity adds to the humor. This is perhaps the same reason why Paik's *TV-Rodin*, in which Auguste Rodin's *Thinker* replaces the Buddha, was not received with the same acclaim. Whereas the Buddha is perceived by Western audiences as ancient, static, something incongruous with the modern world, and representative of the Orient, Rodin's *Thinker* is not seen to be as representative of Western or European culture. It does not stand in for an enlightened cosmopolitanism, particularly because the West sees itself as dynamic and heterogeneous. The West also sees itself as modern, which also inevitably means technologically advanced. Thus, when Rodin's *Thinker* sits in front of a camera, contemplating its image on the TV screen, it seems more redundant rather than whimsical or profound. The success of *TV-Buddha* lies in the significance that the Western audiences view the Buddha as a metonymy for the Orient as it sits vis-à-vis (a perceived Western) technology.

As an Asian artist working in the West, however, Paik recognizes that he can be a cultural curiosity, existing in a space that neither affords him the luxury of calling New York or Düsseldorf truly "home" while realizing that he was able to escape the tumultuous years of Korean history and receive an education because of his family's affluence. For Paik, living in Japan, where ethnic Koreans are treated as inferior, then moving to Germany as an Asian avant-garde among white Europeans and Americans, his ethnicity and race definitely mattered. His distaste for Daisetz Teitero "D. T." Suzuki and what Paik once called Suzuki's "selling of our culture" points not to Paik's alliance with Suzuki as a fellow Asian, but to Suzuki's marketing of a practice that further fueled the belief in an essentialized East Asia and the belief that Westerners and East Asians are fundamentally different (Rhee 48). It is this belief in the essential Asian mystical wisdom that has appealed to many of Zen Buddhism's Western adapts. Furthermore, Zen stands in as a critique and/or a replacement for a number of different Western practices; for John Cage, for instance, it became an alternative to psychoanalysis, whereas for others, like Robert Pirsig and his 1974 *Zen and the Art of Motorcycle Maintenance*, it replaced Western philosophy in general.

Precisely because of the West's fascination with "Eastern" cultural practices and beliefs, it is perhaps tempting to ascribe an uncritically cosmopolitan identity on someone like Paik, who has lived in a number of different countries. Yet, here I will revisit Paik's life: In the 1950s, as Japan tried to recover from the aftermath of a costly war and rapidly rebuilt its infrastructure, Paik looked to the West as the pinnacle of modernity and artistic modernism. But instead of going to New York, the capital of postwar artistic modernism, Paik went to Munich, Germany, Japan's former ally that was also recovering from the same war. Although he spent less than a decade in Munich, it was here that he made the relationships that would result in lifelong friendships and collaborations. Ironically, it was also in Germany that he first became familiar with works of Japanese avant-gardes such as Yoko Ono, Shigeko Kubota (whom he would later marry), and others. During this time, he did not return to Korea and spent minimal time in Japan. Once he left Korea, in fact, he did not return for thirty years, and only after he had already received international recognition.

Indeed, John Cage and the works of other Fluxus artists have had a tremendous impact on how Paik has approached his art. Fluxus as a movement was extensively international in nature, with approximately two dozen Japanese artists participating in various aspects of the movement during its existence, influencing it greatly. Furthermore, as a neo-Dada movement, Fluxus wanted to challenge the established art world. This motive is seen clearly in George Maciunas's 1963 *Manifesto*, which outlines the basic tenets of what Fluxus was trying to do as a movement. *Manifesto* is composed of three strips of reverse negative dictionary definitions of the word "flux," placed on a piece of paper, and under each strip are handwritten directives for the practitioners of Fluxus. Much like Tristan Tzara's *Dada Manifesto* a half century earlier, Maciunas wanted to deinstitutionalize art. In the first directive, Maciunas makes a call to "*Purge* the world of bourgeois sickness, 'intellectual,' professional & commercialized culture, PURGE the world of dead art, imitation, artificial art, abstract art, illusionistic art, mathematical art,—PURGE THE WORLD OF 'EUROPANISM' [sic]!" Much as the horrors of World War I made the Dadaists reevaluate the relevance of institutionalized art, the events of the atomic age following Hiroshima and Nagasaki led the Fluxus artists to do the same. In this sense, Fluxus was not only Orientalist in its embrace of East Asian beliefs but also cosmopolitan in its rejection of "Europanism"; in this sense this movement was ardently antiestablishment and anticapitalist.

Maciunas's *Manifesto*—and later that of Joseph Beuys, who merely replaced "Europanism" with "Americanism"—was a declaration of cosmopolitan ideology. It is, then, no surprise that the Fluxus artists would want to replace the capitalism of the West and of Western art with a form of Zen Buddhism. In rebelling against the institutionalized ideals of European Enlightenment and modernism, the originators of Fluxus, through the influence of John Cage, were drawn to East Asian philosophies. As Alexandra Munroe explains, within Fluxus, "[t]he Japanese were welcomed as a collective manifestation of an Eastern sensibility that corresponded with such Flux-ideas as chance, minimalism, poetics, and the investigation of the simple and habitual acts of everyday life and their inherent relation to art" (218).

In the midst of these philosophical tensions, Paik, whose interest in Schoenberg brought him to Germany, caught between his desire for the modern and his Asian body and cultural heritage, found himself decidedly in an ambivalent position. In many ways, his art reflects this cosmopolitan/Orientalist expectation placed upon him. This is a tricky proposition because for non-Western cosmopolitans, there exists the danger of self-Orientalizing as a countermeasure to the pressures of modernism and globalization. Often, this self-Orientalism manifests itself as an essentialized past that is premodern and precapitalist, and therefore "pure" and free of the corrupting influences of the West. For someone like Paik, self-Orientalization was an element that he not only dealt with but also utilized in his work. This is not meant as a criticism but only to reiterate that an Asian artist in Europe or the United States is more likely to gain acceptance when he or she melds Eastern and Western elements together. Paik certainly incorporated—or even appropriated—Zen as a motif in his works.

Nonetheless, Paik also worked with one of the hallmarks of midcentury Western culture: television. In light of a piece like *TV-Buddha*, one could make the argument that he sought to destroy the divide between "East" and "West"—to allow, even force, the twain to meet and fuse—through the incorporation of televisual technology. Yet often his works are read through the lens of techno-Orientalism in which "Asian" becomes synonymous with "the image of a culture that is cold, impersonal and machine-like, an authoritarian culture lacking emotional connection to the rest of the world" (Morley and Robins 169). In this context, *TV-Buddha* takes on a more sinister twist and becomes not an antidote to Maciunas's "Europanism" or Beuys's "Americanism" of midcentury, but the symptom of a rising Asian technological dominance of the late twentieth century. The willful reading of Paik's works as "Asian," rather than as Continental European, means that Paik is further essentialized and his use of technology becomes naturalized as an expression of his "Asianness." In other words, rather than seeing his use of Zen principles and technology as equal strategies for "entertaining" his audiences, critics see Paik as expressing something essential to his nature.

Perhaps, then, it would be misleading to look at Paik as someone melding Eastern and Western cultures, despite the temptation to do so. For instance, to say that he is bringing together the East and the West is to say that there is an essential East and a West, distinctively antithetical or inherently opposed to one another that can be mixed together into a cultural medley with recognizable parts. Paik is neither a bridge nor a conduit, at least not in the sense of connecting two opposites. Instead, he is someone who is expressing the sum of his experiences, as a Korean who has lived in Japan at a time when Korea was still very much a third world country and Japan was quickly refocusing its resources on international economic competition, *and* as an Asian living in Europe and the United States when "Asian beliefs" were very much in vogue even if Asian peoples were not. The fact that the television and the camera are incorporated with the Buddha statue should not be read as an invitation to read *TV-Buddha* as a reflection of Asian "dehumanized technological power" (Morley and Robins 170). Rather, it should be read in light of Paik's experiencing multiple cultural modalities simultaneously; Paik is expressing Abdul JanMohamed's specular border, and the technology is merely a means to that end.

What Paik presents through his work is the ease with which various cultures and traditions come together and are changed through these contacts. Paik's Buddha is one who has already been changed through several millennia of intercultural contact among India, Central Asia, and East Asia in terms of the doctrines that surround him as well as in the way he is represented artistically. Paik's Buddhism, encountered through its Western practitioners such as Cage, is one that has already changed through its mutations in East Asia and through its exportation to Europe and America. This brings us to the case of *TV-Rodin*. The differing receptions to *TV-Buddha* and *TV-Rodin* reveal an inherent Western bias to art and technology. What scholars of video art do not understand, or fail to mention, is that Rodin was an influential figure for prewar Japanese sculptors, greatly influencing the works of Ogiwara Morie and Takamura Kotaro. For many Japanese art lovers, however, their exposure to Rodin was mostly through photographs in Japanese-language art magazines. If we follow Walter Benjamin's argument regarding mechanically reproduced art, then surely these photographs in magazines have lost their aura. Indeed, seeing a two-dimensional photo reproduction of a three-dimensional sculpture leaves a great much to be desired. The significance of *TV-Rodin*, then, lies in the way many Japanese art lovers experience Western art, which is to say, via an intermediary medium such as print or TV. Furthermore, for many Asian museumgoers, Western art is mediated by differing histories and cultures that are foreign and at times incomprehensible. Those Japanese who embraced Rodin were in effect embracing the West at a time when Japan as a whole was modernizing (read: Westernizing) and rapidly industrializing. Western culture was seen as a necessary evil in Japan in the late nineteenth and early twentieth centuries as a way to prevent the colonialism that rendered China and India impotent against the West. Rodin represented just one element in this overall embrace of Western culture in prewar Japan.

In this regard, both *TV-Buddha* and *TV-Rodin* are a part of the same investigation into the cultural exchanges that occur and are mediated by technology that makes cultural encounters even more frequent and fluid. For Paik, however, inhabiting an Asian body, when he utilizes "Asian" themes, art critics assume that he is drawing from insider/native knowledge to an extent that does not happen for Euro American artists. But by juxtaposing various technologies, artifacts, and themes, he demonstrates the encounters and changes that have been occurring specifically throughout the twentieth century in East Asia, Europe, and the United States, not to mention in himself as an "Oriental" in the West. Both *TV-Buddha* and *TV-Rodin* are the result of these intercultural encounters; not exactly an equal melding of two distinctive and unique, diametrically opposed, parts, it implies the multiple crossings of real and imagined borders and the mutations in religions and cultures throughout history. Ultimately, *TV-Buddha* in particular is an artifact that is already embodying these multiplicities, it being just the next incarnation in this cycle.

Notes

1. For a more in-depth discussion of such readings, see Jieun Rhee and Lee Yongwoo.
2. Of course, Paik's ability to see TV and video as a powerful medium is in no way new or revolutionary. Marshall McLuhan and Norbert Weiner saw the impact that new modes of transmitting information could have on modern society. McLuhan's

explanation of the "global village" in *The Gutenberg Galaxy: The Making of Typographic Man* (1962) expressed the potential of technology—especially electronic mass media—to allow people to live and communicate in collapsed time-space, empowering individuals to be much more global in their everyday lives. Weiner's discussion in *Cybernetics* (1948) of the flow and feedback of information influenced the way scientists and theorists began rethinking human-machine interface and human interactions in general. George Orwell certainly saw the sinister implications of this medium in his vision of a not-too-distant dystopian future.

Desiring Machines, Repellant Subjects

A Conclusion

DAVID S. ROH, BETSY HUANG,
AND GRETA A. NIU

> The problem's plain to see:
> too much technology
> Machines to save our lives.
> Machines dehumanize.
> —Styx, "Mr. Roboto," 1983

> I'm from the future—you should go
> to China.
> —*Looper*, 2012

In "Two Cheers for Sweatshops" and *Thunder from the East*, Pulitzer Prize–winning journalists Nicholas Kristof and Sheryl WuDunn chronicle their journey from chastising the exploitive nature of Asian sweatshops to praising their economic efficacy. This is not without a measure of moral conflict, they explain, but despite their best efforts to retain their indignation over sweatshop conditions, they can no longer deny the economic benefits, which are simply too enticing: "Fourteen years ago, we moved to Asia. . . . Like most Westerners, we arrived in the region outraged at sweatshops. In time, though, we came to accept the view supported by most Asians: that the campaign against sweatshops risks harming the very people it is intended to help" (Kristof and WuDunn, "Two Cheers for Sweatshops"). It is not that they have become soulless neoliberal subjects, they insist, but that they have been convinced by loud objections coming from an unexpected corner—the sweatshop laborers themselves:

> "It's dangerous work," Mongkol added. "Twice the needles went right through her hands. But the managers bandaged up her hands, and both times she got better again and went back to work."
> "How terrible," we murmured sympathetically.
> Mongkol looked up, puzzled. "It's good pay," he said. "I hope she can keep that job. There's all this talk about factories closing now, and she said there are rumors that her factory might close. I hope that doesn't happen...."

How do they reconcile the horrendous reality of the work conditions with their first-world guilt and noblesse oblige? They are not blind to sweatshop conditions, and fully acknowledge that "some managers are brutal in the way they expose children to dangerous chemicals, deny bathroom breaks, force people to work double shifts, dismiss anyone who tries to organize a union, or demand sexual favors from employees" (129). Instead of banning them altogether, the authors suggest, perhaps more measured steps might benefit all involved, for "improved safety conditions can be helpful, just as it was in 19th-century Europe." The underlying logic here appears to be that the West has already undergone the painful industrialization period, and now, perhaps, it is the East's turn (Kristof and WuDunn, "Two Cheers for Sweatshops"). Moreover, they note, Eastern laborers may just think differently: "Nothing captures the difference in mind-set between East and West more than attitudes toward sweatshops.... [S]weatshops that seem brutal from the vantage point of an American sitting in his living room can appear tantalizing to a Thai laborer getting by on beetles" (Kristof and WuDunn, "Two Cheers for Sweatshops"). In other words, conditions may be deplorable, but if the Asian worker demands his or her hours ultimately resulting in a higher standard of living, then perhaps the sweatshop is an efficient—if painful—means to an end that the West should not deny.

Far from being free-market ideologues, Kristof and WuDunn are prominent sociocultural critics who lean toward progressivism. How, then, can their seemingly paradoxical—and to be fair, somewhat self-aware—position on sweatshop labor be explained? We contend that this disconnect can be contextualized within a broader, quite recognizable, discourse. Essentialist language notwithstanding, Kristof and WuDunn mime frequently repeated phrases used to describe the economic "miracles" of South Korea, Taiwan, Hong Kong, and Singapore, the so-called Asian Tigers (and Japan), dependent not on a wealth of natural resources, but on human capital. For laborers in these resource-poor nations are reputed to be quite willing to spurn the Western nine-to-five workday for an Eastern five-to-nine. Theories abound as to why they are such exemplary workers: East Asian laborers have more discipline, drive, and desire; they are more culturally and socially obsequious to authority; or they simply enjoy working, not needing the same luxuries of the coddled Western worker. Indeed, opine the authors, "The rise of Asia in the post–World War II era came at the sacrifice of hundreds of millions of young people who worked thirteen-hour days and saved every yen, won, and fen. The characteristic sound of Asia has not been a shout of joy but the hum of *machinery*" (Kristof and WuDunn, *Thunder from the East* 119, emphasis added).

Elements of their rhetoric may sound uncannily familiar, for it is essentially the same language used to describe coolie labor, which was recycled to explain Japan's meteoric rise as an economic world power after World War II. We also detect strains of the aforementioned language in Kenneth Hough's analysis (Chapter 1), which shows how mechanistic rhetoric fueled wartime hysteria against the Japanese. A more recent shift, as Aimee Bahng demonstrates, is a conflation of neoliberal economics with the speculative future (Chapter 12). That this language has persisted throughout the decades in one form or another indicates there is another mechanism behind the material apparatus.

Techno-Orientalism, then, is not so much a narrow discourse marking the posthuman cybernetic body as distinctly Asian, nor is it about the latest bleeding-edge widget being assembled by dexterous, scarred fingers in Guangdong, China—these are instead signifiers of a larger project. Rather, we trace the "techno" in techno-Orientalism to *techne*, a process instead of literal tool, for "revealing" a technology's true presence (*wesen*) and "enframing" of the world according to humankind's vision (Heidegger 3–35). It is, in a sense, a doubling of Orientalism, a means of constructing and reifying an Occidentalist worldview in a more sophisticated way. Techno-Orientalism accounts for—and then dismisses—Eastern modernity as both process and product of dehumanization, of which the West is an economic and ontological beneficiary; but should that modernity ever transition to hypermodernity (and threat), its dehumanizing means and ends reaffirm the West's monopoly over liberal humanism. The speculative narratives of textual and visual media are the vehicles through which this disciplinary process travels.

As the American empire wanes—or is reconfigured—in the West and China rises in the East, the logic of techno-Orientalism continues to exert its influence over emerging cultural productions. Recent examples abound: The 2012 remake of the Philip K. Dick–inspired film *Total Recall* (1990) redesigns the cityscape to resemble the Hong Kong skyline; Gary Shteyngart's satirical *Super Sad True Love Story* (2010) envisions a future New York City placed at the precipice of the U.S. economy's implosion and subsequent takeover by the Chinese; Junot Diaz's postapocalyptic novel in progress, *Monstro*, projects the Chinese renminbi replacing the U.S. dollar as the dominant international currency—a phenomenon predicted by many economic prognosticators in recent years (Cox). The film *Looper*'s (2012) speculative sequence was set in Shanghai to signal its futurity; Daniel Wilson's novel *Robopocalypse* (2011) contains an obligatory subplot involving a Japanese roboticist whose love for his android wife leads to the discovery of a critical component for humanity's survival. These works continue on a well-trodden path—the techno-Orientalized element is, at times, an alien environment, existential threat, economic competitor, or technological bridge and always, invariably, a vehicle through which the Western-encoded subject undertakes his or her journey. Likewise, this volume has identified and critiqued numerous examples of uncritical framing: Jason Crum's scrutinizing of how early radio broadcasts programs underscored Asian premodernity (Chapter 2); Victor Bascara's investigation into the erasure of Asian bodies integral in a nineteenth-century work about the twenty-first century (Chapter 3); Warren Liu's racialization of temporality (Chapter 4); Abigail De Kosnik's tracing of the sublimation of race in three techno-Orientalist films (Chapter 6); Jinny Huh's analysis of the mixed-race imaginarium of *Battlestar Galactica* (Chapter 7); and Dylan Yeats's exegesis of the historical rhetoric and politics of Orientalized enemy "bots" in video games (Chapter 9). The West desires Eastern machinery but resists recognizing the human toll or a humanistic center.

Still, there are wrinkles and complications, particularly when techno-Orientalism is appropriated by spaces of counterdiscourse. For instance, Korean American filmmaker and comic book author Greg Pak exploits techno-Orientalist logic in *Robot Stories* (2003), an exploration of posthumanism, race, and relationships in the guise of a genre film. Pak's series of vignettes superficially mime techno-Orientalist tropes—in this case, the dehumanized, machine-like Asian laborer represented at different points by a ruthless businesswoman, a software coder with Asperger syndrome, an android, a disembodied consciousness—and the film proceeds to deconstruct them by reinscribing the humanity behind each iteration. *Robogeisha* (2009), a Japanese film belonging to a subgenre equal parts grotesque and camp, takes the Western gaze to its logical conclusion. Completely self-aware and parodic in tone, the film's loose plot centers on two orphaned sisters who grow up to become cyborg geisha assassins, one of whom ends up in the thrall of an evil conglomerate. The film's strongly nationalist and absurdist denouement, in which a corporation plans the destruction of Mt. Fuji to unite Japan against its enemies, shows how techno-Orientalist aesthetics can be used for other ends.[1] It is on this front that additional contributors to this volume also scrutinize deformations of techno-Orientalist discourse: Julie Ha Tran's examination of

William Gibson's fictional geographies reveals an unexpected critical bidirectionality (Chapter 10); Kathryn Allan's discussion of *Maul* and *Salt Fish Girl* shows how a new subgenre may recuperate the cybernetic Asian female figure (Chapter 11); Douglas Ishii's exposition of Joss Whedon's population of Asian artifacts and depopulation of Asian peoples in his universe creates room for his own critical intervention (Chapter 13); Tzarina Prater and Catherine Fung (Chapter 14) reveal how Larissa Lai's *Automaton Biographies* grants *Blade Runner*'s Rachael a voice to "talk back" to Ridley Scott's Asian-infused vision of dystopic Los Angeles; and media artist Nam June Paik's work, expertly analyzed by Charles Park, operates a similar aesthetic through which the mechanisms of human creativity and activity are fetishized *and* critiqued (Chapter 15).

National and cultural authorship of the discourse notwithstanding, our historically conscious exegesis indicates that, thus far, techno-Orientalism is strongly tied to geopolitics, economics, and race, and we see no reason to suspect that will change. If compelled to speculate, we would first note the material consequences of a rising consumer class in China—partly a consequence of neoliberal trade agreements creating favorable manufacturing conditions—and how quickly the landscape changes in response. In some ways, very little work is required to translate Orientalist tropes: the invading horde of barbarians is replaced by a horde of robotic factory workers, kept at a distance by multinational corporations and shipping routes. They are uncreative, less than human (although complicated by reports of poor working conditions driving some to suicide), and always already mechanized—a narrative that persists even in the realm of leisure, as Steve Choe and Se Young Kim describe in their analysis of the disparity of rhetoric surrounding Eastern as opposed to Western gamers (Chapter 8). Still, on closer examination complications emerge, for while Japan, South Korea, Singapore, and Taiwan were economic "miracles" of a hypercapitalist frenzy, the strong role of the communist state cannot be ignored in China's rise. And lest we are accused of ignoring the rest of Asia, we note how the outsourcing of high-tech labor to South Asian nations via information networks may also complicate a techno-Orientalist logic that is nothing if not supple and elastic. One emerging commonality we detect—and we are curious to see how this will be integrated into cultural discourse that must discipline—is the role of pollution in developing nations as manufacturing booms. Already, news reports teem with stories of poor air quality over the largest metropolitan cities in China, Beijing in particular. It may be that the techno-Orientalized subject may take on an ecocritical slant, as we begin to move away from cyberspace-oriented discourse characterizing the future as ephemeral and diaphanous; instead, it may be polluted, riddled with the detritus of ex-gen technology, haunted by the specter of Asian manufacturing (indeed, already a hallmark of post-cyberpunk tropes). The message conveyed by the rhetoric of "pollution" is that even as Asia has finally reached modernity, it does so irresponsibly, without regard for the supposed lessons learned by the West during its periods of rapid industrialization over the course of the twentieth century. The final irony, then, is while the human toll in Asia can be effaced from Western consciousness, environmental pollutants traveling over wind and water currents more efficient than any shipping route will persist, leading to inescapable, catastrophic effects on a global scale. Asia's major economies—Japan, China, South Korea, and India—are, in the eyes of the West, behaving like recalcitrant children, refusing to abide by its tutelage, insisting on growing up too quickly, and thus warranting its constant surveillance.

If Seo-Young Chu is correct in characterizing stereotypes as "a technology meant to facilitate mental shortcuts" (Chapter 5), then techno-Orientalism has become a technology that facilitates the containment of a perceived mass threat. "We all create images of things we fear or glorify," writes Sander Gilman in his extended psychoanalytic study of stereotypes. But while some of us retain the capacity to recognize the distinction between the individual and the stereotyped class, Gilman explains, "[t]he pathological personality does not develop this ability, and sees the entire world in terms of the rigid lines of difference. The pathological personality's mental representation of the world supports the need for the line of difference, whereas for the nonpathological individual the stereotype is a momentary coping mechanism, one that can be used and then discarded once anxiety is overcome. The former is consistently aggressive toward the real people and objects to which the stereotypical representations correspond; the latter is able to repress the aggression and deal with people as individuals" (18). The prospect that such "aggressions" will abate remains nil, however, partly because the "individual" is by now a quaint notion of a bygone American cultural mythology, and partly due to the West's perception of Asia as historically and persistently collectivist. Drawing on Gilman's formulation, then, techno-Orientalism is a form of pathology, necessitated by the "Rising East" rhetoric and rationalized by the neoliberal logic of (Asian) humans as mortal engines of modernity and economic growth. Thus, techno-Orientalist studies must be vigilantly developed and deployed as a critical countertechnology for negotiating the complex, taut lines of a discourse ensconced in racial and international politics.

Note

1. In contrast, David Mack's graphic novels *Kabuki* (1994–2010), which feature a hypersexualized geisha assassin from the future, is completely earnest. The eponymous Kabuki signifies the "purity" of Japan, through which Mack subtextually argues the corruption of Japanese culture by Western influences; one wonders if the irony of Mack's own Orientalist rendition of that "purity" is lost on him.

Bibliography

Ahmed, Sara. *The Promise of Happiness.* Durham, NC: Duke University Press, 2010.
Alexander, Leigh. "Kaos Descends: How *Homefront*'s Developer Met Its End." *Gamasutra* 6 Jul. 2012.
Ali Baba and the Forty Thieves. Dir. Thomas Edison. Edison Manufacturing Company, 1902.
Allen, Robertson. "The Unreal Enemy of America's Army." *Games and Culture* 6.1 (2011): 38–60.
Alsultany, Evelyn. "Selling American Diversity and Muslim American Identity through Nonprofit Advertising Post-9/11." *American Quarterly* 59.3 (2007): 593–622.
American Federation of Labor, et al. *Some Reasons for Chinese Exclusion, Meat vs. Rice, American Manhood against Asiatic Coolieism: Which Shall Survive?* San Francisco: Asiatic Exclusion League, 1902.
Amy-Chinn, Dee. "'Tis Pity She's a Whore: Postfeminist Prostitution in Joss Whedon's *Firefly?*" *Feminist Media Studies* 6.2 (2006): 175–189.
Asada, Sadao. *From Mahan to Pearl Harbor: The Imperial Japanese Navy and the United States.* Annapolis, MD: Naval Institute Press, 2006.
Ashcraft, Brian. "The Country That Loves PC Gaming So Damn Much." *Kotaku* 14 Nov. 2011.
———. "Learn StarCraft from a Full Blooded Korean." *Kotaku* 1 Jul. 2009.
———. "StarCraft on Korean TV." *Kotaku* 17 May 2006.
———. "Stink at StarCraft? Live in Korea? Look Abroad." *Kotaku* 6 Feb. 2007.
———. "Why Is StarCraft So Popular in Korea?" *Kotaku* 24 Jul. 2010.
Asimov, Isaac. *Prelude to Foundation.* New York: Bantam, 2004.
Assman, Jan and John Czaplicka. "Collective Memory and Cultural Identity." *New German Critique* 65 (Spring–Summer 1995): 125–133.
Austin Powers: International Man of Mystery. Dir. Jay Roach. New Line Cinema, 1997.
Balsamo, Anne. "The Virtual Body in Cyberspace." *Technologies of the Gendered Body: Reading Cyborg Women.* Durham, NC: Duke University Press, 1996. 116–132.
"Banzai—How Japan Fought the U.S.—and Lost." *New York Times* 12 Jul. 1908: SM5.
Barr, Marlene. "'We're at the Start of a New Ball Game and That's Why We're All Real Nervous': Or, Cloning—Technological Cognition Reflects Estrangement from Women." *Learning from Other Worlds: Estrangement, Cognition, and the Politics of Science Fiction and Utopia.* Ed. Patrick Parrinder. Durham, NC: Duke University Press, 2001. 193–207.

Barry, Tom. "US: Danger, Danger Everywhere." *Asia Times Online* 23 Jun. 2006.
Bart, Peter. "Doing It McVeigh's Way." *Variety* 19 Jun. 1997: 2.
Battlestar Galactica (2003–2009). *Battlestar Galactica: The Complete Series*. Universal Studios, 2010.
  "Daybreak, Part 2." Writ. Ronald Moore, Dir. Michael Rhymer.
  "Epiphanies." Writ. Joel Anderson Thompson, Dir. Rod Hardy.
  "The Farm." Writ. Carla Robinson, Dir. Rod Hardy.
  "Flight of the Phoenix." Writ. David Weddle and Bradley Thompson, Dir. Michael Nankin.
  "Kobol's Last Gleaming, Part II." Writ. David Eick, Dir. Michael Rhymer.
  "A Measure of Salvation." Writ. Michael Angeli, Dir. Bill Eagles.
  Miniseries Pilot. Writ. Ronald D. Moore, Dir. Michael Rymer.
  "The Plan." Writ. Jane Espenson, Dir. Edward James Olmos.
Beale, Howard K. *Theodore Roosevelt and the Rise of America to World Power*. Baltimore, MD: Johns Hopkins University Press, 1956.
Beard, Charles. *An Economic Interpretation of the Constitution of the United States*. New York: Free Press, 1986.
Bederman, Gail. *Manliness & Civilization: A Cultural History of Gender and Race in the United States, 1880–1917*. Chicago: University of Chicago Press, 1995.
Bellamy, Edward. *Looking Backward 2000–1887*. Cambridge, MA: Belknap, 1967.
Benjamin, Park. "Battleships, Mines and Torpedoes." *Review of Reviews* Jul. 1904: 65–71.
Benjamin, Walter. "The Work of Art in the Age of Mechanical Reproduction." *Illuminations: Essays*. New York: Schocken Books, 1968. 217–251.
Bennett, Eve. "Deconstructing the Dream Factory: Personal Fantasy and Corporate Manipulation in Joss Whedon's *Dollhouse*." *Slayage: The Journal of the Whedon Studies Association* 9.1 (2011).
———. "Techno-butterfly: Orientalism Old and New in *Battlestar Galactica*." *Science Fiction Film and Television* 5.1 (Spring 2012): 23–46.
Bergson, Henri. *Matter and Memory*. Trans. N. M. Paul and W. S. Palmer. New York: Zoned Books, 1994.
Berlant, Lauren. *Cruel Optimism*. Durham, NC: Duke University Press, 2011.
———. "On Her Book Cruel Optimism." Rorotoko.com 5 Jun. 2012. http://rorotoko.com/interview/20120605_berlant_lauren_on_cruel_optimism/.
Blackhawk, Ned. *Violence over the Land: Indians and Empires in the Early American West*. Cambridge, MA: Harvard University Press, 2008.
Blade Runner. Dir. Ridley Scott. Warner Brothers, 1982.
Bonacich, Edna and Lucie Cheng, eds. *Labor Immigration under Capitalism: Asian Workers in the United States before World War II*. Berkeley: University of California Press, 1984.
Bould, Mark, et al., eds. *The Routledge Companion to Science Fiction*. Reprint. Routledge, 2009.
Bowman, Sylvia E. *Edward Bellamy*. Boston: Twayne, 1986.
Bowser, Rachel and Brian Croxall. "Introduction: Industrial Evolution." *Neo-Victorian Studies* 3.1 (2010): 1–45.
Boyer, Paul S. "Selling Star Wars: Ronald Reagan's Strategic Defense Initiative." *Selling War in a Media Age: The Presidency and Public Opinion in the American Century*. Ed. Kenneth Osgood and Andrew K. Frank. Gainesville: University Press of Florida, 2010. 196–223.
Brands, H. W. *T. R.: The Last Romantic*. New York: Basic Books, 1997.

Braun, Bruce and Sarah Whatmore. "The Stuff of Politics: An Introduction." *Political Matter: Technoscience, Democracy, and Public Life*. Ed. Bruce Braun and Sarah Whatmore. Minneapolis: University of Minnesota Press, 2010. ix–xl.
Brooke, James. "South Koreans React to Video Games' Depictions of North Koreans." *New York Times* 7 Dec. 2005.
Brooker, Will. *Using the Force: Creativity, Community and Star Wars Fans*. London: Continuum, 2002.
Buck, Pearl S. *The Good Earth*. New York: Harper & Row, 1977.
Bukatman, Scott. *Blade Runner* (BFI) Classics. London: British Film Institute, 1997.
Bush, George W. "Veteran's Day Address." Ronald Reagan Building and International Trade Center, Washington, DC. 11 Nov. 2003.
Butch, Richard. *The Making of American Audiences: From Stage to Television, 1750–1990*. Cambridge: Cambridge University Press, 2000.
Butler, Judith. *Gender Trouble: Feminism and the Subversion of Identity*. New York: Routledge, 1990.
Cahn, Anne Hessing. *Killing Détente: The Right Attacks the CIA*. University Park: Pennsylvania State University Press, 1998.
Carr, Brian. "At the Thresholds of the 'Human': Race, Psychoanalysis, and the Replication of Imperial Memory." *Cultural Critique* 39 (Spring 1998): 129–131.
Carr, Harry C. "*The Invasion* Captures Quick Popular Approval." *Los Angeles Times* 15 Nov. 1909: 15.
Cassell's History of the Russo-Japanese War. New York: Cassel, 1905.
Castronova, Edward. *Synthetic Worlds: The Business and Culture of Online Games*. Chicago: University of Chicago Press, 2005.
Challener, Richard D. *Admirals, Generals, and American Foreign Policy, 1898–1914*. Princeton, NJ: Princeton University Press, 1973.
Chang, Iris. *The Chinese in America: A Narrative History*. New York: Penguin, 2004.
Chatterjee, Partha. *The Black Hole of Empire: History of a Global Practice of Power*. Princeton, NJ: Princeton University Press, 2012.
Chauncy, George. *Gay New York: Gender, Urban Culture, and the Making of the Gay Male World, 1890–1940*. New York: Basic Books, 1994.
Chen, David. "Racism and Ethnic Stereotypes in 'Star Wars: The Phantom Menace.'" *The Life and Times of David Chen*. 10 Feb. 2012.
Cheng, Anne Anlin. *The Melancholy of Race: Psychoanalysis, Assimilation, and Hidden Grief*. New York: Oxford University Press, 2001.
Cheng, Lucie and Philip Yang. "The 'Model Minority' Deconstructed." *Contemporary Asian America: A Multidisciplinary Reader*. Ed. Min Zhou and James Gatewood. New York: New York University Press, 2000. 459–482.
"Chinese Man Drops Dead after 3-Day Gaming Binge." *Fox News* 18 Sep. 2007.
Cho, Jae-hyon. "Collegian Dies after 12 Hours of Online Gaming." *Korea Times* 28 Dec. 2010.
Choi, Ho-kyung. "tvN, Special Documentary 'Lim Yo-Hwan's Wings' Airs on the 27th." *GameDonga* 26 Nov. 2010.
Choi, Y. H. "Advancement of IT and Seriousness of Youth Internet Addiction." *International Symposium on the Counseling and Treatment of Youth Internet Addiction*. Seoul: National Youth Commission, 2007.
Chow, Rey. "The Age of the World Target." *America's Wars in Asia: A Cultural Approach to History and Memory*. Ed. Philip West, et al. Armonk, NY: M.E. Sharpe, 1998. 221–232.
"Chronicle's Oriental War Correspondence." *San Francisco Chronicle* 12 Feb. 1904: 1.

Chu, Seo-Young. *Do Metaphors Dream of Literal Sleep? A Science-Fictional Theory of Representation.* Cambridge, MA: Harvard University Press, 2010.
Chuh, Kandice. *Imagine Otherwise: On Asian Americanist Critique.* Durham, NC: Duke University Press, 2003.
Chun, Wendy Hui Kyong. *Control and Freedom: Power and Paranoia in the Age of Fiber Optics.* Cambridge, MA: MIT Press, 2006.
———. "Race and Software." *Alien Encounters: Popular Culture in Asian America.* Ed. Mimi Thi Nguyen and Thuy Linh Nguyen Tu. Durham, NC: Duke University Press, 2007. 305–334.
"Civilization and Savagery." *Los Angeles Herald* 15 Aug. 1905: 4.
Clarke, I. F. *Voices Prophesying War, 1763–1984.* London: Oxford University Press, 1966.
Cloud Atlas. Dir. Tom Tykwer, Andy Wachowski, and Lana Wachowski. Warner Bros., 2012.
Conrad, Joseph. *Heart of Darkness.* New York: Norton, 2006.
Cook, David A. *Lost Illusions: American Cinema in the Shadow of Watergate and Vietnam 1970–1979.* Berkeley: University of California Press, 2000.
Cornyetz, Nina and Keith Vincent. *Perversion and Modern Japan: Psychoanalysis, Literature, Culture.* London: Routledge, 2010.
Cowan, Ruth Schwartz. *More Work for Mother: The Ironies of Household Technology from the Open Hearth to the Microwave.* New York: Basic Books, 1983.
Cox, Jeff. "Is the Dollar Dying? Why US Currency Is in Danger." CNBC.com. n.d.
Csicsery-Ronay, Istvan, Jr. *The Seven Beauties of Science Fiction.* Middletown, CT: Wesleyan University Press, 2008.
Cumings, Bruce. *North Korea: Another Country.* New York: New Press, 2004.
Dangerous Days: Making Blade Runner. Dir. Charles de Lauzirika. Warner Bros., 2007.
Daniels, Roger. *The Politics of Prejudice: The Anti-Japanese Movement in California and the Struggle for Japanese Exclusion.* Berkeley: University of California Press, 1977.
"Death Dealing Whitehead Torpedo, Terror of Modern Warfare, Used by Japanese Navy." *Boston Daily Globe* 12 Feb. 1904: 4.
"Death of Net Addict Alert Others." *Xinhua Online* 1 Nov. 2005.
de Certeau, Michel. *The Practice of Everyday Life.* Trans. Steven Randall. Berkeley: University of California Press, 1984.
Decker-Phillips, Edith. *Paik Video.* Trans. Marie-Genvieve Iselin, Karin Koppensteiner, and George Quasha. Barrytown, NY: Station Hill Press, 1998.
Debrix, François. "The Sublime Spectatorship of War: The Erasure of the Event in America's Politics of Terror and Aesthetics of Violence." *Millennium: Journal of International Studies* 343 (2005): 767–791.
Deis, Christopher. "Erasing Difference: The Cylons as Racial Other." *Cylons in America: Critical Studies of Battlestar Galactica.* Ed. Tiffany Potter and C. W. Marshall. New York: Continuum, 2008. 156–166.
Deleuze, Gilles. *Dialogues II.* New York: Columbia University Press, 2007.
———. *Cinema 2: The Time Image.* Trans. Hugh Tomlinson and Robert Galeta. Minneapolis: University of Minnesota Press, 1989.
Delpar, Helen. *The Enormous Vogue of Things Mexican: Cultural Relations between the United States and Mexico, 1920–1935.* Tuscaloosa: University of Alabama Press, 1992.
de Matos, Xav. "THQ Enlists North Korean 'Soldiers' to Promote Homefront." *Joystiq* 16 Jun. 2010.
Denning, Michael. *The Cultural Front: The Laboring of American Culture in the Twentieth Century.* New York: Verso, 1997.
Dick, Philip K. *Do Androids Dream of Electric Sheep?* New York: Del Rey, 1996.

Die Another Day. Dir. Lee Tamahori. Metro-Goldwyn-Mayer, 2002.
Dixon, Peter. *Radio Writing.* New York: Century Co., 1931.
Dollhouse: Season One. Created by Joss Whedon. Twentieth Century Fox, 2009.
Dollhouse: Season Two. Created by Joss Whedon. Twentieth Century Fox, 2010.
Doris, David. "Zen Vaudeville: A Medi(t)ation in the Margins of Fluxus." Institute of Broken and Reduced Languages, n.d.
Dorwart, Jeffery M. *The Pigtail War: American Involvement in the Sino-Japanese War of 1894–1895.* Amherst: University of Massachusetts Press, 1975.
Douglass, Frederick. "What to the Slave Is the Fourth of July?" *The Norton Anthology of African American Literature.* Ed. Henry Louis Gates, Jr. and Nellie Y. McKay. New York: Norton, 2003. 462–474.
Dr. Horrible's Sing-Along Blog. Dir. Joss Whedon. New Video Group, 2008.
Duggan, Lisa. *The Twilight of Equality? Neoliberalism, Cultural Politics, and the Attack on Democracy.* Boston: Beacon, 2004.
Dulles, Foster Rhea. *Forty Years of American-Japanese Relations.* New York: D. Appleton Century, 1937.
Edelman, Lee. *No Future: Queer Theory and the Death Drive.* Durham, NC: Duke University Press, 2004.
Edwards, Paul N. *The Closed World: Computers and the Politics of Discourse in Cold War America.* Cambridge, MA: MIT Press, 1996.
"Eggs from Young Asian Women in High Demand." *CBS San Francisco* 14 Nov. 2011.
Eng, David L. *The Feeling of Kinship: Queer Liberalism and the Racialization of Intimacy.* Durham, NC: Duke University Press, 2010.
Englehardt, Tom. *The End of Victory Culture: Cold War America and the Disillusioning of America.* Amherst: University of Massachusetts Press, 1998.
Equilibrium. Dir. Kurt Wimmer. Miramax, 2002.
Esthus, Raymond A. *Double Eagle and Rising Sun: The Russians and Japanese at Portsmouth in 1905.* Durham, NC: Duke University Press, 1988.
———. *Theodore Roosevelt and the International Rivalries.* Waltham, MA: Ginn-Blaisdell, 1970.
Fackler, Martin. "In Korea, a Boot Camp for Web Obsession." *New York Times* 18 Nov. 2007.
Fahey, Mike. "Another Chinese Man Dies from Gaming." *Kotaku* 17 Sep. 2007.
Farrell, Nick. "Second Gamer Dies after Massive Binge." *V3.co.uk.* 22 Oct. 2002.
Fejes, Fred. *Imperialism, Media, and the Good Neighbor.* Ramsey, NJ: Alex, 1986.
Ferguson, Roderick A. *Aberrations in Black: Toward a Queer of Color Critique.* Minneapolis: University of Minnesota Press, 2003.
Firefly: The Complete Series. Created by Joss Whedon. Twentieth Century Fox, 2003.
"First Detailed History of a Modern Siege." *San Francisco Call* 4 Nov. 1904: 2.
Fong, Timothy P. *The Contemporary Asian American Experience: Beyond the Model Minority.* 2nd ed. Upper Saddle River, NJ: Prentice Hall, 2002.
Foster, Thomas. *The Souls of Cyberfolk: Posthumanism as Vernacular Theory.* Minneapolis: University of Minnesota Press, 2005.
Foucault, Michel. *History of Sexuality.* Vol. 1. New York: Vintage, 1990.
Fowler, Edward. *San'ya Blues.* Ithaca, NY: Cornell University Press, 1996.
Franklin, H. Bruce. *Vietnam and Other American Fantasies.* Amherst: University of Massachusetts Press, 2000.
———. *War Stars: The Superweapon and the American Imagination.* New York: Oxford University Press, 1988.

Freeman, Elizabeth. *Time Binds: Queer Temporalities, Queer Histories.* Durham, NC: Duke University Press, 2010.
Fritz, Ben and John Horn. "Reel China: Hollywood Tries to Stay on China's Goodside." *Los Angeles Times* 16 Mar. 2011.
Furst, Lilian R. *Before Freud: Hysteria and Hypnosis in Later Nineteenth-Century Psychiatric Cases.* Lewisburg, PA: Bucknell University Press, 2008.
Galloway, Alexander R. *The Interface Effect.* Cambridge: Polity, 2012.
Gattaca. Dir. Andrew Niccol. Columbia Pictures, 1997.
Gaudiosi, John. "North Korea Invades America in Controversial 'Homefront' Game." *Hollywood Reporter* 16 Mar. 2011.
Gauntier, Gene. "Blazing the Trail." *Woman's Home Companion* Nov. 1928: 15–16, 132–134.
"Genius Asian Egg Donor." Advertisement. *The Tech* 30 Nov. 2012: 14.
Giap, General Vo Nguyen. "Cable News Network Interview with General Vo Nguyen Giap." Handout, Oakland Museum of California, 1996.
Gibson, William. *All Tomorrow's Parties.* New York: Berkley Books, 1999.
———. *Idoru.* New York: Berkley Books, 1996.
———. "Modern Boys and Mobile Girls." *Guardian* 31 Mar. 2001.
———. *Mona Lisa Overdrive.* New York: Bantam Books, 1988.
———. "My Own Private Tokyo." *Wired* Sep. 2001.
———. *Neuromancer.* New York: Ace Books, 1984.
———. *Pattern Recognition.* New York: Putnam, 2003.
———. *Virtual Light.* New York: Bantam Books, 1993.
Gibson, William and Bruce Sterling. *The Difference Engine.* New York: Bantam Books, 1991.
Gilman, Sander L. *Difference and Pathology: Stereotypes of Sexuality, Race, and Madness.* Ithaca, NY: Cornell University Press, 1985.
"Gives America All of the Credit for the Rapid Progress of Japan." *San Francisco Call* 13 Mar. 1904: 22.
Gluck, Caroline. "South Korea's Gaming Addicts." *BBC News* 22 Nov. 2002.
Goslinga-Roy, Gillian. "Body Boundaries, Fiction of the Female Self: An Ethnography of Power, Feminism and the Reproductive Technologies." *Feminist Studies* 26.1 (Spring 2000): 113–140.
Goswami, Neelam. "Chinese Man Dies after Playing Video Games Non-stop for 3 Days." *MedGuru* 23 Feb. 2011.
Gotanda, Neil. "A Critique of 'Our Constitution Is Color-Blind.'" *Critical Race Theory.* Ed. Kimberle Crenshaw, Neil Gotanda, Gary Peller, and Kendall Thomas. New York: New Press, 1995. 257–275.
Gottlieb, Bruce. "The Merchant of Menace." Slate.com 27 May 1999.
Griffth, Nancy Snell. *Edward Bellamy: A Bibliography.* Metuchen, NJ: Scarecrow Press, 1986.
Hacking, Ian. *The Taming of Chance.* Cambridge: Cambridge University Press, 1990.
Halberstam, Judith. *In a Queer Time and Place: Transgender Bodies, Subcultural Lives.* New York: New York University Press, 2005.
Hall, Linda and Don Coerver. *Revolution on the Border: The United States and Mexico, 1910–1920.* Albuquerque: University of New Mexico Press, 1988.
Halpern, Sue. "Virtual Iraq." *New Yorker* 19 May 2008.
Halter, Ed. *From Sun Tzu to Xbox: War and Video Games.* New York: Thunder's Mouth Press, 2006.
Hammond, J. R. *An H. G. Wells Companion: A Guide to the Novels, Romances, and Short Stories.* London: Macmillan, 1979.
Hanzal, Carla. "Traversing the Worlds of Nam June Paik." *Sculpture Magazine* Jun. 2001.

Haraway, Donna. "Situated Knowledges: The Science Question in Feminism and the Privilege of Partial Perspective." *Feminist Studies* 14.3 (1988): 575–599.
Hartshorn, Peter. *I Have Seen the Future: A Life of Lincoln Steffens*. Berkeley, CA: Counterpoint, 2011.
Hasan, Zaki. "Interview: Producer Tripp Vinson Talks *Red Dawn* Remake." Huffington Post 20 Nov. 2012.
Heidegger, Martin. *The Question Concerning Technology, and Other Essays*. New York: Harper Perennial, 1982.
Henderson, E. F. "Japanese Are Fighting 'White Man's Battle.'" *Los Angeles Herald* 14 Mar. 1905: 12.
Henderson, Mary. *Star Wars: The Magic of Myth*. New York: Bantam Books, 1997.
Heuser, Sabine. *Virtual Geographies: Cyberpunk at the Intersection of the Postmodern and Science Fiction*. Amsterdam: Rodopi, 2003.
Hevia, James L. "The Archive State and the Fear of Pollution: From the Opium Wars to Fu-Manchu." *Cultural Studies* 12.2 (1998): 234–264.
Hicks, Heather. "Striking Cyborgs: Reworking the 'Human' in Marge Piercy's *He, She and It*." *Reload: Rethinking Women and Cyberculture*. Ed. Mary Flanagan and Austin Booth. Cambridge, MA: MIT Press, 2002.
The Hidden Fortress. Dir. Akira Kurosawa. Toho Company, Ltd., 1958.
Hobsbawm, Eric. *The Age of Empire, 1875–1914*. New York: Pantheon, 1987.
Hofstadter, Richard. *The Age of Reform: From Bryan to FDR*. New York: Vintage, 1955.
Hogg, Trevor. "Assembly Required: A Walter Murch Profile." FlickeringMyth.com 21 Jul. 2010.
Höglund, Johan. "Electronic Empire: Orientalism Revisited in the Military Shooter." *Game Studies* 8.1 (Sep. 2008).
Hong, Grace Kyungwon. *The Ruptures of American Capital: Women of Color Feminism and the Culture of Immigrant Labor*. Minneapolis: University of Minnesota Press, 2006.
Hong, Grace Kyungwon and Roderick A. Ferguson. *Strange Affinities: The Gender and Sexual Politics of Comparative Racialization*. Durham, NC: Duke University Press, 2011.
"How to Tell Japs from the Chinese: Angry Citizens Victimize Allies with Emotional Outburst at Enemy." *LIFE* 22 Dec. 1941: 81–82.
Hsu, Hua. "The End of White America?" *The Atlantic*. Jan./Feb. 2009.
Huang, Betsy. "Reorientations: On Asian American Science Fiction." *Contesting Genres in Asian American Fiction*. New York: Palgrave Macmillan, 2010. 95–140.
———. "Premodern Orientalist Science Fictions." *MELUS* 33.4 (Winter 2008): 23–43.
Huggins, Nathan Irvin. *Harlem Renaissance*. London: Oxford University Press, 1971.
Huizinga, Johan. *Homo Ludens: A Study of the Play Element in Culture*. New York: Harper, 1970.
Hune, Shirley. "The Politics of Chinese Exclusion: Legislative-Executive Conflict, 1876–1882." *Amerasia Journal* 9 (1982): 5–27.
Hung, Eric. "The Meaning of 'World Music' in *Firefly*." *Buffy, Ballads, and Bad Guys Who Sing: Music in the Worlds of Joss Whedon*. Ed. Kendra Preston Leonard. Lanham, MD: Scarecrow Press, 2011. 255–273.
Hunt, Darnell and David K. Yoo, eds. "Los Angeles since 1992: Commemorating the 20th Anniversary of the Uprisings." *Amerasia Journal* 38.1 (2012).
Hu-Pegues, Juliana. "Miss Cylon: Empire and Adoption in Battlestar Galactica. *MELUS* 33.4 (Winter 2008): 189–209.
Indiana Jones (film series). Dir. Steven Spielberg. Paramount, 1981–2008.

Iriye, Akira. "Introduction: The Russo-Japanese War in Transnational History." *The Russo-Japanese War in Global Perspective: World War Zero*. Vol. 2. Ed. David Wolff, et al. Leiden: Brill, 2006. 1–9.

Irwin, Robert. "A Thousand and One Nights at the Movies." *Middle Eastern Literatures: Incorporating Edebiyat* 7.2 (Jul. 2004): 223–233.

Iwamura, Jane Naomi. *Virtual Orientalism: Asian Religions and American Popular Culture*. New York: Oxford University Press, 2011.

Jacobson, Matthew Frye. *Barbarian Virtues: The United States Encounters Foreign Peoples at Home and Abroad, 1876–1917*. New York: Hill & Wang, 2000.

Jamison, Peter. "Anti-North Korea Rally, Inspired by 'Homefront' Video Game, Planned for SF." *SFWeekly Blogs*.

"Jap Tactics Highlighted." *Los Angeles Times* 21 Jul. 1942: 12.

"Japan Has a Submarine." *San Francisco Call* 6 Apr. 1904: 3.

"Japan May Buy Fleet of Airships from Inventor Gerth." *San Francisco Call* 25 Feb. 1904: 5.

"Japanese Astonish the Torpedo Experts." *New York Times* 11 Feb. 1904: 2.

"Japanese Calm." *Living Age* 15 Jul. 1905: 189–191.

"The Japanese Invasion." *New York Dramatic Mirror* 10 Jul. 1909: 17.

"A Japanese Military Airship in Use." *Popular Mechanics* Feb. 1905: 203.

Jeffords, Susan. *Hard Bodies: Hollywood Masculinity in the Reagan Era*. New Brunswick, NJ: Rutgers University Press, 1994.

Jenkins, Stephen. "Uriu, Admiral of Japan." *New York Times* 21 Feb. 1904: 7.

Johnson, Julian. "The Local Week." *Los Angeles Times* 14 Nov. 1909: III.1.

Johnston, Paul K. "A Puritan in the Wilderness: Natty Bumppo's Language & America's Nature Today." *James Fenimore Cooper: His Country and His Art (No. 11)*. Oneonta: State University of New York at Oneonta Cooper Seminar, English Department, 1999.

Jukes, Geoffrey. *The Russo-Japanese War 1904–1905*. Oxford: Osprey, 2002.

Kagan, Robert and William Kristol, eds. *Present Dangers: Crisis and Opportunity in American Foreign and Defense Policy*. San Francisco: Encounter Books, 2000.

Kang, Hee-jong. "Starc Is Business." *iNews24.com* 27 Aug. 2000.

Kang, Laura Hyun Yi. "The Uses of Asianization: Figuring Crises, 1997–98 and 2007–?" *Race, Empire, and the Crisis of the Subprime*. Ed. Paula Chakravartty and Denise Ferreira da Silva. Spec. issue of *American Quarterly* 64.3 (2012): 411–436.

Kawai, Yuko. "Stereotyping Asian Americans: The Dialectic of the Model Minority and the Yellow Peril." *Howard Journal of Communications* 16.2 (2005): 109–130.

Kearney, Reginald. *African American Views of the Japanese: Solidarity or Sedition?* Albany: State University of New York Press, 1998.

Keevak, Michael. *Becoming Yellow: A Short History of Racial Thinking*. Princeton, NJ: Princeton University Press, 2011.

Kelly, James Patrick and John Kessel, eds. *Rewired: The Post-Cyberpunk Anthology*. San Francisco: Tachyon, 2007.

Kessler, John. "The Body Electric." *Artforum* Apr. 2006.

Kim, Claire Jean. *Bitter Fruit: The Politics of Black-Korean Conflict in New York City*. New Haven, CT: Yale University Press, 2003.

Kim, Elaine H. "Interstitial Subjects: Asian American Visual Art as a Site for New Cultural Conversations." *Fresh Talk, Daring Gazes: Conversations on Asian American Art*. Ed. Elaine H. Kim, Margo Machida, and Sharon Mizota. Berkeley: University of California Press, 2003. 1–50.

Kim, Hyung-Chan. *Asian Americans and Congress: A Documentary History*. Westport, CT: Greenwood, 1996.

Kim, Tae-heung. *Starcnomics*. Seoul: Soft Bank Media, 2000.
Kim, Yong-woo. "'Full Return' Pro Gamer Lee Joong Heon 'I Want to Stand on a Big Stage.'" *Daum Sports* 28 May 2012.
Kim Watson, Jini. *The New Asian City: Three-Dimensional Fictions of Space and Urban Form*. Minneapolis: University of Minnesota Press, 2011.
Kipling, Rudyard. "The Ballad of East and West." Online-Literature.com n.d.
Kiyoshi, Aizawa. "Differences Regarding Togo's Surprise Attack on Port Arthur." *The Russo-Japanese War in Global Perspective: World War Zero*. Vol. 2. Ed. David Wolff, et al. Leiden: Brill, 2006. 81–104.
Knorr-Cetina, Karin and Urs Bruegger. "Global Microstructures: The Interaction of Practices of Financial Markets." *The Sociology of the Economy*. Ed. Frank Dobbin. New York: Russell Sage Foundation, 2004. 157–189.
Koizumi, Kenkichiro. "In Search of *Wakon:* The Cultural Dynamics of the Rise of Postwar Manufacturing in Japan." *Technology and Culture* 43.1 (Jan. 2002): 29–49.
Kowner, Rotem. "Becoming an Honorary Civilized Nation: Remaking Japan's Military Image during the Russo-Japanese War, 1904–1905." *Historian* 64.1 (Fall 2001): 18–38.
———. *Historical Dictionary of the Russo-Japanese War*. Lanham, MD: Scarecrow Press, 2006.
———, ed. *The Impact of the Russo-Japanese War*. London: Routledge, 2007.
Krämer, Peter. *The New Hollywood: From Bonnie and Clyde to Star Wars*. London: Wallflower Press, 2005.
Kristof, Nicholas D. and Sheryl WuDunn. *Thunder from the East: Portrait of a Rising Asia*. New York: Knopf, 2000.
———. "Two Cheers for Sweatshops." *New York Times* 24 Sep. 2000.
Krock, Arthur. "Six Months after Pearl Harbor." *New York Times* 7 Jun. 1942: SM3.
Kurashige, Scott. *Shifting Grounds of Race: Black and Japanese Americans in the Making of Multiethnic Los Angeles*. Princeton, NJ: Princeton University Press, 2008.
LaFeber, Walter *The Clash: U.S.-Japanese Relations throughout History*. New York: Norton, 1997.
Laffey, John. *Imperialism and Ideology: An Historical Perspective*. Montreal: Black Rose Books, 2000.
Lai, Larissa. *Automaton Biographies*. Vancouver: Arsenal Pulp Press, 2009.
———. "Rachel." *So Long Been Dreaming: Postcolonial Science Fiction and Fantasy*. Vancouver: Arsenal Pulp Press, 2004. 53–60.
———. *Salt Fish Girl*. Toronto: Thomas Allen, 2008.
Lane, A. T. "American Trade Unions, Mass Immigration and the Literacy Test: 1900–1917." *Nativism, Discrimination, and Images of Immigrants*. Ed. George Pozzetta. New York: Garland, 1991. 345–365.
Langer, Jessica. "The Familiar and the Foreign: Playing (Post)colonialism in World of Warcraft." *Digital Culture, Play and Identity: A World of Warcraft Reader*. Ed. Hilde G. Corneliussen and Jill Walker Rettberg. Cambridge, MA: MIT Press, 2008. 87–108.
Lavery, David and Rhonda V. Wilcox, eds. *Fantasy Is Not Their Purpose: Joss Whedon's Dollhouse*. Spec. issue of *Slayage: The Journal of the Whedon Studies Association* 8.2–3 (2010).
Lawrence of Arabia. Dir. David Lean. Columbia Pictures, 1962.
Le, Mike. "Frustrations of an Asian American Whedonite." Racebending.com 17 Jul. 2012.
Lea, Homer. *The Valor of Ignorance*. New York: Harper & Brothers, 1909.
Lee, James Kyung-jin. "Appropriations of Blackness." *Urban Triage: Race and the Fictions of Multiculturalism*. Minneapolis: University of Minnesota Press, 2004. 64–99.

———. *Urban Triage: Race and the Fictions of Multiculturalism.* Minneapolis: University of Minnesota Press, 2004.

Lee, Jiyeon. "South Korea Pulls Plug on Late-night Adolescent Online Gamers." *CNN* 22 Nov. 2011.

Lee, Robert G. *Orientals: Asian Americans in Popular Culture.* Philadelphia, PA: Temple University Press, 1999.

Lee, Tara. "Mutant Bodies in Larissa Lai's *Salt Fish Girl:* Challenging the Alliance between Science and Capital." *West Coast Line* 38.2 (Fall 2004): 1–11.

Lee Yongwoo. "Technology as Art: The Legacy of Video Artist Paik Nam June." *Koreana* 20.2 (Summer 2006): 36–39.

"Legal Map." LovingDay.org n.d.

Lenihan, John H. "Superweapons from the Past." *Beyond the Stars: Studies in American Popular Film, Volume 3: The Material World in American Popular Film.* Ed. Paul Loukides and Linda K. Fuller. Bowling Green, OH: Bowling Green State University Popular Press, 1993. 164–174.

Levinson, Paul. "Battlestar Galactica Series Finale: Not Goodbye for See You." *Open Levinson* 21 Mar. 2009.

Levy, Pierre. *Becoming Virtual: Reality in the Digital Age.* Trans. Robert Bononno. New York: Plenum, 1998.

Lewis, Reina. *Gendering Orientalism: Race, Femininity and Representation.* New York: Routledge, 1996.

Li, Shan. "Asian Women Demand Premium Prices for Egg Donation in the U.S." *Los Angeles Times* 4 May 2012.

Licht, Mellissa Vera. "Warring Opinions: An Investigation into the Sublime Aesthetic Narratives of Contemporary Warfare." PhD Diss. University of Minnesota, 2010.

Liew, Sonny. *Malinky Robot: Collected Stories & Other Bits.* Berkeley, CA: Image Comics, 2011.

Limerick, Patricia Nelson. *The Legacy of Conquest: The Unbroken Past of the American West.* New York: Norton, 1988.

Linn, Brian McAllister. *The Philippine War: 1899–1902.* Lawrence: University Press of Kansas, 2000.

Lippmann, Walter. 1922. *Public Opinion.* Project Gutenberg.

LiPuma, Edward and Benjamin Lee. *Financial Derivatives and the Globalization of Risk.* Durham, NC: Duke University Press, 2004.

Lissak, O. M. "What the World Has Learned from the Russo-Japanese War." *Harper's Weekly* 6 May 1905: 642–646.

Little, Douglas. *American Orientalism: The United States and the Middle East since 1945.* Chapel Hill: University of North Carolina Press, 2002.

Lively, Robert L. "Remapping the Feminine in Joss Whedon's *Firefly.*" *Channeling the Future: Essays on Science Fiction and Fantasy Television.* Ed. Lincoln Geraghty. Lanham, MD: Scarecrow Press, 2009. 183–197.

Locke, Brian. "White and 'Black' versus Yellow: Metaphor and *Blade Runner*'s Racial Politics." *Arizona Quarterly: Journal of American Literature, Culture, and Theory* 65.4 (Winter 2009): 113–138.

London, Jack. *Revolution and Other Essays.* New York: Macmillan, 1912.

———. "The Unparalleled Invasion." *McClure's* Jul. 1910: 308–315.

Looper. Dir. and writ. Rian Johnson. Endgame Entertainment, 2011.

Lowe, Lisa. *Critical Terrains: French and British Orientalisms.* Ithaca, NY: Cornell University Press, 1994.

———. *Immigrant Acts: On Asian American Cultural Politics.* Durham, NC: Duke University Press, 1996.
———. "Imagining Los Angeles in the Production of Multiculturalism." *Immigrant Acts: On Asian American Cultural Politics.* Durham, NC: Duke University Press, 1996. 84–96.
———. "The Intimacies of Four Continents." *Haunted by Empire: Geographies of Intimacy in North American History.* Ed. Ann Laura Stoler. Durham, NC: Duke University Press, 2006. 191–212.
Mack, David. *Kabuki: Volume 1, Circle of Blood.* Marvel Comics, 2010.
MacKenzie, Donald, Fabian Muniesa, and Lucia Siu, eds. *Do Economists Make Markets? On the Performativity of Economics.* Princeton, NJ: Princeton University Press, 2007.
Mahbubani, Kishore. *The New Asian Hemisphere: The Irresistible Shift of Global Power to the East.* New York: PublicAffairs, 2008.
———. "Why Asia Stays Calm in the Storm." *Financial Times* 28 Oct. 2008.
Mahtani, Shibani. "Thursday's the Day to Go All the Way for Civic Duty in Singapore: New Ad Campaign Urges Locals to Help Spike Birthrate; 'Make Fireworks Ignite.'" *Wall Street Journal* 10 Aug. 2012.
"Major Describes Moves." *New York Times* 8 Feb. 1968: 14.
Marchetti, Gina. *Romance and the "Yellow Peril": Race, Sex, and Discursive Strategies in Hollywood Fiction.* Berkeley: University of California Press, 1993.
Martin, Randy. *Financialization of Daily Life.* Philadelphia: Temple University Press, 2002.
The Mask of Fu Manchu. Dir. Charles Brabin. Metro-Goldwyn-Mayer, 1932.
Massumi, Brian. *Parables for the Virtual: Movement, Affect, Sensation.* Durham, NC: Duke University Press, 2002.
The Matrix (film series). Dir. The Wachowski Siblings. Warner Brothers, 1999–2003.
McAlister, Melanie. *Epic Encounters: Culture, Media, and U.S. Interests in the Middle East, 1945–2000.* Berkeley: University of California Press, 2001.
McClernand, Edward J. *Reports of Military Observers Attached to the Armies in Manchuria during the Russo-Japanese War.* Part V. Washington, DC: GPO, 1906.
McCully, Newton A. *The McCully Report: The Russo-Japanese War, 1904–05.* Annapolis, MD: Naval Institute Press, 1977.
McKay, Steven C. *Satanic Mills or Silicon Islands: The Politics of High-Tech Production in the Philippines.* Ithaca, NY: IRL/Cornell University Press, 2006.
McNary, Dave. "Milius Joins Military Training Op at USC." *Variety* 11 Jun. 2000.
Meier, Matt S. and Feliciano Ribera. *Mexican Americans/American Mexicans: From Conquistadors to Chicanos.* New York: Hill & Wang, 1993.
Melamed, Jodi. *Represent and Destroy: Rationalizing Violence in the New Racial Capitalism.* Minnesota: University of Minnesota Press, 2011.
Mellencamp, Patricia. "The Old and the New: Nam June Paik." *Art Journal* 54.4 (1995): 41–47.
Menaugh, John A. "Surprise at Port Arthur." *Chicago Tribune* 19 Apr. 1942: E8.
Mendible, Myra. "Post Vietnam Syndrome: National Identity, War, and the Politics of Humiliation." *Radical Psychology* 7 (2008).
Miller, Edward S. *War Plan Orange: The U.S. Strategy to Defeat Japan, 1897–1945.* Annapolis, MD: Naval Institute Press, 1991.
Miller, John. "Best Conservative Movies." *National Review* 23 Feb. 2009.
Mitchell, David. *Cloud Atlas: A Novel.* New York: Random House, 2004.
Mitchell, William J. *City of Bits: Space, Place, and the Infobahn.* Cambridge, MA: MIT Press, 1996.
Mo and Will. *Life and Love in the Petri Dish.* Blogger 4 Jun. 2013.

Monroy, Douglas. *Rebirth: Mexican Los Angeles from the Great Migration to the Great Depression*. Berkeley: University of California Press, 1999.

Morley, David and Kevin Robins. *Spaces of Identity: Global Media, Electronic Landscapes, and Cultural Boundaries*. 1st ed. London: Routledge, 1995.

Morris, Edmund. *Theodore Rex*. New York: Random House, 2001.

Morris, Robyn. "'What Does It Mean to Be Human?' Racing Monsters, Clones and Replicants." *Foundation* (Summer 2004): 81–96.

Mortal Kombat. Dir. Paul W. S. Anderson. New Line Cinema, 1995.

Munro, Dana. *Intervention and Dollar Diplomacy in the Caribbean, 1900–1921*. Princeton, NJ: Princeton University Press, 1964.

Munroe, Alexandra. "A Box of Smile: Tokyo Fluxus, Conceptual Art, and the School of Metaphysics." *Japanese Art after 1945: Scream Against the Sky*. Ed. Alexandra Munroe. New York: H. N. Abrams, 1994. 215–225.

"Music and the Stage." *Los Angeles Times* 2 Nov. 1909: II.5.

Nakamura, Lisa. "After/Images of Identity: Gender, Technology, and Identity Politics." *Reload: Rethinking Women and Cyberculture*. Ed. Mary Flanagan and Austin Booth. Cambridge, MA: MIT Press, 2002. 321–331.

———. *Cybertypes: Race, Ethnicity, and Identity on the Internet*. New York: Routledge, 2002.

———. *Digitizing Race: Visual Cultures of the Internet*. Minneapolis: University of Minnesota Press, 2008.

———. "Race In/For Cyberspace: Identity Tourism and Racial Passing on the Internet." *The Cybercultures Reader*. Ed. David Bell and Barbara Kennedy. New York: Routledge, 2000. 712–720.

———. "Race In/For Cyberspace: Identity Tourism and Racial Passing on the Internet." *Reading Digital Culture*. 1st ed. Ed. David Trend. New York: Wiley-Blackwell, 2001. 226–235.

Nakashima, Cynthia L. "Servants of Culture: The Symbolic Role of Mixed-Race Asians in American Discourse." *"Mixed-Race" Studies: A Reader*. Ed. Jayne O. Ifekwunigwe. New York: Routledge, 2004. 271–275.

"Nam June Paik: Performance Artist and Sculptor Whose Pioneering Work with Video May Be Said to Have Changed the Course of Modern Art." *Times* [London] 31 Jan. 2006: 55.

National Intelligence Council. "Global Trends 2030: Alternative Worlds." 10 Dec. 2012.

Neculau, Radu. "The Sublimity of Violence: Kant and the Aesthetic Response to the French Revolution." *Symposium* 12.1 (2008): 29–43.

Neu, Charles E. *An Uncertain Friendship: Theodore Roosevelt and Japan, 1906–1909*. Cambridge, MA: Harvard University Press, 1967.

Nevins, Jess. "Prescriptivists vs. Descriptivists: Defining Steampunk." *Science Fiction Studies* 38.3 (2011): 513–518.

Nguyen, Mimi Thi. *The Gift of Freedom: War, Debt, and Other Refugee Passages*. Durham, NC: Duke University Press, 2012.

Ninkovich, Frank. *The United States and Imperialism*. Malden, MA: Blackwell, 2001.

Nishime, LeiLani. "Aliens: Narrating U.S. Global Identity through Transnational Adoption and Interracial Marriage in *Battlestar Galactica*." *Critical Studies in Media Communication* 28.5 (2011): 450–465.

———. "The Mulatto Cyborg: Imagining a Multiracial Future." *Cinema Journal* 44.2 (Winter 2005): 34–49.

Niu, Greta A. "Techno-Orientalism, Nanotechnology, Posthumans, and Post-Posthumans in Neal Stephenson's and Linda Nagata's Science Fiction." *MELUS* 33.4 (2009): 73–96.

Nixon, Nicola. "Cyberpunk: Preparing the Ground for Revolution or Keeping the Boys Satisfied?" *Cybersexualities: A Reader on Feminist Theory, Cyborgs, and Cyberspace.* Ed. Jenny Wolmark. Edinburgh: Edinburgh University Press, 1999. 191–207.
"No Quarter Asked or Given." *New York Times* 19 Dec. 1904: 5.
Nye, David E. *American Technological Sublime.* Cambridge, MA: MIT Press, 1994.
Oboler, Arch, and Stephen Longstreet. *The Free World Theatre: Nineteen New Radio Plays.* New York: Random House, 1944.
Oda, Masanori. "Welcoming the Libido of the Technoids Who Haunt the Junkyard of the Techno-Orient; or, The Uncanny Experience of the Post-Techno-Orientalist Moment." *The Uncanny: Experiments in Cyborg Culture: Experiments in Cyborg Culture.* Ed. Bruce Grenville. Vancouver: Arsenal Pub Press, 2002. 249–273.
O'Gorman, Marcel. "Angels in Digital Armor: Technoculture and Terror Management." *Postmodern Culture* 20.3 (May 2010).
Okihiro, Gary Y. *Margins and Mainstreams: Asians in American History and Culture.* Seattle: University of Washington Press, 1994.
Olender, Piotr. *Russo-Japanese Naval War 1905, Volume 2: Battle of Tsushima.* Sandomierz: Stratus, 2010.
Omar, the Wizard of Persia. 1931. Mutual Broadcasting Network.
Omi, Michael and Howard Winant. *Racial Formation in the United States: from the 1960s to the 1990s.* 2nd ed. New York: Routledge, 1994.
Ong, Aiwha. *Flexible Citizenship: The Cultural Logics of Transnationality.* Durham, NC: Duke University Press, 1999.
———. *Neoliberalism as Exception: Mutations in Citizenship and Sovereignty.* Durham, NC: Duke University Press, 2006.
———. *Spirits of Resistance and Capitalist Discipline: Factory Women in Malaysia.* Albany: State University of New York Press, 2010.
Ono, Kent A. "To Be a Vampire on *Buffy the Vampire Slayer:* Race and ('Other') Socially Marginalizing Positions on Horror TV." *Fantasy Girls: Gender in the New Universe of Science Fiction and Fantasy Television.* Ed. Elyce Rae Helford. Lanham, MD: Rowman & Littlefield, 2000. 163–186.
Pak, Greg. *Robot Stories and More Screenplays.* San Francisco: Immedium. 2005.
Palumbo-Liu, David. *Asian/American: Historical Crossings of a Racial Frontier.* Stanford: Stanford University Press, 1999.
———. "Universalisms and Minority Culture." *Difference: A Journal of Feminist Cultural Studies* 7.1 (1995): 188–203.
Parikh, Crystal. *An Ethics of Betrayal: The Politics of Otherness in Emergent U.S. Literatures and Culture.* New York: Fordham University Press, 2009.
Park, Jane Chi Hyun. *Yellow Future: Oriental Style in Hollywood Cinema.* Minneapolis: University of Minnesota Press, 2010.
Parreñas, Rhacel Salazar. *Servants of Globalization: Women, Migration, and Domestic Work.* Stanford: Stanford University Press, 2001.
Patai, Daphne, ed. *Looking Backward 1988–1888: Essays on Edward Bellamy.* Amherst: University of Massachusetts Press, 1988.
Patrikeeff, Felix and Harry Shukman. *Railways and the Russo-Japanese War: Transporting War.* New York: Routledge, 2007.
Patterson, Orlando. *Slavery and Social Death: A Comparative Study.* Cambridge, MA: Harvard University Press, 1982.
Peace Envoys at Portsmouth, New Hampshire. American Mutoscope and Biograph Company, 1905.

Pelkey, Stanley C. "Still Flyin'? Conventions, Reversals, and Musical Meaning in *Firefly.*" *Buffy, Ballads, and Bad Guys Who Sing: Music in the Worlds of Joss Whedon.* Ed. Kendra Preston Leonard. Lanham, MD: Scarecrow Press, 2011. 209–242.
Perry, John. *Jack London, an American Myth.* Chicago: Nelson-Hall, 1981.
Pietz, William. "The 'Post-Colonialism' of Cold War Discourse." *Social Text* 19/20 (Autumn 1988): 55–75.
Pipes, Richard. "What Is the Soviet Union Up To? (April 4, 1977)." In *Alerting America: The Papers of the Committee on the Present Danger.* Ed. Charles Tyroler II. Washington, DC: Pergamon-Brassey's, 1984. 6–15.
"Plays Waiting Game." *Los Angeles Times* 1 Feb. 1904: 1.
Power, Marcus. "Digitized Virtuosity: Video War Games and Post 9/11 Cyber Deterrence." *Security Dialog* 38.2 (Jun. 2007): 271–288.
"Prisoner of War." Display advertisement 193. *Los Angeles Times* 25 Mar. 1905: VI.1.
Puar, Jasbir. *Terrorists Assemblages: Homonationalism in Queer Times.* Durham, NC: Duke University Press, 2007.
Ray, Gene. "History, Sublime, Terror: Notes on the Politics of Fear." *The Sublime Now.* Ed. Luke White and Claire Pajaczkowska. Newcastle upon Tyne: Cambridge Scholars, 2009. 133–154.
Reagan, Ronald. "Remarks during a Visit to Walt Disney World's EPCOT Center" and "Address to the National Association of Evangelicals in Orlando, Florida." 8 Mar. 1983. *Public Papers of the President of the United States.*
Reesman, Jeanne Campbell. *Jack London's Racial Lives: A Critical Biography.* Athens: University of Georgia Press, 2009.
Reid, Michelle. "Rachel Writes Back: Racialized Androids and Replicant Texts." *Extrapolation* 49.3 (2008): 353–367.
Rhee, Jieun. "Reconstructing the Korean Body: Nam June Paik as Specular Body." *Oriental Art* 48.4 (2002): 48.
Robinson, Richard H. and Willard L. Johnson. *The Buddhist Religion: A Historical Introduction.* 4th ed. Belmont, CA: Wadsworth, 1997.
Rodriguez, Robyn. *Migrants for Export: How the Philippine State Brokers Workers to the World.* Minneapolis: University of Minnesota Press, 2010.
Rogers, Ralph. *Dos and Don'ts of Radio Writing.* Boston: Association of Radio Writers, 1937.
Rogin, Michael. *Ronald Reagan: The Movie, and Other Episodes of Political Demonology.* Berkeley: University of California Press, 1988.
Rohmer, Sax. *The Insidious Dr. Fu-Manchu: Being a Somewhat Detailed Account of the Amazing Adventures of Nayland Smith in His Trailing of the Sinister Chinaman.* Mineola, NY: Dover, 1997.
Roosevelt, Theodore. *The Strenuous Life.* New York: Review of Reviews Co., 1901.
Rosenberg, Emily S. *A Date Which Will Live: Pearl Harbor in American Memory.* Durham, NC: Duke University Press, 2003.
Roy, Ananya and Aihwa Ong, eds. *Worlding Cities: Asian Experiments and the Art of Being Global.* West Sussex, UK: Wiley-Blackwell, 2011.
Said, Edward W. *Orientalism.* New York: Vintage, 1979.
Sammon, Paul M. *Future Noir: The Making of Blade Runner.* New York: HarperCollins, 1996.
Sanders, Jerry Wayne. *Peddlers of Crisis: The Committee on the Present Danger and the Politics of Containment.* Boston: South End Press, 1983.
Sandoval, Stephen. "Attack of the Killer App." *Futurama.* Comedy Central 1 Jul. 2010.
Sassen, Saskia. *Cities in a World Economy.* Thousand Oaks, CA: Pine Forge Press, 2006.

———. "Global Cities and Survival Circuits." *American Studies: An Anthology*. Ed. Janice A. Radway, Kevin Gaines, et al. West Sussex, UK: Wiley-Blackwell, 2009. 185–194.

———. *Globalization and Its Discontents*. New York: New Press, 1998.

———. *Territory, Authority, Rights: From Medieval to Global Assemblages*. Princeton, NJ: Princeton University Press, 2006.

Sato, Kumiko. "How Information Technology Has (Not) Changed Feminism and Japanism: Cyberpunk in the Japanese Context." *Comparative Literature Studies* 41.3 (2004): 335–355.

Schell, Orville. *Discos and Democracy: China in the Throes of Reform*. New York: Pantheon, 1988.

Sconce, Jeffrey. "Mediums and the Media." *Technological Visions: The Hopes and Fears That Shape New Technologies*. Ed. Marita Sturken, Douglas Thomas, and Sandra J. Ball-Rokeach. Philadelphia: Temple University Press, 2004. 56–63.

Sears, Roebuck and Co. and Joseph J. Schroeder. *1908 Catalogue: No 117: The Great Price Maker*. 1908. Chicago: Gun Digest Co., 1969.

Sedgwick, Eve Kosofsky. *Touching Feeling: Affect, Pedagogy, Performativity*. Durham, NC: Duke University Press, 2003.

"Seek to Avert War." *Washington Post* 1 Feb. 1907: 1.

Senna, Denzy. "The Mulatto Millennium." *Half and Half: Writers on Growing Up Biracial and Bicultural*. Ed. Claudine C. O'Hearn. New York: Pantheon, 1998. 12–27.

Serenity. Dir. Joss Whedon. Universal Pictures, 2005.

Serwer, Jacquelyn D. "Nam June Paik: 'Technology.'" *American Art* 8.2 (Spring 1994): 90.

Sharf, Frederic Alan, Anne Nishimura Morse, and Sebastian Dobson. *A Much Recorded War: The Russo-Japanese War in History and Imagery*. Boston: MFA, 2005.

Sharp, Patrick B. *Savage Perils: Racial Frontiers and Nuclear Apocalypse in American Culture*. Norman: University of Oklahoma Press, 2007.

Shatan, Chiam F. "Bogus Manhood, Bogus Honor: Surrender and Transfiguration in the U.S. Marine Corps." *Psychoanalytic Review* 64.4 (1977): 585–610.

Shim, Doobo. "From Yellow Peril through Model Minority to Renewed Yellow Peril." *Journal of Communication Inquiry* 22.4 (1998): 385.

Shirer, William. "By Wireless from Berlin." *Radio Guide* 29 Oct. 1938: 1.

Shohat, Ella. "Gender and the Culture of Empire: Toward a Feminist Ethnography of Cinema." *Visions of the East: Orientalism in Film*. Ed. Matthew Bernstein and Gaylyn Studlar. London: I.B. Tauris, 1997. 19–66.

Siek, Stephanie and Joe Sterling. "Fewer White Babies Being Born." *CNN* 17 May 2012.

Silver, Peter Rhoads. *Our Savage Neighbors: How Indian War Transformed Early America*. New York: Norton, 2008.

Silverman, Kaja. "Back to the Future." *Camera Obscura* 27 (Sep. 1991): 109–132.

Simon, Zoltán. *The Double-Edged Sword: The Technological Sublime in American Novels between 1900 and 1940*. Budapest: Akadémiai Kiadó, 2003.

Sinbad the Sailor. Dir. Richard Wallace. RKO, 1947.

"Singapore in the Future—The Future in Singapore." Annual Report 2007–2008.

Singel, Ryan. "Richard Clarke's *Cyberwar*. File Under Fiction." *Wired.com* 22 Apr. 2010.

Sirota, David. *Back to Our Future: How the 1980s Explains the World We Live in Now—Our Culture, Our Politics, Our Everything*. New York: Random House, 2011.

"Slew the Helpless." *San Francisco Examiner* 20 Dec. 1894: 1.

Smith, Roberta. "Nam June Paik, 73, Dies; Pioneer of Video Art Whose Work Broke Cultural Barriers." *New York Times* 31 Jan. 2006: B8.

Sohn, Stephen Hong. "Introduction: Alien/Asian: Imagining the Racialized Future." *MELUS* 33.4 (2008): 5–22.
Son of Sinbad. Dir. Ted Tetzlaff. RKO, 1955.
Spence, Jonathan D. *The Search for Modern China*. New York: Norton, 1991.
Stahl, Roger. "Have You Played the War on Terror?" *Critical Studies in Media Communication* 23.2 (2006): 112–130.
Star Wars Episode I: The Phantom Menace. Dir. George Lucas. Twentieth Century Fox, 1999.
Star Wars Episode IV: A New Hope. Dir. George Lucas. Twentieth Century Fox, 1977.
"Star Wars and Neo-Nazis: George Lucas' Empire Gets Its Revenge." FreeRepublic.com 5 Jul. 2005.
Stearns, Peter N. *American Fear: The Causes and Consequences of High Anxiety*. London: Routledge, 2006.
Steinberg, John W. and David Wolff. *The Russo-Japanese War in Global Perspective: World War Zero*. Leiden: Brill, 2005.
Stephenson, Neal. *The Diamond Age; or, A Young Lady's Illustrated Primer*. 1995. New York: Bantam, 1996.
Sturken, Marita, Douglas Thomas, and Sandra J. Ball-Rokeach. *Technological Visions*. Philadelphia: Temple University Press, 2004.
Styx. "Mr. Roboto." A&M, 1983.
"Submarine Boats Wreaked Destruction on Russians." *Los Angeles Herald* 15 Apr. 1904: 2.
Sullivan, Tricia. *Maul*. San Francisco: Night Shade Books, 2006.
Sussman, Herbert. "*The Difference Engine* as Alternative Victorian History." *Victorian Studies* 38.1 (1991): 1–23.
"Sustainable Population for a Dynamic Singapore." Population White Paper Jan. 2013.
Sutter, John D. "Wired for Success or Destruction?" *CNN* 5 Aug. 2012.
Szkupinski Quiroga, Seline. "Blood Is Thicker Than Water: Policing Donor Insemination and the Reproduction of Whiteness." *Hypatia* 22.2 (Spring 2007): 143–161.
Tatsumi, Takayuki. *Full Metal Apache: Transactions between Cyberpunk Japan and Avant-Pop America*. Durham, NC: Duke University Press, 2006.
———. "A Very Soft Time Machine." *Robot Ghosts and Wired Dreams: Japanese Science Fiction from Origins to Anime*. Ed. Christopher Bolton, Istvan Csicsery-Ronay Jr., and Takayuki Tatsumi. Minneapolis: University of Minnesota Press, 2007. 250–260.
Tavernise, Sabrina. "Whites Account for Under Half of Births in U.S." *New York Times* 17 May 2012.
TeamLiquid ESPORTS. "StarCraft II eSports Transition Conference." *TeamLiquid* 2 May 2012.
The Thief of Baghdad. Dir. Raoul Walsh. United Artists, 1924.
Thompson, Nathaniel. "Son of Sinbad." TCM.com n.d.
Thompson, Richard Austin. *The Yellow Peril, 1890–1924*. New York: Arno Press, 1978.
Tison, Alexander. "The Genius of Japan." *World's Work* Apr. 1904: 4699–4700.
"To Blow Up Ship." *Los Angeles Herald* 30 Mar. 1905: 1.
Toothaker, Christopher. "Venezuela to Outlaw Violent Video Games, Toys." Associated Press 4 Oct. 2009.
———. "Video Game Simulating Invasion of Venezuela Raises Ire of Chavez Allies." Associated Press 24 May 2006.
Torok, John Hayakawa. "Asians and the Reconstruction Era Constitutional Amendments and Civil Rights Laws." *Asian Americans and Congress: A Documentary History*. Ed. Hyung-Chan Kim. Westport, CT: Greenwood, 1996. 13–70.
Totilo, Stephen. "China Is Both Too Scary and Not Scary Enough to Be Video Game Villains." *Kotaku* 13 Jan. 2011.

———. "A Video Game That Dares To Make Americans Angry." *Kotaku*. 5 Nov. 2010.
Turner, Frederick Jackson. *The Frontier in American History*. New York: Holt, Rinehart and Winston, 1920.
Ueno, Toshiya. "Japanimation and Techno-Orientalism." *The Uncanny: Experiments in Cyborg Culture*. Ed. Bruce Grenville. Vancouver: Arsenal Pulp Press, 2002. 223–236.
Villarica, Hans. "Meet Sonny Liew, Southeast Asian Comic Book Hero." *Atlantic* 21 Jul. 2011.
Vincent, Danny. "China Used Prisoners in Lucrative Gaming Work." *Guardian* 25 May 2011.
Waller, Gregory A. "Narrating the New Japan: Biograph's *The Hero of Liao-Yang* (1904)." *Screen* 47.1 (Spring 2006): 43–65.
"Want to Be a Dad." Dear Prudence (Emily Yoffe). Slate.com 29 Nov. 2012.
"War on the System." Display advertisement. *Los Angeles Times* 1 Aug. 1904: 3.
"War Spirit in Sweet Names." *Los Angeles Times* 26 Feb. 1904: 1, pt. II.
Wark, McKenzie. *Gamer Theory*. Cambridge, MA: Harvard University Press, 2007.
Wells, David and Sandra Wilson. *The Russo-Japanese War in Cultural Perspective, 1904–05*. New York: St. Martin's, 1999.
Wells, H. G. *The War in the Air, and Particularly How Mr. Bert Smallways Fared While It Lasted*. London: G. Bell and Sons, 1908.
"What the World Has Learned from the Japanese War." *Harper's Weekly* 6 Mar. 1905: 642.
Whedon, Zack and Joss Whedon. *Serenity: The Shepherd's Tale*. Milwaukie, OR: Dark Horse Comics, 2010.
White, Richard. *The Roots of Dependency: Subsistence, Environment, and Social Change among the Choctaws, Pawnees, and Navajos*. Lincoln: University of Nebraska Press, 1983.
Wilcox, Rhonda V. and Tanya R. Cochran, eds. Firefly *and* Serenity. Spec. issue of *Slayage: The Journal of the Whedon Studies Association* 7.1 (2008).
———, eds. Investigating Firefly *and* Serenity: *Science Fiction on the Frontier*. New York: I.B. Tauris, 2008.
Wilson, Daniel. *Robopocalypse*. New York: Doubleday, 2011.
Wilson, James F. *Bulldaggers, Pansies, and Chocolate Babies: Performance, Race, and Sexuality in the Harlem Renaissance*. Ann Arbor: University of Michigan Press, 2011.
Wohl, Robert. *A Passion for Wings: Aviation and the Western Imagination, 1908–1918*. New Haven, CT: Yale University Press, 1994.
Wolff, David. "Portsmouth, Regionalism, and the Birth of Anti-Americanism in Northeast Asia." *The Treaty of Portsmouth and Its Legacies*. Ed. Steven J. Ericson and Allen Hockley. Hanover, NH: Dartmouth College Press, 2008. 125–141.
Wong, Eugene Franklin. "The Early Years: Asians in the American Films Prior to World War II." *Screening Asian Americans*. Ed. Peter X. Feng. Piscataway, NJ: Rutgers University Press, 2002. 53–70.
Wu, Frank H. "The Best 'Chink' Food: Dog Eating and the Dilemma of Diversity." *Gastronomica* 2.2 (2002): 38–45.
Wu, Yong. "Obese Online Gamer Dies Playing." *China Daily* 28 Feb. 2007.
Yokote, Shinji. "Political Legacies of the Portsmouth Treaty." *The Treaty of Portsmouth and Its Legacies*. Ed. Steven J. Ericson and Allen Hockley. Hanover, NH: Dartmouth College Press, 2008. 106–122.
Yu, Timothy. "Oriental Cities, Postmodern Futures: *Naked Lunch, Blade Runner*, and *Neuromancer*." *MELUS* 33.4 (2009): 45–71.
Zakaria, Tabassum. "U.S. Intelligence Sees Asia's Global Power Rising by 2030." *Reuters* 10 Dec. 2012.
Zimbardo, Philip G. "'The Demise of Guys': How Video Games and Porn Are Ruining a Generation." *CNN* 24 May 2012.

Contributors

KATHRYN ALLAN completed her PhD (English literature) at McMaster University in 2010. Her doctoral thesis, "Bleeding Chrome: Technology and the Vulnerable Body in Feminist Post-Cyberpunk Science Fiction," is available on her blog, Bleeding Chrome. She operates an academic coaching and copyediting business, Academic Editing Canada, as she pursues independent scholarly research into (feminist/cyberpunk) science fiction. She writes for both academic and fan audiences, and is editor of *Disability in Science Fiction* (Palgrave Macmillan, 2013).

AIMEE BAHNG is an assistant professor of English at Dartmouth College with affiliations in women's and gender studies, Asian American studies, and Asian & Middle Eastern studies. Her work on postcolonial science fiction has appeared in *MELUS* and *Critical Studies*. Her current book manuscript on speculation examines competing narratives of futurity in contemporary fiction, film, and finance.

VICTOR BASCARA is associate professor in the Department of Asian American Studies at the University of California, Los Angeles, where he specializes in Asian American cultural politics and the critical study of colonial discourse. He is the author of *Model Minority Imperialism* (University of Minnesota Press, 2006), and his writings have been published in journals such as *American Quarterly, American Literature, Journal of Asian American Studies, Amerasia Journal*, and *Asian American Law Journal* (Boalt Hall), and in collections such as *Strange Affinities: The Gender and Sexual Politics of Comparative Racialization, Imagining Our Americas: Toward a Transnational Frame*, and *East Main Street: Asian American Popular Culture*.

STEVE CHOE is an assistant professor in the Department of Cinema and Comparative Literature at the University of Iowa. He teaches and writes on the cinemas of Germany and South Korea. He is the author of *Afterlives: Allegories of Film and Mortality in Early Weimar Germany* (Bloomsbury, 2014).

SEO-YOUNG CHU is assistant professor of English at Queens College, CUNY. She is the author of *Do Metaphors Dream of Literal Sleep? A Science-Fictional Theory of Representation* (Harvard University Press, 2011). Her current book project is tentatively titled "Science-Fictional North Korea."

JASON CRUM is a lecturer at the University of San Diego, where he teaches courses on multiethnic U.S. literature, contemporary fiction, and graphic novels. He recently received his PhD from the University of California, San Diego and was a fellow at UCSD's California Cultures in Comparative Perspective Center. He has written papers on community agency in Los Angeles radio, objectivist poetry, and science fiction and fantasy cultures. His current research is on transborder communities in early twentieth-century U.S. radio culture.

ABIGAIL DE KOSNIK is an assistant professor at the University of California, Berkeley, in the Berkeley Center for New Media and the Department of Theater, Dance & Performance Studies. She is the coeditor, with Sam Ford and C. Lee Harrington, of *The Survival of Soap Opera: Transformations for a New Media Era* (University Press of Mississippi, 2010). Her articles on popular culture and digital technologies have appeared in the *Drama Review*, *International Journal of Communication*, and *Transformative Works and Cultures*.

CATHERINE FUNG is assistant professor of English and media studies at Bentley University. She is published in the journal *Novel: A Forum on Fiction* and is currently working on a book manuscript about memory of the Vietnam War in Asian American literature, titled "Perpetual Refugee." She serves on the executive board for the Association for Asian American Studies and as book reviews editor for *MELUS*.

KENNETH HOUGH is a PhD candidate and lecturer in the history department at the University of California, Santa Barbara. He is currently completing his study "Fear of the Rising Sun: The Japanese Invasion Sublime in American Culture," which examines Japanese war scares and speculative war culture in the United States and the effect this tension had on the media, the military, domestic politics, and relations between the two Pacific nations.

BETSY HUANG is an associate professor of English and chief officer of diversity and inclusion at Clark University. Her first book, *Contesting Genres in Contemporary Asian American Fiction* (Palgrave Macmillan, 2010), examines the political implications of narrative form for Asian Americans who write highly conventionalized "genre fiction"—immigrant fiction, crime fiction, and science fiction. Her current book project traces the history of robots and other automata in science fiction and how such a history reflects human ambivalences toward physical and intellectual labor. Her work has appeared in *Journal of Asian American Studies*, *MELUS*, and the *Asian American Literary Review*.

JINNY HUH is an assistant professor of English at the University of Vermont. Her areas of specialization and research interests include comparative race studies, detective fiction, passing narratives, cultural studies, and speculative fiction. Her current book explores the anxiety of race detection in African American and Asian American narratives of detection and passing. Another book project examines transracial adoption, race and pedagogy, and scenes from a small New England town.

DOUGLAS ISHII is a PhD candidate in American studies at the University of Maryland. His research brings together the fields of critical ethnic studies, queer theory, and U.S. popular culture. His dissertation, "On the Middlebrow Dialectics of Panethnicity," theorizes the racialization of class in post-9/11 U.S. culture by examining Asian Pacific American activist interventions in a range of middlebrow cultural forms. He is also an assistant editor for the *Asian American Literary Review*.

SE YOUNG KIM is a film studies PhD candidate in the Department of Cinema and Comparative Literature at the University of Iowa. His research areas include contemporary East Asian cinema, contemporary U.S. cinema, nationalism, state violence, and cinematic violence.

WARREN LIU received his PhD from the University of California, Berkeley, and is an assistant professor of English at Scripps College, where he teaches courses on Asian American literature, American literature, and creative writing. His research focuses on Asian American literature, with a particular emphasis on how formal experimentation enacts and dramatizes the complex and often conflicted relationship between aesthetics and politics in contemporary Asian American discourse. He is currently working on a project focusing on representations of "Asian futures" in contemporary American fiction, poetry, and visual culture.

GRETA A. NIU earned her PhD in English from Duke University. Her research and teaching investigate issues of sexuality, gender, ethnicity, postcolonialism, diaspora, and globalization in literature, film, and digital media. Her research has been published in *National Women Studies Association Journal, Continuum: Journal of Media & Cultural Studies,* and *Quarterly Review of Film & Video,* among others. She has taught at State University of New York–College at Brockport, University of Rochester, and St. John Fisher College. In addition, she teaches video and digital media production to students ranging from middle school through college.

CHARLES PARK is an instructor at Northampton Community College in Bethlehem, Pennsylvania. He received his PhD in American studies at Purdue University, where his research focused on Asian Americans and the construction of the model minority myth and the reinforcement of the American dream within the consumer culture of postwar America.

TZARINA T. PRATER is an assistant professor of English in Bentley University's English and Media Studies Department. She teaches African American and Anglophone Caribbean literature as well as gender and cultural studies. She has published articles on the work of Michelle Cliff, Patricia Powell, and U.S. spectatorship of Hong Kong action cinema and is currently working on several articles relating to the Asian diaspora in the Caribbean and her book project, "Cinematic Vernacular in Black Fiction."

DAVID S. ROH is assistant professor of American literature and digital humanities at Old Dominion University. He is author of *Illeal Literature: Toward a Disruptive Creativity* (University of Minnesota Press, 2015), which examines how the intersection of intellectual property policy, digital networks, and subcultural texts influences literary development. He is writing a second book investigating the transnational conversation between America and Japan in formulating diasporic subjectivity in Korean American and *zainichi* (Korean Japanese) literature. His work has previously appeared in *Law & Literature* and *MELUS.*

JULIE HA TRAN is a doctoral candidate in the English department with a specialization in twentieth and twenty-first-century American literature at the University of California, Davis. She is interested in postmodernism, science fiction, posthumanism, ecocriticism, and urban studies. More specifically, her work examines how science fiction cities rewrite and reinvigorate the classic trope of the body politic.

DYLAN YEATS is a doctoral candidate in history at New York University. His dissertation traces the often-unacknowledged (and sometimes unintentional) role of the U.S. federal government in promoting and shaping a national culture before World War I. Yeats is coeditor with John Kuo Wei Tchen of *Yellow Peril! An Archive of Anti-Asian Fear* (Verso, 2014), a collection of essays, images, and historical documents that demonstrates the long tradition of "Yellow Peril" fears of Asia shaping popular ideas of "the West" and modern America.

Index

9/11, post-, 185, 188–189, 207

Abe, Shuya, 209
abjection, 18, 119, 194
adoption, 104, 106, 247
Afghanistan, 131, 134
Africa, 73, 129, 151; Sub-Saharan, 201
African, 201, 152; North, 47, 28, 202
African American, 19n, 57, 106–107, 148, 195; literature, 247, 248
agency, 49, 157, 161–162, 189
alien, 9, 19n, 45, 73–74, 79, 80, 109, 119, 134, 139, 141, 147, 155, 164, 168, 171, 207, 224
alienation, 201
All Tomorrow's Parties, 139, 141–142, 148. See also Bridge trilogy
American exceptionalism, 188, 191
American Graffiti, 98
Americanism, 217–218
America's Army, 134
Amy-Chinn, Dee, 186
android, 4, 18, 54, 60, 224
anime, 10, 143, 150n
anti-Asian, 90, 183, 190, 199
Apple, Inc., 11, 13
appropriation(s), 9, 99, 119, 124, 202, 217, 224; racial, 155-156. See also reappropriation
Arab, 201–202
Arabian Nights, 94
artist, non-Western, 211
Ashcraft, Brian, 117–118

Asian, South, 13, 201, 225
Asian/American, 92–93
Asian Americans, 181, 183, 190–192
Asian American Studies, 10, 182
Asian economy, -ies, 2, 17, 123, 165, 167
Asianness, 103, 156, 182, 194, 206, 210, 218
Asimov, Isaac, 87
assimilation, 118, 199–200
assisted reproductive technology (ART), 103–105
Assman, Jan, 89
asynchrony, 69–74, 145
Austin Powers: International Man of Mystery, 53–54
automaton, 11, 13, 16, 33, 73–74, 164, 206–207
Automaton Biographies, 194–195, 197, 225
avant garde, 210, 214, 216
avatar, 120, 123, 148, 153–157, 159, 161

Babbage, Charles, 65
Baghdad, 94
Balsamo, Anne, 155
Bangladesh, 167
Banzai!, 35
Battle of Yalu, 26
Battlestar Galactica, 17, 57, 102–103, 107–111, 224
Baudrillard, Jean, 3
Bedouin, 45–46
Beijing, 115, 207n1, 225

251

Bellamy, Edward, 16, 53
Benjamin, Walter, 53, 58, 219
Bergson, Henri, 146
Berlant, Lauren, 17, 165, 176, 178
Beuys, Joseph, 217–218
Biograph, 27
biopower, 105
biotechnology, 102–103, 105, 107, 110, 157–158, 167
bishōnen, 143
black and white, 196; binary, 112n; discourse, 193; procreation, 109; relations, 108; topography, 194
blackness, 17–18, 103, 105–109, 111, 148, 182, 185–186, 189–190, 194–195, 201, 206–208n
Blade Runner, 2, 4, 9, 16, 18, 53–54, 57, 60–63n, 100, 164, 193–195, 197, 199, 202, 206–207, 225
Blizzard Entertainment, 14–15
body (-ies), 10, 143, 147–148, 150–151, 153–159, 161–162, 194, 196, 206, 223; Asian, 10–11, 159–161, 189, 215, 217, 219; black, 106, 109, 148, 186, 190, 195, 201; Chinese, 11; female, 151, 159, 161, 196; Korean, 83–84; national, 41, 43–44, 49–50, 168; posthuman cybernetic, 223; white, 158; white male, 160
Bolton, Christopher, 6
border(s), 26, 46, 105, 153–154, 205–206, 210–211; specular, 214–215, 218–219
Bradbury Building, 195
Braun, Bruce and Sarah Whatmore, 75n
Bridge trilogy, 17, 140–141, 144, 149. *See also All Tomorrow's Parties*; Gibson, William; *Idoru*; *Virtual Light*
Britain, 68, 73–74
broadband, 116, 119
Brooker, Will, 97
Brown, Rebecca M., 180
Buck, Pearl, 41, 49
Buddha, 90, 213, 215, 218
Buddhism. *See* Zen Buddhism
Buffy the Vampire Slayer, 180–181
Burke, Edmund, 28
Burroughs, William S., 7
Bye Bye Kipling, 210–211

Cage, John, 210, 214, 218
Call of Duty: Modern Warfare, 136
capital, 2–6, 15, 120–123, 164, 196, 203, 205–207, 223; colonial, 196, 205; human, 223; information, 18; Western, 196
capitalism, 43, 54, 56, 58, 60, 62, 91, 115, 120–123, 152, 158, 160, 165–166, 174, 217; anti-, 217; industrial, 124; information, 3; finance, 165; global, 161, 169; globalized, 157; laissez-faire, 59; late, 122, 161; neoliberal, 173
capitalist(s), 54; amorality of, 157; anti-, 217; economy, 91; global, 160, 166; hyper, 225; logic, 124; notion of work and play, 122; overproduction, 169; pre-, 217; subject, 124; time, 120; tool of domination and exploitation, 158
Carter, Jimmy, 129, 132
Casablanca, 200
Castronova, Edward, 122
Center for Security Policy, 133
Charlie Chan, 204
chi, 98. *See also* qi
Chin, Vincent, 11
China (People's Republic of China), 1–4, 11, 15, 93, 115–116, 119, 122, 126, 128, 133, 157, 183, 186, 191, 207, 219, 223, 225, 226; economy of, 11
"chinaman," 198, 202
China Mountain Zhang, 2
China to America, 41, 49–50
Chinatown, 186–187, 201
Chinese Exclusion Acts, 10, 33, 45, 55, 59, 92
Cho, Seung-Hui, 119
Chow, Rey, 133
Christianity, 47, 130, 200
Chun, Wendy Hui Kyong, 6, 139, 140, 151, 188
cinematic, 9, 83, 100, 194
citizen(s), 44, 46, 49, 51, 79, 167–168
Citizens Against Government Waste, 11
citizenship, 44, 92, 167, 179n
civilization, 55, 67, 73, 128, 183–186; Western, 28
Civil War (U.S.), 185–186, 188
class, 55, 144, 167, 184, 190
Clinton, Hillary, 125
cloning, 157, 159–161
Close Combat: First to Fight, 134
Closed World, The, 99
Cloud Atlas, 13
code, 149, 205–206; code switching, 180

Cold War, 39, 54, 56, 94–95, 126, 128–129, 132–133, 188, 207
colonialism, 58, 79, 195–196, 219; British, 84
colonial racism, 202
Columbine High School, 119
Comic-Con, 181
comics (graphic novel), 19n, 44, 169, 170–171, 173–174, 176, 178, 180, 185, 224
Committee on the Present Danger (CPD), 128–129, 133
commodity, 155; culture, 148
Communism, 96, 127–130, 133; anti-, 128–129
Communist state, 225
Confederate South, 183
console cowboy, 141–142, 152, 162
Control and Freedom, 139–140
Cook, David, 97
coolie, 19, 91, 194
Cornea, Christine, 6
corporation, 157; Japanese, 207; multinational, 141, 161, 178, 225
corporatism, 188–189, 205
corporeality, ix, 149
cosmopolitanism, 143, 167, 210, 215–217; non-Western, 217
counterdiscourse, 7, 9, 17, 74, 166, 224
Count Zero, 139. *See also* Sprawl trilogy
courtesan, 183, 203
Csicsery-Ronay, Jr., Istvan, 6
cyberpunk, 3, 6, 8, 17, 100, 139–141, 143–144, 151–154, 157, 159–161, 169, 189; feminist post-, 17, 152–153, 157, 161–162; post-, 152, 226
cyberspace, 9, 143, 146–147, 149, 152, 155
cyborg(s), 8, 15, 17, 164
Cylon, 58, 102–103, 107–112n; -human hybrid, 108, 110

Dadaism, 216–217
Daoism (Taoism), 98–100, 213, 215
Death Note, 150
Debrix, Francois, 29
de Certeau, Michel, 170
Decker-Phillips, Edith, 213
Deis, Christopher, 108
Deleuze, Gilles, 146
Democratic People's Republic of Korea (DPRK), 86
Depression, the, 41, 45, 173

dialectic, 14, 17, 144
Diamond Age, The, 2
Diaz, Junot, 224
Dick, Philip K., 7, 18, 63n, 99, 194, 223
Die Another Day, 77, 83–88
Difference Engine, The, 16, 64–65, 139
DNA, 160, 206; transplant, 83–84
Do Androids Dream of Electric Sheep?, 18, 194
Dollar Diplomacy, 42–43, 51n
Dollhouse, 18, 181–182, 186–190, 192
Douglass, Frederick, 63
dragon lady, 40, 44
Dr. Horrible's Sing-along Blog, 190
Dubai, 188
Du Bois, W.E.B., 28
Dusseldorf, 210, 216
dystopia, 52, 54–55, 152, 182, 194

Eames, Charles and Ray, 56
Edelman, Lee, 175
Edison Company, 27
Edwards, Paul N., 99
Eisenhower, Dwight D., 96
electronic superhighway, 209
El Salvador, 131
emigration, 59. *See also* immigration
Emperor Meiji, 25
empire, 60, 73; American, 223; British, 126
engineer: European, 1; Japanese, 209
engineering: Asian, 199; electrical, 209
England, 59
Enlightenment, 28, 55, 217
enslavement, 14, 61, 194–195. *See also* slavery
eSports, 116–117, 119–120, 122
ethnic cleansing (genocide), 38
eugenics, 104, 106, 196
Europe, 117
expansion, Westward, 184

Facebook, 119
Fahey, Mike, 115–116
fantasy, -ies: anti-Asian and antiblack, 183; gaming, 115–116, 122; genre, 15, 46, 48, 94, 97; of Japan, 164; liberationist, 18; masochistic, 131; Middle Eastern country, 136; neoliberal, 164, 168; Orient as Western, 17; Orientalist, 79, 96; racial, 191; racist, 182; sexual, 94;

fantasy (*continued*)
  of social control, 156; technological, 4; techno-Orientalist, 129, 133, 169; tropes, 46; Western, 115, 166–167; Westernized cyber-, 157; Western penetration of the East, 150; of Western subject, 114; Western technological supremacy, 126
Fallujah, 135
femininity, 44, 69, 74, 148, 154, 203, 208n; ultra-, 96
feminism, 151–152, 157, 182
feminist post-cyberpunk, 152–153, 157
fertility, 104, 180
financial crisis of 2008, 12, 167, 207
Firefly, 2, 18, 100, 180–186, 188, 190–191
Fluxus movement, 210–211, 214, 216–217
Foster, Thomas, 143, 148
Foucault, Michel, 105
Frankenstein, 83
Franklin, H. Bruce, 35
Free World Theatre, 41, 48–49, 51
Fu Manchu, 1–3, 12, 40, 79, 81–84, 90, 92–93, 97, 126, 198, 204
Fu Manchu, The Mask of, 17, 90–92, 100
Full Spectrum Command, 134–135
Full Spectrum Warrior, 134
Futurama, 12–13
futurity, 8, 16, 165–167, 174–176, 178, 207, 224

Galloway, Alexander R., 124
gamer(s), 17, 113, 115, 123–124, 225; death, 115–118; South Korean, 14–15, 17; theory, 120. *See also* gaming
gamespace, 121–123
gaming, 14–15, 113–120, 124, 135; First-Person Shooter (FPS), 115, 134
Garden of Allah, The, 41
Gattaca, 104
Gee, Yun, 215
geisha, 187, 206, 224, 226
gender, 17, 144, 152–157; fluidity, 154–155; gendered body, 151, 154; gendered racialization, 55, 58, 62; gendered stereotypes, 144
genealogy, 197, 198, 203–205
genetic engineering, 157, 161
genetics, 160–161
Genghis Khan, 91, 198
Germany, 211
Ghosh, Amitav, 7

Ghost in the Shell, 8, 91
Gibson, William, 2, 7–9, 16–17, 75n, 144–148, 225. *See also* Bridge trilogy; Sprawl trilogy
Gibson, William and Bruce Sterling, 16, 65, 74n
Gilman, Sander, 226
Ginsberg, Allen, 214
globalism, 3, 8
globalization, 2–3, 15, 17, 141, 152, 157, 183, 217
Global South, 166
gold farming, 15, 114, 122–124
Good Morning, Mr. Orwell, 210
Goslinga-Roy, Gillian, 105
Great Recession. *See* financial crisis of 2008
Greenspan, Alan, 164
Grenada, invasion of, 131

Hahn, Otto, 214
Haig, Alexander, 130
Hannibal, 198
Hanzal, Carla, 211
hanzi, Chinese, 184
Haraway, Donna, 75n
harem girl, 202, 206
Harlem Renaissance, 201
hegemony, 8, 164, 166, 199
Heidegger, Martin, 52, 58, 223
heteronormativity, 154, 165, 173, 204
Heuser, Sabine, 154
Hevia, James, 92, 126
Hezbollah, 132
Hidden Fortress, The, 97
Hill, Gary, 212
Hiroshima, 217
Hollywood, 90, 94, 195
Homefront, 125, 127–128, 134–136
Hong, James, 61, 197
Hong Kong, 145, 206, 211–223
Hoover, Herbert, 45
Houston, Sam, 71
Huang, Betsy, 19n, 33, 59, 92, 99, 184
Hughes, Howard, 93, 96
Hugo Award, 141
Huizinga, Johan, 121
human, 168, 182–183, 190–192, 197–199; inhuman, 11, 74, 92, 118, 182, 191, 196. *See also* nonhuman
humanity, 158, 161, 188, 190–192, 196; in-, 183, 188, 190
Hung, Eric, 182, 185

Hussein, Saddam, 133
hybrid, 92, 108, 110, 203, 211
hybridity, 18, 191, 204, 206

identity, 24, 29, 30, 40, 42, 47, 50–51, 61, 123, 152–153, 155, 157, 159, 161, 188, 194; national, 168, 206; tourism, 155–157
Idoru, 139, 141, 143, 145–149, 160n. *See also* Bridge trilogy; Gibson, William
immigrant, 156, 195, 199–200, 205–206; anti-, 57, 90
Immigrant Acts, 91
immigration, 6, 45, 49, 51, 57, 59; Chinese, 19n, 92; European, 45; Japanese, 23; Mexican, 45
Immigration Act of 1917, 45
imperialism, 29, 52, 179n, 196; anti-, 63; British, 84, 166; Dutch, 166; Japanese, 25, 27, 39, 50, 90, 166; Portuguese, 166; US (American), 29; Western, 24
imperialist(s), 6, 8, 31, 51, 127
India, 4, 41, 43, 71, 73, 175, 218–219, 226
Indiana Jones, 100
Indians (Native Americans), 71, 131. *See also* Native Americans
Indonesia, 167
industrialization, 10, 11, 93, 222, 226
Industrial Revolution, 9, 16
information, 2–3, 27, 41, 81, 95, 126, 139, 142, 147–148, 206, 219–220n, 225
inhuman. *See* human
inhumanity. *See* humanity
Institute for Creative Technologies, 134
Interface Effect, The, 124
Internet, 114–119, 124, 144, 147, 159
internment, Japanese American, 31, 79, 160
intersectionality, 28
Iran, 129, 135. *See also* Persia
Iranian, 95, 134
Iraq, 133–135
Iraq War, 29, 127, 134
Iron Man 3, 2, 207
Islam, 47, 133
Iwamura, Jane, 98

James Bond, 76–77, 83
JanMohamed, Abdul, 214–215, 218
Japan, 3–4, 6, 8–9, 11, 15, 16, 23, 73–74, 92–93, 114, 140–141, 164, 169, 195, 197, 210–211, 216, 218–219, 222, 226

Japanese, 27, 71, 73–74, 139, 140, 142; anti-, 23; mimicry, 38; navy, 24
Japanese American internment. *See* internment, Japanese American
Japanese Invasion, The, 35–36
Japaneseness, 8, 114
Japanophile, 28
Jewish, 153, 156, 159
Johnny Mnemonic, 207
Joyrich, Lynn, 6
Juliani, Alessandro, 112n

Kabuki, 187, 202
Kabuki, 226n
Kant, Immanuel, 28–29
Kaos Studios, 125
Kelly, James Patrick and John Kessel, 152
Kerouac, Jack, 214
Kessler, Jon, 213
Khan, Genghis. *See* Genghis Khan
Khayyam, Omar, 51
Kim, Elaine, 215
Kipling, Rudyard, 210
Kissinger, Henry, 128
Kline, Franz, 214
Korea, 14, 92, 196, 210–211, 216, 218; Koreans, 216, 218; North, 77, 83, 86, 125–127, 134–136, 207; South, 15, 17, 86, 115–117, 119, 122, 126, 134, 222, 225–226
Korean American, 153, 155
Korean War, 90, 96, 128, 211
Kotaku, 115, 118
Kotaro, Takamura, 219
Kowloon Walled City, 145
Kowner, Rotem, 31
Kramer, Peter, 97
Kristof, Nicholas and Sheryl WuDunn, 221–223
Kubota, Shigeko, 216
Kurosawa, Akira, 97

labor, 4–5, 10–11, 15, 120–121, 124, 157, 160–161, 164, 166–167, 184, 190; Asian, 157–162, 166–167, 169, 178, 198, 221–225; Chinese, 4; coolie, 19, 31, 91–92, 194, 223; exploitation, 53; immigrant, 205–206; Indian, 4; sexual, 196–197, 203; temporary capitalist, 123; union, 10, 45; white American, 198

laborer, 157, 160–161, 164, 205, 222–233; Asian, 224; Chinese, 10, 206; European, 11; migrant, 167, 178
Lachman, Dichen, 181
Lai, Larissa, 7, 18, 151–153, 157–162, 193–207
Last Starfighter, The, 134
latina/o, 155–156, 204
Latour, Bruno, 167
Lawrence of Arabia, 98
Laws of Robotics, 87
League of Legends, 114, 116
Lebanon, 132
Lee, Chang-rae, 88
Lee, Christopher, 83
Lee, Tara, 161
Lee, Will Yun, 83
Le Guin, Ursula K., 7, 99
leisure, 122–123, 225. *See also* play
Le, Mike, 181
Lenihan, John H., 94
Levy, Pierre, 146
liberal humanism, 5, 8, 10–11, 14, 182, 223
Liew, Sonny, 165–179
LIFE, 80
Lippmann, Walter, 77
Locke, Brian, 195
London, Jack, 36–38
London Underground (subway), 71–75
Looking Backward 2000–1887, 16, 55–57, 59–60
Loong, Lee Hsien, 175
Looper, 221, 224
Los Angeles, 9, 31, 35, 48, 54–55, 57, 60–61, 134, 141, 186–188, 194–195, 204–225
Lowe, Lisa, 91–92, 182, 190–191
Lucas, George, 98
lynching, 28, 59

Machine Age, 28
Maciunas, George, 217–218
Magnus, David, 107
Mahbubani, Kishore, 163–164
mail-order bride, 202
Malaysia, 163, 166–167
male gaze, 149, 151
Malinky Robot, 17, 166–179
Manet, Eduard, 203
manga, 10, 143, 150n
Manifesto, 217

Marchetti, Gina, 30, 198
marginalized: bodies, 158, 161; characters, 153; identity, 155; Other, 156; subject, 194
martial arts, Asian, 98, 100, 186
Marx, Karl, 122
masculinity, 11, 43, 48, 85, 152, 154; American (U.S.), 41, 49; hyper, 44; Japanese, 27; nonnormative, 186; primal, 152; white, 40, 185–186
Mask of Fu Manchu, The, 90, 92
Massachusetts Institute of Technology, 101
Massumi, Brian, 146–147
Matrix, The, 2, 100
Maul, 17, 151–159, 161, 162n, 225
McAlister, Melanie, 50
McHugh, Maureen, 2
McLuhan, Marshall, 213, 219
McVeigh, Timothy, 133
Mellencamp, Patricia, 212
Mercenaries: Playground of Destruction, 134
Mercenaries 2: World in Flames, 134
Mercury Theatre Company, 41, 46–47, 51
meritocracy, 167
metanarrative, 9
Middle East, 29, 127, 136, 184, 188, 201
Middle East Forum, 133
migrant worker. *See* laborer, migrant
militarism, 30; military weaponry, 26
Milius, John, 134
minoritization, 155–156, 159, 183, 192
minstrelsy, 202
miscegenation, 91, 102, 108, 148, 196; anti-, 92
Mists of Pandaria, The, 14–15
Mitchell, David, 13
Mitchell, William J., 145
MMORPG (Massively Multi-player Online Role-Playing Games), 14–15, 122
model minority, 102, 105, 189, 199
modern, 7, 70, 73; pre-, 7, 74; uber-, 74
modernism, 216–217
modernity, 3, 8, 71, 73, 124, 182, 216, 223, 226; Asian, 73; Japanese, 38; US, 29, 50–51; Western, 3, 72, 100, 180
Mona Lisa Overdrive, 75, 139. *See also* Sprawl trilogy
Mongols, 94–95, 130
Mori, Masahiro, 16, 76, 78
Morie, Ogiwara, 219

Morley, Kevin and David Robins, 2–3, 114, 164, 212, 218
Morris, Robyn, 157, 159–161
Mortal Kombat, 100
mulatta/o, 193, 196, 206
"Mulatto Millennium," 104
multiculturalism, 61, 63n, 104
multiraciality, 188–189
Munich, 210, 216
Munroe, Alexandra, 217
Murder in the Air, 130
music composition, 113, 211–212
mutually assured destruction (MAD), 56. See also nuclear war
My Faust: Technology, 215

Nagasaki, 217
Nakamura, Lisa, 7, 14, 61, 144, 148, 153, 155–157, 182
nanotechnology, 148
narrative, 165–166, 168–169, 183, 187, 189–190, 195; counter-, 166
nationalism, 37, 165, 208; consolidated through process of racialization, 165; German, 208n; militaristic Western, 37
nationalist, 8, 41, 168, 224
National Night, 175–176, 179n
National Security Council, 129
Native Americans, 106, 110, 130; Cheyenne, 69. See also Indian
Native Speaker, 88
Nauman, Bruce, 212
Nebula Award, 141
neoconservatism, 129, 132–133
neo-Dada, 216
neoliberalism, 17–18, 122–123, 164–165, 167–168, 173, 178, 190, 222–223, 225–226
neoliberal trade agreements, 225
Neuromancer, 2, 9, 75n, 139, 141, 143, 146, 151–152, 164. See also Sprawl trilogy
newly industrialized country (NIC), 4, 5
New York (City), 183, 210, 212, 216, 223
Nguyen, Mimi Thi, 6, 182
Nicaragua, 131
nihonjinron, 6, 8
Niu, Greta, 19n, 75n, 140, 150n, 181
Nixon, Nicola, 152
nonhuman, 58, 160–161, 168
Northern Ireland, 129

NSC-68, 128
nuclear war, 130. See also mutually assured destruction
nuclear weapons, 94–95, 99–100, 129
Nye, David, 28, 31

Occident, the, 10, 120, 124, 223
Oda, Masanori, 10
O'Gorman, Marcel, 119
Olympia, 203
Olympus Has Fallen, 207
Omar, the Wizard of Persia, 40–41, 43–45, 51
Omi, Michael and Howard Winant, 42
One Thousand and One Nights, 93
Ong, Aihwa, 68, 179n
Ono, Kent A., 180
Ono, Yoko, 216
Operation Red Dawn, 133
Operation Rolling Thunder, 132
Operation Urgent Fury, 131
Orient, the, 124, 127, 139, 141, 149, 215
Orientalism, 3, 6–8, 15, 29, 50–52, 58, 66, 73, 76, 79, 90, 94, 97, 103, 109–110, 114, 117, 120, 123, 129, 151, 180–181, 185, 190, 194–195, 202, 217, 223, 225; palimpsestic, 181–184, 187, 189–191; past-turning, 181–182, 184; premodern, 3, 7, 18n, 74, 182, 184, 217; self-, 217; spiritual, 187
Orwell, George, 220
otaku, 143–144; techno-, 143
Other, 11, 16, 118, 123–124, 139, 155–156; Asian, 41, 44, 51, 114–115; Oriental, 184, 201
Otherness, 158, 191, 194; racial, 201, 206
Outsourced, 4
outsourcing, 4, 225

Pacific Rim, 207
Paik, Nam June, 15, 18, 209–215, 225
Pak, Greg, 224
Palestine, 129
Palumbo-Liu, David, 42, 92–93
Park, Grace, 57, 103
Park Hong, Cathy, 88
Park, Jane Chi Hyun, 195
passing, 155, 193, 205
patriarchy, 41, 106, 161, 204
Pearl Harbor, 39, 79, 93
performance art, 212, 214
Perry, Commodore Matthew, 32, 35

Persia, 94, 95. *See also* Iran
Philippine-American War, 29
Philippines, The, 167, 196
phrenology, 196
Pipes, Richard, 129
Pirsig, Robert, 216
play, 120–121, 124. *See also* leisure
PlayStation, 113, 124
Plessy v. Ferguson, 55
pollution, 170, 225–226
Pope Paul VI, 212
Port Arthur, Manchuria, 24–25, 27, 30, 32, 39
Portsmouth Treaty. *See* Treaty of Portsmouth
post-Fordist, 3, 121
posthumanism, 17, 86, 224
postindustrial, 123
postmodernism, 3, 140, 182
Post-Orientalist, 10
postracial, 190
post-traumatic stress disorder (PTSD), 135
Pound, Ezra, 142
premodernity, 182, 218
primitive, the, 67, 72–73
production, 197, 203, 205
Project for a New American Century (PNAC), 133
propaganda, 26–27, 49; World War II, 76
pseudoscience, 79
psychoanalysis, 216, 226
Public Opinion, 77

qi, 98
queer, 67, 69, 70–73, 153, 178, 189

R2-D2, 78
race, 17, 72, 74, 101–102, 104–105, 110–111, 139, 144, 146, 155–156, 182–183, 188, 193–196, 203, 224; racial contamination, 105; racial mixing, 102–103
racialization, 55, 102–103, 109, 111, 155, 157, 160, 165, 181–185, 188, 190, 194, 224; of time, 66
racism, 101, 103, 105–106, 123, 158, 165, 181–183, 185; anti-black, 183
Radio Writing, 47
railroads, 10, 28
Rambo: First Blood, 130–132
Rambo: First Blood Part II, 132

rape, 186, 188, 198, 200
Reagan, Ronald, 129, 131–132
Real, The, 5, 121, 144, 146, 150, 206
Realism, Literary, 140
Real-Time Strategy (RTS) game, 114–115, 120. *See also* gaming
reappropriation(s), 7, 16–18, 140, 144, 148. *See also* appropriation
recession of 2008, 207. *See also* financial crisis of 2008
Red Dawn, 126–128, 130–131, 136, 207
reparative practices, 165, 169, 171
replicant, 5, 58, 164, 193, 195–201, 203, 205
representation, 183, 196
reproduction, 159, 175–176, 204
Rhee, Jieun, 214–215
rights: abuses of, 125; Asian, 92; Bill of, 63; civil, 51; declaration of, 14; human, 182; white, modern subject of, 191; white-defined human, 18
Rising Sun, 207
Robeson, Paul, 49
Robogeisha, 224
Robopocalypse, 224
robot, 15, 97, 168; humanoid, 110
robotics, 19n, 59, 76, 78, 87, 209
Robot K-456, 209
Robot Stories, 224
Rodin, Auguste, 219
Rohmer, Sax, 1, 18, 76, 79, 81–82, 90
Romeo and Juliet, 200, 204
Roosevelt, Theodore, 23, 76, 32, 34, 42, 130
Rorty, James, 41
Rosenberg, Julius and Ethel, 95
Russian, 136, 166
Russo-Japanese War, 24, 26–27, 30–31, 39, 92

sadism, 185
Said, Edward, 8, 94, 116, 127, 156, 180
Salt Fish Girl, 17, 151–153, 157–162
Sato, Kumiko, 2, 6, 8
Schoenberg, Arnold, 211
science, 1, 68, 117
science fiction, 6, 144
Science Fiction Studies, 6
Scott, Ridley, 16, 193, 225
Secret Identities: The Asian American Superhero Anthology, 88
Sedgwick, Eve, 165, 169

Selig Polyscope, 27
Senna, Danzy, 104
Seoul, 211
Serenity, 63, 181, 183–186
Serwer, Jacquelyn, 215
sexuality, 186, 188; female, 109, 119
sexual tourism, 196–197
Shakespeare, William, 82, 200, 204
Shanghai, 47, 224
Shatan, Chaim, 135
"shock and awe," 29, 136
Shohat, Ella, 202
Showa Hanako, 78
Shteyngart, Gary, 2, 223
simulacrum, 9
Sinbad the Sailor, 93
Singapore, 47, 163–168, 175, 178–179n, 199, 222, 225
Sino-Japanese War, 27, 49
sky.com, 113
Skywalker, Luke, 97
Slate.com, 103
slavery, 58, 61, 108–109, 184, 190, 194, 196; neo-, 195
slave(s), 61, 108–109, 184, 189–190, 195–196. *See also* enslavement
Smith, Walter, 213
Snow Crash, 151
Snyder, Gary, 214
software, 152, 205
Sohn, Stephen Hong, 7
Son of Sinbad, 17, 90, 93–94, 100
Soviet Union, 126–129, 131–133
Space Race, 127
Spanish-American War, 29
speculation, 169
speculative fiction, 5, 164–165, 182–183; feminist, 152, 154
spirituality, 185, 190
Sprawl trilogy, 139, 141, 149, 152–153. *See also Count Zero*; *Mona Lisa Overdrive*; *Neuromancer*
StarCraft, 114–123; *StarCraft II*, 120, 124
Star Trek, 1, 57, 63n
Star Wars I: The Phantom Menace, 97
Star Wars Episode IV: A New Hope, 17, 90, 97–100
steampunk, 57, 65, 74–75n
Stephens, Toby, 83

Stephenson, Neal, 2, 7, 151
stereotype, 16, 76–79, 103, 114, 139, 141–142, 144, 148, 150, 155–156, 201, 226; ethnic, 77, 79; technology of, 78, 87
Sterling, Bruce, 16, 65, 74n. *See also* Gibson, William and Bruce Sterling
Stone, Alan, 97
Strategic Defense Initiative (SDI) or Star Wars, 130, 134
subaltern, 4
subject, 152, 165; Asian, 140; colonized, 200; male, 8; marginalized, 194; neoliberal, 222; technologized Asian, 8; techno-Oriental, 207; western, 1, 140; white, 186; white modern, 191
subjectivity, 8, 17, 149,
Sullivan, Tricia, 151–157, 161, 162n
Suzuki, Daisetz Teitero, 216
sweatshops, 221–222
Syria, 134
Szkupinski Quiroga, Seline, 105–106

tai chi, 187
Taiwan, 113–116, 163, 199, 222, 225
Tancharoen, Maurissa, 181, 190–192
Tatsumi, Takayuki, 6, 190, 140, 144
technoculture, 119–120
technological sublime, 28
technology, 49, 52–53, 58, 72, 158, 160–161, 190, 196; Japanese, 212; memory, 16, 89; military, 126–127; reproductive, 101, 103, 109; telecommunication, 210; televisual, 218; Western, 1
techno-Orientalism, ix, 2–5, 7–8, 10–15, 18, 24, 48, 51, 66–67, 74, 76, 90, 92, 94, 97–98, 100, 103, 110, 114–115, 123, 126, 129, 133–134, 136, 139–140, 144, 149–151, 153, 157, 159, 160–162, 164–166, 169, 178, 181–184, 187, 196, 212, 218, 223–226
techno-primitivism, 182
Tech, The, 101–102
telecommunication, 26
Terminator, The, 78
terrorism, 95, 109, 133–134, 185, 189, 207
Terry and the Pirates, 40–41, 44
Thailand, 196
Thief of Baghdad, The, 93
Thompson, Nathaniel, 93
Thousand and One Nights, 93, 100

time travel, 53–54
Tokyo, 9, 164, 169, 187
Tokyo Rose, 44
Total Recall, 223
Totilo, Stephen, 135
transcultural dialogue, 144, 211, 219
transistor, 211
Treaty of Portsmouth, 26, 34, 39
Tu, Thuy Linh Nguyen, 6
TV-Buddha, 211–213, 215–216, 218–219
TV-Rodin, 215, 219
Tzara, Tristan, 217

Ueno, Toshiya, 2–3, 9
uncanny valley, 76
United States, 4, 57, 117, 183, 191, 211
Universal Declaration of Human Rights, 87
universality, 72, 182, 190
urbanism, 142
urban planning, 60
utopia, 56, 158

video art, 209, 212, 219
video artist, 212
video game addiction, 118
Viet Cong, 127
Vietnam, 196; North, 99
Vietnam Syndrome, 128–129, 132, 135
Vietnam War, 90, 96, 98–99, 127–129, 132–135
Vinson, Tripp, 127
Viola, Bill, 212
Virginia Tech, 119
Virtual Light, 139. *See also* Bridge trilogy
virtual reality, 155, 158
virtual realization, 171
Virtual Realm, 143–150

wakon yosai, 24
Wang-hsia, 214
Wark, McKenzie, 120–121

War of the Worlds, The, 46
War Plan Orange, 30
weapons, 26. *See also* nuclear weapon
Weiner, Norbert, 219–220
Welles, Orson, 41, 46–47, 51
Wells, H.G., 36–37, 46
Whedon, Joss, 2, 18, 63, 180, 182, 225
Whedonverse, 180, 182, 191
whiteness, 182, 185–186, 189, 195–196, 203
white supremacy, 183, 185
Wild West, 183–184
Wilson, Woodrow, 43, 45
work. *See* labor
World Cyber Games, 117
World of Warcraft, 14–15, 114–116, 120, 122
World War I, 42
World War II, 16, 44, 79, 90, 93–96, 127, 160, 211

xenophobia, 183, 188, 198
Xu, Zhang, 214

Yamashita, Karen Tei, 7
yellowface, 83
yellow journalism, 27
yellow peril, 2, 6, 11, 31–30, 38, 76, 81, 83, 85–86, 90, 109–110, 114, 198–199
Yoffe, Emily, 103–104
Young, LaMonte, 214
YouTube, 119
Yukikaze, 8
Yune, Rick, 84

Zen, 99, 100, 213–218
Zen and the Art of Motorcycle Maintenance, 216
Zen Buddhism, 214, 216–217
Zen for Film, 214
Zen for Head, 214
Zen for TV, 214
Zen for Walking, 214

www.ingramcontent.com/pod-product-compliance
Lightning Source LLC
Chambersburg PA
CBHW021822300426
44114CB00009BA/284